Learning Disabilities in Adulthood: Persisting Problems and Evolving Issues

EDITED BY

Paul J. Gerber, Ph.D.
SCHOOL OF EDUCATION, VIRGINIA COMMONWEALTH UNIVERSITY,
RICHMOND, VIRGINIA

Henry B. Reiff, Ph.D.
DEPARTMENT OF EDUCATION, WESTERN MARYLAND COLLEGE,
WESTMINSTER, MARYLAND

WITH 24 CONTRIBUTING AUTHORS

Andover Medical Publishers

Boston London Oxford Singapore Sydney Toronto Wellington

Andover Medical Publishers is an imprint of
Butterworth-Heinemann.

∞ Recognizing the importance of preserving what has been
written, it is the policy of Butterworth-Heinemann to
have the books it publishes printed on acid-free paper,
and we exert our best efforts to that end.

Library of Congress Cataloging-in-Publication Data
Learning disabilities in adulthood : persisting problems and evolving
  issues / edited by Paul J. Gerber, Henry B. Reiff ; with 24
  contributing authors.
      p.   cm.
  Includes bibliographical references (p.) and index.
  ISBN 1-56372-066-3
  1. Learning disabled—Education—United States.   2. Learning
disabled—Vocational guidance—United States.   3. Learning disabled-
-United States —Psychology.   I. Gerber, Paul Jay.   II. Reiff, Henry
B.,   1953–
LC4818.5.L43   1993
371.9—dc20   93-37478
                                                        CIP

British Library Cataloguing-in-Publication Data.
A catalogue record for this book is available from the British Library.

Butterworth-Heinemann
80 Montvale Avenue
Stoneham, MA 02180

10 9 8 7 6 5 4 3 2 1

Printed in the United States of America

To our wives
Veronica Geran Gerber and Jacqueline Conord Reiff

Contents

PART IV / Vocational Issues

Contributors

C. WILSON ANDERSON, M.ED.
Menninger Clinic, Topeka, Kansas

ROBIN S. BARTON, ED.D.
Georgia Southern University, Statesboro, Georgia

DIANE S. BASSETT, PH.D.
Assistant Professor of Education, University of Northern Colorado, Greeley, Colorado

LORING C. BRINCKERHOFF, PH.D.
Boston University, Boston, Massachusetts

DALE S. BROWN, B.A.
President's Committee for the Employment of People with Disabilities, Washington, D.C.

JOHN CORCORAN, B.S.
Board Member, National Institute for Literacy, Oceanside, California

SHARON DEFUR, ED.D.
Associate Specialist/Special Education Transition, Virginia Department of Education, Richmond, Virginia

CAROL A. DOWDY, ED.D.
Associate Professor, University of Alabama, Birmingham, Alabama

KEN DRUCK, PH.D.
Clinical/Consulting Psychologist, Del Mar, California

BARBARA S. FUHRMANN, ED.D.
Professor of Education and Director of Assessment, Virginia Commonwealth University, Richmond, Virginia

RICK GINSBERG, PH.D.
University of South Carolina, Columbia, South Carolina

PAUL D. GROSSMAN, J.D.
Oakland, California

KATHERINE J. INGE, M.ED., O.T.R.
Rehabilitation Research and Training Center on Supported Employment, Virginia Commonwealth University, Richmond, Virginia

MICHAEL MCCUE, PH.D.
Behavioral Neuropsychology Associates, Pittsburgh, Pennsylvania

JOAN M. MCGUIRE, PH.D.
The University of Connecticut, Farmington, Connecticut

DARYL F. MELLARD, PH.D.
Assistant Scientist, Institute for Research in Learning Disabilities, Lawrence, Kansas

ESTHER H. MINSKOFF, PH.D.
Professor of Special Education, James Madison University, Harrisonburg, Virginia

JAMES R. PATTON, ED.D.
Adjunct Professor, University of Texas at Austin, Pro-Ed Publishers, Austin, Texas

EDWARD A POLLOWAY, ED.D.
Professor of Education, Lynchburg College, Lynchburg, Virginia

MARSHALL H. RASKIND, PH.D.
The Frostig Center, Los Angeles, California

STAN F. SHAW, PH.D.
The University of Connecticut, Farmington, Connecticut

TOM E.C. SMITH, ED.D.
Associate Director, University of Arkansas, Little Rock, Arkansas

GEORGE TILSON, ED.D.
TransCen, Inc., Rockville, Maryland

ELIZABETH H. WIIG, PH.D.
Professor Emeritus, Boston University, Boston, Massachusetts

Foreword

In the study of human development, professionals in various fields have tried to chart the stages of development along a variety of dimensions in an effort to understand normal and abnormal development and to determine when an individual reaches maturity. Fields of study have also been described using the analogy of the life cycle. For example, new fields of inquiry are "born"; some fields are "young"; and others reach maturity, peak, and then fade into obscurity.

Where is the field of learning disabilities in the life cycle? In the decade of the 1980s, we observed the dramatic confluence of two events: (1) the emergence of advocates who themselves have learning disabilities and are articulate spokespersons for increased understanding, the removal of attitudinal barriers, and the availability of accommodations and services to meet their needs; and (2) the dramatic increase in interest among professionals in the field of learning disabilities in the manifestations of learning disabilities in adults, problems they face, and ways to help them. This text is unique in that it exemplifies the importance of the contribution of both professionals in the field of learning disabilities and adults with learning disabilities to the understanding of the changing manifestations of learning disabilities in light of the demands of the developmental phases of adulthood. In this text, one

might say, the field of learning disabilities has "come of age." The focus of learning disabilities is shifted from childhood to adolescence, young adulthood, and beyond, from basic skills deficits and intervention to social/emotional, post-secondary, and vocational/employment issues. In each of these arenas of life, the authors provide real-life examples and descriptions of the problem areas as well as some model programs, strategies, and interventions.

Drs. Gerber and Reiff are the right professionals to have set out to accomplish this task. Through their groundbreaking research involving retrospective interviews of adults with learning disabilities, they began to identify the multifaceted and changing nature of the persisting problems and evolving issues of learning disabilities in adulthood. Their research provided the foundation for this text and this next step, namely, to provide state-of-the-art knowledge regarding problems, issues, concerns, and effective practices. This text should be required reading for all present and future professionals in the field so that they can forge their own alliance with adults with learning disabilities to work together to achieve a level of accomplishment commensurate with their highest abilities and aspirations.

Susan Vogel, Ph.D.
DeKalb, Illinois

Preface

By now, most of us are relatively familiar with issues of learning disabilities during the twelve or so years of schooling. But what happens over the next 60 or 70 years? A book such as this probably could not have been written a decade ago. At that time, adult issues were just beginning to creep into the thinking of those in the field of learning disabilities. As a profession, we realized that the children who had engaged our attention for a generation were growing up. More importantly, even though they were no longer involved with formal mechanisms that identified them as learning disabled, problems persisted and issues evolved.

Adults have gradually attained their rightful place on the learning disabilities agenda. They are the focus of much research and writing, and they are becoming a recognized constituency within human services professions. Two phenomena may account for this paradigm shift in the field. First, learning disabilities persist from childhood through adulthood with lifelong implications. Second, although organic or neurological conditions presumably remain constant, new and different issues evolve over time through a variety of adjustments, adaptations, and transitions involving home, school, community, and the workplace.

This book provides a multifaceted view of learning disabilities in adulthood. Our focus spans from young to late adulthood and reflects state-of-the-art knowledge and the best practices of the field. We do not, however, address gerontological issues. In acknowledging the expanse of time in this last and longest stage of human development, we believe that our approach is unique in the field of learning disabilities. The learning disabilities literature tends to include adults most often in their early to mid 30s, occasionally in their 40s, and rarely in their 50s or beyond.

This text represents the efforts of many contributors who offer a diversity of perceptions and expertise. In order to capture the spirit of evolving issues, we have clustered the topic areas into educational, social/emotional and daily living, and vocational sections, with an introductory section of several chapters that establishes an overall foundation for these discussions. We have used these clusters in our previous investigations of adults with learning disabilities and have found that they present a multifaceted approach to the topic. In order to offer an original perspective to these issues, we have asked adults with learning disabilities to share their personal insights and experiences, which provide a "human touch" to each of the topic clusters.

This text should be of interest to a variety of audiences. The book can be used as a primary or supplementary text for undergraduate and graduate courses in special education, rehabilitation counseling and psychology, and other helping professions. Employers, supervisors, and trainers should find this book helpful in realizing the goals of the recently implemented Americans with Disabilities Act. And adults with learning disabilities, parents, and advocacy organizations may find the book to be a valuable reference both as a practical guide and as a validation of issues presented by learning disabilities in adulthood.

The editors would like to thank the contributing authors, whose effort, expertise, and patience have made this book possible. We also offer our profound gratitude and appreciation to all the adults with learning disabilities who have crossed our paths, for they are the driving force that inspired and sustained our vision of this work.

P.J.G.
H.B.R.

PART I
OVERVIEW

Chapter 1

Perspectives on Adults with Learning Disabilities

PAUL J. GERBER, PH.D.
HENRY B. REIFF, PH.D.

"Don't worry, your child will outgrow it." For years the conventional wisdom prophesied that adulthood would bring deliverance from the difficulties of learning disabilities. To an extent, the field of learning disabilities, with its agenda on children and adolescents, denied that learning disabilities could persist through the lifespan. Although adults account for two thirds of the American population (Rice, 1986), the study of adults and lifespan issues has traditionally lagged behind the professional research and writing on children.

At the beginning of the P.L. 94-142 era in 1975, adults with learning disabilities had not entered fully into the thinking of policymakers and professionals, even though the law guaranteed a free and appropriate education to all students with disabilities up to the age of 21. But in the almost twenty years that have intervened, a whole generation of children who accessed special education services are today's young adults. It was inevitable that adults with learning disabilities would eventually attract the attention of a field that once concentrated its efforts solely on children and youths. The persisting nature of learning disabilities knows no developmental boundaries (Gerber, Schneiders, Paradise, Reiff, Ginsberg, & Popp, 1990).

The learning disabilities population is the largest of the disability groups (Interagency Committee on Learning Disabilities, 1987; SRI International, 1990). Each year, thousands of people with learning disabilities enter adulthood and begin a new stage of their lives, unlike as in previous years when schooling was a primary concern and independence seemed to be an abstraction. Providing services for 12 years of schooling has proved to be complex; addressing the needs of the learning disabled population for as many as the next 70 years will involve a realization of the myriad effects of learning disabilities on employment, home, community, and possibly even gerontological issues.

Bodies of research data have been developing on the issues of transition, four- and two-year college programming, technological and assistive aids, vocational rehabilitation services, adult literacy, and employment and employability issues. Concomitantly, areas such as basic learning disabled adult development, dependency, mental health issues, and aging are waiting to be investigated. In addition, research on learning disabilities beyond the age of 40 is meager. The field is acknowledging a spectrum of issues pertaining to learning disabilities in adulthood and setting a full agenda. Even greater

3

importance lies in the development and application of new bodies of knowledge to create better services and delivery systems, thereby enhancing the quality of life for adults with learning disabilities.

Chronology of Events

A confluence of developments beginning in the early 1980s catalyzed much of the thinking about adults with learning disabilities. Within the federal government a number of initiatives and activities moved the field of learning disabilities beyond school-age issues. Upon her appointment as Assistant Secretary of Education to lead the Office of Special Education and Rehabilitation Services, Madeline Will's (1984) transition initiative energized the field and prompted professionals to look formally beyond school-age years and ask, "In transition to what?" Never before had issues of preparing individuals with learning disabilities for adulthood garnered so much concerted attention. Parents, professionals, and advocacy and professional organizations focused initially on the transition from school to work and later on the transition from secondary to post-secondary education. Conference proceedings of organizations such as the Association for Children with Learning Disabilities adopted titles on the theme of "Coming of Age" (Cruickshank & Lerner, 1982). Moreover, the concept of lifespan instruction for persons with learning disabilities began to appear in the literature (e.g., Wiederholt, 1982).

At about the same time the issue of eligibility for vocational rehabilitation services confronted the Rehabilitation Services Administration (RSA) at the federal level. Historically, only mental or physical disabilities that substantially limited employment predicated eligibility for services. Despite a movement in reconceptualizing learning disabilities as a mental disorder (cf., American Psychiatric Association, 1987), RSA declined to qualify learning disabilities as a mental or physical disorder when they re-

wrote their amendments in 1978. But the climate was changing significantly (Gerber, 1981). Individuals with learning disabilities and consumer groups fought the proposed amendments. In 1980 a federal-level task force forged the way for eligibility and formulated the first definition pertaining to adults with learning disabilities. These developments precipitated new thinking and efforts concerning definitions, services, and quality of life issues in adulthood in the field of learning disabilities.

In concert with this new-found interest, the National Institute of Handicapped Research of the United States Department of Education (now the National Institute for Disability Research and Rehabilitation) convened leading professionals and consumers in May, 1983 for a state-of-the-art conference on special rehabilitation needs of adults with learning disabilities (Gerber, 1983). With a focus on planning and determining future research needs and priorities, the participants pared 17 priorities to a final list of seven (Gerber & Mellard, 1985):

1. Identify the condition of learning disabilities in adulthood. Identify the subgroups and where they are located. Determine severity factors and how professionals should work with multihandicapped individuals who have a learning disability.
2. Determine what social skills are at issue for adults with learning disabilities.
3. Identify the vocational skills that are at issue for adults with learning disabilities.
4. Conduct a state-of-the-art conference to determine what programs exist for adults with learning disabilities.
5. Establish definitions of community adjustment. Determine which ones apply to adults with learning disabilities.
6. Develop strategies for involving the family in order to help remedy the problems facing adults with learning disabilities.
7. Identify and investigate the setting demands in post-secondary training.

Building on the growing interest in adults with learning disabilities, this meeting established a set of research priorities and concerns to attract and challenge the attention of the field. The agenda posed many questions about adults with learning disabilities with a paucity of research and writing to provide answers. Furthermore, existing data from advanced special education and rehabilitation systems, such as those in the Netherlands and Denmark, raised other important issues about the extent to which the United States was willing to commit services to adults with learning disabilities.

In studying the Dutch and Danish systems, Gerber (1984) illuminated a nexus for the learning disabilities field in the United States. The Dutch viewed learning disabilities as an education-specific issue, whereas the Danish believed learning disabilities to be a problem with lifelong implications. Commensurate with these philosophical differences, the Dutch system provided minimal services to adults with learning disabilities. On the other hand, the Danish system had incorporated *kurators*, school and community transition specialists, who were making significant inroads in vocational and community adjustment. Due to this model and other innovations and initiatives, adults with learning disabilities in Denmark could boast of an unemployment rate lower than the national average (Gerber, 1984). In searching for their own model, policymakers in the United States would have to weigh the costs and cost-effectiveness of such different approaches.

Capitalizing on the momentum generated in the first half of the 1980s, the National Joint Committee on Learning Disabilities (NJCLD), a body of eight constituent professional and advocacy organizations (e.g., Orton Dyslexia Society, National Association of School Psychologists, Association for Children and Adults with Learning Disabilities), issued "A Call to Action" (1987). This paper articulated the following concerns:

1. Learning disabilities are both persistent and pervasive throughout an individual's life. The manifestations of the learning disability can be expected to change throughout the lifespan of the individual.

2. At present there is a paucity of appropriate diagnostic procedures for assessing and determining the status and needs of adults with learning disabilities. This situation has resulted in the misuse and misinterpretation of tests that have been designed for and standardized on younger people.

3. Older adolescents and adults with learning disabilities frequently are denied access to appropriate academic instruction, prevocational preparation, and career counseling necessary for the development of adult abilities and skills.

4. Few professionals have been prepared adequately to work with adults with learning disabilities.

5. Employers frequently do not have the awareness, knowledge of, nor sensitivity to the needs of adults with learning disabilities. Corporate as well as public and private agencies have been unaware and therefore have failed to accept their responsibility to develop and implement programs for adults with learning disabilities.

6. Adults with learning disabilities may experience personal, social, and emotional difficulties that may affect their adaptation to life tasks. These difficulties may be an integral aspect of the learning disability or may have resulted from past experiences with others who were unable or unwilling to accept, understand, or cope with the person's disabilities.

7. Advocacy efforts on behalf of adults with learning disabilities are currently inadequate.

8. Federal, state, and private funding agencies concerned with learning disabilities have not supported program development initiatives for adults with learning disabilities (p. 172).

The work of the NJCLD spawned a variety of professional and advocacy efforts on behalf of adults with learning disabilities. Equally important, for the first time adults with learning disabilities took the initiative to organize and advocate for themselves in the 1980s. For example, young adults with learning disabilities in the Learning Disabilities Association of America created their own section. Likewise, the National Network for Learning Disabled Adults was formed and expanded to about 25 chapters across the United States.

As the decade of the 1980s came to a close, a series of developments resulted in the emergence of employability as a key issue for adults with learning disabilities. A number of research reports indicated that both unemployment and underemployment were more pervasive among adults with learning disabilities than among the general population. Moreover, the passage of the Americans with Disabilities Act (ADA) in 1990 was generating a paradigm shift in public policy. The letter of the law guaranteed a workplace-friendly environment to all people with disabilities, including those with learning disabilities. The spirit of the law envisioned increased opportunity, productivity, and independence.

Consistent with the initiatives of the federal government, the President's Committee for the Employment of People with Disabilities (PCEPD) convened a consensus conference on the employability of persons with learning disabilities (Gerber & Brown, 1990). Participants from 21 states represented government agencies, national advocacy organizations, business and industry, unions, higher education, and state education and included a significant number of adults with learning disabilities. Tackling a myriad of issues such as transition, entry, maintenance, advancement, and leadership roles, the participants developed a plan on employment and employability for adults with learning disabilities. This plan consisted of priorities and action steps for eight topic areas: (1) work preparation; (2) vocational entry; (3) reasonable accommodation; (4) job advancement; (5) socio-adaptability; (6) attitudes; (7) policy and legislation; and (8) definition and

diagnosis. A blueprint for addressing employment issues in the era of the ADA, the document that emerged from the PCEPD, emphasized the need for collaborative efforts from adults with learning disabilities, professionals, policymakers, advocacy organizations, and business and industry. The realization of the action steps would depend on responses not only at the national level, but, more importantly, at state and local levels as well.

By the end of the 1980s, a flurry of activities had put adults with learning disabilities fully on the learning disabilities agenda. As the mid-1990s approach, professional are poised to address the lifespan issues of learning disabilities. A chronology that focuses primarily on the initiatives of government and policymakers does not do justice to the endeavors of those individuals, groups, and organizations who presented the case and provided the rationale to bring the field to its current state. The unsung heros in this movement are adults with learning disabilities themselves. They have advocated effectively for themselves and for those who will follow. Many issues are still developing, with program and service delivery systems in an embryonic state. The work is just beginning.

Definition

Historically, the field of learning disabilities has struggled to reach consensus on a definition (Hammill, 1990). Despite debate and controversy, the definitions of P.L. 91-230 (Children with Specific Learning Disabilities Act of 1969) and P.L. 94-142 (Education for All Handicapped Children's Act of 1975) have driven funding and services for students with learning disabilities. Perceived limitations of these definitions have led professionals to attempt to develop more acceptable definitions. For example, the NJCLD unanimously agreed on a consensus definition in 1981 (Hammill, Leigh, McNutt, & Larsen, 1981).

Definitional debates have centered on children and youths. Definitions for learning disabilities in adulthood have received little consideration. RSA has made one of the few attempts to formulate a definition that focuses on work (RSA, 1985). Another example comes from a model designed by the California Community College System to provide a definition for its adult students (Mellard, 1990). In addition to commonly accepted components, adaptive behavior and measured achievement deficit in a specific skill (including vocational areas) constitute new concerns in this definition. To date, the literature has offered little or no examples of definitions of learning disabilities in adulthood, but the emergence of definitions seems likely.

For example, research on highly successful adults with learning disabilities (Gerber, Ginsberg, & Reiff, 1992) may provide a source for a definition. Reiff, Gerber, and Ginsberg (in press) analyzed how adults conceptualize their learning disabilities. The responses tended to cluster around three issues typical of learning disabilities definitions—processing difficulties, specific functional limitations, and underachievement determination—and a fourth, learning disabilities as differences, an issue that most definitions preclude. Reiff et al. (1993) proposed a synthesized definition from the diversity of responses:

> Learning disabilities in adulthood affect each individual uniquely. For some, difficulties lie in only one specific functional area; for others, problems are more global in nature, including social and emotional problems. For many, certain functional areas of adult life are limited compared to other areas. Adults with learning disabilities are of average or above-average intelligence, but intelligence oftentimes has no relation to the degree of disability. Learning disabilities persist throughout the lifespan, with some areas improving and others worsening. Although specific deficits associated with learning disabilities are real and persistent, such deficits do not necessarily preclude achievement and, in some cases, may have a positive relationship with achievement. In almost all cases, learning disabilities necessitate alternative approaches to achieve vocational and personal success (pp. 19–20).

Risk and Resilience

Risk and resilience are concepts that extend throughout the developmental continuum of persons with learning disabilities. Traditionally, the field of learning disabilities has concentrated heavily on risk and has built a set of assumptions that, in spite of intuitive logic, do not necessarily correlate with research on risk in adulthood (Gerber, 1991). Risk patterns in childhood may increase the likelihood of adult difficulties but do not necessarily dictate negative adult outcomes (Gerber et al., 1992; Gerber & Reiff, 1991; Rogan & Hartman, 1976, 1990). Conversely, an absence of risk does not automatically ensure satisfactory adulthood. For persons with learning disabilities, research has indicated that early intervention does not guarantee an adaptive adult (Rogan & Hartman, 1976, 1990); at the same time, many successful adults with learning disabilities had problem-laden childhoods with little or no formal support or assistance (Gerber et al., 1992; Gerber & Reiff, 1991).

Interrelated with risk but virtually ignored by the field of learning disabilities, resilience poses a degree of conceptual complexity. Both internal and external factors comprise resilience. The interaction of individual characteristics and attributes with the ecological relationship of the individual to the environment serves as the foundation for one's degree of resilience. The extent to which adults with learning disabilities shape their own lives within their interests and capacities, a concept related to goodness-of-fit, seems to figure prominently in their resilience (Gerber et al., 1992). Confidence and adaptiveness typically emerge when the individual with learning disabilities removes the shackles of school-age demands and confronts the choices of adulthood (Gerber & Reiff, 1991). A certain amount of risk may even catalyze resilience as highlighted by retrospective interviews of adults with learning disabilities that portray the trials and tribulations found in education, vocation, family, daily living, and social/emotional issues from childhood through adulthood (Gerber & Reiff, 1991).

A Glance into the Future

A transformation of perspectives during the 1980s poses concrete challenges for the 1990s. The development and initiation of policy and programs by the field itself will play a significant role in the future of adults with learning disabilities. But the field must be mindful of broader societal patterns that will have tremendous impact on adults with learning disabilities for the rest of the decade and into the twenty-first century; examples include future training (Cetron, 1985), demographics in the workforce (Johnston & Packer, 1987), and current trends (SRI International, 1990). Conversely, adults with learning disabilities will have an impact on those broader societal patterns. They will be living in an increasingly technologically sophisticated and complex world. That world will be more economically competitive and socially demanding. That world will also provide more opportunities for a normalized life than ever before. The challenges of the future may be far more subtle and progress may be difficult to measure. Nevertheless, the movement that has advocated for the rights and opportunities for adults with learning disabilities will continue to evolve. Further, adult quality of life issues in home, work, and community will improve, albeit in a familiar way—marked with struggle and determination.

References

American Psychiatric Association. (1987). *Diagnostic and statistical manual of mental disorders* (3rd ed., revised). Washington, D.C.: American Psychiatric Association

Americans with Disabilities Act. P.L. 101-336. July, 1990.

Cetron, M. (1985). *Schools of the future.* New York: McGraw-Hill.

Children with Specific Learning Disabilities Act. P.L. 91-230. February, 1969.

Cruickshank, W. M., & Lerner, J. W. (eds.). (1982). *Coming of age: Volume 3, The best of ACLD.* Syracuse: Syracuse University Press.

Education for All Handicapped Children's Act. P.L. 94-142. February, 1975.

Gerber, P. J. (1981). Learning disabilities and eligibility for vocational rehabilitation services: A chronology of events. *Journal of Learning Disabilities, 14*, 422–425.

Gerber, P. J. (1983). Conference summary and generation of final research priorities. In *The special rehabilitation needs of learning disabilities adults.* (pp. 50–61.) Washington, D.C.: The National Institute for Handicapped Research.

Gerber, P. J. (1984). *A study of the school to work transition for learning disabled students and the learning disabled adult in society in the Netherlands and Denmark.* New York: World Rehabilitation Fund.

Gerber, P. J. (1991, June). *Successful adults with learning disabilities: Factors of risk, elements of resilience.* Paper presented at the conference on Risk and Resilience in Individuals with Learning Disabilities: An International Focus on Intervention Approaches and Research. Brittany, France.

Gerber, P. J., & Brown, D. (1990). Report of the pathways to employment consensus conference on employability of persons with learning disabilities. *Learning Disabilities Research and Practice, 6*, 99–103.

Gerber, P. J., Ginsberg, R., & Reiff, H. B. (1992). Identifying alterable patterns in employment success for highly successful adults with learning disabilities. *Journal of Learning Disabilities, 25*, 475–487.

Gerber, P. J., & Mellard, D. (1985). Rehabilitation of learning disabled adults: Recommended research priorities. *Journal of Rehabilitation, 51*, 62–64.

Gerber, P. J., & Reiff, H. B. (1991). *Speaking for themselves: Ethnographic interviews with adults with learning disabilities.* Ann Arbor: The University of Michigan Press.

Gerber, P. J., Schneiders, C. A., Paradise, L. V., Reiff, H. B., Ginsberg, R., & Popp, P. A. (1990). Persisting problems of adults with learning disabilities: Self-reported comparisons from their school age years. *Journal of Learning Disabilities, 23*, 570–573.

Hammill, D. D. (1990). On defining learning disabilities: An emerging consensus. *Journal of Learning Disabilities, 23*, 74–85.

Hammill, D. D., Leigh, J. E., Mcnutt, G., & Larsen, S. (1981). A new definition of learning disabilities. *Learning Disabilities Quarterly, 4*(4), 336–342.

Interagency Committee on Learning Disabilities. (1987). *Learning disabilities: A report to Congress.* Bethesda, MD: National Institutes of Health.

Johnston, W. B., & Packer, A. H. (1987). *Workforce 2000.* Indianapolis: Hudson Institute.

Mellard, D. F. (1990). The eligibility process: Identifying students with learning disabilities in California's community colleges. *Learning Disabilities Focus, 5,* 75–90.

National Joint Committee on Learning Disabilities. (1987). Adults with learning disabilities: A call to action. *Journal of Learning Disabilities, 20,* 172–175.

Reiff, H. B., Gerber, P. J., & Ginsberg, R. (1993). Definitions of learning disabilities from adults with learning disabilities: The insiders' perspective. *Learning Disability Quarterly, 16,* 114–125.

Rice, P. R. (1986). *Adult development and aging.* Boston: Allyn and Bacon.

Rogan, L. L., & Hartman, L. D. (1976). *A follow-up study of learning disabled children as adults.* Washington, D.C.: United States Department of Health, Education, and Welfare, Office of Education, Bureau of Education for the Handicapped.

Rogan, L. L., & Hartman, L. D. (1990). Adult outcomes of learning disabled students ten years after initial follow-up. *Learning Disabilities Focus, 5*(2), 91–102.

RSA. (1985, January). *Program policy directive.* Washington, D.C.: U.S. Office of Special Education and Rehabilitation Services.

SRI International. (1990). *The national longitudinal transition study of special education students, Volume 2: Youth categorized as learning disabled.* Washington, D.C.: Office of Special Education Programs, United States Department of Education.

Vocational Rehabilitation Act of 1973. Amendments to the Vocational Rehabilitation Act of 1986.

Wiederholt, J. L. (ed.). (1982). Lifespan instruction for the learning disabled. *Topics in Learning and Learning Disabilities, 2*(3), 1–89.

Will, M. (1984). *OSERS programming for the transition of youth with disabilities: From school to working life.* Washington, D.C.: United States Department of Education.

Chapter 2

Learning Disabilities: Perspectives on Adult Development

DIANE S. BASSETT, PH.D.
EDWARD A. POLLOWAY, ED.D.
JAMES R. PATTON, ED.D

The field of learning disabilities has grown and evolved over more than a quarter of a century. The individuals with disabilities who have inspired several decades of dedicated professionals coincidentally have also grown and developed. A field that once had primary concerns for early identification and elementary curricula and methods increasingly, both by choice and necessity, has altered its focus to embrace concerns for those persons who continue to experience learning disabilities in adulthood. Thus, a cohort of individuals with learning disabilities and the field of learning disabilities have progressed together; Levine (1989) refers to it as the "early adulthood of a maturing concept" (p. 1).

Clearly, regardless of disability or absence thereof, adults continue to age, facing new sets of tasks and responsibilities throughout their lives. Research on adult development is a relatively new phenomenon, beginning during the mid-twentieth century and continuing to the present. Only recently have these developmental constructs been used in relation to adults whose learning disabilities are acknowledged to continue throughout the lifespan (Patton & Polloway, 1992). Attention to these concerns gives rise to key questions: Do these disabilities have an impact on adult development as it is generally understood? If they do, how and to what degree do they affect the spectrum of adult life?

This chapter provides a context for understanding adult adjustment in individuals with learning disabilities. It focuses on several salient models of adult development with ties to relevant research on adults with learning disabilities as appropriate.

Learning Disabilities in Adulthood

As Zigmond (1990) noted, only a limited body of literature addressed the needs of adolescents prior to the passage of P.L. 94-142, with even less attention given to adults. This neglect in the literature did not imply that adults' learning disabilities did not exist, but rather that they were not perceived as a "distinct population with distinct characteristics and programming needs" (p. 1). The focus on adults in the literature has increased significantly since the mid-1970s (Patton & Polloway, 1992). Although the relationship has not been a linear, ever-increasing one, it has produced steady change within the field. It is now commonly accepted that many students with learning disabilities do not outgrow their learning or social difficulties, a concept that was relatively unexplored in the 1970s. Although many adults appear to have developed successful compensatory strategies to aid in coping with their disabilities (Adelman & Vogel, 1990; Polloway, Schewel, & Patton, 1992), the difficulties of adults with learning disabilities may increase in complexity and, for certain situations, appear to be exacerbated with age (e.g., Gerber et al., 1990; Malcolm, Polatajko, & Simons, 1990; Minskoff, Sautter, Sheldon, Steidle, & Baker, 1988). Thus, as Lieberman (1987) noted, the learning disabilities field increasingly has established adults as a unique group of individuals requiring interventions distinct from those used for children and adolescents.

While it is recognized that adults travel through various phases on their developmental journeys, such transitions may pose particular difficulties for adults with learning disabilities (Gerber et al., 1990; Polloway, Smith, & Patton, 1984). Although Gerber, Ginsberg, & Reiff (1992) were able to identify the key variables, such as taking control of one's life, persistence, learned creativity, a goodness-of-fit between one's abilities and the environment, and a pattern of personal support that enhanced the lives of successful adults with learning disabilities, a more typical description of this population may be a profile of an early history of academic problems compounded by social and organizational difficulties, resulting in higher unemployment rates than those of the general population (Malcolm et al., 1990). Edgar's (1987) data on graduating secondary students with mild disabilities emphasized ineffective programming for adolescents that may result in recurrent difficulties for them as adults.

As consideration is given to adult-relevant concerns, it becomes quite clear that adults with learning problems should not be viewed simply as children with disabilities who have grown up. Rather, the adjustment of adults in general provides the context for addressing their characteristics and needs. Consideration of this perspective requires an orientation rooted in adult development,

similar to the way that the study of children with learning disabilities begins with an understanding of child development. Lifespan models provide a framework for understanding adulthood and thus a foundation from which to examine the adulthood of individuals with learning disabilities. Analysis then begins from the perspective of variation on normative developmental events rather than from one of the continuing pathologies of childhood.

Adult Development Models

A negative myth has molded the concept of adulthood for many persons. That myth has instructed us that to be an adult is to be a finished product. Children have grown up assuming that when they are adults, they will have finished the development period of their lives and will be prepared for any curve life throws at them. From such a view, adults are not expected to grow, develop, or change; rather, adults only age. Thus, adulthood may unfortunately be seen as a single-lane drive down a long hill (Smith, 1991).

The field of developmental psychology has gradually evolved from reflecting adulthood as essentially "aging" to a lifespan approach that acknowledges that becoming an adult is not becoming a finished product. Several reasons may account for this increasing recognition of the complexity of adult development. Certainly, the dramatic lengthening of life during this century has made a difference. At the turn of the century, when psychology was being formulated as a science and personality theories were first being constructed, the average lifespan in Europe and the United States was significantly shorter than it is today. Where the average lifespan fell somewhere between four and five decades, there was much less concern about phases or stages of adult life. Since surviving childhood was an accomplishment, adults were seen as the fortunate products of that survival.

The changing demographic age distribution created by the "baby boom" cohort has also contributed to the change in development thought. It has created a "market" for adult development literature and adult development services. Longer lives, better health, projected early retirement, and greater affluence have all contributed to an environment that has clearly made adult life more interesting to more persons. These factors have consequently created a need for greater insight into the changes and challenges that may characterize the respective stages of adulthood (Smith, 1991).

Adult theorists are divided in their approaches to the developmental spectrum. Although all agree that adults continue to grow and change, some theorists believe that development progresses in sequential fashion, following predetermined age delineations. These stage theorists include Erikson (1950, 1968), Havighurst (1972), Levinson (1978), and Gould (1978). There is not consensus regarding the precise length, timing, or characteristics of stages; they can vary according to social class, economic conditions, and culture (Rogers, 1980). Other theorists believe in a pluralistic approach of lifespan development less dependent on a linear progression of age-related factors (Baltes, Reese, & Lipsitt, 1980). Life events may be grouped into age-graded events, history-graded events, or non-normative events. Finally, others (Gilligan, 1982; Loevinger, 1976) focus on ego and moral development as determinants to adult development. They also remind us that adult developmental patterns may manifest themselves differently for men and women. The following sections will provide a brief overview of representative models in order to promote further understanding and continuing research on the needs of adults with learning disabilities.

Erik Erikson

Erikson (1950, 1968) was the first personality theorist to extend developmental concepts into adult life. His work describes eight stages of life that represent a series of psychological conflicts. Each stage involves tension between possibilities, a psychosocial crisis that must be resolved before further development may proceed (Smith, 1991). Thus, each stage offers both increased vulnerability and potential. Through these stages, past and future issues must continually be mediated. The final four life stages presented by Erikson are particularly helpful in viewing the unique aspects of adult development. A brief discussion of each stage follows.

Identity v. Role Confusion: An adult identity consists of the goals, values, manners, and relationships that are chosen as part of the way that a person wishes to define himself/herself. Erikson observed that the search for an adult identity may last a long time, perhaps into the thirties. If this search is not resolved positively, identity confusion may result in a lack of certainty about one's role in life.

Intimacy v. Isolation: The individual does not become truly capable of intimate relationships until an identity crisis is resolved. Erikson's conceptualization of intimacy includes the willingness to fuse one's identity with that of others. It includes the capacity of commitment to affiliations and partnerships, although these relationships subsequently may require sacrifices and compromises (Smith, 1991). For the most part, intimacy manifests itself in a romantic attachment; it can also help to form sustaining friendships and working relationships. The opposite of intimacy results in distantiation, that is, isolation from others.

Generativity v. Stagnation: Generativity refers to an altruistic sense of leaving one's mark on producing something that will outlive the individual. It may be achieved through parenthood or occupational accomplishments. The stage is also marked by a feeling of caring—about people, institutions, traditions, or other aspects of community and culture. It acts as the precursor to the final stage—that of feeling a sense of fulfillment in life. Stagnation, the negative resolution of this stage, may occur through boredom, lack of commitment to others, or overconcern for self.

Integrity v. Despair: The final stage in the model stresses the finiteness of life and the closeness of death. It presents a tension between one's sense of integrity regarding worth and self-acceptance or a sense of despair resulting from disappointment and embitterment. Hamachek (1990) notes that those who achieve a sense of integrity have come to accept and believe in their own life choices and have accepted death as an inevitable part of the life cycle; they feel a sense of personal wholeness and completion.

Each of these four stages presents unique challenges to growth for adults, which may be exacerbated for adults with learning disabilities. In establishing a sense of identity, for example, Shaw and Brinkerhoff (1990) stress the importance of the acceptance of a learning disability as a critical step in positive development. If one is not able resolve this issue, ensuing development may be significantly altered. Similarly, many adults with learning disabilities may have difficulties maintaining relationships (Chelser, 1982; Fafard & Haubrich, 1981; Haig & Patterson, 1980), which could present particular concerns at the intimacy stage. A sense of isolation may result, coloring future patterns of development.

Erikson speaks of development as a series of turning points evolving in a predictable sequence and at similar times. This model may not prove as predictable for some adults with learning disabilities who may take longer periods of time through which to develop within each stage. For example, they may have particular difficulties with trust because of histories of school failure or social isolation. Although Erikson believes that past and future issues are continually being mediated, the complex nature of this task may also be perplexing for adults with learning disabilities as they struggle with the relationship of cause and effect.

Robert Havighurst

Havighurst is considered to be one of the most socially oriented adult theorists; his work describes specific tasks that arise around certain age-defined periods in the lives of men and women. The inability to accomplish these tasks may have serious deleterious effects on future growth. Havighurst outlines three sources of tasks through which individuals must develop: the physical maturation process; cultural pressure from society; and the personal values and aspirations of each individual. As these factors actively intertwine with each other, developmental tasks emerge.

Havighurst (1972) presents a series of "dominant concerns" for each period of life. Three major stages of life take into account the maintenance of an economic standard of living, establishment of family and occupation, and adjustment to health and aging conditions. During the first stage, early adulthood (age 18 to 30 years), individuals typically begin adult life by selecting a mate, starting a family, beginning a career, and managing a home. Middle age (age 30 to 60 years) is marked by the achievement of adult social and civic responsibility, the attainment of goals in one's occupation, and adjustment to the demands of adolescents and older parents. The final stage, adult maturity, begins at age 60 years and focuses on the decrease in strength and health, retirement, and death of a spouse.

Havighurst's model has come into question because of the rigidity of the stages of development; that is, not all adults may develop within the same circumscribed age divisions. This may be particularly true for adults with learning disabilities who may arrive at developmental tasks at differing time periods. On the other hand, this model may be more appropriate for these adults as it stresses specific vocational and social goals as part of developmental growth. For example, the early adulthood stage includes marriage, beginning a family, and starting an occupation. These events may prove a turning point for adults with learning disabilities; for example, development could be enhanced by marrying a supportive spouse who is accepting of the disability or by working in a challenging job that requires future training or education. Conversely, lack of such support or challenge could result in atrophy or rigidity where fear and low self-esteem may prevent future possibilities.

Daniel Levinson

Just as Havighurst emphasized the important role of occupations, so also does Levinson (1978, 1986; Levinson, Darrow, Klein, Levinson, & McKee, 1974) correlate the importance of occupation to identity and psychological adjustment. Based on a biographical study of 40 men aged 35 to 45 years drawn from four groups (i.e., hourly workers, executives, academic biologists, and novelists), Levinson (1978) sought to construct a universal developmental sequence. He concluded that adulthood is characterized by alternating periods of stability (of 6 or 7 years' duration) when individuals solidify their life structure and periods of transition (of 4 to 5 years' duration) when that structure is reexamined and modified.

Levinson's first era, early adult transition, begins at age 17 and continues to age 22. It provides the link between adolescence and early adulthood. During this period, the individual must terminate the preadult self and take the preliminary step into the adult world. This involves making explorations and choices. It parallels the onset of the second era, early adulthood (age 17 to 45 years). This period represents the peak years of biological and intellectual functioning. An individual attempts to establish the balance between keeping options for change open while striving to create a stable life structure in personal and occupational choices. It is within this era that an individual transforms from a novice adult to a full-fledged adult. Middle adulthood (age 40 to 65 years) is often marked by a significant life event such as job change or divorce that sets into place the polarities of young and old, creativity and destruction, and separation and attachment. This era is seen as critical if an individual is to attain true fulfillment and creative growth.

Levinson's work has been criticized because of its strict chronological adherence and because of its focus on only males. However, this theory may be applicable to adults with learning disabilities on several levels. First, he acknowledges the difficulties of leaving the support of family to establish one's own life. This challenge has been corroborated by studies of adults with learning disabilities who continue to live at home with family (Affleck, Edgar, Levine, & Kortering, 1990; Rogan & Hartman, 1976, 1990; Smith, 1992). He also speaks of the importance of striking a balance between a stable life while being open to new alternatives as they arise. Adults with learning disabilities may swing to either end of that continuum; they may become rigidly set into a vocational or personal pattern that is hard to disrupt, or they may vacillate into middle age without finding occupational or personal satisfaction. These possibilities suggest rich veins to be mined by researchers in the future. Are the stages of adult development different in individuals with learning disabilities? Do they mature more slowly than their adult counterparts who are nondisabled? Do catalytic events specific to adults help to drive their development or does internal control begin to play a larger role in self-determination?

Roger Gould

Gould (1978) perceives adulthood as a dynamic, changing time where growth is not only inevitable, but an obligation. As he stated:

> With each step, the unfinished business of childhood intrudes, disturbing our emotions and requiring psychological work. With this in mind, adults may now view their disturbed feelings at particular periods as a possible sign of progress, as part of their attempted movement toward a fuller adult life (p. 14).

Gould describes the time of adulthood as one of mastery. He stresses the acknowledgement of a childhood consciousness continually being modified through the passage of age-related stages and the occurrence of marker events. He places great significance on events such as marriage, divorce, job change, and illness as catalysts for further development. He also specifies age periods general to adult development: age 16 to 22—the individual leaves the known world of family; age 22 to 28—occupational choices are formulated; age 28 to 34—initial questioning of those choices, lack of role clarity; age 35 to 45—intense discontent and introspection; age 45 to 50—turning inward, resigned to finite time; 50s—mellower, warmer, mortality felt.

Gould's model may be especially pertinent to adults with learning disabilities for two key reasons. First, Gould addresses the ongoing struggle adults experience between their child and adult personae. Indeed, this struggle may be exacerbated for many adults experiencing learning problems because they may not be able to shed the childhood scripts of failure and isolation they have experienced. Second, Gould states that as adults pass through life stages, they need to be tolerant of their questions and changes because these elements are critical to continued growth. Just as we have come to be accepting of the learning strengths and weaknesses of children, so is it important to acknowledge a parallel structure in adult development. This concern is particularly relevant to adults with learning disabilities because they may possess neither the self-assurance nor the coping abilities to be able to readily embrace independence and change. Support personnel must have a heightened sensitivity to the trepidations faced by these adults and encourage them through the self-doubts and challenges that change inevitably brings.

Jane Loevinger and Carol Gilligan

The preceding theories share two similar attributes: they focus on stages of adult development, and they have used males as the subjects for their research. Loevinger (1976) and Gilligan (1982) criticized these models because they may not apply to the development of females. For example, in her discussion of Erikson, Gilligan notes that the life cycle is defined in terms of the male experience. While identity precedes intimacy in Erikson's model, Gilligan claims that these two developmental tasks are melded together in women's development. A woman defines herself and is defined by her relationships with others. Gilligan also speaks to Levinson's model as consisting only of males in a rigidly prescribed context of age that correlates identity and adjustment with job satisfaction. She adheres instead to a model of moral development that knows no gender specificity or age delineations.

Loevinger (1976) also dismisses stage development and the total reliance on male subjects in favor of a hierarchical model of ego development in which an adult learns to cope with increasingly deeper problems. Development is viewed as a process beginning with an impulsive child-like stage and moving through the sequence of self-protection, conformism, conscientious conformism, conscientiousness, autonomy, and integration. The ego acts as a mediator that determines how one views and relates to the world.

These two theorists bring special relevance to the field of learning disabilities since few investigations have focused on the learning patterns of females with learning disabilities (Vogel, 1990). Future research must seek to determine if significant gender differences exist. Further, modern society has changed to the extent that specific stages defined by age may not be relevant. Models incorporating other means of addressing development may help to clarify adult roles in these times. For adults with learning disabilities, alternative perspectives may provide additional insight into the heterogeneous nature of this population. For example, one adult may still be exhibiting self-protective behavior where there is little responsibility taken and external factors are blamed for failure experiences. Conversely, another adult may be autonomous in understanding her limitations and being accepting of them. This paradigm promotes development of the self in relation to external influences rather than in relation to one's own actions. A model that does not rely on defined gender or stages may aid in understanding the developmental process of adults with learning disabilities.

Pluralistic Approach to Development

Baltes and colleagues (1980) proposed an integrative model of lifespan development. This model differs from the stage theories of adult development discussed above in several ways. First, developmental processes may begin at any point in life and may differ in intensity and duration. Second, these processes may not follow in linear fashion but may be curvilinear; that is, they may be very important in early and late life but not necessarily in between. Third, development can begin at virtually any age, increase to a maximum, and decrease slowly if at all. Finally, tremendous variation between individuals increases in complexity with age.

Therefore, basic elements described by Baltes and co-workers (1980) define development as pluralistic in nature. It can begin at different times and affect individuals in different ways. Further, they indicate that specific influences also affect development in different forms. These include:

1. *Normative age-graded* events consisting of biological and environmental influences correlated with age. These might include marriage, birth of a child, and menopause.
2. *Normative history-graded* influences including cultural events correlated with historical time. Economic depression, political upheavals, and major epidemics play a role in the developmental context of a generation. The decade of the 1960s provides an apt example of such a sequence of events.
3. *Non-normative* events affecting a particular individual but not tied to age or history-graded influence. They occur idiosyncratically and may include such things as automobile accidents, winning a lottery, religious conversions, or divorce.

The pluralistic model offers a unique perspective for considering the development of adults with learning disabilities. Because this population is acknowledged to be widely heterogeneous, individuals may vary greatly in the ages and stages at which they develop. Further, it is obvious that other influences have already altered their lives in ways that may set them apart from their nondisabled counterparts. By viewing adult development as pluralistic, one can begin to recognize the extreme variation and impact of life experiences at all ages and design interventions accordingly.

A related concept that facilitates an application of a lifespan developmental model is that of mediating variables. Polloway and associates (1984), building on the concept of resources to facilitate adaptation of life events advanced by Lieberman (1975), Hultsch and Deutsch (1981), and Vaillant (1977), stressed the role that such variables may play. The four variables they identified included *biological and intellectual variables* (e.g., physical health, energy, attention, memory); *personal and social variables* (e.g., social relationships, support systems); *past experience and anticipatory socialization* (i.e., the role of past experiences as a basis for responding to current tasks, specifically, the influence of previous successes or failures); and *locus of control* (i.e., perceptions of degree of control one has over life events). Each of these variables has implications for a variety of challenges (e.g., vocational, financial, personal, social) facing adults with learning disabilities.

Concluding Comments: Adjustment Within Adult Contexts

Inspection of the growing number of adult outcome studies conducted with students who have learning disabilities reveals an alarming picture. The scenario for many young adults is characterized by unemployment and/or underemployment, low pay, part-time work, frequent job changes, nonengagement with the community, limitations in independent functioning, and limited social lives (Chelser, 1982; Hoffman et al., 1987; Smith, 1992). Although other more personal outcomes (e.g., happiness, self-esteem, sense of achievement) have not been adequately studied, it is likely that individuals with learning disabilities do not fare well in these areas either.

Cronin, Patton, and Polloway (in press) have concluded that many individuals who were formerly in special education programs are not being prepared adequately for the multidimensional demands of adulthood. They suggest that the major life demands of adulthood can be categorized into six domains: employment-education, home and family, leisure pursuits, community involvement, emotional and physical health, and personal responsibility and relationships. These domains provide a framework for examining the successful adjustment of young adults with learning disabilities as well as providing a "top-down" perspective for curriculum development.

Clearly adjustment problems in any of the six areas can have a significant impact both on the choices one makes in life and how successful one is within one's chosen path. Within a lifespan perspective, the relative importance of selected domains will change throughout an individual's life, whereas the absolute importance of all domains remains constant.

While concerns have been raised about problematic areas, increased attention has been directed at factors associated with success. The investigations of Gerber and co-workers (1992) have elicited the characteristics of acceptance of the disability, perseverance, goal-setting, self-directedness, and use of strong support networks. Spekman, Goldberg, and Herman (1992) discovered parallel traits. Key factors point to a strong sense of self, flexibility and adaptability, persistence, goal-directedness, and use of support systems. A new paradigm of adult development must take into account these success-related factors to be relevant to adults with learning disabilities.

To achieve a positive quality of life, appropriate supports must be available to enhance the likelihood of successfully dealing with the demands of adulthood. The word *supports* serves as a broader term than *services* since it has particular relevance for adulthood. The concept moves beyond the idea of special services within the school context and also includes personal supports from individuals themselves and natural supports from the environment (e.g., family, friends, neighbors). Thus, while agency services are important, they may not necessarily be the key variables in determining success for an individual in an adult-relevant context.

The significant heterogeneity of the population of adults with learning disabilities must be matched with an equally broad spectrum of available supports and services. Addressing adult characteristics within the context of a model of needed supports serves to dispel the deficit model common to the field of special education and to de-emphasize irrelevant (e.g., child-oriented) characteristics. Instead, such an orientation stresses adult-referenced needs tied to effective systems of support.

Portions of this paper have been adapted from Patton and Polloway (1992) and Polloway, Smith, and Patton (1984) and used with permission.

The authors acknowledge the assistance provided by J. David Smith relative to lifespan developmental concepts in general and the work of Erikson in particular.

References

Adelman, P. B., & Vogel, S. A. (1990). College graduates with learning disabilities—Employment attainment and career patterns. *Learning Disability Quarterly, 13,* 154–162.

Affleck, J., Edgar, E., Levin, P., & Kortering, L. (1990). Post-school status of students classified as mildly retarded, learning disabled, or nonhandicapped: Does it get better with time? *Education and Training in Mental Retardation, 25,* 315–324.

Baltes, P. B., Reese, H. W., & Lipsitt, L. D. (1980). Lifespan developmental psychology. *Annual Review of Psychology, 31,* 65–110.

Chelser, B. (1982). ACLD vocational committee completes survey on LD adults. *ACLD Newsbrief, 5* (46), 20–23.

Cronin, M. E., Patton, J. R., & Polloway, E. A. (in press). Preparing for adult outcomes: A model for a life skills curriculum. *Remedial and Special Education.*

Edgar, E. (1987). Secondary programs in special education: Are many of them justifiable? *Exceptional Children, 53,* 555–561.

Erikson, E. (1950). *Childhood and society.* New York: Norton.

Erikson, E. (1968). *Youth, identity, and crisis.* New York: Norton.

Fafard, M. B., & Haubrich, P. A. (1981). Vocational and social adjustment of learning disabled young adults: A follow-up study. *Learning Disability Quarterly, 4,* 122–130.

Gerber, P. J., Ginsberg, R. J., & Reiff, H. B. (1992). Identifying alterable patterns in employment success for highly successful adults with learning disabilities. *Journal of Learning Disabilities, 25,* 475–487.

Gerber, P. J., Schneiders, C. A., Paradise, L. V., Reiff, H. B., Ginsberg, R. J., & Popp, P. A. (1990). Persisting problems of adults with learning disabilities: Self-reported comparisons from their school-age and adult years. *Journal of Learning Disabilities, 23,* 570–573.

Gilligan, C. (1982). *In a different voice: Psychological theory and women's development.* Cambridge, MA: Harvard University Press.

Gould, R. L. (1978). *Transformations: Growth and change in adult life.* New York: Simon & Schuster.

Haig, J. M., & Patterson, B. H. (1980, March). *An overview of adult learning disabilities.* Paper presented at the Annual Meeting of the Western College Reading Association, San Francisco. (ERIC Document Reproduction Service No. ED 197 563)

Hamachek, D. (1990). Evaluating self-concept and ego status in Erikson's last three psychosocial stages. *Journal of Counseling and Development, 69,* 677–684.

Havighurst, R. (1972). *Developmental tasks and education* (3rd ed.). New York: D. McKay Co.

Hoffman, F., Shelden, K., Minskoff, E., Sautter, S., Steidle, E., Baker, D., & Bailey, M. (1987). Needs of learning disabled adults. *Journal of Learning Disabilities, 20,* 43–52.

Hultsch, D., & Deutsch, F. (1981). *Adult development and aging: A life-span perspective.* New York: McGraw-Hill.

Levine, M. D. (1989). Learning Disabilities at 25: The early adulthood of a maturing concept. *Learning Disabilities, 1*(1), 1–11

Levinson, D. J. (1978). *Seasons of a man's life.* New York: Knopf.

Levinson, D. J. (1986). A conception of adult development. *American Psychologist, 41,* 3–13.

Levinson, D. J., Darrow, C. M., Klein, E. B., Levinson, M. H., & McKee, B. (1974). The psychosocial development of men in early adulthood and the mid-life transition. In D. F. Ricks et al.

(Eds.), *Life history research in psychopathology* (Vol. 3). Minneapolis: University of Minnesota Press.

Lieberman, L. M. (1987). Is the learning disabled adult really necessary? *Journal of Learning Disabilities, 20,* 64.

Lieberman, M. A. (1975). Adaptive processes in later life. In N. Datan & L. H. Ginsberg (Eds.), *Lifespan developmental psychology: Normative life crises.* New York: Academic Press.

Loevinger, J. (1976). *Ego development: Conceptions and theories.* San Francisco: Jossey-Bass.

Malcolm, C. B., Polatajko, H. J., & Simons, J. (1990). A descriptive study of adults with suspected learning disabilities. *Journal of Learning Disabilities, 23,* 518–520.

Minskoff, E. H., Sautter, S. W., Sheldon, K. L., Steidle, E. F., & Baker, D. P. (1988). A comparison of learning disabled adults and high school students. *Learning Disabilities Research, 3,* 115–123.

Patton, J. R., & Polloway, E. A. (1992). Learning disabilities: The challenged of adulthood. *Journal of Learning Disabilities, 25,* 410–416.

Polloway, E. A., Schewel, R., & Patton, J. R. (1992). Learning disabilities in adulthood: Personal perspectives. *Journal of Learning Disabilities, 25,* 520–522.

Polloway, E. A., Smith, D. J., & Patton, J. R. (1984). Learning disabilities: An adult development perspective. *Learning Disabilities Quarterly, 7,* 179–186.

Rogan, L. L., & Hartman, L. D. (1976). *A follow-up study of learning disabled children as adults.* Final report. Evanston, IL: Cove School Research Office. (ERIC Document Reproduction Service No. ED 163 728)

Rogan, L. L., & Hartman, L. D. (1990). Adult outcomes of learning disabled students ten years after initial follow-up. *Learning Disabilities Focus, 5,* 91–102.

Rogers, D. (1980). *Issues in adult development.* Monterey, CA: Brooks/Cole.

Shaw, S., & Brinkerhoff, L. (1990, October). *Training for independence: Preparing LD students for postsecondary education.* Paper presented at the annual conference of the Council for Learning Disabilities, Austin, TX.

Smith, J. D. (1991). *Adult development models.* Unpublished manuscript, Lynchburg College, Lynchburg, VA.

Smith, J. O. (1992). Falling through the cracks: Rehabilitation services for adults with learning disabilities. *Exceptional Children, 58,* 451–460.

Spekman, N. J., Goldberg, R. J., & Herman, K. L. (1992). Learning disabled children grow up: A search for factors related to success in the young adult years. *Learning Disabilities Research & Practice, 7,* 161–170.

Vaillant, G. E. (1977).*Adaptation of life.* Boston: Little, Brown.

Vogel, S. (1990). Gender differences in intelligence, language, visual-motor abilities, and academic achievement in students with learning disabilities: A review of the literature. *Journal of Learning Disabilities, 23,* 44–52.

Zigmond, N. (1990). Rethinking secondary school programs for students with learning disabilities. *Focus on Exceptional Children, 23*(1), 1–21.

Chapter 3

Developing Issues for the Learning Disabled Community under Employment Discrimination Laws

PAUL D. GROSSMAN, J.D.*

A New Civil Right

As a matter of law, persons with "specific learning disabilities" are entitled to be free from employment discrimination in certain work settings. The Americans with Disabilities Act of 1990 (ADA) will extend this legal protection to nearly every workplace in America. This legal protection is a "civil right," one that expands on legal and social principles established predominantly by people of color, language minority communities, and women. The principle of nondiscrimination in employment, with regard to disability, was achieved in large measure by some very politically astute and courageous[1] persons with disabilities. The right of individuals with learning disabilities to be free from discrimination in employment presents

the learning-disabled community with a promising and exciting challenge.

Optimism about the implementation of the ADA must be tempered by the well-known fact that persons with learning disabilities are often perceived as "careless, inattentive, lazy, stupid," and worse. Judges are not immune to the prejudices of our society.[2] A comprehensive review of court decisions concerning persons with learning disabilities demonstrates that it will not always be easy to convince employers and judges that individuals with learning disabilities are covered by disability discrimination laws, that such persons are competent to meet the business expectations of an employer, or that individuals with learning disabilities are entitled to "reasonable accommodation" in order to perform their jobs effectively.

Legal Authorities

The Rehabilitation Act

As it is implemented, title I of the ADA[3] will be the primary tool for creating equal em-

---

*The author of this chapter is in practice with a federal civil rights agency and an adjunct professor at the Hastings College of Law, teaching disability law. This chapter was written exclusively in his capacity as a private citizen. No endorsement by his employers or any other agency has been expressed or implied.

This chapter is designed to provide a useful overview of the subject matter covered. However, if legal advice is required, the services of a competent professional should be sought.

ployment opportunity for America's disabled population.[4] Before implementation of the ADA, the single most important law prohibiting employment discrimination on the basis of disability has been title V of the Rehabilitation Act of 1973.[5] Title V of the Rehabilitation Act contains three substantive sections that are germane to employment discrimination on the basis of disability. Section 501 prohibits discrimination and requires affirmative action on behalf of qualified individuals with disabilities in federal employment.[6] Section 503 establishes fundamentally the same duties with regard to federal contractors.[7] Section 504 prohibits discrimination in employment against qualified individuals with disabilities by recipients of federal financial assistance.[8] Section 504 contains no affirmative action provisions. In short, title V covers the federal government, every entity that receives financial assistance from the federal government, and everyone who does business with it. Because section 504 principles figured prominently in the development of the ADA, section 504 will be covered more extensively in this chapter than the other two sections of title V.

The Americans with Disabilities Act

On July 26, 1990, President Bush signed P.L. 101-336, the ADA, which will greatly reduce the barriers that prohibit people with disabilities from fully participating in American society as employees, customers, consumers, and public service beneficiaries. Like title V of the Rehabilitation Act, the ADA pertains to every aspect of the employment relationship: pre-employment testing and screening, selection, promotion, pay, training, employee benefits, and so forth. However, while the Rehabilitation Act is limited in the employers it covers, the ADA is expansive. With rare exception,[9] as of July 26, 1992, title I of the ADA,[10] which concerns employment discrimination, applies to every entity with 25 or more employees.

Under section 506 of the Rehabilitation Act of 1992, Congress amended section 504 to achieve greater uniformity with title I of the ADA. As to an alleged act of *employment* discrimination occurring after October 29, 1992, any institution subject to section 504 will have its conduct measured by the "standards" of title I of the ADA.[10A] This amendment did not alter section 504 jurisdiction or procedure.

Except as it amends the Rehabilitation Act, the ADA affects the rights of only a very limited group of federal employees. However, title I and subpart A of title II of the ADA, taken together, cover virtually every state and local government employer.[11] The ADA is estimated to affect the rights of 43 million persons[12] and cover 3.9 million business establishments of 660,000 employers.[13] Like the Rehabilitation Act, this law applies to persons with visible disabilities (such as persons in wheelchairs) as well as to persons with "invisible disabilities" (such as individuals with learning disabilities).

Three Major Issues

The answers to three fundamental questions provide a comprehensive framework for anyone who wishes to become familiar with title I of the ADA and section 504 of the Rehabilitation Act. These questions are the following:

1. Who is an individual with a disability?
2. What are the essential functions of a job?
3. What is reasonable accommodation?

Who Is "Disabled" within the
Meaning of Section 504 and
the ADA?

Section 504 and the ADA protect only persons who meet the statutory definition of "disabled." The ADA and the Rehabilitation Act cover persons who are disabled, have been disabled, or are perceived as disabled.[14]

Specifically, these laws apply to any person in the United States who:

1. Has "a physical or mental impairment which substantially limits one or more major life activities."
2. Has "a record of such an impairment."
3. Is "regarded as having such an impairment."[15]

First Definition. The first of the above three definitions is the one most often used to establish jurisdiction. Therefore it will be discussed at greater length than the other two.

WHAT IS AN "IMPAIRMENT?" [16] No matter which of the three definitions an individual seeks to use, he or she must first establish the existence or perceived existence of an "impairment." "Specific learning disabilities" are clearly included in the definition of a "mental impairment."[17] No particular learning disability is mentioned in the ADA or its employment regulation, part 1630. Dyslexia is the only learning disability specifically mentioned in the appendix to part 1630. However, the list of impairments mentioned in the regulation is in no way intended to be exhaustive. Persons with dysgraphia or dyscalculia, for example, would do well to analogize to dyslexia to establish that they have an impairment. Persons with attention deficit disorder (ADD) or attention deficit hyperactive disorder (ADHD) may wish to cite guidance issued by the U.S. Department of Education stating that children with ADD or ADHD *may* be "handicapped [disabled]" within the meaning of section 504, "depending on the severity of their condition."[18]

The presence of an impairment is determined without taking into account mitigating measures such as medication or assistive devices. Thus, a person with ADD will not be found unimpaired because of the positive effect of medication on his or her behavior. Nor do electronic dictionaries remove persons who are learning disabled from the definition of disabled.

WHAT IS A "MAJOR LIFE ACTIVITY?"[19] Under the ADA or the Rehabilitation Act, establishing that a person has an impairment is only the first step to proving, in a legal sense, that the individual is "disabled." The individual must further establish that the impairment "substantially limits major life activity."[20] The regulations implementing these laws define major life activities to include basic functions that the average person can perform with little or no difficulty. These functions include seeing, hearing, speaking, learning, and working.[21] This list is not intended to be exhaustive. By analogy, the courts could be encouraged by learning-disabled litigants to adopt "processing visual or auditory information" as major life activities. Some support for this proposition may be found in the technical assistance manuals explaining the ADA issued by the Equal Employment Opportunity Commission and the Department of Justice (hereinafter the *EEOC* and *DOJ TA Manuals*).[22]

WHAT MAKES AN IMPAIRMENT "SUBSTANTIAL?"[23] Many impairments, even those affecting a major life activity, do not adversely affect an individual's life to the degree necessary to constitute a disabling impairment. If everyone could qualify as "disabled," the ADA and the Rehabilitation Act would become useless. Nonetheless, the inability to do what most people can do is highly relevant to determining who is disabled within the meaning of the ADA and the Rehabilitation Act. The inability of an uneducated person to read anything will not be evidence of a disability. But if an educated person cannot comprehend the first written page of a book, there is a strong inference of an impairment that substantially limits a major life activity. There is no question that persons with learning disabilities whose impairments are sufficiently great are covered by title I of the ADA and title V of the Rehabilitation Act.[24]

It makes sense that these laws do not cover persons with insubstantial impairments or persons whose impairments affect them adversely only in the narrowest of situations. Nonetheless, the learning disabled community should be concerned that judges, ill-informed about learning disabilities, will misapply these legitimate and necessary legal requirements to the detriment of the community. For example, one Iowa state court concluded that a person who alleged that he was dyslexic had not established that he was disabled because he was captain of the employer's bowling team, dated, had a driver's license and drove, was of "essential[ly] normal" intelligence, and responded well to questions at trial.[25] The court did not find persuasive the fact that someone of essentially normal intelligence had never progressed beyond bag-boy after several years of employment with a grocery store, had to repeat several grades in school, never fully mastered the cash register, and engaged in aberrant behavior while at the worksite.[26]

Each person seeking protection under the ADA or the Rehabilitation Act must be well prepared to establish on an individual basis that he or she is disabled within the meaning of the law. But this burden should not be seen as excluding persons who are learning disabled from the protection of the law.[27] A comprehensive search of legal decisions reveals at least seven cases in which the courts accepted the fact that a plaintiff with a learning disability was a disabled person within the meaning of employment discrimination law.[28] Some summary observations can be made about what courts consider relevant to showing that an individual's learning disability is, or is not, a substantially limiting impairment. The courts seem to require little evidence before concluding that a person who is learning disabled has incurred a substantial impairment if it is established that he or she has incurred other more serious limitations to major life activities such as mental retardation or a serious emotional illness such as schizophrenia.[29] Academic difficulties, even for an individual who has completed his or her education, are germane.[30] Difficulties encountered in actual job performance are also relevant.[31] Formal testing, such as testing for reading grade level, will be taken into evidence.[32] A determination by a rehabilitation agency or service that a person is disabled or eligible for special programs for the severely disabled will do a great deal to persuade a court

that a person with a learning disability is handicapped within the meaning of the Rehabilitation Act.[33]

Second Definition: "A Record of Such an Impairment." [34] This definition of who is disabled was written primarily to protect persons from discrimination because they have been misclassified as disabled.[35] The word "record" may include educational records or a history of a disability.

As with many other obligations under the ADA, a key requirement of this definition is that the employer know of the record. Take the situation of a typist who, *unknown to the employer*, had a learning disability in elementary school but, through remediation, has fully compensated for his or her impairment. One day the employer fires the typist for attendance problems. Logically, this individual could not then claim that his or her elementary school record served to prejudice the employer. Nor would such a person be entitled to a reasonable accommodation for his or her former disabling condition.

Third Definition: "Is Regarded as Having Such an Impairment." [36] This definition is for persons who have an impairment that is not substantially limiting, but who are perceived (believed) by the employer to have a substantially limiting impairment. This definition will not often be of consequence to the learning-disabled community. Nonetheless, it should not be overlooked. For example, this definition would be useful in a case where an employer believes that there is a strong genetic link to dyslexia and refuses to hire someone because the employer knows that the applicant's brother is severely dyslexic or where an employer limits the types of assignments given to a person the employer mistakenly believes is learning disabled.

Other Bases for Coverage Under Title I of the ADA and Title V of the Rehabilitation Act. In addition to the third definition, there are other ways a nondisabled person may be covered by the ADA and the Rehabilitation Act. First, both laws prohibit retaliation for either filing claims of discrimination, opposing that which is prohibited by these laws (e.g., participating in a peaceful demonstration opposing employment discrimination on the basis of disability), and/or cooperating in an investigation of alleged discrimination (e.g., serving as a witness).[37] Second, the regulations implementing the ADA, but not those implementing the Rehabilitation Act, explicitly prohibit discrimination against persons because they associate or have a relationship with a disabled individual.[38] This protection would apply to the circumstances of an employer who knows that a job applicant is the parent of a child who has ADD. Under the ADA, the employer would be prohibited from refusing to hire the applicant because he or she fears that the applicant will frequently miss work for parent/teacher meetings or that the child's medical needs will adversely affect the employer's health insurance premium rate.

What Are the Essential Functions of a Job?[39]

Under the ADA and the Rehabilitation Act, it is illegal to discriminate against a "qualified individual with a disability." Thus far, this chapter has explored for the learning disabled community three ways in which an individual with a learning disability may meet the legal definition of "disabled." The next step is to determine if the disabled individual is "qualified." This is best examined through a two-part analysis. The first element is to determine whether the individual meets the employer's *legitimate*[40] job prerequisites, such as possessing the required years of experience, holding the necessary licenses, or having attained a required degree. This is sometimes referred to in the Rehabilitation Act case law as determining whether an individual is "otherwise qualified" for employment. The second element is to determine whether the disabled person can perform the "essential functions" of the position (held or sought) with (or without) the benefit of reasonable accommodation.

The relationship between the two elements of this process is exemplified by the case of a person with a learning disability who seeks employment with a law firm as a summer clerk. Assume that the law firm will hire only persons who have successfully completed two years of law school and an applicant, despite his or her best efforts, has completed only one semester of law school. It will do the applicant no good to argue that requiring completion of two years of law school is discriminatory, even though, but for having a learning disability, the applicant would have already graduated from law school. However, if an applicant with a learning disability has completed two years of law school, the law firm may not refuse to hire the student as a summer clerk on the grounds that it does not wish to go to the expense of buying software that would check his or her spelling.

It is unlawful to fail to hire, retain, or promote an individual with a disability because he or she cannot perform the nonessential or marginal elements of a job. If the law were otherwise, it would merely protect persons who can do everything the employer expects, reasonable or not, in spite of their disabilities. Neither Congress in enacting the ADA and the Rehabilitation Act nor the agencies implementing civil rights laws intend such a limited purpose for them.

Determining essential functions begins with looking at what the employer actually expects to be accomplished by persons holding the job. This will be revealed through examining a number of sources, including preexisting job descriptions, the terms of collective bargaining agreements, the nature of the skills needed to competently perform the job in question, the time prior incumbents spent on performing a given function, the consequences of not performing a given function, the experience of past incumbents, and the experience of incumbents in similar jobs.[41] Although some of these factors pertain to what the employer requires on paper, when properly conducted, this inquiry will be more concerned with what requirements the employer actually imposes on the employees.

Except where standards are selected for the purpose of excluding persons with disabilities, the inquiry into essential functions should not second-guess an employer's business judgment with regard to actual production standards, whether qualitative or quantitative. If an employer actually requires its proofreaders to review 20 pages of text an hour, an individual who can read only 15 pages an hour is not relieved of the higher standard by virtue of being disabled within the meaning of the ADA and section 504.

It is the very unevenness of the mental abilities of persons with learning disabilities that defines their disabilities (e.g., a person who can comprehend the writings of Plato but not those of Rand McNally). Persons who are learning disabled may perform some essential functions of a job, including ones requiring judgment or higher intellectual skill, with great proficiency and at the same time fall far short of employer expectations in other areas requiring seemingly simple skills, such as knowing right from left. As a consequence, learning disabilities cases are well-suited to raising the question, "What are the essential functions of the job?" Two federal court cases serve as sound examples of how this issue will continue to be prominent in employment discrimination litigation brought by the learning-disabled community.

In *DiPompo v. West Point Military Academy*,[42] a legal action was brought in federal district court under section 501 of the Rehabilitation Act. When not under stress, Mr. DiPompo could read at the level of an advanced first grader; when under stress he became illiterate. Mr. DiPompo sued the Academy because it would not hire him as a "structural firefighter" on the grounds that he could not read at the twelfth-grade level. The plaintiff lost. Holding that a firefighter's job "is defined at almost every turn by the potential for disaster to himself and others," the court concluded that Mr. DiPompo's inability to read posed an undue safety haz-

ard[43] for himself and other firefighters. This conclusion was based on the fact that, at West Point, many structures contained hazardous materials. Firefighters relied on a five-digit code marked on the side of each building indicating what materials were inside. The plaintiff could not make efficient use of the code. The judge stated that requiring another firefighter to read the material to him was simply not a reasonable accommodation. Reading was an essential function of the job that could not be shifted to others.

The matter of *Fitzgerald v. Green Valley Area Education Agency*[44] contrasts well with *DiPompo*. Fitzgerald, an individual impaired by hemiplegia and dyslexia, graduated from a well-recognized teacher preparation program. He sought employment with a special education consortium as a teacher of children with disabilities. The consortium's offer of a job interview was withdrawn when it was revealed that, due to his disabilities, Mr. Fitzgerald could not drive a school bus, purportedly an essential element of a teaching position with the consortium. The court concluded that the plaintiff was a victim of employment discrimination. Although it did not find for Mr. Fitzgerald under section 504, it concluded that under the "affirmative steps" provision of the Education of the Handicapped Act (now the IDEA),[45] the District had a duty to accommodate the plaintiff by finding another way to meet its transportation needs. For a teacher, bus driving was not an essential function.

What Is Reasonable Accommodation?

If an individual with a disability cannot accomplish the essential functions of a job as it is currently constituted, the question arises whether with "reasonable accommodation" the individual can perform the job. If the answer is no, the person in question is not a "qualified individual with a disability" and the employer may lawfully choose not to hire, maintain, or promote the person because his or her disability creates an insurmountable barrier to accomplishing the purpose of the job.[46]

Fortunately, disability antidiscrimination law recognizes that most impairments of persons with disabilities do not erect insurmountable barriers to competent and productive employment. If impairments create barriers to doing a job well, they are usually surmountable barriers. Reasonable accommodation compels employers to take those reasonable steps necessary to overcome surmountable barriers.

WHAT DUTIES ARE ENCOMPASSED WITHIN THE CONCEPT OF REASONABLE ACCOMMODATION? "The obligation to make reasonable accommodation is a form of nondiscrimination. It applies to all employment decisions and to the job application process."[47] For persons with learning disabilities the most common accommodations include modification of pre-employment tests, job restructuring, changes in how information is communicated (e.g., how a supervisor's directives are transmitted to subordinates; the way training information is acquired; how the employee communicates back to the supervisor), separating the employee from extraneous noise, and providing the employee with "assistive devices" such as word processors and spellcheckers. It should be noted that nothing in the law prohibits employers from providing accommodations beyond those required by title I of the ADA or section 504.

In the part 1630 regulations and the explanatory appendix to part 1630, issued by the EEOC, the Commission projects that in a post-ADA world, the process of identifying an appropriate reasonable accommodation should be the product of joint cooperation between the disabled individual and the employer.[48] "The appropriate reasonable accommodation is best determined through a flexible, interactive process. . ." in which the employer (1) determines the essential functions of the job; (2) consults with the disabled individual to ascertain his or her limitations and how they could be overcome; (3) assesses the effectiveness of each potential accommodation; (4) "consider[s] the preference of the individual" and (5) implements the accommodation that is "most appropriate for the employee and the employer."[49]

According to the EEOC, if more than one accommodation will make it possible for an employer to accomplish the essential functions of a job, the preference of the applicant or employee is to be given "primary consideration." However, the employer has the "ultimate discretion" to choose between effective accommodations. Nothing under the section 504 regulation or title I prohibits the employer from selecting the least expensive, most convenient, effective accommodation. An obvious point for dispute is whether the accommodation chosen by the employer, in fact, is effective.

Reasonable accommodation also includes permitting individuals to provide their own accommodation, including ones the employer may not be required or able to provide. An example, of this might be to permit a person who is learning disabled to put personalized assistive software he or she has developed on the computer at his or her work station.

A significant emerging question for the learning-disabled community under the ADA is what are the limits of the right to make use of self-accommodation. For instance, does this right protect the opportunity of a business executive or college professor who is learning disabled to take his or her written work home every night for proofreading by a literate companion who does not have learning disability? An individual who is learning disabled could argue that as long as the work is turned in on time, up to the standards of the employer, and accomplished without compromising the security of the employer's business, there is no undue hardship on the employer. An employer, opposed to such a practice, might argue that reliance on another individual in this manner is, in effect, restructuring an essential function of the employee's job. The ADA does not require restructuring an essential job function. In effect, the need to take work home for proofreading demonstrates that the employee is not a *qualified* individual with a disability.

When analyzing a situation like the preceding one, the disabled community must never lose sight of the fact that many things employers may wish to characterize as "reasonable accommodation" are really no more than equal treatment required by law. For example, the person with a learning disability who wishes to take his or her work home at night might defend this form of self-accommodation on the grounds that non-disabled employees frequently take their work home.

An employer cannot require an individual to make use of a particular accommodation. But if a lawful necessary accommodation is refused, the individual is not a "qualified individual with a disability." As a consequence, the individual is no longer protected by the ADA or the Rehabilitation Act.[50]

ON WHAT GROUNDS MAY AN EMPLOYER DECLINE TO PROVIDE REASONABLE ACCOMMODATION? The concept of "undue hardship" was developed as a check or limit on the duty to provide reasonable accommodation. According to the EEOC,

> [t]he term "undue hardship" means significant difficulty or expense in, or resulting from, the provision of the accommodation. The "undue hardship" provision takes into account the financial realities of the particular employer or other covered entity. However, the concept of undue hardship is not limited to financial difficulty. "Undue hardship" refers to any accommodation that would be unduly costly, extensive, substantial, or disruptive, or that would fundamentally alter the nature or operation of the business.[51]

For example, an assembly welder whose learning disability makes him or her highly susceptible to distraction could not ask General Motors to spend millions of dollars to make its assembly line silent. But if no significant safety problem were created,[52] such a person would be entitled to wear special sound-reduction equipment or, absent a conflict with a collective bargaining provision,[53] be reassigned from welding to something quieter, such as painting.

In *Nelson v. Thornburgh*,[54] a leading case on the factors used to determine whether a requested accommodation presents an undue hardship, blind "income-maintenance" (social) workers brought an action under section 504 of the Rehabilitation Act to get a court order and damages requiring the Pennsylvania Department of Public Welfare to provide and absorb the cost of readers, electronic devices, and braille translations of agency manuals to accommodate their disability. The court handled the question of undue hardship by placing it in the context of the agency's budget, as well as social policy. The agency dispersed over $4 billion and spent $300 million on administering the funds. The court found that the cost per visually impaired employee for a reader would be $6,638 per year. Taking into account the small percentage of the agency's total budget represented by that sum of money and the high productivity of the blind employees who already had made use of readers, the court found no undue burden and ordered the state to pay for the accommodations sought by the plaintiffs.

What Accommodation Issues Are Particularly Important to Individuals with Learning Disabilities? The EEOC states that there are three categories of reasonable accommodation. These are "(1) accommodations that are required to ensure equal opportunity in the application process; (2) accommodations that enable the employer's employees with disabilities to perform the essential functions of the position held or desired; and (3) accommodations that enable the employer's employees with disabilities to enjoy equal benefits and privileges of employment as are enjoyed by employees without disabilities."[55] All three forms of accommodation pertain to persons with learning disabilities.

TESTS AND EXAMINATIONS. The ADA, part 1630, and the regulations implementing section 504 prohibit discrimination in testing of applicants and employees.[56] The ADA and part 1630 specifically list modification of the application process, including testing, as a form of reasonable accommodation.[57] Thus, 29 C.F.R. § 1630.2(o) (reasonable accommodation), 29 C.F.R. § 1630.11 (administration of tests), and 29 C.F.R. § 1630.10 (qualifications standards) read together require that employment tests be administered to eligible applicants or employees who have a disability that "impairs sensory, manual, or speaking skills" in a manner that does not require use of the impaired skill, unless it is the impaired skill that the employer is *legitimately* testing. The appendix written by the EEOC to clarify title I of the ADA and the EEOC and DOJ technical assistance manuals make clear that individuals who are learning disabled, such as individuals with dyslexia, are included within the group of persons who have impaired "sensory, manual or speaking skills."[58]

These legal provisions may be used by an individual with dyslexia, who has substantial difficulty with reading, to obtain additional time to take a written examination, or to take the test in an alternate format (such as orally),[59] unless what the employer is legitimately testing is the ability to read or read quickly.[60] The term "legitimate" is used to indicate that an employer can test for speedy reading, or reading, if these are the particular skills it is intending to measure. Further, if these skills relate to *marginal* job functions, poor performance on this test may not be a basis for screening out the applicant. On the other hand, if these skills relate to an *essential* job function,[61] poor performance may be used to screen out an applicant unless reasonable accommodation would enable the individual to do the job competently.

With very limited exception, the employer is required to provide reasonable accommodation in testing only if it knows in advance of conducting the examination that a disabled individual with impaired sensory skills wishes to take the test.[62] It is not an uncommon experience for a person with a moderate learning disability to expect to be able to perform a test without accommodation and then realize after the test has begun that accommodation is necessary. In the explanatory appendix to part 1630, the EEOC suggests that under such circumstances the applicant or employee should discontinue the test and request an accommodated retest.

Since test modification is a form of reasonable accommodation, the ADA regulation does not require that an employer offer an applicant with a learning disability the format of his or her choice. The format chosen merely needs to comply with the standards of the regulation.

The concept of accommodated testing may also be applied to licensing and credentialing procedures, a traditional barrier to the employment of individuals with learning disabilities in trade and professional positions. A person with a learning disability who has taken a credential or license examination, and has been unsuccessful, may try to hold the employer responsible for using a discriminatory selection criterion, as was attempted in a federal court case described below (*Pandazides v. Virginia Board of Education and the Educational Testing Service*). However, a more effective strategy may be to seek an accommodation, in the form of test modification, directly from the licensing or credentialing agency.

Under section 504, few licensing or credentialing agencies or their examinations could be reached for a legal challenge, because such agencies usually do not receive federal financial assistance.[63] However, all licensing or credentialing agencies operated by a state or local government may be reached under subtitle A of title II of the ADA. In essence, subtitle A of title II prohibits discrimination on the basis of disability in any program, service, or activity of a public entity. The nondiscrimination requirements of subtitle A of title II are the same as those to be found under section 504.[64]

Congress recognized that licensing and credentialing examinations may be given by entities that are neither operated by a state and local government nor receive federal financial assistance. To close a potential loophole, Congress included section 12189 in the ADA. This provision of title III of the ADA prohibits discrimination by "persons" rather than entities. It reaches licensing and credentialing authorities as well as the persons who operate licensing courses such as bar examination review services.[65] Although this provision is of great importance to any individual with a disability who must take a licensing or credentialing examination, unlike the other provisions discussed above, it is limited to issues of access to examinations, such as their format and where and how they are given. This provision is unlikely to provide sound legal authority for challenging the content, as opposed to the form, of an examination. Finally, this provision reaches licensing and credentialing for most, but not quite all, professions.[66]

Several important cases concerning the duty to provide this form of reasonable accommodation under the Rehabilitation Act concern persons who are learning disabled.[67] One of the first of these cases, *Stutts v. Freeman*, served as a model for legislating this obligation into the ADA.[68] Mr. Stutts, a dyslexic individual, was denied entry into a Tennessee Valley Authority (TVA) construction apprenticeship program on the grounds that he could not pass a paper-and-pencil entry examination, the General Aptitude Battery Test (GABT). The appellate court concluded that, "Where an employer like TVA chooses a test that discriminates against handicapped persons as its sole hiring criterion, and makes no meaningful accommodation for a handicapped applicant, it violates the Rehabilitation Act."[69] The appellate court sent the case back to the district court for further consideration. The appellate court instructed that the district court could still find Stutts unqualified but not on the basis of the GATB. The appellate court suggested that Stutts be reexamined "either with the help of a reader or by other means."[70]

Most recently, in *Pandazides v. Virginia Board of Education and the Educational Testing Service*,[71] the subject of testing has been explored by the United States District Court for the Eastern District of Virginia and the appellate court that reviews its decisions, the Fourth Circuit Court. Following graduation from college, Ms. Pandazides was employed as a special education teacher. Pursuant to state law she received a one-year appointment under a probationary teaching certificate and was required within this period to pass the National Teacher Examination (NTE) or lose her certificate. Ms. Pandazides passed two portions of the examination, but over a period of two years she repeatedly failed the third portion, communication skills (listening, reading, and writing). Following these difficulties, Ms. Pandazides sought, but failed to receive, an exemption from the NTE licensure requirements by the Virginia Board of Education. However, Ms. Pandazides was able to obtain several test accommodations from the Educational Testing Service on the grounds that she had an auditory learning disability. Accommodations given the plaintiff included time and one-half on the examination, a written script to follow when receiving taped listening-skills questions, a machine on which to play the taped questions at a slower speed, and an isolated test-taking environment. She requested, but did not receive, an "intermediary" who would deliver oral questions and with whom she could interact. She was also denied unlimited time to provide a response to the questions.

When Ms. Pandazides continued to fail to pass the third section of the NTE, she went to the district court, arguing that section 504 entitled her to the exemption she sought or at least additional test accommodations. She was not successful. The district court held that an individual who had sought employment as a school teacher but who failed to pass the NTE was not an "otherwise qualified handicapped [qualified individual with a disability]" individual under section 504.

The appellate court reversed the ruling of the district court on the basis that the lower court had failed to make a truly individualized consideration of Ms. Pandazides' skills and had merely dismissed as unqualified an individual who could not pass the NTE. The appellate court was apparently impressed with Ms. Pandazides' academic accomplishments, her student and probationary employee teaching record, the fact that she had passed two sections of the NTE, and expert testimony on her behalf as to her sensitivity to the needs of special education students.[72]

The appellate court instructed the district court to reconsider her case.

> [D]efendants cannot merely mechanically invoke any set of requirements and pronounce the handicapped applicant. . . not otherwise qualified. . . . [N]o factual determinations were made as to whether the NTE requirements represented the essential functions of the job, whether she could perform the essential functions of the position, and whether a test waiver was a reasonable accommodation.[73]

Despite the directives of the appellate court, matters did not go well for the plaintiff when her case returned to the district court.[74] As was underscored at the beginning of this chapter, it is critical to almost every type of disability discrimination case that the plaintiff be able to establish that he or she is disabled. In the opinion of the district court, at her rehearing, Ms. Pandazides was unable to meet this burden. The expert documentation supporting Ms. Pandazides was ambiguous. Some contained statements such as she "might" have a learning disability. The court interpreted this ambiguity against her for a number of reasons. The credentials of the expert testifying against Ms. Pandazides were well established. The plaintiff alleged she was learning disabled only after she had been unsuccessful a number of times in passing the NTE. Her diagnosed area of greatest deficiency, auditory processing, did not correspond to the areas in which she had the most difficulty passing the third section of the NTE.

The district court also based its conclusion on an independent second ground. The court concluded that even if Ms. Pandazides was disabled within the meaning of the Rehabilitation Act, she was not qualified to be a licensed teacher because she could not perform the essential functions of a teaching position. In the opinion of the court, someone who received the extensive test accommodations received by the plaintiff but remained unable to demonstrate the skills tested on the NTE could not function capably as a classroom teacher. For example, in response to Ms. Pandazides' unsuccessful request for unlimited time to respond to test questions,

the court stated, "The ability to read intelligently, to comprehend written and spoken communication accurately, effectively and quickly, and to respond to written and spoken communications professionally, effectively and quickly, are 'essential functions' of a special education, public school teacher in Virginia."[75]

Finally, there was a fundamental difference of perception as to whether Ms. Pandazides' teaching record demonstrated that she has been an effective teacher thus far in her career. The rehearing record of the district court suggested she had some difficulties as a teacher. Such a record, if accurate, can be very damaging as it logically supports the court's view that the NTE accurately distinguishes between persons who will or will not serve as competent teachers, even when the persons taking the test are disabled.

The Pandazides case underscores the degree to which test validation for persons with disabilities is an area of science and law in need of further development. The learning disabled community should not lose sight of the fact that the principles enunciated by the appellate court remain good law, even if they did not ultimately vindicate the efforts of Ms. Pandazides to become a special education teacher.

In *Wynne v. Tufts University School of Medicine*[76] the First Circuit Court of Appeals affirmed the conclusion of a federal district court that section 504 did not compel Tufts Medical School to give a particular student with a learning disability essay or oral examinations in lieu of multiple-choice examinations.

Wynne was dismissed from medical school after failing eight of fifteen courses (one three times) during repeated attempts to complete his first year of school.[77] In the course of Wynne's second attempt at the first year, the school provided him with multiple accommodations ["academic adjustments"] including a free evaluation, counselors, a learning tutor, taped lectures, note-takers, and retesting. These accommodations improved his performance, but he continued to fail biochemistry. Wynne introduced expert evidence that he had difficulty interpreting the type of complexly arrayed multiple choice examinations used in biochemistry. He asserted that the failure to test him in a manner appropriate to his disability was the cause of his continuing academic deficiencies.

Following a lengthy and complex series of court proceedings,[78] Wynne was unable to attain the form of test modification he sought or reinstatement to medical school. The Supreme Court recently declined to review the decision of the First Circuit.[79]

The decision of the First Circuit has been criticized for, according to Tufts, too much deference in making academic decisions. An element of this critique is that the court failed to require the medical school to fully comply with certain Department of Education regulations implementing section 504. These regulations require postsecondary education institutions to utilize examinations that test a disabled student's level of knowledge and skills rather than his or her disability.[80]

The court merely required Tufts to demonstrate that its decision was a "rationally justifiable conclusion."[81] According to the court, the medical school could demonstrate that it had met this responsibility by showing that the "hierarchy" of Tufts had made an individualized decision, considered alternate accommodations and had examined their feasibility.[82] This exploration of accommodations could include consideration of their cost and the effect on the academic standards of the institution. In sum, the scrutiny of the First Circuit focused on whether and how Tufts reached its conclusion, not on the substance or outcome of the consideration process.[83]

Those who cite Wynne with approval hold that the First Circuit's opinion is well grounded in logic and judicial precedent. To begin, Wynne did not clearly convince the court he was disabled.[84] Like the unsuccessful plaintiff in Pandazides, his evaluation results were ambiguous. His claim of incompatibility between his purported disability and multiple-choice examinations was diminished by the fact that he had taken and passed several multiple-choice examinations.[85] Similarly, the court was troubled by the fact that Wynne did not know or report that he was disabled until after he had failed the first year of school once. Prior to Wynne or Tufts discovering his disability, as a matter of logic and law, Tufts had no duty to provide him with an accommodation.[86]

Those who agree with the Wynne decision also argue that the deference accorded to Tufts, if not entirely compatible with the words of the applicable section 504 regulations, is consistent with the consideration traditionally accorded medical schools and other institutions of higher education in employment discrimination cases[87] and by the Supreme Court in the seminal section 504 case, Southeastern Community College v. Davis.[88]

Finally, it was undeniable that Tufts had given Wynne numerous accommodations and many chances to improve his academic record. Tufts could not be accused of intending to dismiss Wynne because of his status as a disabled person.[89] Though the court did not comment directly on Wynne's qualifications, his failures in the face of all these opportunities could not help but raise a serious doubt on the part of the court as to whether it should increase his chances of becoming a doctor.[90]

Ultimately, the issue for the learning disabled community will not be the wisdom of the reasoning of the First Circuit but rather, how narrowly or broadly the case will be applied as a precedent. Wynne is not an employment discrimination case. The First Circuit even sought to limit its application within academia:

> Although both parties to this litigation invite us to paint with a broad brush, we decline their joint invitation. The issue before us is not whether a medical student, authoritatively diagnosed as a dyslexic and known to the school to be so afflicted, is ever entitled, upon timely request, to an opportunity to take an examination orally. Rather, we are limited to the idiosyncratic facts of Wynne's case.[91]

Despite the limiting words of the First Circuit, business and industry can be expected to urge judges to apply Wynne broadly, thereby securing for employers great discretion in deciding what is an adequate accommodation.[92] The disabled community will need to guard against the application of *Wynne* beyond its unique facts and particular context. Of course, *Wynne* could be used effectively by the community in cases where employers or educational institutions have failed to even meet the standards articulated by the First Circuit.

COMMUNICATION. The decision of the federal district court in *Sedor v. Postmaster General*[93] suggests that an employer that knows that an employee has a disability adversely affecting communication must take steps to address the communication deficiency before holding the employee responsible for the substance of the communication.[94] In *Sedor*, the plaintiff, who had a learning disability, was hired through a program for the "severely handicapped." After working with Mr. Sedor for a period of time during which he received many accommodations, the Postal Service proposed to dismiss him for attendance problems. The court denied a request by the Postal Service for a summary judgment against Mr. Sedor. The court would not ratify his dismissal because it wanted the opportunity to determine whether the Postal Service had made clear to Mr. Sedor what was expected of him with regard to attendance and how the agency's disciplinary procedures operated.

HOW WORK IS ORGANIZED. In *American Fed. Government Emp., Local 51 v. Baker*,[95] the plaintiffs were long-term Treasury Department employees who assembled coin proof sets for sale to the public. The plaintiffs' disabilities covered a wide range of mental impairments, including retardation and learning disabilities. The Treasury Department sought to dismiss the plaintiffs because they could not achieve production goals after the system of set assembly was converted from assembly line to work stations. Under the authority of section 501 of the Rehabilitation Act, the federal district court concluded that the Treasury Department could not take adverse action against the plaintiffs until it had hired an expert

"with training and experience [in the particular disabilities of the plaintiffs]; training and experience in job analysis, job restructuring and making recommendations to employers regarding accommodating handicapped employees; and knowledge in rehabilitation engineering."[96] The court ruled that having failed to take such action, the Treasury Department could not establish that it had fulfilled its affirmative duty to consider reasonable accommodation.[97]

READERS. Earlier this chapter discussed the case of the blind income maintenance workers who were successful in suing the State of Pennsylvania for readers as a reasonable accommodation (*Nelson v. Thornburgh*).[98] This case is frequently cited by courts when exploring the methodology for ascertaining undue burden. For the learning-disabled community another part of the opinion may also prove to be important. With regard to the ability to read as an essential function, the district court stated,

> The capacity to read without aid is certainly helpful in carrying out the duties of the job, as are the abilities to hear or to move about without help. The essential qualifications for this career, however, are dedication to the work, sufficient judgment and life experience to enable one accurately to assess the legitimate needs of clients, and the ability to work effectively under the pressure of competing demands from clients and supervisors.[99]

The above-quoted portion of the *Nelson* decision underscores another emerging legal issue for the learning-disabled community. That is, to what degree are the accommodations available for "visually impaired" persons also available to persons with impairments in processing visual information? Although accommodations such as readers are usually thought of in terms of assistance to visually impaired persons, in title I as well as in part 1630, readers are merely listed as a form of accommodation without reference to any particular disability.[100] The *EEOC TA Manual*, concerning title I of the ADA, explains the circumstances under which provision of a reader to a person with a learning disability may be an appropriate form of accommodation for pre-employment testing. This is consistent with the accommodations that the TVA was ordered to consider by the court in *Stutts*. This explanation implies that under certain circumstances this form of accommodation also would be appropriate to post-selection employment.[101] The *DOJ TA Manual*, concerning title III of the ADA, provides similar guidance with respect to making college entrance examinations and professional and licensing examinations accessible to individuals with learning disabilities.[102]

The learning-disabled community would do well to carefully follow court precedents concerning visually impaired persons and to support their efforts and those of other disabled communities to assert their rights under the ADA and the Rehabilitation Act.

Procedures and Remedies

Title I of the Americans with Disabilities Act

An individual cannot bring an action under title I of the ADA in federal court without first properly filing a charge with the EEOC or a state Fair Employment Practices (FEP) agency. In jurisdictions that do not have an FEP agency, a charge must be filed with the EEOC within 180 days of the alleged discrimination.[103] In jurisdictions that do have an FEP agency with jurisdiction over discrimination on the basis of disability, the charge must be filed with the EEOC within 300 days of the alleged discrimination.

The EEOC will investigate any timely filed charge and determine whether there is or is not "reasonable cause to believe" that discrimination occurred. In cases where the EEOC finds discrimination, it will attempt to reach a voluntary settlement of the violation between the charging party and the responsible employer. If the attempt at voluntary resolution fails, the EEOC has authority to file a lawsuit in federal court on behalf of the charging party and seek the relief to which

the person is entitled. The person may rely on the EEOC's suit, may join into the lawsuit brought by the EEOC, or may bring his or her own action independent of the EEOC's lawsuit.

If the EEOC determines that discrimination did not occur, it will issue a "right to sue" letter to the charging party. This letter is required before an individual may go into federal court on his or her own behalf. The individual may request a "right to sue" letter at any time after the 180th day following the filing of a charge, even if the EEOC has not finished its investigation or made its determination. Once the right to sue letter is issued, the charging party must file suit in court within 90 days of receipt of the letter.

The primary forms of relief available under title I of the ADA are back pay, front pay, restored benefits, reinstatement, or an offer of employment. Another common form of relief is correction of the discriminatory condition, such as removal of a physical barrier or a discriminatory employment criterion, the provision of a reasonable accommodation, or modification of an employee selection procedure. Under the Civil Rights Act of 1991, punitive and compensatory damages for violation of the employment provisions of the ADA will be available in certain instances of intentional discrimination.[104]

Section 504 of the Rehabilitation Act of 1973

Under section 504 there is no "right to sue letter" process. Federal courts have heard section 504 employment claims from private citizens that were not presented first to a federal agency.[105] The time limits for filing a section 504 claim directly in federal court are established by reference to analogous state statutes, such as a state civil rights act.[106] Thus, persons contemplating a court action under section 504 or the ADA are advised to seek the advice of a qualified attorney.

The Rehabilitation Act does not specify what remedies are available to plaintiffs who bring a suit in federal court, and the scope of the remedies available to a plaintiff in a private federal court lawsuit under section 504 is under change. The federal courts have available to them the broad authority to award "all appropriate remedies" in a section 504 case.[107] It is established that federal courts may redress employment practices held to violate section 504 through "equitable remedies" such as reinstatement, back pay, and reform of the employer's personnel practices.[108]

A recent decision of the Supreme Court, *Franklin v. Gwinnett County Public Schools*,[109] and new federal legislation, the Civil Rights Act of 1991,[110] leave little doubt that to redress "intentional discrimination"[111] under section 504 federal courts also have the authority to award "general or compensatory damages."[112] Examples of compensatory damages include money for pain and suffering or for loss of job responsibilities, status, and promotion potential.[113] With regard to punitive damages, in the 1991 Civil Rights Act, Congress both recognized that punitive damages are available in some instances under section 504 and limited the amount of those damages.[114]

Although individuals who wish to file a claim under section 504 in federal court have not been required to "exhaust" their claim by filing first with a federal agency, there may be good practical reasons for using an office for civil rights (OCR) of an appropriate federal agency instead of, or before, filing an action in federal court. Generally claims must be filed with an OCR within 180 days of the date of the discriminatory act.[115] If an OCR takes a case, it will investigate the matter, issue findings, and, where a violation has been found, obtain a remedy, without expense to the complainant. Thus, filing an administration complaint with an OCR may present the opportunity to resolve a matter more efficiently than going through the federal courts.

There may also be disadvantages to filing a claim with an OCR. An OCR does not represent persons who file complaints. Rather, it uses their complaints to ensure that the statutory and agency objectives of section 504 are met. As a result, an individual may file a complaint of employment discrimination, obtain a violation finding, but fail to receive the remedy he or she desired.

Conclusion

The protections secured for persons with learning disabilities under the Rehabilitation Act and the ADA are now a part of American civil rights history. Lessons learned from past advances make it clear that civil rights can be subject to reversal and diminution, particularly when not thoughtfully or vigorously exercised. These laws have much that will be open to interpretation by the courts. Nothing guarantees that the courts will be understanding of the particular needs of the learning-disabled community. Now is the moment to set precedents that are favorable to the learning-disabled community. The community must reject cases that suggest that the ADA or the Rehabilitation Act is a guarantee of employment to individuals with learning disabilities or that Congress intended these laws to provide reasonable accommodations that would have others do the essential functions of a job for community members. However, the community must press the case that its members are included within the definition of disabled, even for individuals who are high functioning in some skill areas. Further, the community, perhaps in an alliance with persons with visual impairments, must get the courts and employers to carefully distinguish between when reading or writing is merely the traditional way of accomplishing a job and when such skills are truly necessary. Finally, the community must educate the courts and employers as to the full range of accommodations that eliminate surmountable barriers to employment.

One looks forward to the day when a work force populated by skillful and hard-working individuals with learning disabilities will dispel the ignorance that exists about the learning-disabled community. Such a day will arrive only after respected employees with learning disabilities reveal their status as members of the community[116] and demonstrate their determination to obtain the full measure of their rights under the Rehabilitation Act of 1973 and the Americans with Disabilities Act.

Research Sources

The most useful sources to gain an understanding of the meaning of title I of the ADA and section 504 and that have primarily been relied on in this chapter are volume 29, part 1630, and volume 34, part 104, of the *Code of Federal Regulations*. Part 1630 and other regulations pertaining to aspects of the ADA were published on July 26, 1991 in volume 56 of the *Federal Register* at pages 35, 455–765. Part 1630 in particular is found at pages 35, 734–39. The *Code of Federal Regulations* is available at law schools and law libraries. The *Federal Register* can be found in law libraries as well as in many public libraries. In addition, these documents are available through the Government Printing Office, by writing to the EEOC, and in the publications of several law book services such as the *National Disability Law Reporter*, published by LRP Publications, and *Employment Practices Decisions*, published by Commerce Clearing House. Further, part 1630 and its appendix may also be obtained in alternative formats, such as in large print, by calling the EEOC at (202) 663-4395.

Additional sources are technical assistance manuals published or supported by the DOJ and the EEOC under the titles:

> Department of Justice, *Americans with Disabilities Act of 1990, U.S. Department of Justice Technical Assistance Manuals Titles II & III* (Commerce Clearing House, 1992)
>
> Equal Employment Opportunities Commission, *Technical Assistance Manual for the Americans with Disabilities Act* (1992)
>
> The Association of Handicapped Student Services Programs in Postsecondary

Education with support from the U.S. Department of Justice, *Testing Accommodations for Persons with Disabilities: A Guide for Licensure, Certification, and Credentialling* (1992)

End Notes

1. A prime example of the kind of courage and political savvy that had to be displayed by disabled persons to achieve equal employment opportunity is the story of how a group of disabled individuals, including persons with severe disabilities, engaged in acts of civil disobedience to force the federal government to issue regulations implementing the Rehabilitation Act of 1973. For a discussion of this history, see Timothy J. Cook, *The Scope of the Right to Meaningful Access and the Defense of Undue Burdens under Disability Civil Rights Laws*, 20 Loy. L.A. L. Rev. 1471 (1987).

2. It may certainly be true that learning disabled persons do not succeed in school or in business, . . . but this inequality stems from their inability to perform the writing-based skills essential to business success. . . . Plaintiff produced no evidence before the agency [the U.S. Small Business Administration] that either he personally or his group in general is or was discriminated against because they are perceived with a cultural prejudice or bias by American society or any significant segment thereof, on account of the fact of their disability. In short, the inequality plaintiff suffers in competitive position is an unfortunate result of the nature of the handicap itself, rather than of society's attitude towards it.

   Doe & Maryland Assoc. for Children with Learning Disabilities, Inc. v. Small Business Admin., 671 F. Supp. 1081, 1083 (D. Md. 1987). *See also* Trobaugh v. Hy-Vee Food Stores, Inc., 392 N.W. 154, 157 (Iowa 1986).

3. The Americans with Disabilities Act of 1990, P.L. No. 101-336, 104 Stat. 327, 330–37 (codified at 42 U.S.C.A. §§ 12101–12213 (West Supp. 1991)). Hereinafter title I of the ADA will be referred to as title I.

   Federal agencies responsible for implementing the ADA have several ways in which they issue interpretations and guidance concerning the ADA. The most important source is a regulation. The next most important source is an "appendix" to the regulation. Both the Department of Justice (DOJ) and the Equal Employment Opportunity Commission (EEOC) have issued appendices to their respective regulations. More guidance, generally referred to as "technical assistance," may be expected from agencies with implementation responsibilities. Both the DOJ and the EEOC have issued technical assistance manuals.

The lead agency with responsibility for coordination of implementation of the ADA is the United States Justice Department. On July 26, 1991, the DOJ published in the *Federal Register* regulations and an appendix, containing a "section by section" analysis clarifying subtitle A of title II of the ADA as well as certain provisions of titles III and V. 56 Fed. Reg. 35,694, 35,696–702 (to be codified as 28 C.F.R. pt. 35, app. A). Title II of the ADA concerns state and local government agencies. *See infra* note 11. Title III of the ADA concerns public accommodations and services operated by private entities.

Additional guidance by the DOJ may be expected. *See,* e.g., DEPARTMENT OF JUSTICE, AMERICANS WITH DISABILITIES ACT OF 1990, U.S. DEPARTMENT OF JUSTICE TECHNICAL ASSISTANCE MANUALS TITLES II & III (Commerce Clearing House, 1992) [hereinafter DOJ TA MANUAL]. This document may be obtained through the DOJ or Commerce Clearing House, a law book publishing company.

As explained in *"Tests and examinations,"* the regulation, appendix, and technical assistance published by the DOJ are of particular interest to persons who are learning disabled because of the treatment of licensing and credentialing examinations found in these legal authorities. *See infra* notes 56–76 and accompanying text.

For citations to the EEOC regulations, appendix, and technical assistance manual, *see infra* notes 14, 17.

4. The Americans with Disabilities Act amends, but does not repeal, the Rehabilitation Act. ADA § 501(a), 104 Stat. at 369.

5. The Rehabilitation Act of 1973, P.L. No. 93–112, §§ 500–504, 87 Stat. 355, 390–94 (current version at 29 U.S.C. § 790–794d) [hereinafter Rehabilitation Act]. Hereinafter title V of the Rehabilitation Act will be referred to as title V.

6. 29 U.S.C. § 791 (1988).

7. 29 U.S.C. § 793 (1988). Federal contractors are primarily entities that provide the federal government services and supplies, such as defense contractors, research institutions, and companies engaged in federally assisted con-struction. Section 503 is administered by the United States Department of Labor (DOL).

8. 29 U.S.C. § 794 (1988). Typical entities that receive federal financial assistance are educational institutions of all types such as elementary and secondary schools as well as colleges, universities, and museums. Other major recipients of federal financial assistance covered by section 504 of the Rehabilitation Act of 1973 include hospitals and state and local government health and human services programs such as welfare and rehabilitation programs. More than 80 federal agencies have issued section 504 regulations, based on a U.S. Justice Department prototype. Nondiscrimination on the Basis of Disability in State and Local Government Services, 56 Fed. Reg. 35,694–701 (1991) (to be codified at 28 C.F.R. pt. 35).

9. Title I of the ADA contains certain limited exemptions for religious entities. 42 U.S.C.A. § 12113(c). The definition of a covered "entity" (employer) does not include bona fide private membership clubs (other than labor unions) or Indian tribes. 42 U.S.C.A. § 12111(5)(B).

10. 42 U.S.C.A. §§ 12111–12117.

10A. Section 506 of the Rehabilitation Act Amendments of 1992, P.L. 102–569, 106 Stat. 4344.

11. Title I covers state and local government agencies with the requisite number of employees. Smaller state and local government agencies are covered by subtitle A of title II of the ADA, 42 U.S.C.A. §§ 12131–12134, which concurrently covers the state and local entities also covered by title I. Subtitle A extends the anti-discrimination requirements of section 504 to all state and local programs and activities, including those that do not receive federal financial assistance. Taken together, these provisions of the ADA cover an entity as large as a state department of human services or as small as a one room school district.

12. 42 U.S.C.A. § 12101(a)(1) (Congressional findings in the ADA).

13. N.Y. TIMES, Sept. 17, 1989, at E5.

14. 42 U.S.C.A. § 12102(2); Equal Employment Opportunity for Individuals with Disabilities, 56 Fed. Reg. 35,726, 35,735 (to be codified at 29 C.F.R. § 1630.2(g)-(k)); Nondiscrimination on the Basis of Handicap in Programs and Activities Receiving Federal Financial Assistance, 34 C.F.R. § 104(3)(j) (1991); Appendix to part 1630—Interpretative Guidance on Title I of the Americans with Disabilities Act, 56 Fed. Reg. 35,726, 35,740–43 (1991) (to be codified at 29 C.F.R. § 1630, app. A) [hereinafter Appendix]. *See* Mantolete v. Bolger, 767 F.2d 1416, 1422 (9th Cir. 1985)

15. 42 U.S.C.A. § 12102(2). The 1973 Rehabilitation Act originally defined "handicap" exclusively in terms of employability. 87 Stat. 355, 361. The current definition was adopted in 1974. 88 Stat. 1617, 1619.
16. 42 U.S.C.A. § 12101; 56 Fed. Reg. 35,735 (to be codified at 29 C.F.R. § 1630.2(h)); 34 C.F.R. § 104.3(j)(2)(i); Appendix, *supra* note 14, 56 Fed. Reg. at 35,740–41.
17. Part 1630, the EEOC regulation implementing title I of the ADA, at 29 C.F.R. § 1630.2(h)(2), expressly states that "specific learning disabilities" are an impairment. 56 Fed. Reg. 35,735 (to be codified at 29 C.F.R. § 1630.2(h)(2)). For the equivalent DOJ regulation implementing subtitle A of title II of the ADA, see Nondiscrimination on the Basis of Disability in State and Local Government Services, 56 Fed. Reg. 35,964 (1991) (to be codified at 35 C.F.R. § 35.104(l)(ii). *See also supra* note 11.

    Numerous agency regulations implementing the Rehabilitation Act contain the same language. For example, specific learning disabilities are stated as an impairment in 34 C.F.R. § 104.3(j)(2)(i)(B). The appendix to part 1630, at three points, includes individuals who are learning disabled either within the definition of impairment or in examples concerning someone defined as a disabled individual. For instance, the appendix to part 1630 distinguishes between a person who cannot read due to a lack of education and a person who is unable to read due to dyslexia in order to explain what is an impairment under the ADA. "[A]n individual who is unable to read because of dyslexia would be an individual with a disability because dyslexia, a learning disability, is an impairment." Appendix, *supra* note 14, 56 Fed. Reg. at 35,741. The appendix also discusses how the ADA protects persons who are misclassified as learning disabled. *Id.* Finally, the appendix cites and discusses at some length the case of Stutts v. Freeman, 694 F.2d 666 (11th Cir. 1983), a case establishing the duty of employers to give accommodated selection tests to individuals with disabilities, particularly persons disabled by dyslexia. Appendix, *supra* note 14, 56 Fed. Reg. at 35,749

    Persons with dysgraphia may wish to cite to the appendix to part 1630 at page 35,744 where it discusses persons "with a disability that inhibits the ability to write. . . ." The technical assistance manual of the EEOC uses treatment of persons with learning disabilities to clarify the requirements of title I. EQUAL EMPLOYMENT OPPORTUNITIES COMMISSION, TECHNICAL ASSISTANCE MANUAL FOR THE AMERICANS WITH DISABILITIES ACT, at II-2, III-29, V-18, V-19 (1992) [hereinafter EEOC TA MANUAL]. For discussion of "hidden disabilities" *see id.* at III-8, V-4. The U.S. Department of Justice technical assistance manual for titles II and III of the ADA includes advice on how to modify college entrance examinations and professional and licensing examinations for individuals with learning disabilities. DOJ TA MANUAL, *supra* note 3, at II-4.6, III-4.61.
18. ROBERT R. DAVILA ET AL., MEMORANDUM TO CHIEF STATE SCHOOL OFFICERS CONCERNING CLARIFICATION OF POLICY TO ADDRESS THE NEEDS OF CHILDREN WITH ATTENTION DEFICIT DISORDERS WITH GENERAL AND/OR SPECIAL EDUCATION 6 (1991). This document may be obtained under the Freedom of Information Act through the United States Department of Education.
19. 42 U.S.C.A. § 12102(2)(A); 56 Fed. Reg. 35,735 (to be codified at 29 C.F.R. § 1630.2(i); 34 C.F.R. § 104.3(j)(2)(ii); Appendix, *supra* note 14, 56 Fed. Reg. at 35,741.
20. Jasany v. United States Postal Serv., 755 F.2d 1244 (6th Cir. 1985); E. E. Black, Ltd. v. Marshall, 497 F. Supp. 1088 (D. Hawaii 1980).
21. 56 Fed. Reg. 35,735 (to be codified at 29 C.F.R. § 1630.29(i)); 34 C.F.R. § 104.3(j)(2)(ii); Appendix, *supra* note 14, 56 Fed. Reg. at 35,741.
22. Support for this position is found in the EEOC technical assistance manual for the ADA that explains that persons with substantially impaired "sensory skills" are entitled to accommodation in testing. Along with the sensory skills found in the ADA, hearing and seeing, the manual adds "process[ing] information." EEOC TA MANUAL, *supra* note 17, at V-18. Other support for information processing as a major life activity may be found in the portion of the *DOJ TA Manual* concerning title III of the ADA. The *Manual* states that "problems perceiving and processing written information" may make individuals with learning disabilities eligible for the assistance of "auxiliary aids," such as readers, while taking college entrance and professional licensing examinations. DOJ TA MANUAL, *supra* note 3, at III-4.6100. *See also infra* notes 58–59 and accompanying text.
23. 42 U.S.C.A. § 12102(2)(A); 56 Fed. Reg. 35,735 (to be codified at 29 C.F.R. § 1630.2(j); 34 C.F.R. § 104.3(j); Appendix, *supra* note 14, 56 Fed. Reg. at 35,741.
24. *See supra* notes 17, 22. *See infra* notes 58–60, 68.
25. Trobaugh v. Hy-Vee Food Stores, Inc., 392 N.W.2d 154, 155, 157 (Iowa 1986).
26. *Id.* at 155, 157.

27. For other cases where plaintiffs had difficulty proving that they were disabled *see* Wynne v. Tufts University School of Medicine, 932 F.2d 19 (1st Cir. 1991), *remanded to* D. Mass. [unreported], 1992 WL 46077, *affirmed*, 976 F.2d 791 (1st Cir. 1992); Pandazides v. Virginia Bd. of Educ., 946 F.2d 345 (4th Cir. Va. 1991), 804 F. Supp. 794, 1992 (D. Va. 1992); Doe & Maryland Assoc for Children with Learning Disabilities, Inc. v. Small Business Admin., 671 F. Supp. 1081 (D. Med. 1987); Pridemore v. Legal Aid Soc'y of Dayton, 625 F. Supp. 1171 (S.D. Ohio 1985); Beck v. James 793 S.W.2d 416 (Mo. Ct. App. 1980). *See infra* notes 71–75 and accompanying text.

28. Skillern v. Bolger, 725 F.2d 1121 (7th Cir. 1984) (disparate treatment discrimination); Stutts v. Freeman, 694 F.2d 666 (11th Cir. 1983) (accommodation in application process); Sedor v. Postmaster General, 756 F. Supp. 684 (D. Conn. 1991) (modification of due process dismissal procedures as a necessary reasonable accommodation); DiPompo v. West Point Military Academy, 708 F. Supp. 540 (S.D.N.Y. 1989), 770 F. Supp. 887 (S.D.N.Y. 1991) (determination of essential functions of a job); Anderson v. Autoworkers, 738 F. Supp. 441 (D. Kan. 1990) (cause of action for intentional infliction of emotional harm is viable for failure to provide accommodation); Fitzgerald v. Green Valley Area Educ. Agency, 589 F. Supp. 1130 (S.D. Iowa 1984) (determination of essential functions of a job); American Fed. Gov't Emp., Local 51 v. Baker, 677 F. Supp. 636 (N.D. Cal. 1987), *remanded*, 1992 WL 191099 (N.D. Cal. Jan. 28, 1992) (relationship of production methods to duty to provide reasonable accommodation to federal employees); Koeppel v. Wachtler, 141 A.D.2d 613, 529 N.Y.S.2d 359 (1988) (duty to accommodate form of bar examination). *See also* Biberos v. Dayco Products, Inc., No. CV90-L-23, 1990 WL 302888 (D. Neb. Dec. 17, 1990); Love v. Dep't of Justice, Bureau of Prisons, EEOC decision number 01903553 (Mar. 5, 1991); McKoy v. Secretary of the Army, EEOC decision number 05900101 (May 4, 1990); *and* Beck v. James, 793 S.W.2d 416 (Mo. Ct. App. 1990).

29. *See* Anderson v. Autoworkers, 738 F. Supp. 441 (D. Kan. 1990); American Fed. of Gov't Emp., Local 51 v. Baker, 677 F. Supp. 636 (N.D.Cal. 1987), *remanded*, 1992 WL 191099 (N.D. Cal. Jan. 28, 1992).

30. *See* Fitzgerald v. Green Valley Area Educ. Agency, 589 F. Supp. 1130 (S.D. Iowa 1984); Love v. Dep't of Justice, Bureau of Prisons, EEOC decision number 01903553 (Mar. 5, 1991); Beck v. James, 793 S.W.2d 416 (Mo. Ct. App. 1990); Koeppel v. Wachtler, 141 A.D.2d 613, 529 N.Y.S.2d 359 (1988); Trobaugh v. Hy-Vee Food Stores, Inc., 392 N.W.2d 154 (Iowa 1986). *But see* Pandazides v. Virginia Bd. of Educ., 946 F.2d 345 (4th Cir. 1991), 804 F. Supp. 794 (D. Va. 1992).

31. American Fed. of Gov't Emp., Local 51 v. Baker, 677 F. Supp. 636 (N.D. Cal 1987), *remanded*, 1992 WL 191099 (N.D. Cal. Jan. 28, 1992). *But see* Pandazides v. Virginia Bd. of Educ., 946 F.2d 345 (4th Cir. 1991), 804 F. Supp. 794, (D. Va. 1992).

32. DiPompo v. West Point Military Academy, 770 F. Supp. 887 (S.D. N.Y. 1991).

33. *See* Sedor v. Postmaster General, 756 F. Supp. 684 (D. Conn. 1991); American Fed. of Gov't Emp., Local 51 v. Baker, 677 F. Supp. 636 (N.D. Cal 1987), *remanded*, 1992 WL 191099 (N.D. Cal. Jan. 28, 1992); Love v. Dep't of Justice, Bureau of Prisons, EEOC decision number 01903553 (Mar. 5, 1991); McKoy v. Secretary of the Army, E.E.O.C. decision number 05900101 (May 4, 1990).

34. 56 Fed. Reg. 35,735 (to be codified at 29 C.F.R. § 1630.2(k)); 34 C.F.R. § 104.3(j)(2)(iii), Appendix, *supra* note 14, 56 Fed. Reg. at 35,742.

35. The appendix to part 1630 specifically states that, "individuals misclassified as learning disabled are protected from discrimination on the basis of that erroneous classification." Appendix, *supra* note 14, 56 Fed. Reg. at 35,742.

36. 42 U.S.C.A. § 12102(2)(A); 56 Fed. Reg. 35,735 (to be codified at 29 C.F.R. § 1630.2(i)); 34 C.F.R. § 104.3(j).

37. 42 U.S.C.A. § 12203(a); 56 Fed. Reg. 35,737 (to be codified at 29 C.F.R. § 1630.12) (EEOC); 56 Fed. Reg. 35,719 (to be codified at 28 C.F.R. § 35.134) (DOJ). The various regulations implementing section 504 prohibit retaliation through incorporation of regulations implementing title VI of the Civil Rights Act of 1964, 42 U.S.C. § 2000d (1988). This provision is incorporated into the Department of Education section 504 regulation at 34 C.F.R. § 104.61. *See, e.g.*, Nondiscrimination under Programs Receiving Federal Assistance through the Department of Education Effectuation of Title VI of the Civil Rights Act of 1964, 34 C.F.R. § 100.7(e) (1991) (anti-retaliation provision of the Department of Education).

38. 42 U.S.C.A. § 12112(b)(4); 56 Fed. Reg. 35,737 (to be codified at 29 C.F.R. § 1630.8).

39. 42 U.S.C.A. 12111(8); 56 Fed. Reg. 35,735 (to be codified at 29 C.F.R. § 1630.2(n); 34 C.F.R. § 104.3(k)(1); Appendix, *supra* note 14, 56 Fed. Reg. at 35,735.

40. The word "legitimate" is used here to indicate that not all employers' job standards are lawful. 42 U.S.C.A. §§ 12112–12114; 56 Fed.

Reg. 35,736, 35,737 (to be codified at 29 C.F.R. §§ 1630.4, 1630.7, 1630.9, 1630.15); 34 C.F.R. §§ 104.11(a)(3), 104.13; Appendix, supra note 14, 56 Fed. Reg. at 35,746, 35,751–52. For example, it is not legitimate to require that all prospective employees be in "good health." See Treadwell v. Alexander, 707 F.2d 473 (11th Cir. 1983); Bentivegna v. Dep't of Labor, 694 F.2d 619 (9th Cir. 1982); Prewitt v. United States Postal Serv., 662 F.2d 292 (5th Cir. Unit A 1981); Coleman v. Casey County Bd. of Educ., 510 F. Supp. 301 (D. Ky. 1980). See also cases concerning prerequisites to post-secondary education programs, County of Los Angeles v. Kling, 769 F.2d 532 (9th Cir. 1985); Pushkin v. Regents of the University of Colorado, 658 F.2d 1372 (10th Cir. 1981); Doe v. New York University, 666 F.2d 761 (2d Cir. 1981).

41. 56 Fed. Reg. 35,735 (to be codified at 29 C.F.R. § 1630.2(n)); Appendix, supra note 14, 56 Fed. Reg. at 35,744–45. The fact that a particular function is performed only occasionally does not render it per se nonessential. Treadwell v. Alexander, 707 F.2d 473, 477 (11th Cir. 1983); Appendix, supra note 14, 56 Fed. Reg. at 35,744. For an extensive exploration of how to determine the essential functions of a job under the Rehabilitation Act, see Simon v. St. Louis County, 656 F.2d 316 (8th Cir. 1981), 753 F.2d 1082 (8th Cir. 1984), cert. denied 455 U.S. 1034. The plaintiff, a once able-bodied police officer, became a paraplegic as the result of a shooting. He unsuccessfully challenged a police department rule that all officers be able to effect a forcible arrest.

42. 708 F. Supp. 540 (S.D.N.Y. 1989) (opposing motions for summary judgment); 770 F. Supp. 887 (S.D.N.Y. 1991) (decision in favor of the Academy on the merits).

43. See infra note 52.

44. 589 F. Supp. 1130 (S.D. Iowa 1984).

45. 34 C.F.R. § 104.11(a)(2) (1991). Appendix A to the Department of Education's section 504 regulation, further explains that

> [s]ection 606 of the EHA obligates elementary and secondary school systems that receive EHA funds to take positive steps to employ and advance in employment qualified handicapped persons. . . . Congress chose the words "positive steps" instead of "affirmative action" advisedly and did not intend section 606 to incorporate the types of activities required . . . under section 501 and 503 of the Rehabilitation Act of 1973.

34. C.F.R. pt. 104, app. A.

The IDEA, 20 U.S.C. § 1405, was formerly known as the Education of the Handicapped

Act (EHA), the Education of All Handicapped Children Act (EAHCA), and Public Law 94-142 until it was changed by the Education of the Handicapped Act Amendments of 1990. P.L. No. 101-476, 104 Stat. 1103, to the Individuals with Disabilities Education Act (IDEA).

46. The only exception that exists to this rule under title I of the ADA pertains to persons who are qualified to receive the benefit of the form of reasonable accommodation known as "reassignment to a vacant position."

The appendix to part 1630 explains the rules of reassignment as follows:

> [R]eassignment should be considered only when accommodation within the individual's current position would pose an undue hardship. Reassignment is not available to applicants. . . . An employer may reassign an individual to a lower graded position if there are no accommodations that would enable the employee to remain in the current position and there are no vacant equivalent positions for which the individual is qualified with or without reasonable accommodation. An employer, however, is not required to maintain the reassigned individual with a disability at the salary of the higher graded position if it does not so maintain reassigned employees who are not disabled. It should also be noted that an employer is not required to promote an individual with a disability as an accommodation. See Senate Report at 31–32; House Labor Report at 63.

Appendix, supra note 14, 56 Fed. Reg. at 35,744. See also infra notes 52–54 and accompanying text.

While reassignment to a vacant position is one of the additional accommodations specified in the ADA, it is not currently authorized by section 504. However, at the time of the writing of this chapter, Congress was considering legislation that would amend section 504 to adapt the employment discrimination standards of title I of the ADA. Passage of this law is considered very likely. See H.R. 5482, 102d Cong., 2d Sess. § 506 (1992).

47. Id. at 56 Fed. Reg. at 35,747.

48. 56 Fed. Reg. 35,736 (to be codified at 29 C.F.R. § 1630.2(o)(3)); Appendix, supra note 14, 56 Fed. Reg. at 35,748–49.

49. Appendix, supra note 14, 56 Fed. Reg. at 35,744.

50. 56 Fed. Reg. 35,737 (to be codified at 29 C.F.R. § 1630.9(d)).

51. Appendix, supra note 14, 56 Fed. Reg. at 35,744.

52. Part 1630 expressly provides that an employer's qualification standards may include a requirement that an individual shall not pose "a direct threat to the health or safety of the individual or others in the workplace." 42 U.S.C.A. § 12113(d); 56 Fed. Reg. 35,736 (to be codified at 29 C.F.R. § 1630.2(r)). Like any other qualification standard, the standard must apply to all individuals, not just to disabled persons. If no reasonable accommodation exists that will reduce the risk to a reasonable level, the employer need not hire the person or maintain him or her as an employee. The assessment of harm must be based on objective evidence and not on stereotypes, irrational or generalized fears, or mere speculation. Appendix, *supra* note 14, 56 Fed. Reg. at 35,745; School Bd. v. Arline, 480 U.S. 273, 287–88 (1987). *See also* Rehabilitation, Comprehensive Services, and Developmental Disabilities Amendments of 1978, P.L. No. 95-602, § 122(a), 92 Stat. 2955, 2984 (codified as amended in scattered sections of 29 U.S.C. title VII (1988)).

    This provision of the ADA would justify, for example, refusing to hire as an airline pilot a person who due to a learning disability has a poor sense of direction. However, "a law firm could not reject an applicant with a history of disabling mental illness based on a generalized fear that the stress of trying to make partner might trigger a relapse of the individual's mental illness. . . ." Appendix, *supra* note 14, 56 Fed. Reg. at 35,745.

53. Under section 504, reasonable accommodation that conflicts with a collective bargaining agreement may be an undue hardship. Carter v. Tisch, 822 F.2d 465, 469 (4th Cir. 1987). *See also* Jasany v. United States Postal Serv., 755 F.2d 1244 (6th Cir. 1985); Carty v. Carlin, 623 F. Supp. 1181, 1189 (D. Md. 1985); Bey v. Bolger, 540 F. Supp. 910 (E.D. Pa. 1982). "An employer cannot be required to accommodate a handicapped employee by restructuring a job in a manner which would usurp the legitimate rights of the employees of a collective bargaining agreement." *Jasany,* 755 F.2d at 1252.

    The relationship between undue hardship, the terms of a collective bargaining agreement, and reasonable accommodation in the form of reassignment is an emerging issue under the ADA. Some insight into this issue is provided by the *EEOC TA Manual,* which suggests by way of example that reassignment contrary to a seniority system established through collective bargaining "might be an undue hardship. . . . However, since both the employer and the union are covered by the ADA's requirements . . . the employer should consult with the union and try to work out an acceptable accommodation." EEOC TA Manual, *supra* note 17, at III–16.

54. 567 F. Supp. 369 (E.D. Pa. 1983), *aff'd without opinion,* 732 F.2d 147 (3d Cir. 1984), *cert. denied,* 469 U.S. 1188 (1985).

55. Appendix, *supra* note 14, 56 Fed. Reg. at 35,744.

56. 42 U.S.C.A. § 12112(b)(3), (6), (7); 56 Fed. Reg. 35,737 (to be codified at 29 C.F.R. §§ 1630.7, 1630.10, 1630.11); 34 C.F.R. § 104.13.

57. 42 U.S.C.A. § 12111(9); 56 Fed. Reg. 35,736, 35,737 (to be codified at 29 C.F.R. §§ 1630.2(o)(i), 1630.11).

58. **II-4.6100 Examinations.** Examinations covered by this section include examinations for admission to secondary schools, college entrance examinations, examinations for admission to trade or professional schools, and licensing examinations such as bar exams, examinations for medical licenses, or examinations for certified public accountants. , . . A private entity offering an examination covered by this section is responsible for selecting and administering the examination in . . . a manner that . . . accurately reflects an individual's aptitude or achievement level or other factor the examination purports to measure, rather than reflecting the individual's impaired sensory skill . . . (except where those skills are the factors that the examination purports to measure). . . . Where necessary, an examiner may be required to provide auxiliary aids or services, unless it can demonstrate that offering a particular auxiliary aid or service would fundamentally alter the examination or result in an undue burden. . . . [S]ome individuals with learning disabilities may need auxiliary aids or services, such as readers, because of problems in perceiving and processing written information. See III-4.300 for a general discussion of auxiliary aids and services.

    DOJ TA Manual, *supra* note 3, at III-4.6100. *See also* Appendix, *supra* note 14, 56 Fed. Reg. at 35,749; EEOC TA Manual, *supra* note 17, at V-18; and *infra* note 68.

59. "Providing extra time to take a test may be a reasonable accommodation for people with certain disabilities, such as visual impairments, learning disabilities, or mental retardation." EEOC TA Manual, *supra* note 17, at V-19. Other examples provided by the EEOC include: "oral rather than written testing unless reading is an essential job function, . . . record[ing] test answers by tape recorder, dic-

tation, or computer" and "tak[ing] a test in a separate room, if a group test setting is not relevant to the job itself." *Id.* at III-29, V-21. *See also supra* notes 22, 58.

60.   A person with dyslexia should be given an opportunity to take a written test orally, if the dyslexia seriously impairs the individual's ability to read. But if ability to read is a job-related function that the test is designed to measure, the employer could require that a person with dyslexia take the written test. However, even in this situation, reasonable accommodation should be considered. The person with dyslexia might be accommodated with a reader, unless the ability to read unaided is an essential job function, unless such an accommodation would not be possible on the job for which s/he is being tested, or would be an undue hardship. For example, the ability to read without help would be essential for a proofreader's job.

EEOC TA MANUAL, *supra* note 17, at V-19.

[A]n employer could require that an applicant complete a test within an established time frame if speed is one of the skills that the test is designed to measure. However, the result of a timed test should not be used to exclude a person with a disability unless the test measures a particular speed necessary to perform an essential function of the job, and there is no reasonable accommodation that would enable this person to perform that function within prescribed time frames, or the accommodation would cause an undue hardship.

Id.

See *infra* notes 76–77 and accompanying text, discussing Wynne v. Tufts University School of Medicine, wherein the First Circuit Court stated that a medical school had the authority to conclude that quick reading skills were essential to being qualified to become a doctor.

61.   See **"What Are the Essential Functions of a Job?"** *supra* notes 39–45 and accompanying text.

62.   Generally, an employer is only required to provide such an accommodation if it knows, before administering a test, that an accommodation will be needed. Usually, it is the responsibility of the individual with a disability to request any required accommodation for a test. It has been suggested that the employer inform applicants, in advance, of any tests that will be administered as part of the application process so that they may request an accommodation, if needed. The employer may require that an individual with a disability request an accommodation within a specific time period before administration of the test. The employer also may require that documentation of the need for accommodation accompany such a request.

EEOC TA MANUAL, *supra* note 17, at V-20.

The requirement that an employee give advance notice of his or her need for an accommodated test is circumscribed by the general principle under the ADA and section 504 that an employer should not make an inquiry into the nature of an individual's disability prior to making an offer of employment. Employers are permitted to make a "pre-offer" inquiry into the ability of an applicant to perform "job-related" functions. 42 U.S.C.A. § 12112(c); 56 Fed. Reg. 35,737–38 (to be codified at 29 C.F.R. § 1630.14); 34 C.F.R. § 104.14; Appendix, *supra* note 14, 56 Fed. Reg. at 35,750–51. Thus the proper inquiry is not, "What is the cause of your paraplegia?" but rather, "Can you operate a word processor?" An employer may ask how an individual with a "known disability" can perform the essential functions of a job, even though it does not make a general inquiry of this nature of all job applicants. *Id.* at 56 Fed. Reg. at 35,750; 34 C.F.R. pt. 104, app. A.

63.   A notable exception to this are some agencies conducting law enforcement and bar examinations that receive funds from the DOJ. The DOJ issued regulations implementing section 504 with regard to DOJ funding in 1984. *See* Enforcement of Nondiscrimination on the Basis of Handicap in Programs or Activities conducted by the Department of Justice, 49 Fed. Reg. 35,723 (1984) (codified at 28 C.F.R. pt. 39 (1991)). 28 C.F.R. § 39.130(b)(6) provides, in pertinent part, "The agency may not administer a licensing or certification program in a manner that subjects qualified handicapped persons to discrimination on the basis of handicap. . . . However, the programs or activities of entities that are licensed or certified by the agency are not, themselves covered by this part [of the law]." *Id.*

64.   42 U.S.C.A. § 12131. *See supra* note 11. With regard to licensing and credentialing by agencies subject to subtitle A of title II, the DOJ regulation found at 28 C.F.R. § 35.130(b)(6) repeats the prohibition against discrimination in licensing and certification issued in the earlier section 504 regulation of DOJ found at 28 C.F.R. § 39.130(b)(6). *See supra* notes 58 and 63 and accompanying text.

65.   42 U.S.C.A. § 12189 provides: "Any person that offers examination or courses related to

application, licensing, certification, or credentialing for secondary or post-secondary education, professional, or trade purposes shall offer such examinations or courses in a place and manner accessible to persons with disabilities or offer alternative accessible arrangements for such individuals." *Id. See supra* note 58.

66. 42 U.S.C.A. § 12189.

67. Pandazides v. Virginia Bd. of Educ., 946 F.2d 345 (4th Cir. 1991), 804 F. Supp. 794, (E.D. Va. 1992); Stutts v. Freeman, 694 F.2d 666 (11th Cir. 1983). *See also* Wynne v. Tufts University School of Medicine, 932 F.2d 19 (1st Cir. 1991), *remanded* to D. Mass. [unreported], 1992 WL 46077, *affirmed*, 976 F.2d 791 (1st Cir. 1992).

68. 29 C.F.R. § 1630.11 concerns administration of tests. 56 Fed. Reg. 35,737 (to be codified at 29 C.F.R. § 1630.11). This provision requires that employment tests be administered to eligible applicants or employees with disabilities that impair sensory, manual, or speaking skills in formats that do not require the use of the impaired skill. *Id.* Regulations implementing section 504 require the same form of accommodation. However, there has been debate as to whether they were meant to apply to persons with learning disabilities. The question has been whether such persons have impaired sensory, manual, or speaking skills. The EEOC has put this issue to rest, at least by implication; individuals with learning disabilities are considered to have impaired "sensory skills." The appendix to part 1630 states: "[I]t would be unlawful to administer a written employment test to an individual who has informed the employer, prior to the administration of the test, that he is disabled with dyslexia and unable to read. In such a case, as a reasonable accommodation and in accordance with this provision, an alternative oral test should be administered to that individual." Appendix, *supra* note 14, 56 Fed. Reg. at 35,749.

69. *Stutts,* 694 F.2d at 669.

70. *Id.*

71. 946 F.2d 345 (4th Cir. 1991), 804 F. Supp. 794, (E.D. Va. 1992).

72. *Id.* at 348. *See also* The Uniform Selection Guidelines, 45 C.F.R. 60–3.

73. *Id.* at 349–50.

74. 804 F. Supp. 794 (E.D. Va.).

75. *Id.* at 803.

76. Wynne v. Tufts University School of Medicine, 932 F.2d 19 (1st Cir. 1991), *remanded* to D. Mass. [unreported], 1992 WL 46077, aff'd, 976 F.2d 791 (1st Cir. 1990), *cert. denied*, 113 S.Ct. 1845, __ U.S. __ (April 19, 1993).

77. 976 F.2d at 792.

78. For insight into the myriad of ways Wynne's case could be analyzed, a review of its unusually complex procedural history, including withdrawn opinions, may prove useful. Wynne v. Tufts University School of Medicine, 1990 WL 52715 (1st Cir. Cir., April 30, 1990), *panel opinion withdrawn, judgment vacated* (August 21, 1990), *opinion superseded on rehearing*, 932 F.2d 19 (1st Cir. 1991), *remanded* to D. Mass. [unreported], 1992 WL 46077, *aff'd*, 976 F.2d 791 (1st Cir. 1990), *cert. denied*, 113 S.Ct. 1945, __ U.S. __ (April 19, 1993).

79. *Cert. denied*, 113 S.Ct. 1845, __ U.S. __ (April 19, 1993).

80. 34 C.F.R. § 104.44(c) [Academic adjustments—Course examinations] provides:

> In its course examination or other procedures for evaluating students' academic achievement in its program, a recipient [college or university] shall provide such methods for evaluating the achievement of students who have a [disability] that impairs sensory, manual, or speaking skills as will best ensure that the results of the evaluation represent the student's achievement in the course, rather than reflecting the student's impaired sensory, manual, or speaking skills (except where such skills are the factors that the test purports to measure).

81. 976 F.2d at 973, 794 citing 932 F.2d at 26.

82. *Id.* at 793–95.

83. The court, citing its pre-remand decision in *Tufts* stated, "The point is that Tufts, after undertaking a diligent assessment of available options, felt obligated to make a 'professional, academic judgment that [a] reasonable accommodation [was] simply not available.' " 976 F.2d at 795 citing 932 F.2d at 27–28. At a later point in the opinion the court tightened this standard by noting that, "Of course the effort [to explore alternate accommodations] requires more than mere lip service, it must be sincerely conceived and conscientiously implemented." 976 F.2d at 795.

84. 976 F.2d at 792, 793 n.2, 796.

85. *Id.* at 796.

86. *Id.* at 795, 796 n.3. *See also* Nathanson v. Medical College of Pa., 926 F.2d 1368, 1381 (3d Cir. 1991).

87. *Id.* at 793, 796.

88. *Id.* at 795. Southeastern Community College v. Davis, 442 U.S. 397 (1979).

89. *Id.* at 795–96.

90. *See Id.* at 795.

91. *Id.* at 796.

92. The district court in *Pandazides* cited *Wynne* in support of its finding against Ms. Pan-

dazides. Pandazides v. Virginia Bd. of Educ., 804 F. Supp. 794, 802 (E.D. Va. 1992).

93. 756 F. Supp. 684 (D. Conn. 1991).

94. This case was decided under Section 501 of the Rehabilitation Act. This provision of law pertains only to federal employees. In addition to nondiscrimination, it requires "affirmative action." 29 U.S.C. § 791 (1988). Because section 501 is unique with regard to its affirmative action requirement, precedents under section 501 may not always be applied to cases brought under section 504 or title I of the ADA.

95. 677 F. Supp. 636 (N.D. Cal. 1987), *remanded*, 1992 WL 191099 (N.D. Cal. Jan. 28, 1992).

96. *Id.* at 639.

97. Following the initial district court decision, the parties selected a specialist who determined the proper accommodations for the plaintiffs. The expert recommended among other measures that the plaintiffs should be assigned to a different area of the Mint to reasonably accommodate them. In spite of these instructions, the Treasury refused to implement any of the expert's recommendations. Subsequently, plaintiffs sought a permanent injunction to force the Treasury to comply with the Rehabilitation Act of 1973 and make the suggested changes. The district court granted the injunction because the Mint had made no attempt to accommodate the plaintiffs. Further, the court found that the new production standards of the Mint were neither part of the minimum requirements of the job, nor were they reasonable and attainable. 1992 WL 1991099 (N.D. Cal. 1992).

This case may be limited in the degree to which it will be applied to private sector employment. This case was brought under section 501 of the Rehabilitation Act, which concerns federal employees. The courts have tended to expect more from the federal government than from other employers subject to the Rehabilitation Act.

98. 567 F. Supp. 369 (E.D. Pa. 1983), *aff'd without opinion*, 732 F.2d 147 (3d Cir. 1984), *cert. denied*, 469 U.S. 1188 (1985).

99. *Id.* at 373.

100. 42 U.S.C.A. § 12111(9)(B); 56 Fed. Reg. 35,736 (to be codified at 29 C.F.R. § 1630.2(o)(2)(ii).

101. *See supra* note 68.

102. *See supra* notes 57–58. As to licensing, *see* DOJ TA MANUAL, supra note 3, at II-3700.

103. The Supreme Court, in Delaware State College, 449 U.S. 250 (1980), and Chardon v. Fernandez, 454 U.S. 6 (1981), has held that the time period in which a person must file a charge of discrimination begins to run when the person first becomes aware that the alleged discriminatory action will be taken. For example, the time period begins to run when a teacher is told that his or her teaching contract will not be renewed and not when the old contract expires.

104. The amendment to the employment provisions of the ADA and the Rehabilitation Act is set forth in section 102 of the Civil Rights Act of 1991, PL. No. 102-166, 105 Stat. 1071. These amendments are affected by the addition of a new section to follow section 1981, as 42 U.S.C. § 1981a.

105. The Supreme Court has made clear that a private cause of action may be brought under section 504 to redress employment discrimination. Consolidated Rail Corp. v. Darrone, 465 U.S. 624 (1984). The Supreme Court has not explicitly stated that no duty to exhaust exists in section 504 employment matters. However, it has never refused to hear an employment action under section 504 on the grounds that the plaintiff failed to first file his or her claim with an Office for Civil Rights. *See, e.g.*, School Bd. v. Arline, 480 U.S. 273 (1987). Numerous federal courts have held no such duty to exhaust exists with regard to section 504 actions. *See, e.g.*, Doe v. Garret, 903 F.2d 1455, 1460 (11th Cir. 1990); Pushkin v. Regents of University of Colorado, 658 F.2d 1372, 1381 (10th Cir. 1981); Kling v. County of Los Angeles, 633 F.2d 876, 879 (9th Cir. 1980).

Under section 794a(a)(2) of the Rehabilitation Act, also enacted as Rehabilitation Amendments of 1978, P.L. No. 95-602, 92 Stat. 2955, the procedural requirements of section 504 are essentially the same as those of title VI of the Civil Rights Act of 1964, 42 U.S.C. § 2000d. The Supreme Court has also heard title VI cases without requiring exhaustion through an OCR. *See, e.g.*, Lau v. Nichols, 414 U.S. 563 (1974).

Under section 794a(a)(1) of the Rehabilitation Act, the procedural requirements of section 501 are essentially the same as those of title VII of the Civil Rights Act of 1964, 42 U.S.C. § 2000e-16 (1988). Thus, federal employees who wish to file a lawsuit under section 501 of the Rehabilitation Act **must** exhaust their claims administratively prior to filing in federal court. Doe v. Garrett, 903 F.2d 1455, 1461 (11th Cir. 1990); Prewitt v. United States Postal Serv., 662 F.2d 292, 302–04 (5th Cir. Unit A 1981).

For a comprehensive discussion of "exhaustion" under title V of the Rehabilitation Act, *see* LAURA F. ROTHSTEIN, RIGHTS OF PHYSICALLY HANDICAPPED PERSONS § 4.13, n.133 (Shepard's/McGraw-Hill, 1984 & Supp. 1991) [hereinafter RIGHTS].

106. Since the enforcement provisions for section 504 contain no time limit for bringing a private cause of action, the federal district court will look to the most appropriate time limit provided by analogous state law. Johnson v. Railway Express, 421 U.S. 454, 462 (1975); Beard v. Robinson, 563 F.2d 331, 334 (7th Cir. 1977). The most likely source for time limits are those provided under state fair employment laws. *See, e.g.,* Andrews v. Consolidated Rail Corp., 831 F.2d 678 (7th Cir. 1987).

107. Tanberg v. Weld County Sheriff, 787 F. Supp. 970, 972–73 (D. Colo. 1992). *See* Franklin v. Gwinnett County Public Schools, __ U.S. __, 112 S.Ct. 1028, 1032 (1992). "[W]e presume the availability of all appropriate remedies unless Congress has expressly indicated otherwise." *Id.*

108. Consolidated Rail Corp., 465 U.S. at 630, n.9. For a comprehensive list of cases cited to awarding monetary damages (both equitable and compensatory) under section 504, see RIGHTS, *supra* note 88, at § 4.13, n.202.

109. In Franklin v. Gwinnett, __ U.S. __, 112 S.Ct. 1028 (1992), the Supreme Court held that under title IX of the Education Amendments of 1972, 20 U.S.C. §§ 1681–1688 (1988), compensatory damages are available to redress sexual harassment of a student by her teacher. There is little basis, if any, for distinguishing the remedies available in federal court under title IX and those available under section 504. It is important, however, to note that *Gwinnett* entailed intentional discrimination.

110. Civil Rights Act of 1991, PL. No. 102-166, 105 Stat. 1071.

111. *See* Guardians Assoc. v. Civil Serv. Comm'n of New York, 463 U.S. 582 (1983). It is important to remember that under traditional civil rights law precedents, "intentional discrimination" encompasses a great deal more than just overt discrimination. In fact, in most cases intent is shown through inference rather than direct evidence.

112. *Gwinnett,* 112 S.Ct. at 1035; *Tanberg,* 970 F.2d at 972–73. *See also* King v. County of Los Angeles, 769 F.2d 532, 534 (9th Cir. 1985), *reversed and remanded on other grounds,* 474 U.S. 936 (1985); Greater Los Angeles Council on Deafness, Inc. v. Zolin, 812 F.2d 1103, 1107 (9th Cir. 1987). Although not focused on remedies for employment discrimination, for an insightful analysis of damages and remedies under section 504, *see* DEBORAH A. MATTISON, STEWART R. HAKOLA, THE AVAILABILITY OF DAMAGES AND EQUITABLE REMEDIES UNDER THE IDEA, SECTION 504, AND 42 U.S.C. SECTION 1983 (LRP Publications, 1992).

113. Smith v. Barton, 914 F.2d 1330, 1337–38 (9th Cir. 1990); *Tanberg,* 787 F. Supp. at 973.

Although less likely, these new sources of law raise a possibility that federal courts will conclude that they also have the authority to award monetary damages for some instances of disparate impact (unintentional discrimination) and punitive damages for particularly egregious instances of intentional discrimination.

With regard to disparate impact, to award compensatory damages, a federal court would have to conclude that such a remedy is "appropriate" as articulated in *Gwinnett* and that Congress has in no manner expressed its intention to the contrary. In Alexander v. Choate, 469 U.S. 287 (1985), the Supreme Court indicated that it might find compensatory damages appropriate to remedy *some forms* of disparate impact discrimination. 469 U.S. at 294, 294 n.11, 297–99, 297 n.17.

114. 42 U.S.C. § 1981a(a)(2). *See supra* note 89.

115. *See, e.g.,* Nondiscrimination under Programs Receiving Federal Assistance through the Department of Health and Human Services Effectuation of Title VI of the Civil Rights Act of 1964, 45 C.F.R. § 80.7 (1991). This regulation permits extension of the period for filing a timely complaint by the "responsible Department official or his designee."

Under agency section 504 regulations, recipients of federal financial assistance are required to establish internal grievance procedures for hearing allegations of discrimination on the basis of disability. *See, e.g.,* 45 C.F.R. § 84.7. Some agencies extend the 180-day time period to accept complaints filed promptly after the exhaustion of an internal employer grievance procedure, provided the grievance alleged discrimination on the basis of disability. *See, e.g.,* UNITED STATES DEPARTMENT OF HEALTH AND HUMAN SERVICES, INVESTIGATION PROCEDURES MANUAL, at B-5 (1983).

Many employers are covered by both the ADA and section 504. In order to prevent duplication of investigative effort by federal agencies such as the EEOC, or OCR, and the Justice Department, the federal government is in the process of issuing rules that will regulate how disability employment complaints that concern overlapping jurisdictions will be processed. Persons intending to make use of an OCR to address alleged employment discrimination under section 504 may want to contact the appropriate OCR first to determine whether any procedures have been adopted that will effect the handling of their complaint.

116. As a social experience, there is nothing new to the question of whether people with learning disabilities should reveal their disabilities to their employers. This same question has been faced by "light-skinned" African Americans, English-fluent Hispanics, gays and lesbians, *etc.* For each group the time to stop "passing" was or will be determined by changes in personal perceptions of their own value and transformation of social attitudes, as well as advances in the law. Of course, there is a cyclical element to this process. The more persons reveal their true identity, the more society is able to substitute positive experiences with real people for negative stereotypes about hypothetical persons; in turn, society becomes more open to the moral imperatives of creating legislation to protect the newly emerging group from discrimination. Thus, for the author, "yes" is only a historically correct answer to the question, "Should I reveal my disability?"

Chapter 4

Personal Perspective—Problems and Promises: Adults with Learning Disabilities in the Past and in the Present

DALE S. BROWN, B.A.

I was asked to write this chapter because of my unique perspective as a leader in the self-help movement for people with learning disabilities, a writer in the field, and a Program Manager for the President's Committee on Employment of People with Disabilities. Although my work at the President's Committee has affected my perspective, I ask the reader to consider these comments as my views as a private citizen only.

When several leaders of people with learning disabilities began the self-help movement in the late 1970s, conventional wisdom stated that persons with learning disabilities would outgrow them. When we reached adulthood, our disabilities supposedly disappeared. When many of us forged ahead and founded self-help groups, we were ridiculed and ran into immediate job discrimination. There were no standardized tests at that time to determine if adults had learning disabilities. If vocational rehabilitation counselors recommended services, they had to claim that we were "visually impaired" or "mentally retarded." There were so few services for adults with learning disabilities that most of the speeches I presented around the country stated, "We must help each other. There is no other help available."

Today much has changed. A variety of programs exist for adults with learning disabilities, and few reputable professionals claim that we outgrow our disabilities. Sadly, just yesterday, a woman with a learning disability told me that her boss was trying to fire her because he found out she was dyslexic. And it is not uncommon for people with learning disabilities to be denied entry into their profession of choice because they cannot pass a standardized test. More work needs to be done by advocates. For example, a recent booklet on the Americans with Disabilities Act written by the National Alliance of Business (1991) lists 20 disabilities and leaves out people with learning disabilities.

Confusion Over Terminology

The most frustrating aspect of the past years has been the chronic confusion over defining learning disabilities. When we began self-help groups for people with learning

46

disabilities, many of the local groups were overwhelmed by people with mental retardation and emotional disturbance who wanted to join. However, they really did not fit into these groups because of differing experiences and needs. Yet, since most groups were nonprofit and met in public locations such as libraries and churches, they could not turn anyone away, nor did they want to do so. However, the majority of members of the self-help groups wanted to discuss difficulties that were particular to classic "specific learning disabilities." For example, a person who appeared intelligent and articulate ran into tremendous scorn when it was discovered that he could not read or calculate simple math or when a co-worker saw his handwriting.

For a self-help group to work well, it is helpful if the people who join have similar problems and issues. This similarity and group rapport were not achieved in the self-help movement for people with learning disabilities on a large-scale basis. Burnout of leaders who were learning disabled became a major problem. Many people who were intelligent and learning disabled felt put down and misunderstood when they met the others in the group. College-based programs and some support groups limited to people with dyslexia have been among the few that have served "truly" learning-disabled persons (people with average or above average intelligence).

The confusion between people with learning disabilities and those with mental retardation continues. The definition of mental retardation excludes people with IQs over 70 (Grossman, 1983). As a consequence, people with IQs over 70 have been unable to get services unless they can say they have learning disabilities or if their low IQ is a result of another neurological disability. Too often, I discover a program for people with learning disabilities only to find it is aimed at those who have intellectual and maturational impairments.

The media oftentimes use the terms *learning disabilities* and *mental retardation* almost interchangeably. In a recent issue of *Reader's Digest* (Nathanson, 1992), an article entitled "Unforgettable Scott Wagner" begins, "Eight learning disabled men and women dressed in T-shirts and running shorts stood waiting at the Haven Center, a lifetime care facility for mentally retarded adults in Miami, Florida. I had volunteered to teach them jogging" (p. 64). In the *Washington Post* (McCarthy, May 16, 1992), an article describes a program for deinstitutionalized people with mental retardation. One sentence reads, ". . . Chepko and Harris are citizens with mental retardation. Chepko, who also cooks and sets tables, has learning disabilities which prevent full intellectual retention" (p. A25).

Today, I am often ashamed to say that I have learning disabilities, despite having spent the last decade promoting pride in that term and understanding of its meaning. The term *learning disabilities* continues to conjure images of intellectual ineptitude. Some people feel more comfortable with the label *dyslexia*, but dyslexia implies inability to read, and my reading skills are excellent. Until we find words that explain our disability and that do not imply lack of intelligence, we will have great difficulty conceptualizing appropriate treatment strategies.

Ironically, the problem is perpetuated when we do not take a strong stand on services, civil rights, and dignity for people who have mental retardation or people who are simply not smart. The stigma of stupidity is significant in our society. We fail to recognize the gifts of people with mental retardation or milder intellectual impairments. A man with learning disabilities complained that he was treated as if he were retarded. He needs to understand that no one should be "treated as if they were retarded," if that implies being treated with condescension, authoritarianism, and rudeness. Our goal should be to encourage dignified and equal treatment for all. Too often we appear to say that people with learning disabilities should not be treated with disrespect because we are superior to people with mental retardation. This type of thinking serves neither group well.

Issues of Life Adjustment

When I started the self-help movement, learning disabilities were perceived very narrowly as academic disabilities. When professionals in the field found out about my learning disabilities, they were often surprised that I graduated from college, worked as a writer, and did not live with my parents. Although hyperactivity and behavioral problems were recognized, much of the diagnosis focused on academic difficulties in school. As a matter of fact, my book *Steps to Independence for People with Learning Disabilities* (Brown, 1980), was virtually the first attempt to grapple with issues such as independent living, employment, and social skills.

The transition initiative of the U.S. Department of Education (Will, 1984) caused the entire field of special education, including that involving learning disabilities, to focus on these issues. Today, most programs recognize these needs. For example, most professionals in the field agree that lack of social skills causes many problems in terms of work and quality of life for persons with learning disabilities. Books such as *Nobody to Play With* (Osman & Blinder, 1982) and numerous programs at conferences reiterate the importance of social skills. More people can get along without reading than can get along without other people. Yet secondary and post-secondary special education programs rarely have a social skills component. With no organized service-delivery system, social skills programs for adults with learning disabilities are virtually nonexistent. In the Washington, D.C. area, parents tell me that my program (an eight-week program that meets for one hour each week) is the only one they have found. Many more programs in independent living skills, employment, and social skills are necessary.

The Need for Information about Learning Disabilities

Over the past decade, learning disabilities have become more widely known and diagnosis as "learning disabled" in the school system has become more common. In 1989 to 1990, 49% of students with disabilities who were served by special education had learning disabilities (U.S. Department of Education, 1991). As a consequence, the need for information on learning disabilities has blossomed.

Several trade books have been published to meet this need, but the information and referral system is currently fragmented and difficult to access. How do parents find a diagnostician in their area? If a person with a learning disability wants to know how to file a discrimination complaint, where does that person turn?

For years, I was inundated with telephone calls. I love helping people over the telephone, but it could easily fill up my entire working day, which requires many other important responsibilities. Today, many national organizations fill some of the information and referral needs. Unfortunately, more such organizations are needed. Parents and professionals report having to spend long periods of time on the telephone tracking down information.

I have found that many of the people who telephone me do not want information, but they want to discuss their situation with a knowledgeable and concerned person. Has our breakdown of family and community left people who are facing crisis to fall "between the cracks?" I have spoken to emotionally upset people who are calling stranger after stranger hoping that someone will listen to them. They become angry when they learn I cannot let them express their experiences for an extensive amount of time. I have learned how to end these conversations swiftly, if needed, but nevertheless, these people need help and human contact. My dream is the establishment of a national center that assists people via the telephone. It would consist of a combination of counseling and information services. Staff would spend the time that people need to let them ventilate their feelings, receive information, and develop a plan of action.

Information and referral systems are more important today than they were in the past.

In the past, there were virtually no services, other than special education, to which people could be referred. Today, vocational rehabilitation services, Job Training Partnership Act (JTPA) programs, Recordings for the Blind, and the National Library for the Blind and Physically Handicapped allow people with learning disabilities to access their services. Rehabilitation Services Administration (RSA) has named "learning disabilities" as a funding priority and has published a program assistance circular (RSA, 1990) to guide counselors on how to determine if the client's learning disability is "severe." Many states cannot serve all of the people who request assistance. They use an "order of selection," a prioritizing system, which, should the money run out, means only people with "severe" disabilities can be served.

The U.S. Department of Labor published *The Learning Disabled in Employment and Training Programs* (1991), a study of the current state-of-the-art programs and proposed recommendations. The study estimated that 15 to 23% of the JTPA Title IIA participants may have learning disabilities. In addition, a network of private tutors, classes, and community activities has sprung up in some middle-class communities to assist young adults with learning disabilities.

The growth of services is encouraging, particularly because I remember when there was none. On the other hand, the service-delivery system is fragmented. Many services are funded privately, limiting them to people whose incomes are middle class and above. Supported employment, which can be potentially helpful to people with learning disabilities in employment settings, currently has few programs for us.*

In addition, the "disability community" still tends to look askance at people with learning disabilities as "not severely disabled." We are believed not to need resources as much as people who have obvious disabilities such as blindness and deafness. Yet, in many conversations, I find that people with learning disabilities have functional impairments that frequently are worse

than obvious disabilities. Several people who use wheelchairs and have learning disabilities have confided in me that they find their learning disabilities more challenging than their mobility impairments.

Learning Disabilities in the Workplace

The field of learning disabilities has been profoundly affected by the civil rights movement of people with disabilities. People with all disabilities and their allies worked hard to ensure the passage of the Americans with Disabilities Act. Sitting in the White House Rose Garden during the signing ceremony, I could not help but reflect that the law would make it illegal for an employer to tell me that I could not be hired because of my learning disabilities. This law may make it safer for people with learning disabilities to request "reasonable accommodation." Certainly, it has increased respect for people with disabilities in the United States.

On the other hand, accommodating learning disabilities brings particular problems. Some accommodations for people with learning disabilities are considered privileges. Sign language interpreters and Brailled materials are easily accepted by co-workers because they themselves do not need them. Everyone appreciates ramps, but ramps do not have a higher status than stairways. However, many people want enhanced clerical help, flexible hours, or privacy and quiet at work, and giving them to employees with learning disabilities can cause undue jealousy. It is crucial, but not always easy, for the manager and the person with learning disabilities to justify accommodation as a need rather than a desire.

Whether or not persons with learning disabilities can gain accommodation often depends on the culture of the business, agency, or corporation where they work. A rigid and bureaucratic culture that has difficulty accommodating diversity may feel that following the rules is more important than the productivity of the individual. Fortunately, the entrance of women and minorities into the workplace and the need to innovate

---

*See Chapter 17 for trends in supported employment.

swiftly to meet foreign competition among corporations and government have created new opportunities for people with learning disabilities. Business books stress flexibility, for example, *Teaching Elephants to Dance* (Moss-Kanter, 1989), *Reinventing Government* (Osborne & Gaebler, 1992), and *Theory Z* (Ouchi, 1982), and many other books advocate openness to change and worker participation. This may make it easier for people with learning disabilities to function in employment situations. To some extent it already has.

Greater Visibility Leading to New Challenges

Ironically, even as some barriers to success for people with learning disabilities have increased, the stigma experienced by people with learning disabilities seems to be decreasing as celebrities publicly discuss their learning disabilities. Dexter Manley, a former National Football League star, testified at a Congressional Hearing about his learning disabilities. Richard Cohen, a nationally syndicated newspaper columnist, wrote a column discussing his dyslexia. When George Bush was Vice President, he spoke proudly of his son Neil and often mentioned his son's problems as a person with dyslexia. Barbara Bush speaks publicly as a parent of a child with learning disabilities and has become a leader in national literacy efforts. Other celebrities who have recently accepted honors for overcoming their learning disabilities include Governor Gaston Caperton of West Virginia; former Governor Tom Keene of New Jersey; Paul J. Orfalea, President of Kinkos Printing; and Fred W. Friendly, a distinguished journalist and professor.

In addition, general publicity about dyslexia has increased. *The Secret*, a television movie about a man with dyslexia, was aired on national television during the 1992 Easter Sunday weekend. Numerous national magazines and newspapers, particularly in education columns, include material about learning disabilities and dyslexia.

This awareness leads to better acceptance of the concept of learning disabilities and of people with learning disabilities. However, the American custom of slanting stories to stress individual determination rather than the teamwork such a triumph often requires can cause a negative effect of raising expectations to unrealistic levels. Accommodations and help received from others are too often underplayed.

In short, watching the field develop over the last decade has been a fascinating process. We have increased the amount of services available for people with learning disabilities. The civil rights movement for people with disabilities has improved our legal protections and decreased stigmatization. On the other hand, at times, societal forces seem to be against us. This country keeps stressing standardized tests and thus rejects non-standardized human beings. Technology increases pressure and decreases the hiding places for minor human error. Sadly, credentialing requirements cause barriers.

Yet, as a group, we have overcome many of these barriers in many ways. Not a week goes by that I am not inspired by a person who is learning disabled who has found a new way to overcome the odds or get around the bureaucracy. In my roles as a writer, a self-help leader, and a government worker, it is still my dream to change the system so that it supports people with learning disabilities, rather than stands as a barrier to be beaten. We continue to work toward that goal.

References

Brown, D. (1980). *Steps to independence for people with learning disabilities*. Washington, D.C.: Closer Look.

Grossman, H. S. (Ed.) (1983). *Classification in mental retardation*. Washington, DC: American Association on Mental Deficiency.

McCarthy, C. (May 16, 1992). Living normally. *Washington Post*, p. A25.

Moss-Kanter, R. (1989). *Teaching elephants to dance*. New York: Simon and Schuster Publishers.

Nathanson, D. E. (1992, May). Unforgettable Scott Wagner. *Reader's Digest*, pp. 35–41.

National Alliance of Business. (1991). *What you need to know about the Americans with disabilities act: A guide for small and medium size businesses*. Washington, DC: National Alliance of Business.

Osborne, D., & Gaebler, T. (1992). *Reinventing government*. Reading, MA: Addison-Wesley Publishing Company.

Osman, B. B., & Blinder, H. (1982). *Nobody to play with: The social side of learning disabilities*. New York: Random House Publishers.

Ouchi, W. G. (1982). *Theory Z*. New York: Avon Books.

Rehabilitation Services Administration. (September, 1990). *Guidelines for determining whether a person with specific learning disabilities has a severe handicap for vocational rehabilitation programs*. RSA-PAC-90-7. Washington, DC: U.S. Department of Education, Rehabilitation Services Administration.

U.S. Department of Education. (1991). *Thirteenth annual report to Congress on the implementation of the Education of the Handicapped Act*. Washington, DC: U.S. Department of Education.

U.S. Department of Labor. (1991). *The learning disabled in employment and training programs*. Research and Educational Report Series 91-E. Washington, DC: U.S. Department of Labor. US GPO 1991-282-146/45359.

Will, M. (1984). *Bridges from school to working life*. Washington, DC: U.S. Department of Education, Office of Special Education and Rehabilitative Services.

PART II
PSYCHOLOGICAL ISSUES

Chapter 5

Clinical Diagnostic and Functional Assessment of Adults with Learning Disabilities

MICHAEL MCCUE, PH.D.

Evidence that learning disabilities often persist into adulthood and may contribute to substantial adaptive difficulties is now well established. These difficulties are often seen in the area of attaining and maintaining suitable employment and in the ability to cope with the demands of everyday life.

Recently, there have been follow-up studies into adulthood of individuals identified as having learning disabilities in childhood (Horn et al., 1983; Kline & Kline, 1975; Spreen, 1987.) One of Spreen's conclusions based on follow-up of subjects into their mid-twenties was that "Learning problems reflected in academic achievement tests were clearly not overcome, but put learning disabled youngsters at a disadvantage in finding advanced education and vocational opportunities" (p. 134). Johnson (1980) and Bowen and Hynd (1988) reported on the persistence of auditory dysfunction in adults with learning disabilities, and several studies report the persistence of neuropsychological deficits associated with learning disabilities persisting into adulthood (Harvey & Wells, 1989: Lewis & Lorion, 1988; McCue et al., 1986; McCue et al., 1984: O'Donnell et al., 1983). Learning disabilities have been identified in college students, and special programs have been designed to meet their needs (Birely & Manley, 1980; Cordoni, 1979; Kahn, 1980).

Within the vocational rehabilitation system, several studies point to the presence of specific vocational deficits and obstacles to vocational rehabilitation related to learning disabilities (Berkeley Planning Associates, 1989; Mars, 1986; McCue, 1984; Minskoff et al., 1989).

Errors in filling out an employment application because of poor reading or spelling skills is a commonly occurring scenario. Job-related problems frequently arise due to other characteristics commonly associated with learning disabilities, such as executive dysfunction (problems in organization, planning, scheduling, and monitoring), language comprehension and expression difficulties, social skills deficits, and inattention. Correspondingly, the major referral source for adults with learning disabilities is not the school system, but rather vocational rehabilitation agencies that provide counseling, rehabilitative, and placement services for individuals experiencing problems in gaining or maintaining employment. Self-referral and referral through advocacy agencies, such as state and local chapters of learning disabilities associations (LDA), are also not uncommon.

This chapter focuses on the assessment of adults with learning disabilities. In adults, assessment may be targeted to several distinct ends. Traditionally, identification of a discrepancy between an individual's level of performance in a specific academic skill area and level of intellectual capacity constitutes classification of a learning disability. For children and adolescents, the presence of a significant discrepancy enables them to meet criteria for identification as learning disabled, entitling them to special education services.

Clinical Diagnostic Assessment

Beyond the objective of meeting educational entitlement criteria, assessment must take on a clinical diagnostic focus. A significant performance–intellectual *capacity* discrepancy is one criterion necessary to establish a diagnosis of one of the specific developmental disorders using the diagnostic classification of the American Psychiatric Association (*Diagnostic and Statistical Manual of Mental Disorders*) 3rd ed. - revised [DSM-III-R] 1987. Despite the importance of establishing a discrepancy, the clinical identification of processing deficits is a more relevant objective of the assessment process than is discrepancy measurement, particularly in adults. There has been ample criticism of the use of discrepancy formulas for the diagnosis of learning disabilities and for entitlement to special education services. Most frequently, concern is raised over the failure to identify the specific psychological and language-processing abilities and limitations in persons assessed for learning disabilities. In adults (as well as in children), manifestations of learning disabilities are likely to occur outside of academic performance domains. Clinical assessment of performance must be sufficiently comprehensive to identify the breadth of psychological processing variables potentially encountered by persons with learning disabilities, and assessment must be sensitive enough to detect subtle processing deficits that may result in significant ability limitations in functioning.

Finally, assessment of functional ability, defined as measurement of an individual's strengths and weaknesses relative to real-life demands, is the most pragmatic objective of the assessment process. Central to the task of providing services to persons with learning disabilities is obtaining a clear understanding of how the disability impairs or impedes their ability to function in the natural environment, including in employment, in higher education, and in independent living. Discrepancy-based assessment and traditional diagnostic and clinical assessment strategies for the elucidation of abilities and deficits are effective in identifying the broad range of deficiencies that may result from a disorder, but they are not effective in detailing how these might interact with task or environmental demands to impact on the individual's functioning in real-life situations (Cicerone & Tupper, 1990). In fact, results of psychological assessment procedures can be quite misrepresentative of an individual's actual level of functional ability. A person may function far above or far below levels suggested by psychological test results (Naugle & Chelune, 1990). Therefore, a combination of assessment approaches that go beyond psychometric evaluation is required to identify, diagnose, and understand the effects of learning disabilities.

The remainder of this chapter elaborates on approaches to assessment for adults with learning disabilities and provides a discussion of and recommendations for diagnostic, clinical, and functional assessment approaches for adults with learning disabilities.

Diagnosis of Learning Disabilities in Adulthood

Because of the extreme heterogeneity of the learning disabled population, the lack of a clear consensus on one definition of what is meant by *learning disabilities*, and difficulties arising from the basic inconsistencies between a "diagnosis" of learning disabilities and classification as having learning disabilities for eligibility or entitlement purposes, diagnosis of learning disabilities is a complex and controversial process. For the purpose of clarification, it is important to point out that there is no formal "diagnosis" of learning disabilities. *Learning disabilities* is a definitional term, not a diagnosis. In the educational system, the term *learning disabilities* is often used to represent an educational "diagnosis," a requirement for special education entitlement. Eligibility policies have resulted in an operational definition of learning disabilities for the educational system (P.L. 94–142) and a definition of specific learning disability by the vocational rehabilitation system (Rehabilitation Services Administration, 1985). However, such definitions do not constitute a diagnosis. In order to assign a diagnosis, classification using a recognized diagnostic system must be established. Medical diagnostic classification systems include the third edition (revised) of the *Diagnostic and Statistical Manual of the American Psychiatric Association* 3rd edition (American Psychiatric Association, 1987) and the ninth revision of the *International Classification of Diseases* (U.S. Department of Health and Human Services, 1980).

Criteria for diagnosis reflect elements of both a clinical deficit and discrepancy models of identification. The specific developmental disorders grouping of the *DSM-III-R* appears to be the most logical option for adults with learning disabilities. This grouping contains a range of diagnostic options corresponding to several manifestations of learning disabilities, including *academic skills disorders, developmental language disorders, motor skills disorders,* and nonspecific categories of *specific developmental disorders* and *developmental disorders, not otherwise specified* (Table 5-1). The diagnosis of attention deficit disorders, not technically considered to be among the learning disabilities but a condition that may coexist with learning disabilities and/or result in similar functional limitations, is categorized using classifications of *attention deficit-hyperactivity disorder* or *attention deficit disorder, not otherwise specified.*

In assigning one of the *DSM-III-R* diagnoses corresponding to learning disabilities,

Table 5-1 DSM-III-R Diagnostic Options for Learning Disability

Specific Developmental Disorders

Academic Skills Disorders
315.00	Developmental reading disorder
315.10	Developmental arithmetic disorder
315.80	Developmental expressive writing disorder

Language And Speech Disorders
315.39	Developmental articulation disorder
315.31	Developmental expressive language disorder
315.31	Developmental receptive language disorder

Motor Skills Disorder
315.40	Developmental coordination disorder

Other Specific Developmental Disorders
315.90	Specific developmental disorder, not otherwise specified

Disruptive Behavior Disorders

314.01	Attention deficit—hyperactivity disorder
314.00	Attention deficit disorder, not otherwise specified

three sets of fundamental criteria are required. First, there is a general set of "rule-out" criteria. This requirement states that the disorder is not due to a number of factors such as a physical disorder (visual and hearing acuity), and acquired neurological disorder (for example, a head injury), a pervasive developmental disorder (i.e., autism), mental retardation, or deficient educational opportunities. In order to make a diagnosis, the identified deficits should not be a result of such rule-outs; however, learning disabilities may coexist with any of the above conditions.

The second set of criteria relates to clinical identification and documentation of a deficit in a particular area (e.g., inability to understand spatial terms and grammatically complex statements) and a determination that performance is discrepant from that expected based on an individual's intellectual capacity. These criteria are met by comparing performance in a particular domain with a measure of expectancy based on an individual's intellectual capacity.

In making such a comparison, it is important to equate the two measures on a common scale. The use of *standard scores,* as opposed to grade-level scores, is critical to this determination, particularly in adults. Also, "intellectual capacity" is not necessarily equivalent to an individual's summary IQ score. In some cases, this summary score may not reflect the individual's actual intellectual capacity (because the learning disabilities may have interfered with the testing process). In such cases, the verbal IQ score, performance IQ score, a combination of subtest scores, or the results from another instrument may be used to determine intellectual capacity. Evidence may suggest summary IQ test scores do not accurately reflect intellectual capacity, for example when there are very high scores on measures of pure abstract reasoning but low scores overall on tests dependent on acquired knowledge. In these cases, clear psychometric documentation must be present, including actual test scores and a statement of rationale in the psychological test report. This clinical determination should be made by the psychological examiner.

In meeting the third set of criteria used to establish a diagnosis, certification that the "disturbance" significantly interferes with academic achievement and, in the case of adults, activities of daily living or work performance must be established. Therefore, the presence of a discrepancy must be accompanied by clinical evidence that the identified problem has a substantial impact on the individual's ability to function. It is possible that an individual who possesses a discrepancy between performance and capacity would not meet diagnostic criteria if the disturbance were not substantial enough to interfere with his or her functioning.

Assessment Approaches

Psychological Evaluation

Assessment of learning disabilities is typically undertaken through the administration of psychological tests. Nontraditional assessment approaches emphasizing observation and qualitative assessment are also gaining popularity, particularly in classroom assessment with children. This section of the chapter focuses on psychometric evaluation. A discussion of nontraditional assessment procedures for use with adults follows in the section entitled Functional Assessment.

The context of psychological evaluation raises a number of questions. What particular approach is best for the adult with learning disabilities? Should a standard battery be administered to all persons suspected of having learning disabilities, or does the heterogeneity found in learning disabilities warrant different testing approaches depending on the presentation of the individual? Does the administration of a standard psychoeducational battery suffice, or should more in-depth evaluation such as neuropsychological assessment be undertaken? The answers to such questions are addressed in part by the charge that the assessment must meet several basic criteria.

First, the approach must possess sufficient *breadth* to cover the wide variety of potential areas of deficit (and strengths) that may be associated with learning disabilities. In persons with learning disabilities, the evaluation should address a number of content areas thoroughly, including attention, language functions, memory, functional literacy, reasoning and problem solving, perceptual motor skills, and executive functions. Table 5-2 contains a listing of specific functional skills that should be addressed within each of these broad content areas. The examiner should, at a minimum, select assessment approaches that provide reliable screening in the domains listed in Table 5-2, with flexibility for evaluating in greater detail those areas in which potential performance deficits are identified.

Second, the assessment instruments selected should possess adequate *depth* of measurement to address the subtle psychological processing and executive functioning problems that may ultimately result in functional or vocational difficulties. These deficits may present as mild generalized dif-

Table 5-2. Assessment Domains for Learning Disability

Attention

Ability to attend to auditory and visual information
Ability to sustain attention sufficiently for task completion
Freedom from distractibility
Freedom from impulsivity and behavioral disinhibition

Memory

Short-term recall of spoken, written, and diagrammatical information
Learning ability (recall through repeated exposure or practice)
Long-term recall
Prospective memory
Procedual memory (task recall)

Reasoning and Problem Solving

Cognitive flexibility
Ability to describe categorical qualities and see relationships
Sequential logic
Ability to derive abstract meaning and form abstract intent
Insight and self-evaluation
Ability to appraise a problem situation
Ability to generate and evaluate alternate solutions
Ability to generalize from one situation to another, or from the general to the specific
Spatial visualization, spatial reasoning, and nonverbal problem solving

Executive Functions

Ability to identify problems and formulate goals
Ability to plan and organize activities
Ability to initiate, maintain, and disengage from problem-solving activity
Ability to internally structure
Ability to self-monitor
Ability to change in response to failure or feedback

Language Functions

Ability to understand language (simple, complex, spatially based, grammatically
   varied, span of comprehension)
Speech quality, rate, and fluency
Ability to express ideas through speech (content, form)

Functional Literacy

Reading mechanics, oral reading, and comprehension
Ability to express ideas in writing (grammar, spelling, content, handwriting)
Arithmetic calculation and applied math problem solving

Perceptual Motor Skills

Ability to perceive basic and complex visual, auditory, and tactile stimuli
Fine and gross motor skills, coordination, and speed
Ability to guide activity and problem solving from sensory input (e.g., kinesthesis,
   visuoconstruction)

ficulties on psychometric tests, but they may have a pronounced impact on functioning when demands for information processing or organizational skills are more challenging or less structured than in the test situation, or when environmental conditions may not be optimal (e.g., in the presence of distractors). Assessment approaches must be sufficiently challenging to identify the presence of subtle deficits.

Third, assessment must be *flexible* to explore the various manifestations of learning disabilities that might occur from individual to individual and to examine the different ways that processing or executive deficits might impact on an individual's performance. For example, problem-solving tasks should be assessed from multiple input perspectives, as well as requiring multiple output or response modalities, to allow for identification of optimal learning and information-processing style and problem-solving conditions. Flexibility also ensures that the specific referral questions or presenting problems are addressed. For example, if memory complaints are identified on referral, an assessment should be selected to address the scope of potential memory deficits fully.

In addition to breadth, depth, and flexibility, assessment approaches must have demonstrated reliability and validity for the identification and diagnosis of problems related to learning disabilities. Test selection must address the psychometric properties of the approach selected, including such concerns as standardization and normative comparisons. For example, tests developed and normed for school-aged individuals are appropriate for use with adults. Guidelines regarding the use of standardized tests can be found in *Standards for Educational and Psychological Tests* (American Psychological Association, 1974).

Given the above requirements, reliance on a psychoeducational battery alone might result in a failure to identify the disorder, or the potential impact of the disorder, in an individual whose deficits might not be readily gleaned from achievement and intelligence testing. Inaccurate conclusions may derive from inappropriate normative comparisons. Assessment of adults with difficulties resulting from learning disabilities should be accomplished through the administration of a combination of clinical and psychometric tools, including the clinical interview, collection of historical data such as developmental milestones and school records, behavioral observation of the client, and norm-referenced tests. As noted previously, assessment strategies must be selected with

attention to the domains to be measured and to the psychometric properties of the instruments.

Currently, no established "battery" of tests sufficiently addresses all of the cognitive, behavioral, and emotional domains required to evaluate the individual with learning disabilities comprehensively and has established psychometric properties for that purpose. As a result, assessment can be accomplished by combining available instrumentation to cover required areas of functioning.

Neuropsychological approaches such as the Halstead-Reitan Neuropsychological Test Battery (Reitan & Wolfson, 1985) and the Luria-Nebraska Neuropsychological Battery (Golden et al., 1980) have well-documented psychometric properties with respect to assessing brain functions. These batteries, although distinctly different from one another, offer the benefit of obtaining standardized information on a wide variety of cognitive, language, sensory, and motor abilities. Studies have identified profiles of adults with learning disabilities on both the Halstead-Reitan battery (McCue et al., 1986; O'Donnell et al., 1983) and the Luria-Nebraska battery (Harvey & Wells, 1989; Lewis & Lorion, 1988; McCue et al., 1984). From a diagnostic standpoint, neuropsychological tests have demonstrated adequate discriminative validity in distinguishing individuals with learning disabilities from other disability groups and from nondisabled individuals (Lewis & Lorion, 1988; O'Donnell et al., 1983; Selz & Reitan, 1979a, 1979b) and have yielded prototypic patterns of performance on the basis of which learning disabilities might be identified. In this fashion, the application of neuropsychological assessment to individuals suspected of having learning disabilities may assist in the identification and diagnostic process. This is relevant for adults because of the lack of adequate normative data on psychoeducational instruments beyond high school age. The information obtained from a neuropsychological approach is particularly useful when learning disabilities problems fall primarily out of the range of specific academic deficits.

With respect to assessing the various domains or content areas pertinent to learning disabilities, the fixed battery neuropsychological approaches such as the Halstead-Reitan and the Luria-Nebraska appear quite well suited for the task when supplemented by additional measures of intellectual functioning, achievement, and personality. Additionally, since neuropsychological batteries sample such a broad range of strengths and weaknesses, they lend themselves well to generating informed clinical judgments about how cognitive, behavioral, and emotional deficits present as functional limitations in the natural environment. From a clinical standpoint, the capacity of neuropsychological approaches to identify differential patterns of strengths and weaknesses serves as a source of information on which to develop a rehabilitation program. With respect to remediation and rehabilitation, the assessment process may yield information about what the individual can or cannot do as a result of the learning disabilities. Neuropsychological test results may facilitate planning with respect to identification of a realistic vocational goal, delineation of remedial or compensatory strategies that are required, identification of areas in need of skill development (e.g., social skills), and identification of vocational training and placement needs. From a prescriptive standpoint, neuropsychological assessment may be used to identify the best and the worst learning and communication modality, define the optimal environmental considerations that fit the individual, and provide some information regarding the prognosis of involvement in rehabilitation services. Currently, many state vocational rehabilitation programs use neuropsychological tests with the learning disabilities population, and a few states require a neuropsychological evaluation for eligibility on the basis of learning disabilities.

A flexible battery approach using screening tests that cover all of the behavioral domains described above may also be selected.

If deficits are observed on screening, these are explored much more comprehensively. In using this approach, caution must be exercised to ensure that the tests used to screen clients are sensitive enough to identify subtle deficits. Tests such as the Wechsler Adult Intelligence Scale–Revised (WAIS-R), although sampling a wide range of problem-solving abilities, would not be sufficient for such screening.

Interpretation of test findings requires sophistication with respect to the instruments employed and a familiarity with the clinical presentation of learning disability. Although broad-based assessment is expensive and time consuming when compared with more traditional psychological and psychoeducational batteries, the heterogeneous nature of learning disabilities necessitates broad-based assessment.

Functional Assessment

Attention directed to the specific limitations of persons with learning disabilities has focused on the difficulties these individuals have in achieving successful vocational and community integration. Both higher education and the federal–state system of vocational rehabilitation have been significantly challenged in the provision of services to these persons because of the cognitive, behavioral, and psychosocial presentations of the disability. As noted earlier, a critical component of the assessment process is establishing not just the presence of a disability, or elucidation of the deficits that might be associated with learning disabilities, but determining how the disability impairs or impedes vocational and independent living functioning. Unlike the limitations of physical disabilities, the cognitive manifestations of learning disabilities are not easily quantified, and the impact of specific cognitive deficits is difficult to ascertain. Assessment must provide detail as to how deficits might interact with task and environmental demands to impact on the individual's functioning in real-life situations.

For assessment to be optimally useful, results should yield information on how the individual functions in the natural environment, when faced with work, education and training, and independent living demands. Assessment conducted in a vacuum with little relevance to real-world demands is of limited use in the planning and delivery of rehabilitation services. Therefore, functional assessment becomes an integral part of service provision to persons with learning disabilities.

Functional assessment may be defined as the analysis and measurement of specific behaviors that occur in real environments and are relevant to life or vocational goals (Halpern & Fuhrer, 1984). Functional assessment always involves an interaction between the purposeful or "goal-directed" behavior and environmental conditions such as people, rules, physical barriers, or schedules. Because the demands placed on a person differ from one environment to another and from one task to another, functional assessment is always a highly individualized process.

Functional assessment is undertaken to determine the impact of disability on behavior. Medical evaluations, diagnostic evaluations, and psychological testing are measures of disability. In contrast, functional assessment, which relates to purposeful behavior such as performing a specific job task, is a measure of the degree of disability. The *environmental specificity* and *goal directedness* of functional assessment separate it from other types of assessment. Put simply, functional assessment is the measurement of what persons can or cannot do (their strengths and weaknesses) in particular situations, under certain conditions, and in light of unique demands.

The objective of functional assessment is to identify the unique obstacles to goal attainment for the individual with learning disabilities. Obstacles occur as the deficits associated with the learning disabilities (e.g., auditory inattention) interfere with the individual's ability to meet demands and conditions imposed by the environment in which the individual must function (e.g.,

noise and distractions), the goal the person aspires to attain (e.g., accounting clerk), or the specific task requirements of a particular situation the individual must master. The challenge of functional assessment is not only to identify the individual's strengths and weaknesses, but to understand fully the demands and conditions of the environment in which the individual expects to function. The purpose is to delineate the functional obstacles that are likely to occur so that rehabilitation intervention might be systematically applied.

Functional assessment of an individual with learning disabilities should reveal information about assets and about limitations or potential problem areas. An *asset* is defined as a skill, ability, or knowledge that represents a strength area relevant to the rehabilitation goal. Assets should be objectively stated and operationally defined to the extent possible (e.g., when, where, with whom, under what circumstances) and should specify the frequency, duration, and intensity in which the asset occurs. An example of an asset statement is "has excellent verbal communication skills, characterized by good vocabulary, clear expression of thoughts and ideas, good comprehension of spoken technical information, such as medical terms, and pleasant interpersonal affect in work and social situations."

In addition to specifying assets, information regarding functional limitations is obtained. A *functional limitation* is defined as any factor, condition, or situation resulting from a disability that impedes an individual's ability to function independently or attain goals (Miller & Mulkey, 1983). The clinician should always identify functional limitations in behavioral, not in diagnostic, terms. For example, describing a functional limitation as "unable to pay attention to information that is presented auditorially (verbal instruction on the job) when noise from other conversations, radio, etc., occurs. This often happens in the workplace and results in reduced efficiency, effectiveness, and ability to learn," is more useful than simply using "attention deficit disorder." In this example, a specific type of inattention is specified, in a particular situation, and under specific conditions. It also identifies the impact of the behavior.

Functional assessment should span the entire rehabilitation process with an individual. Initial assessment should be conducted within the clinical or rehabilitation setting, with subsequent assessments ultimately performed in the natural environment. Functional assessment data are gathered throughout the entire process, using approaches such as role playing, situational assessments, work simulations, community outings, and field trips, and through direct observation in a number of settings.

Active involvement of the individual with learning disabilities in the assessment process improves the validity and reliability of the information gathered and enhances the individual's understanding of and investment in rehabilitation. Personal involvement in gathering functional assessment information may also provide a therapeutic approach to gaining more accurate self-appraisal and insight into strengths and limitations because it is not a clinical process; rather, it is the observation and recording of real-life behavior.

A functional assessment approach offers a number of advantages. First, functional assessment promotes the pragmatic use of all the assessment information obtained from the onset of involvement with an individual. In this fashion, all information gathered about an individual is applied to the formulation of inferences about what individuals can and cannot do in real environments.

Second, the functional assessment approach encourages ongoing assessment throughout the rehabilitation process. Assessment should not end once a diagnosis or eligibility has been established. Ongoing assessment provides for performance feedback to enhance daily living and vocational functioning.

Third, functional assessment promotes the refined use of specialty evaluations such as vocational evaluation or situational assessment. Based on inferences about assets

and functional limitations generated early in the involvement with a person with learning disabilities, vocational evaluation or other specialty evaluations can be specifically tailored to test these inferences, rather than being generic or redundant with respect to previously obtained information. For example, initial psychological testing may suggest the possibility of attention difficulties due to distractibility. A period of vocational evaluation can then be prescriptively utilized to assess how various types and degrees of distractions influence work performance. This ability to provide precise information about environmentally specific behavior maximizes the utility of specialty evaluations by building on previously gathered information.

Finally, functional assessment is centered around and oriented toward the individual. Information is gathered *with* the individual, not about the individual. Not only does the clinician share all information with the individual, but the individual plays an active role in gathering and recording information.

Functional Assessment Techniques

Functional assessment utilizes a number of specific tools, including obtaining direct information from the individual with learning disabilities and from informants such as family members and others aware of that individual's functional abilities. Information is obtained through interview, the administration of rating scales and questionnaires used to quantify the observations and reports of the individual and other informants, administration of more traditional assessment tools such as psychological and neuropsychological tests, observation of performance on simulations and situational assessments, and direct observation in the natural environment. All information gathered in this process constitutes data on which inferences are made about an individual's ability to meet the demands of the work, vocational training or higher education, and daily living. The various sources of information should be integrated, with successive approaches used to refine impressions regarding functional abilities. Each of the approaches is described below.

Functional Interviewing. The interview is useful to obtain a historical perspective, including the individual's perception of limitations as well as strengths, past history of the problem and limitations imposed, and previous remediation or rehabilitation strategies employed and their effectiveness. Birth and developmental history, medical history, and family information are of functional and diagnostic utility. School information should be obtained, including transcripts, grades, class rank, standard and psychoeducational test scores, and individualized education programs (IEPs), along with qualitative information about learning style, effective teaching approaches, and compensatory abilities. Work history should include the types and duration of jobs held, work skills and interests, and reasons for any job separations or failures. General observation of the individual during the interview is important. Information about social skills, timeliness, dress and hygiene, self-esteem, and receptive and expressive language skills are examples of what should be obtained through behavorial observation during a clinical interview.

Because, as a result of the learning disabilities, individuals may have a limited understanding of their disability and how it affects functioning, it is helpful to interview a person who has knowledge of the individual's functioning in the natural environment, preferably a family member (spouse, parent, or sibling). The interview validates details relating to the early life and developmental and educational history and provides additional information about functional strengths and weaknesses. It may be necessary to interview a number of individuals (teachers, employers, or co-workers) to ensure the collection of all pertinent information.

Rating Scales and Questionnaires. A number of rating scales and questionnaires exist for the purpose of obtaining information about characteristics and impact of learning disabilities, and for obtaining specific data about daily living and school or work performance. For example, the Learning Disabilities Characteristics Checklist (Dowdy, 1990) is an observer-rated instrument developed to be consistent with the U.S. Department of Education, Rehabilitation Services Administration's 1985 definition of specific learning disabilities and is useful in identifying not only the presence of learning disabilities but in documenting the manifestations or impact of learning disabilities. The Patient's Assessment of Own Functioning Inventory (Heaton & Pendleton, 1981) and the Patient Competency Rating Scale (Fordyce, 1983) are examples of instruments used to identify the impact of cognitive and behavioral disorders having a neurological origin. These scales, completed by the individual, also have parallel forms that are rated by a family member on the same dimensions rated by the individual. The use of relatives' forms allows for validation of self-report and may also be of assistance in identifying difficulties in accurate self-appraisal. Whether using a published instrument or one expressly designed to obtain information about a single individual, the use of scales and questionnaires may expand on and quantify performance observations.

Psychological and Neuropsychological Tests. Most psychological and neuropsychological tests were not developed to predict behavior in the natural environment, and extensive validation does not exist for this purpose. However, increasing evidence suggests that standardized measurement of cognitive and behavioral skills on psychological and neuropsychological tests correlates well with performance in the daily living and work environments. Evidence suggests a significant relationship between results of neuropsychological assessment and vocational functioning in neuropsychiatrically disabled individuals (Dennerll et al., 1966; Dikmen & Morgan, 1980; Heaton et al., 1978; Newnan et al., Lehman, 1978; Schwartz et al., 1968). Such findings point to the potential clinical value of these tests to address functional performance in persons with learning disabilities. Combining test data with clinical and rehabilitation knowledge enhances such inferences about real-world behavior.

Clinical inferences about real-world behaviors posed on the basis of psychological and neuropsychological tests can be enhanced if the clinician making predictions demonstrates knowledge and expertise in three areas:

1. A clear, clinical knowledge of the skills and abilities that are being measured, specifically, those behaviors that might be associated with a learning disability. For example, in order to make predictions about how perceptual difficulties would interfere with vocational performance, one would have to have a thorough appreciation for the types, degree, and intensity of perceptual disorders.
2. Technical expertise in the test procedures, including knowledge of behavioral requirements for performance, and strong interpretive skills for addressing difficulties or performance failures.
3. An understanding of and appreciation for the demands of the situation or environment being predicted. Performance on standardized test must relate to the demands of environment for the results to be functionally relevant. For example, knowledge that a particular job task requires a certain degree of auditory attention, moderately complex verbal interactive skills, and fine bimanual coordination would be essential in making inferences about whether or not an individual could perform on the particular job.

Although a rehabilitation psychologist or neuropsychologist is more likely to generate inferences about functional abilities from psychological and neuropsychological tests, a number of professionals working with persons with learning disabilities, including teachers, counselors, and advisors who are knowledgeable in psychometric approaches, can make deductions from test performance.

Situational Assessments and Simulations. Individually designed simulated approaches may be used to test specific everyday and vocational abilities. For example, a situational assessment of the specific demands of a certain job might be developed for an individual. In this approach, a sample of task demands is designed to match as closely as possible the demands that are anticipated on a job, including work site conditions such as noise level, degree of co-worker interaction, and presence of visual distractors. In simulated assessment settings, accommodations, modifications, and compensatory strategies can be identified and tested for their effect on improving performance.

Simulation and role play can also be designed to address difficult-to-assess cognitive and social skills. Functional assessment of cognitive skills can be accomplished through observation of the individual while performing a sequence of simulated real-life tasks. Such tasks can be designed to (1) place demands on the individual in a number of cognitive domains, including memory, communication, problem solving (goal formulation, planning, self-monitoring), organizational skills, sequential skills, initiation, and attention; and (2) replicate the demands in these areas that persons face in their everyday life, either related to daily living or vocational functioning. One benefit of this approach is that tasks are not artificially broken down into components, as is the case in psychological assessment. Rather, the individual is required to organize tasks conceptually in order to proceed with problem solving. Social problem solving and social skills can be assessed similarly.

Executive and organization skills, which are essential in complex daily activities, are difficult to observe in standard psychometric assessment. Executive functions are particularly relevant to success in vocational, educational, and community living activities. Unfortunately, the structure imposed during psychological evaluation of cognitive functions typically does not require the individual to initiate and sustain a plan of behavior. An example of a useful simulation tool for assessing executive abilities in everyday living is the Multiple Errands Test (MET), developed in England by Shallice and Burgess (1991). The MET was designed to assess the ability to act effectively on one's own initiative and to organize nonroutine activities in a real-life setting. The test requires the subject to shop for several items and complete several tasks while complying with time and cost constraints. Using an American adaptation of the MET with a pilot sample, which included persons with learning disabilities, qualitative data were obtained about everyday skills including: (1) comprehension of verbal and written instructions; (2) self-monitoring of comprehension and asking for clarification; (3) spontaneous use of compensatory strategies such as note writing; (4) coping with unexpected changes in plans; and (5) requesting information or assistance in an effective and socially appropriate way (McCue et al., 1992). Results also provided support for the MET's capacity to discriminate between individuals with cognitive disabilities who are judged to be effective (e.g., employed or succeeding in school) and those who are functionally ineffective.

Simulated and situational assessment approaches are an important component of the functional assessment process. These assessments can be tailored to the specific individual needs of the person and can also be used to measure skills and abilities that are not easily discernible from standard psychological and neuropsychological test measures.

Direct Observation. The ideal mechanism for valid study of real-world behavior is to observe individuals directly when confronted by demands in their natural environment. Ongoing observation in the natural environment should be planned as a method of follow-up after educational or rehabilitation intervention. Actual performance measures can serve as a basis for identifying support needs, accommodations, and environmental modifications.

In order to measure cognitive behavior in the natural environment, some method of quantifying and qualifying the behavior is required. Although several functional assessment measures exist, such as the Functional Assessment Inventory (Crewe & Athelstan, 1984) and Rehabilitation Indicators (Diller et al., 1983), these approaches do not adequately address the measurement of cognitive and problem-solving skills pertinent to persons with learning disabilities. A primary limitation of functional assessment instruments has been the restricted range of activities they address (Haffey & Johnston, 1990; Indices, 1979). In order to plan interventions to overcome limitations associated with learning disabilities, procedures must address the functional impact of cognitive disabilities. The Pre-Vocational Checklist (PVC) developed at the New York University Center for Head Trauma and Stroke (Silver, et al., 1988), although developed for use with persons with disabilities resulting from traumatic brain injuries, is an example of a measure of complex cognitive behaviors in the work and educational environments. The PVC provides for detailed behavioral observation and analysis of a wide range of cognitive, language, problem-solving, and work responses and has been used with persons with learning disabilities.

In summary, functional assessment is most effective when a number of approaches are used to obtain information about an individual's strengths and weaknesses. An approach that utilizes and builds on information from multiple sources over an extended period of time, culminating in direct observation in the natural environment, is likely to be the most reliable source of accurate functional information.

Issues in Assessment

There are a number of issues to consider when identifying and selecting an approach to assessment of an individual with learning disabilities. These include the following:

1. The assessment approach selected should meet requirements for establishing a *diagnosis* (i.e., meet diagnostic criteria) and for establishing any definitional and eligibility criteria that might be required (e.g., eligibility for state vocational rehabilitation services)
2. The assessment should be sensitive to the particular needs of individuals with learning disabilities and reflect not only intellectual and academic achievement measures, but also measures of language functioning, sensory perception, motor skills, higher-level cognitive and executive abilities, and emotional factors.
3. Assessment approaches should generate information about functional limitations, assets, and the conditions under which performance is optimal. Information generated from the assessment process should be relevant to making a determination of what an individual can or cannot do, given specific environmental and goal demands.
4. Assessment approaches selected should be able to answer specific referral questions. For example, if there is a question about an individual's memory functions, tests and ancillary procedures should be identified that specifically address memory functions.
5. Identification of an assessment approach must take into consideration logistic concerns such as availability and cost. Although broad neuropsychological approaches may provide a packaged, comprehensive approach to assessment, they are not available in all areas. The use of simulations and situational and direct observational procedures may be time consuming and labor intensive, but they are likely to yield more accurate information about an individual's functional strengths and limitations.

In addition to identifying the type of assessment appropriate for an individual with learning disabilities, the referral process is important. Sound referrals for assessment must include a significant amount of background information and a set of well-formed referral questions. Information required to make a competent referral for assessment includes:

1. *Identifying and contact information.* The individual's name, address, phone number, and demographic information enable the assessment provider to contact the individual. The individual's living situation and other contact information such as the telephone numbers of friends or relatives are of assistance if the individual is difficult to reach at home.
2. *Description of presenting problem.* This description should provide a referral diagnosis, a summary of why the individual is seeking assessment services, and a behavioral description of the presenting problems.
3. *History of presenting problems.* A description of the history of learning disability problems should be provided, including school diagnosis, remedial services, and related difficulties.
4. *Secondary disabilities* or *past history of other problems.* Individuals may have emotional difficulties, psychiatric problems, physical disabilities, or substance-abuse problems, which may be considered secondary disabilities. These should be addressed in the assessment process. Acknowledging these difficulties in the referral process increases the likelihood that they will be comprehensively assessed.
5. *Previous testing.* Any information from previous assessments should be included with an assessment referral, including the names and dates of tests administered, results, and diagnoses. Actual scores are beneficial for comparison with current results.
6. *Precautions, special conditions, contraindications.* Any significant issues that might influence the assessment process should be identified, including

willingness and "motivation," possible scheduling difficulties, and the presence of sensory disabilities and behavioral difficulties that might interfere with testing. Awareness of special conditions prior to scheduling assessments allows for modifications to ensure that assessment reflects the optimal functioning of the individual.

7. *Specific referral questions.* Specific questions must be posed to ensure that assessment responds to the unique needs of the individual. Specific tests may be requested to address specific questions. If no questions are posed, assessment results and reports are likely to be general and lacking in functional information. Referral questions should reflect specific information about the individual's goals, current situation, and environmental conditions, to the degree possible. This information allows for the drawing of inferences regarding an individual's capacity to meet environmental demands and attain stated goals.

Shaping the Assessment Product

A number of strategies might be used to make assessments more useful. These strategies essentially shape the assessment product and ensure that the individual gains from the process. First, the most effective way to make sure that the assessment is useful is to formulate direct questions. As noted above, if no questions are asked, or if questions are general and nonspecific, the assessment report tends to be generic and lacking in information specific to the individual and the individual's situation.

Second, feedback should be given on assessment reports and consultations. Positive and negative feedback to the assessment provider is encouraged, stressing the *utility* (or lack of it) of assessment results provided.

Third, a mechanism for asking follow-up questions is a way to obtain information not available in a test report. For example, at the time an individual is referred for assessment, a specific job goal or environment may not have been identified. Six months after testing, following a period of counseling and vocational exploration, specific information about environmental demands may be available. A follow-up consultation in which specific environmental demands are provided allows for consideration of the individual's performance in light of current demands. It is important to establish a mechanism for posing follow-up questions, for example, in a brief (one-half hour) period scheduled each month in which, via a telephone conversation, a number of individual cases might be discussed. The assessment provider should be contacted in advance to ensure that the appropriate client records are available. It is important not to assume that, once an assessment report has been filed, further consultation may not be obtained.

Fourth, developing specialists for particular needs will enhance the assessment product. One assessment provider may be identified for psychoeducational or neuropsychological approaches, and a community-based facility might provide simulations or on-site assessments. Specialists may be identified for assessing certain types or manifestations or learning disabilities.

Finally, *flexibility* in the assessment process is critical and should be encouraged. All parties should be flexible in their approach to assessment. The counselor or referring person may have to be flexible in structuring assessment batteries, referral procedures, and so forth. For the assessment provider, flexibility may require being available for consultation, modifying report style and format to meet the needs of the individual and referral source, and flexible scheduling to ensure optimal performance by the individual with learning disabilities.

Summary

This chapter has addressed assessment and diagnostic concerns regarding adults with learning disabilities and has raised several key issues and recommendations. Assessment conducted to establish the presence of learning disabilities should provide clinical detail on psychological processing deficits as well as discrepancy-based information. Assessment approaches should be sufficiently comprehensive to evaluate a number of domains believed to be involved in learning disabilities, including attention, language functioning, memory and learning, functional literacy, reasoning and problem solving, perceptual and motor skills, and executive functioning. Assessment should also be challenging enough to detect subtle psychological processing and executive functioning problems that may exist. Comprehensive neuropsychological batteries provide broad-based, sensitive, and flexible assessment for clinical diagnostic purposes.

Central to the task of providing services to individuals with learning disabilities is functional assessment, or the process of obtaining a clear understanding of how the disability impairs or impedes the ability to function at work, in higher education or vocational training, and in independent living. Sound assessment practice encompasses clinical diagnostic and functional assessment approaches. A combination of assessment procedures that go beyond psychometric evaluation is required to identify, diagnose, and understand the effects of learning disabilities. An approach that utilizes and builds on information from multiple methods over an extended period of time is the most reliable source of accurate functional information.

Finally, the assessment process and results can be positively shaped by asking specific questions at referral, establishing a mechanism for ongoing consultation regarding assessment results, and providing feedback regarding the utility of results obtained.

References

American Psychiatric Association. (1987). *Diagnostic and statistical manual of mental disorders* (3rd ed., revised). Washington, DC: American Psychiatric Association.

American Psychological Association (1974). *Standards for educational and psychological tests.* Washington, DC: American Psychological Association.

Berkeley Planning Associates. (1989). *Evaluation of services provided for individuals with specific learning disabilities, 1* (Contract No. 300-87-0112). Washington, DC: Office of Rehabilitation Services Administration.

Birely, M., & Manley, E. (1980). The learning disabled student in a college environment: A report of State University's program. *Journal of Learning Disabilities, 13,* 12–15.

Bowen, S. M., & Hynd, G. W. (1988). Do children with learning disabilities outgrow deficits in selective auditory attention? Evidence from dichotic listening in adults with learning disabilities. *Journal of Learning Disabilities, 21,* 623–631.

Cicerone, K. D., & Tupper, D. E. (1990). Neuropsychological rehabilitation: Treatment of errors in everyday functioning. In D. E. Tupper & K. D. Cicerone (Eds.), *The neuropsychology of everyday life: Issues in development and rehabilitation.* Boston: Kluwer Academic Publications.

Cordoni, B. (1979). Assisting dyslexic college students: An experimental program designed at a university. *Bulletin of the Orton Society, 29,* 263–268.

Crewe, N. M., & Athelstan, G. T. (1984). *Functional Assessment Inventory manual.* Menomonie, WI: University of Wisconsin–Stout.

Dennerll, R. D., Rodin, E. A., Gonzalez, S., Schwartz, M. S., & Lin, Y. (1966). Neuropsychological and psychological factors related to employability of persons with epilepsy. *Epilepsia, 7,* 318–329.

Dikmen, S., & Morgan, S. F. (1980). Neuropsychological factors related to employability and occupational status in persons with epilepsy. *Journal of Nervous and Mental Disease, 168,* 236–240.

Diller, L., Fordyce, W., Jacobs, D., Brown, M., Gordon, W., Simmens, S., Orazem, J., & Barrett, L. (1983). *Final Report: Rehabilitation Indicators project* (Grant No. G008003039). Washington, DC: National Institute of Handicapped Research, U.S. Department of Education.

Dowdy, C. (1990). *LD characteristics checklist.* Birmingham, AL: University of Alabama at Birmingham.

Fordyce, D. J. (1983). *Psychometric assessment of denial of illness in brain injured patients.* Paper presented at the 91st Annual Convention of the American Psychological Association, Anaheim, CA.

Golden, C. J., Hammeke, T. A., & Purisch, A. D. (1980). *The Luria-Nebraska neuropsychological battery: A manual for clinical and experi-*

mental uses. Lincoln, NE: University of Nebraska Press.

Haffey, W. J., & Johnston, M. V. (1990). A functional assessment system for real-world rehabilitation outcomes. In D. E. Tupper & K. D. Cicerone (Eds.), *The neuropsychology of everyday life: Issues in development and rehabilitation.* Boston: Kluwer Academic Publications.

Halpern, A. S., & Fuhrer, M. J. (1984). *Functional assessment in rehabilitation.* Baltimore: Paul H. Brooks Publishing Co.

Harvey, J. R., & Wells, M. (1989, February). *Diagnosis of adult learning disabilities and vocational rehabilitation: A descriptive analysis.* Paper presented at the ACLD International Conference, Miami, FL.

Heaton, R. K., & Pendleton, M. G. (1981). Use of neuropsychological tests to predict adult patients' everyday functioning. *Journal of Consulting and Clinical Psychology, 49* (6), 807–821.

Heaton, S., Chelune, G., & Lehman, R. (1978). Using neuropsychological and personality tests to assess the likelihood of patient employment. *Journal of Nervous and Mental Disorders, 166,* 408–416.

Horn, W. F., O'Donnell, J. P., & Vitulano, L. A. (1983). Long-term follow-up studies of learning disabled persons. *Journal of Learning Disabilities, 16,* 542–555.

Indices, Inc. (1979). *Functional limitations: A state of the art review* (RSA Grant No. 13 P 59220/3 01). Falls Church, VA: Indices, Inc.

Johnson, D. (1980). Persistent auditory disorders in young dyslexic adults. *Bulletin of the Orton Society, 30,* 269–276.

Kahn, M. (1980). Learning problems of the secondary and junior college learning disabled student: Suggested remedies. *Journal of Learning Disabilities, 13,* 445–449.

Kline, C., & Kline, C. (1975). Follow-up study of 216 children. *Bulletin of the Orton Society, 25,* 127–144.

Lewis, R. D., & Lorion, R. P. (1988). Discriminative effectiveness of the Luria-Nebraska Neuropsychological Battery for LD adolescents. *Learning Disability Quarterly, 11,* 62–69.

Mars, L. (1986). Profile of learning disabled persons in the rehabilitation program. *American Rehabilitation, 12* (3), 10–33.

McCue, M. (1984). Assessment of learning disabled adults. *Rehabilitation Counseling Bulletin, 27,* 281–290.

McCue, M., Aitken, S., & Chase, S. (1992). [Scores from the *American Multiple Errands test*]. Unpublished raw data.

McCue, M., Shelly, C., Goldstein, G., & Katz-Garris, L. (1984). Neuropsychological aspects of learning disability in young adults. *The In-*

ternational Journal of Clinical Neuropsychology, 6, 229–233.

McCue, P. M., Shelly, C., & Goldstein, G. (1986). Intellectual, academic and neuropsychological performance levels in learning disabled adults. *Journal of Learning Disabilities, 19,* 233–236.

Miller, J., & Mulkey, W. (1983). *Functional assessment and eligibility determination.* Unpublished training manual, University of Tennessee, Knoxville.

Minskoff, E. H., Hawks, R., Steidle, E. F., & Hoffman, F. J. (1989). A homogeneous group of persons with learning disabilities: Adults with severe learning disabilities in vocational rehabilitation. *Journal of Learning Disabilities, 22,* 521–528.

Naugle, R. I., & Chelune, G. J. (1990). Integrating neuropsychological and "real life" data: A neuropsychological model for assessing everyday functioning. In D. E. Tupper & K. D. Cicerone (Eds.), *The neuropsychology of everyday life: Assessment and basic competencies.* Boston: Kluwer Academic Press.

Newnan, O. S., Heaton, R. K., & Lehman, R. A. (1978). Neuropsychological and MMPI correlates of patients' future employment characteristics. *Perceptual and Motor Skills, 46,* 635–642.

O'Donnell, J. P., Kurtz, J., & Ramanaiah, N. V. (1983). Neuropsychological test findings for normal, learning-disabled, and brain-damaged young adults. *Journal of Consulting and Clinical Psychology, 51,* 726–729.

Rehabilitation Services Administration (1985). *Program policy directive.* RSA-PPD-85-3, January 24.

Reitan, R. M., & Wolfson, D. (1985). *The Halstead-Reitan Neuropsychological Test Battery.* Tucson: Neuropsychology Press.

Schwartz, M., Dennerll, R., & Lin, Y. (1968). Neuropsychological and psychological predictors of employability in epilepsy. *Journal of Clinical Psychology, 24,* 174–177.

Selz, M., & Reitan, R. M. (1979a). Rules for neuropsychological diagnosis: Classification of brain function in older children. *Journal of Consulting and Clinical Psychology, 47,* 258–264.

Selz, M., & Reitan, R. M. (1979b). Neuropsychological test performance of normal learning-disabled, and brain-damaged older children. *Journal of Nervous and Mental Disorders, 167,* 298–302.

Shallice, T., & Burgess, P. W. (1991). Deficits in strategy application following frontal lobe damage in man. *Brain, 114,* 727–741.

Silver, S. M, Ezrachi, O., Kay, T., Rattock, J., Piasetsky, E., & Ben-Yishay, Y. (1988). *Administration manual for the N.Y.U. Prevocational*

Checklist. New York: New York University Medical Center.

Spreen, O. (1987). *Learning disabled children growing up: A follow-up into adulthood.* Netherlands: Swets & Zeitlinger.

U.S. Department of Health and Human Services. (1980). *The international classification of diseases, 9th revision, clinical modification* (2nd ed.). Washington, DC: U.S. Government Printing Office.

Chapter 6

Social/Emotional and Daily Living Issues for Adults with Learning Disabilities

HENRY B. REIFF, PH.D.
PAUL J. GERBER, PH.D.

Adults with learning disabilities face the same social/emotional and daily living issues as all of us. We all have acquired repertoires of social behaviors, some of which tend to be successful and some less so. All of us have certain aspirations for different types of social activities, ranging from our friendships to how we spend our leisure time to how we handle our interpersonal situations. Some of these aspirations are realized; we fall short in others. We are individuals who are at least partially defined by our emotions and find that emotional well-being fluctuates in response to ongoing events as well as to events from the past. And we all find that activities of daily living, from keeping our financial affairs in order to knowing what to order in a fancy restaurant, may invigorate, tire, perplex, or reassure us.

For adults with learning disabilities, such experiences may take on slightly or even radically different hues, for learning disabilities color how a person perceives and responds to the world and how the world perceives and responds to that person. The same complex of problems that makes learning in a classroom difficult may interfere with acquiring the necessary skills to negotiate social situations and everyday activi-

ties. The residual effects of learning disabilities, from frustration about schooling to a lack of satisfaction in one or a number of areas of adulthood, sometimes reverberate in the emotional sphere. For some adults with learning disabilities, a seeming inability to understand why life continues to be a struggle creates a tragic and self-perpetuating cycle of loneliness and despair. Yet for other persons with learning disabilities, adult life offers freedom and opportunities previously denied them. With the shackles of their school years behind them, they can structure their lives within their *own* self-created niche. Social and emotional health may soar while daily living activities become indices of successful adaptation.

This chapter explores some of these issues in the lives of adults with learning disabilities. Social/emotional and daily living issues do overlap, but for the purposes of clarity, we will discuss these two areas separately. As adults with learning disabilities represent a heterogeneous population where every experience is unique, pithy generalizations about these issues will not capture the scope of adaptations made in adulthood. Perhaps the only generalizable finding lies in our inadequate awareness of the social and emotional issues facing adults with

learning disabilities, a critical area of ignorance recognized by the National Joint Committee on Learning Disabilities (1983). Nevertheless, patterns that depict the experiences
of many adults with learning disabilities do
exist. Controlled quantitative research has
unearthed theoretical foundations for such
patterns; ethnographic investigations into
the lives of adults with learning disabilities
(cf., Gerber et al., 1992; Gerber & Reiff, 1991)
will, perhaps, transform theory into the living reality as experienced by these adults.

Social/Emotional Issues

The foundation for investigating social/emo-
tional issues in adults with learning disabilities lies in the massive attention given to
social skills deficits in the learning disabilities literature over the past 15 years. The
most widely cited article in the field of
learning disabilities over the past 10 years is
Bryan's (1976) replication of research examining peer popularity of children with learning disabilities (Swanson & Trahan, 1986).
Many studies indicate that individuals with
learning disabilities are more rejected and
less accepted than nondisabled peers (e.g.,
Bruininks, 1978; Rosenberg & Gaier, 1977;
Schumaker & Hazel, 1984). Looking back on
her childhood, an adult with learning disabilities recounted this social state: "I never
was a member of the group in grammar
school or in high school. I was an outsider,
and my best friends were the rather delinquent 'rejects.' "* As a result, many individuals with learning disabilities exhibit poor
self-concept and have difficulty socializing
(Schumaker & Hazel, 1984).

A number of different explanations account for problems with social skills. On the
one hand, students with learning disabilities

---

* This quotation and all others following, unless otherwise noted, are taken from transcripts of interviews
used as data in Gerber, P. J., Ginsberg, R., & Reiff, H. B.
(1990). *Identifying alterable patterns in employment
success for highly successful adults with learning disabilities.* Final report (Grant No. 133G80500). Washington, DC: U.S. Department of Education, Office of Special
Education and Rehabilitative Services.

tend to experience frustration in the classroom; adults find any number of demands
exasperating. Additionally, painful experiences in school may have long-lasting consequences. Many adults with learning disabilities are plainly bitter about the treatment
they received in school and find that their
academic shortcomings continue to threaten
feelings of self-worth and competence (Gerber et al., 1992). Perhaps the most pervasive
reaction to school failures is a feeling of
being stupid, which in turn may express itself in a spectrum of emotions, ranging from
anger to depression to challenge. Even successful adults with learning disabilities,
who have obviously demonstrated keen intelligence, disclose an overwhelming psychological backlash that undermines social
relationships:

> "I felt so stupid all my life. I still feel stu-
> pid with men that are fairly intelligent,
> so I choose men that aren't. Then I don't
> like them."
> "I always felt dumb around my family
> with their killer vocabulary."
> "I went to school to find out that I was a
> loser. It's that integrity, the human
> spirit, that gets crushed."

The emotional "baggage" that many adults
with learning disabilities carry no doubt
plays a part in less-than-satisfying social
outcomes. Sometimes these outcomes result
in a self-perpetuating negative cycle where
social failings breed further emotional labil-
ity, which in turn sabotages successful social
interaction.

On the other hand, emotional factors do
not fully explain the pervasive nature of social skills deficits in the learning-disabled
population. Cognitive characteristics inher-
ently associated with learning disabilities
may lie at the root of some social skills
deficits, particularly those related to social
perception (Reiff & Gerber, 1989). Social perception difficulties reported in persons with
learning disabilities include (1) the inability
to make central inferences in social settings
(Gerber, 1978); (2) less sensitivity to others'
thoughts and feelings (Dickstein & Warren,

1980; Wong & Wong, 1980); (3) poor judgment of others' moods and attitudes (Lerner, 1993); (4) doing or saying inappropriate things (Lerner, 1993); (5) problems comprehending humor (Pickering et al., 1987); and (6) problems discriminating the response requirements in social situations (Larson & Gerber, 1987). An adult with learning disabilities described some of the difficulties in understanding and employing certain kinds of social behavior: "One of my goals that I am working on is to take a look at how do you enter into a conversation and how do people handle themselves. It's not one of those things that comes natural. I am going to have to stand back and look and try to figure them out." Social perception deficits may lead to and interact with emotional difficulties; characteristics such as aggression, hostility, insecurity, and frustration can result from a failure to interpret social messages correctly (Wiig & Semel, 1976).

Learning problems related to learning disabilities may affect social relations indirectly and subtly, yet significantly. Verbal social intercourse often depends on a shared knowledge base; persons with learning disabilities may have more difficulties in acquiring types of information that most persons take for granted as a normal framework for socializing. Looking back on his childhood, a professor with learning disabilities recollected, "I didn't feel normal. I couldn't remember important things and therefore couldn't discuss what was important to these people. I couldn't get involved for lack of appreciation of the history and rules of these sorts of things."

The relation between characteristics of learning disabilities and social skills deficits implies that social skills are learned. Consequently, opportunities to learn appropriate social behaviors are critical in the development of social competence; some adults with learning disabilities may have missed out on such experiences in childhood. Certainly, a repeated criticism of segregated special education settings has focused on the lack of exposure to "normal" socialization. Students from self-contained classrooms not only have

limited opportunities to socialize with nondisabled peers, they may also have fewer common experiences that provide a foundation for socialization. Even for students in mainstreamed environments, opportunities may be lacking. The increased rejection of these students diminishes their social interaction. Other students may self-impose a degree of isolation. An account from one adult illustrates how compensating for one aspect of learning disabilities led to a new concern:

> I think that because I spent so much time on my studies, I had less time to spend just hanging out, if you will, with the boys and the girls. So I feel like maybe I missed out on the development of some social graces or some social opportunities. Same thing through college. So although, yes, there were some positive things, I missed out on a part of living. . . . I missed out in high school on a lot of social opportunities, and I'm not interested, or afraid to tackle, or I don't want to have anything to do with certain similar social activities now. Has it impacted my life even to this day? Yeah, no question about the fact, in my mind, that it's helped mold my profile of social activity (Gerber & Reiff, 1991, pp. 67–68).

Another adult with learning disabilities remembered that she not only had little time for friendships, she also couldn't handle the ridicule of having to study all the time. Expectations that others will react negatively tend to limit socialization even if the expectations are erroneous. But evidence suggests that persons with learning disabilities are more likely to be the recipients of negative attitudes.

Learning disabilities affect the way one is regarded by others. Children with learning disabilities may grow up in an environment where nondisabled peers, teachers and other adults, and even parents and siblings perceive them as socially incompetent (Reiff, 1987). It is likely that, for at least some persons, the messages received in childhood become self-fulfilling prophecies in the adult years. Additionally, the very issue of the label *learning disabilities* may contribute to atypical social experiences. A wide body of research has consistently delineated the deleterious impact of labels on self-esteem and on the perceptions of others. The label alone may bias how persons with learning disabilities are viewed by others. Negative peer evaluations are predictive of juvenile delinquency (Roff et al., 1972), early school dropout (Ullman, 1957), and psychiatric hospitalization in young adulthood (Cowen et al., 1973). Follow-up and longitudinal studies of adults with learning disabilities have often reported these difficulties of adult adjustment (Gerber & Reiff, 1991).

Up to this point, this chapter has presented compelling evidence that many individuals with learning disabilities are held in low esteem by teachers, parents, and peers, and that negative reactions may have long-term consequences in the development of self-esteem. Contrary to this perception, another body of evidence suggests that at least some individuals with learning disabilities are popular (Dudley-Marling & Edmiaston, 1985). These individuals do not evidence any kind of social or emotional difficulties; rather, they often exhibit a strength in these areas that may significantly compensate for the academic difficulties usually associated with learning disabilities. A retired professor with learning disabilities disclosed that succeeding in school depended on his social charm: "I practiced public relations from the start. I knew there couldn't be a conflict situation with teachers. It's hard enough without having someone dislike you. So I carried their books to the car or would bring them an apple. Tried to be a nice student in class."

Learning disabilities represent a constellation of characteristics in a truly ecological relationship with interpersonal environments. Consequently, the vast number of variables makes the social development for each individual unique. Some persons with learning disabilities may have basically intact social skills but suffer from the emotional stress of coping with a learning problem. Others may cope emotionally with the learning difficulties per se but lack specific skills to achieve satisfactory social outcomes. Still others may have intact emotional and social coping skills. It is probable that most social problems are related to an interaction of these two factors, the proportions being slightly different in every case. And environments range from nurturing to destructive, with the potential to ameliorate or exacerbate inherent social difficulties. No matter what combination of circumstances has led to social/emotional problems, interpersonal failings in childhood may have deleterious consequences in adulthood.

How do social skills difficulties associated with learning disabilities manifest themselves in adulthood? In some cases, the ramifications of social skills deficits intensify in adulthood. A child who is reluctant to make eye contact and is generally deficient with social ingratiation techniques may have trouble making friends or inviting a date to the prom, but to some extent, both family and educational systems are likely to prevent catastrophic consequences. As an adult with persisting social skills difficulties, this individual may have critical difficulty finding and keeping a job or developing a relationship leading to marriage. A young adult with learning disabilities told of becoming impatient at waiting for a job interview and barging in on the employer to express his displeasure. Needless to say, he did not get the job. The same young man experiences anxiety in trying to socialize with young women. "I have a small vocabulary, and so whenever I use big words, sometimes I forget how to use them. And I'll say the wrong word. And sometimes I'll forget what I'm getting at, and then I'll forget which way I'm going. So the chicks will just sit there and look at me, and I will try and talk. I'd make sense, but I wouldn't be able to impress them. I'd just be able to make small talk, conversation. But that'll be a serious jam" (Gerber & Reiff, 1991, p. 103).

In the case of this adult, social skills deficits permeate almost all aspects of his life. For many others, social skills difficulties are not as immediately obvious or pervasive; nevertheless, the impact can be significant. One adult commented that he has learned how "to play the game," but that many social situations continue to make him feel uncomfortable. He has learned to cope by putting "on whatever coat of armor was needed to be put on and go into the fray, knowing that I could win the battle if I fought hard enough. And that's been sort of my approach. Even when I put on my tuxedo, and I've got to go to a large social gathering, I put on my 'Hamlet disguise,' and I'll play the game like anybody else" (Gerber & Reiff, 1991, p. 69). This individual is able to overcome social apprehension in a functional sense but must exert significant energy and will-power to do so.

Although some adults with learning disabilities find ways to overcome or compensate for social skills difficulties, others continue to experience basic shortcomings with social competence. Such deficits interfere with many other components of adult life and independent living, such as use of leisure time and interpersonal relationships, and with the overall socioadaptive repertoire demanded in adult life. The existing literature that examines socialization of adults with learning disabilities offers a rather extensive list of problems with social adjustment, including high anxiety, panic responses, being overwhelmed by stress, and avoidance (Johnson, 1981); overcommitment, withdrawal, alloplastic manners, mood swings, and encapsulation (Rogan & Hartman, 1976); more dependence on friends and relatives (Fafard & Haubrich, 1981); difficulty in making friends (Meyers & Messer, 1981); dissatisfaction with familial relationships and a limited range of social opportunities (White, 1985); and feelings of aloneness and isolation, discomfort in social gatherings, and a sense of boredom and frustration with recreational and leisure time (Gerber & Reiff, 1991). These difficulties assume a greater sense of reality through firsthand accounts.

Anxiety takes many forms for different people, but a recurring theme of anxiety in adults with learning disabilities is related to feeling stupid. A successful businessman stated that he is anxious every morning when he awakes because he doesn't know if he's going to be smart or stupid when he gets to work; vacations offer similar fears of returning to work to find that he's become "stupid." Other adults express anxieties about their perceived academic shortcomings; one professor with learning disabilities has recurring nightmares that her Ph.D. has been taken away because "they" found out she couldn't read. Another professor tries to avoid social situations: "I go to a movie and two days later forget that I even went so how can I manage to survive in a social situation? . . . I'm the most uncomfortable person looking for some way to bow out because I feel vulnerable in these situations."

This same professor offers insight into overcommitment and subsequent problems. "From the age of 35 to 42 I had a rapid series of three breakdowns. The crisis came due to the fact that I was achieving fairly well in my outward work, but in order to do that, I was driving myself beyond reason. . . . There was also alcohol involvement. I used alcohol socially to overcome difficulties that turned out to be related to learning problems."

Of particular importance, social skills deficits, more than academic deficiencies or vocational incompetence, often lead to on-the-job difficulties (Blalock, 1982; Patton & Polloway, 1982). Vocational social skills difficulties are so pervasive and their implication so significant that Pathways to Employment for People with Learning Disabilities (Brown et al., 1990) specifically recommended an action plan to address the issue of socioadaptability in the workplace. The plan emphasizes the lack of awareness about problems with social functioning on the parts of both people with learning disabilities and other people in the workplace, a situation that undoubtedly exacerbates interpersonal tension and ultimately jeopardizes employment suitability. The plan prioritizes the need for information on effective intervention in the work setting (Brown et al., 1990).

In interviewing highly successful adults with learning disabilities (Gerber et al., 1992), perhaps the most prevalent theme centered on a degree of anger felt by many adults. This anger was so pervasive in the sample of subjects that it warrants special commentary. Clearly, many of the adults were angry about the treatment they had received during their years in school, usually at the hands of teachers, sometimes from peers and parents. They were angry that others called them stupid, stubborn, or lazy. They were angry that high school counselors told them not to bother to apply to college; one adult remembers that his counselor told him he was a "J.I.T."—janitor in training. Probably all of us have experiences from childhood that still make us wince when we think about them. For many adults with learning disabilities, those feelings are more than mere memory; the feelings continue to play a part of adult experience, often tinting, sometimes staining, the landscape of their social and emotional lives. "The literate world was my enemy. I wasn't much different than a Jew in Nazi Germany. I took a psychological posture of who the good guys were and who the bad guys were. . . . In this society, learning how to read and write is very basic, and you learn it when you're a child. So psychologically and emotionally we're left in our childhood. And we're left in the emotions and fears of our childhood."

Carrying anger and pain from childhood into adulthood can have a variety of consequences. Some adults basically give up on themselves, allowing the learned helplessness from the classroom to become a generic condition. Others have managed to turn the anger into a motivating force that fuels the fire to persevere and succeed. One adult's purpose in life has been to prove his childhood critics wrong: "I decided, 'I'll show them I'm not an idiot.'" Another adult explained the process of making the pain work for him. "You fight until you can't fight anymore, and then you fight some more. You take the hurt and turn in inward and it becomes part of the burn (to succeed). It has to burn."

Whether anger and pain from childhood are positive or negative forces in adult life, the adult with learning disabilities is carrying emotional baggage that most of us would prefer to leave behind. Some of the adults in the study by Gerber and co-workers (1992) spoke of the need to heal in adulthood from the wounds of the past. The process tends to begin as learning disabilities are fully accepted and, in many cases, acknowledged to others. For one adult, healing and self-awareness are inextricably linked.

> At times it was extremely lonely and painful . . . but I think I got to know myself in that loneliness. I think I really had to pull for myself. I had to learn how to believe in myself very early. . . . I think I identify with people in low self-esteem positions or people who are struggling to believe in themselves because I had that experience so intimately. I'm also rooting for the underdog because I felt like one in some ways. I'm very optimistic and hopeful and persistent so I think I'm a messenger of hope and encouragement for many people. . . . Initially I was trying to rescue other people as a way of healing myself, but that changed early on. I have felt healed for a long time and more.

Although most issues related to learning disabilities focus on the inherent limitations of the disabilities, we would be remiss in neglecting the wonderful examples of success that many adults with learning disabilities experience in social and emotional aspects of their lives. In the Gerber and associates' (1992) interviews, a significant number of respondents had nothing but positive reactions to social and emotional concerns. Many felt great about friendships: "I have networks of people in diverse areas all over the world." Instead of feeling anxious in social situations, many adults with learning disabilities are truly "people persons," entirely at ease with small or large groups. A response from a successful 37-year-old single woman living in New York reflects the situation of many adults with learning disabilities. "I like my social life. I have a real wide variety of friends. I can run the gamut from close friends to acquaintances. And I love theater and film and classical music and go to lots of chamber music concerts. . . . The people that you surround yourself with hopefully are the people that you love and that bring out the best in you."

Daily Living Issues

For adults with learning disabilities, activities of day-to-day living offer concrete evidence of the persistence of learning disabilities through the lifespan. Difficulties and subsequent ways of coping with daily demands vary with the characteristics of individual disabilities as well as the types of tasks with which an adult is routinely involved. Additionally, some adults develop remarkable coping strategies to deal with their daily affairs; some are extremely selective in what they choose to undertake; others may be largely befuddled or overwhelmed by activities that most of us take for granted. In almost all cases, adults feel the impact of learning disabilities in numerous areas of daily living.

The most common difficulty associated with learning disabilities revolves around language-based deficits, especially reading and spelling (Blalock, 1982). We live in a world where it would be nearly impossible to avoid situations that involve reading and writing; adults with significant problems in these areas are continually confronted by the demands of a literate society. Sometimes avoidance poses no threat; many adults who do not read well do not bother to read a newspaper; they can watch the news on television instead. Other adults, in spite of significant reading difficulties, love to read and are willing simply to devote much more time to reading than the average reader or choose texts that are easier to read. And in some cases, when reading a document is absolutely necessary, many adults with learning disabilities cope by relying on someone else to do the reading. The fine line between effective use of support systems and dependence is largely a matter of perspective, but clearly some adults achieve admirable autonomy within the realization that they need assistance with some tasks, whereas others become dependent on support for almost all endeavors.

Coping with spelling provides a number of examples of the challenges of daily living for adults with learning disabilities. Writing checks, specifically in spelling the amount of money, tends to perplex many adults who do not spell well. Several adults have reported an ingenious method for responding to this task. Inside their checkbooks, in place of a calendar or account sheet that most people have next to the checks, these adults have inserted a "crib" sheet that provides the necessary numerical spellings. With this system, they can write checks without requiring assistance and without other persons knowing that they have spelling difficulties. On the other hand, some adults have never resolved this problem and essentially have given up trying to write checks. They either rely exclusively on cash or on someone else to do the shopping.

Learning disabilities may affect numerous other areas of daily living from the mundane to the profound. Citing all examples is beyond the scope of this chapter; instead, we will discuss a sample of issues to present a flavor of life for adults with learning disabilities. In particular, problems associated with visual perception, directionality, and organization will serve as examples.

Difficulties with visual perception extend well beyond reading. One woman with poor visual memory keeps all of her kitchen implements hanging on hooks or otherwise displayed, for if she were to put them in drawers, she would never remember where she had stored them. Another professional woman does not have adequate visual discrimination in either color or design to coordinate her outfits appropriately. To compensate, she has had a professional arrange her clothes into coordinated ensembles that she always hangs together. Other adults have spoken of being visually overwhelmed at the supermarket, and they usually avoid grocery shopping. Problems with depth perception and figure–ground discrimination have resulted in concerns with driving for some adults with learning disabilities.

Most stories related to driving focus on the theme of directionality. Reading maps is nearly impossible for some persons. They rely on visual landmarks to guide them. If they have to travel to a new destination, they will often make a trial run before an actual appointment in order to learn a set of landmarks that they can use. Directionality at its most basic level (i.e., left and right) can have an obvious impact on driving. A number of adults with learning disabilities report that they have significant difficulties distinguishing right from left turns, especially when someone else is giving them directions. Perhaps the most common compensation involves consistently wearing a watch or ring on a given side and referring to that item to locate the direction. Some individuals have found that extending their thumb and index finger on the left hand creates an "L," which serves as a directionality indicator. Directionality problems affect numerous aspects of daily living. The range of compensations is enormous and as varied as the individuals themselves; the degree to which the compensation allows the individual to cope probably has more of an impact on quality of life than the severity of the learning disabilities per se.

Problems with organization constitute a well-documented characteristic of learning disabilities, which, in adulthood, may affect a number of components of daily living. Some adults have found that any disruption to their daily routine causes havoc; therefore, they maintain a meticulous organization of all aspects of their lives. This striving for control may not be unusual in that many adults without learning disabilities exhibit a similar approach. The difference rests in the phenomenon that, without zealous attention to such details, the learning disabilities would overwhelm the individual and make certain functions of daily living impossible. For example, one adult related that she follows exactly the same routine and sequence every morning, from which side of the bed she gets out of to when she brushes her teeth to how she sets the table for breakfast. If the routine is disrupted in any way, she is so overwhelmed that she cannot function. Starting from the beginning (i.e., getting out of bed again) is her only recourse to regaining control.

Other adults with learning disabilities have developed unusual and innovative methods to overcome organizational difficulties. Some rely on other people to help, from doing the shopping, to coordinating outfits, to scheduling appointments. Some have created or utilize organizational prosthetics such as color-coded files, computer programs, or inveterate list-making and note-taking. Other strategies include allowing extra time to do tasks or find places, devoting time every day to organizational concerns, or simply throwing out anything that might cause clutter. Still others have decided not to expend undue energy on organizing their lives. For some, this decision may be an admission of defeat, but for others, it represents a consciousness of and comfort with a degree of disarray that does not necessarily interfere with quality of life. As a successful dermatologist with learning disabilities points out, "Neat is to me a waste of time, not high on my priorities. I have somewhat of a scattered thinking pattern, so leaving things around is just find with me."

Conclusions

Social/emotional functioning and daily living activities represent critical components of an individual's quality of life. Personal independence, constructive community participation, healthy familial relationships, and success in vocational endeavors all hinge, to a large extent, on social/emotional well-being and daily living competence. As we have discussed in this chapter, some adults with learning disabilities fare well in these areas, whereas others find the quality of their lives compromised by social/ emotional and daily living shortcomings.

Clearly, adults with learning disabilities deserve equal opportunities to pursue the quality of life of their choosing. Fairness in employability and access to public accommodations, as mandated in the newly implemented Americans with Disabilities Act, will only partially redress discrimination of persons with learning disabilities if social/emotional functioning and daily living continue to result in lives of frustration, unhappiness, and despair. A recognition of the link between these two issues and the construct of disability is a prerequisite for persons with learning disabilities to receive their "fair shake." Addressing social/emotional and daily living issues demands a holistic approach that highlights the interactive manifestations of learning disabilities in adulthood.

References

Blalock, J. (1982). Persistent problems and concerns of young adults with learning disabilities. In W. Cruickshank & A. Silver (Eds.), *Bridges to tomorrow* (Vol. 2), pp. 3–56. Syracuse, NY: Syracuse University Press.

Brown, D. S., Gerber, P. J., & Dowdy, C. (1990). *Pathways to employment for people with learning disabilities: A plan for action.* New York: National Center for Learning Disabilities.

Bruininks, V. (1978). Peer status and personality characteristics of learning disabled and nondisabled students. *Journal of Learning Disabilities*, 11, 484–489.

Bryan, T. (1976). Peer popularity of learning disabled children: A replication. *Journal of Learning Disabilities*, 9, 307–311.

Cowen, E., Pederson, A., Babijon, H., Izzo, L., & Trost, M. (1973). Long-term follow-up of early detected vulnerable children. *Journal of Consulting and Clinical Psychology*, 41, 438–446.

Dickstein, E., & Warren, D. (1980). Role-taking deficits in learning disabled children. *Journal of Learning Disabilities*, 13, 378–382.

Dudley-Marling, C. C., & Edmiaston, R. (1985). Social status of learning disabled children and adolescents: A review. *Learning Disability Quarterly*, 8, 189–204.

Fafard, M. B., & Haubrich, P. A. (1981). Vocational and social adjustment of learning disabled young adults: A follow-up survey. *Learning Disabilities Quarterly*, 4, 122–130.

Gerber, P. J. (1978). *A comparative study of social perceptual ability of learning disabled and nonhandicapped children.* Doctoral Dissertation, University of Michigan, Ann Arbor.

Gerber, P. J., Ginsberg, R. J., & Reiff, H. B. (1992). Identifying alterable patterns in employment success for highly successful adults with learning disabilities. *Journal of Learning Disabilities*, 25, 475–487.

Gerber, P. J., & Reiff, H. B. (1991). *Speaking for themselves: Ethnographic interviews with adults with learning disabilities.* Ann Arbor, MI: University of Michigan Press.

Johnson, C. (1981). LD adults: The inside story. *Academic Therapy*, 16, 435–442.

Larson, K., & Gerber, M. (1987). Effects of social metacognitive training for enhancing overt behavior in learning disabled and low achieving delinquents. *Exceptional Children*, 54, 210–212.

Lerner, J. (1993). *Learning Disabilities: Theories, diagnoses, and teaching strategies.* Boston: Houghton Mifflin.

Meyers, G. S., & Messer, J. (1981). The social and vocational adjustment of learning disabled/behavior disordered adolescents after h.s.: A pilot survey. *Proceedings from the International Conference on the Career Development of Handicapped Individuals* (pp. 70–83). Washington, DC: National Institute of Education.

National Joint Committee on Learning Disabilities. (1983) *The needs of adults with learning disabilities: A position paper of the National Joint Committee on Learning Disabilities.* Baltimore, MD: National Joint Committee on Learning Disabilities.

Patton, J. R., & Polloway, E. A. (1982). The adult years. *Topics in Learning and Learning Disabilities*, 2, 91–103.

Pickering, E., Pickering, A., & Buchanan, M. (1987). LD and nonhandicapped boys' comprehension of cartoon humor. *Learning Disability Quarterly*, 10, 45–51.

Reiff, H. B. (1987). *Cognitive correlates of social perception in students with learning disabilities.* Unpublished doctoral dissertation.

Reiff, H. B., & Gerber, P. J. (1989). Social cognition and cognitive processing in students with learning disabilities. *Learning Disabilities: A Multidisciplinary Journal*, 1, 56–62.

Roff, M., Sells, S., & Golden, M. (1972). *Social adjustment and personality development in children.* Minneapolis: University of Minnesota Press.

Rogan, L., & Hartman, L. (1976). *A follow-up study of learning disabled children as adults. Final report.* Project #443CH60010, Grant #OEG-0-74-7453. Washington, DC: Bureau of Education for the Handicapped, U.S. Department of Health, Education and Welfare.

Rosenberg, B., & Gaier, E. (1977). The self-concept of the adolescent with learning disabilities. *Adolescence*, 12, 489–498.

Schumaker, J., & Hazel, S. (1984). Social skills assessment and training for the learning disabled: Who's on first and what's on second? *Journal of Learning Disabilities, 17,* 422–431.

Swanson, H., & Trahan, M. (1986). Characteristics of frequently cited articles in learning disabilities. *Journal of Special Education, 20,* 167–182.

Ullman, C. (1957). Teachers, peers, and tests as predictors of adjustment. *Journal of Educational Psychology, 8,* 227–233.

White, W. J. (1985). Perspectives on education and training of learning disabled adults. *Learning Disability Quarterly, 8,* 231–236.

Wiig, E. H., & Semel, E. M. (1976). *Language disabilities in children and adolescents.* Columbus, OH: Merrill.

Wong, B., & Wong, R. (1980). Role-taking skills in normal achieving and learning disabled children. *Learning Disability Quarterly, 3,* (2), 11–18.

Chapter 7

Counseling and Psychotherapy for Adults with Learning Disabilities

ROBIN S. BARTON, ED.D.
BARBARA S. FUHRMANN, ED.D

Adults with learning disabilities seek counseling and psychotherapy for the same reasons as do other adults: marital discord, divorce, substance use and abuse, work problems, and so on. Yet they bring along another set of unique needs and problems. Although therapists may approach therapy from various theoretical perspectives, growth for the client with learning disabilities relies on three factors: (1) the healing inherent in the therapeutic relationship; (2) understanding by the therapist and the client of the person's unique cognitive processing style; and (3) interventions that not only foster growth but also fit the specific cognitive, emotional, and social needs of the client.

Reasons for Seeking Therapy

The needs of adult clients with learning disabilities vary depending on age and life experiences. Most of these clients have problems either with work, school, or relationships. Although those adults who were identified as learning disabled in elementary or secondary school have some different issues than those who are confronting identified learning disabilities for the first time, they share the common effects of learning disabilities, and their treatment may differ only in the degree to which the counselor must help the client to understand the disability itself.

School-identified adults are generally younger, having completed their kindergarten through twelfth-grade education since the implementation of P.L. 94–142. Often they are in school, looking for work, or just beginning jobs. Like other young adults, they are seeking their identities as individuals in society, with the confounding element of their disabilities. Many are trying to apply skills learned in high school to new settings. Others who thought they had conquered their learning disabilities are shocked to find themselves confronting failure again on the job or in the classroom. Some do not fully understand the implications of their disabilities in either work-related or social situations (Blalock, 1981). They lack understanding of how to capitalize on their strengths to compensate for their deficits (Gerber, Ginsberg, and Reiff, 1992). Some have not learned independent living skills and feel confused by the complexity of daily living (e.g., managing time and money) (Blalock, 1981).

CASE EXAMPLE

Michael, age 20, grew up in a small town where his father was on the school board. Throughout school, he received special education services. His teachers tried to meet his educational needs. However, socially he never quite fit in. His mechanical skills were outstanding, but he could not banter in the halls with the guys or flirt with the girls. After high school he attended community college. While he had no difficulty learning computer technology, he was overwhelmed by the need to socialize with peers and to navigate around the campus and through the day. He became so anxious that he wanted to quit school.

Unlike Michael, who knew he had a learning disability but who had trouble assimilating into a new environment, adults learning about their disabilities for the first time have to assimilate a new element into their self-images and confront the experience (and sometimes relief) of a label. In addition, they need to learn new skills and to advocate for their rights, as well as to find the external resources to learn new strategies and skills, all the while maintaining work and family responsibilities. Often these adults have previously seen themselves as lacking intelligence and have consequently lowered their expectations of themselves. Some are shocked, even frightened, to discover that they have average or above-average intelligence. Others are enraged at having been misperceived all their lives.

CASE EXAMPLE

Sherry, who worked two jobs, one as a dentist's receptionist and the other as a bartender, was stunned to learn that her intelligence was well above average and that at the age of 35 her reading skills were also above average. She had spent her entire school career in the "bottom" classes and had barely graduated. She perceived herself as "dumb" and unable to read and write adequately.

What she didn't know was that in the years since high school she had grown cognitively and had improved her reading-comprehension skills on the job. Her school experience defined her perception of her competence. She didn't know that she had, in fact, developed compensatory skills and strategies that evidenced her learning abilities.

Adults with learning disabilities often succeed through a variety of compensatory strategies, and as long as these work, they are not seen in counselor's offices. But when the strategies fail and they no longer can avoid the effects of the disabilities, they come to counseling. They may reappear throughout their adult lives as demands change.

CASE EXAMPLE

For several years, Gene had worked closely with Jeannette as salespersons in a brokerage firm. Jeanette handled the older, more stable accounts, while Gene did the "cold call" selling and handled the recalcitrant accounts. Jeannette's organizational and detail abilities combined with Gene's charming personality to make a dynamic sales team. Their sales records were outstanding, so much so that the company promoted them— to separate offices.

Jeannette adapted easily, although she missed Gene's handling of difficult customers. Gene, however, found himself overwhelmed. He was soon swamped with paper work, his schedule was in disarray, and he was angry and humiliated as his sales dropped while Jeannette's soared. He had lost his support system and was unable to function without it.

These stories of Michael, Sherry, and Gene highlight the effects of learning disabilities. In general, these effects fall into four categories: (1) stress and anxiety resulting from being overwhelmed by the complexity of life's demands; (2) low self-esteem and feelings of incompetence; (3) unresolved grief; and (4) helplessness resulting from limited understanding of learning abilities and disabilities.

Stress and anxiety

"How do I get it all done? It takes so long! I get so tired!" Almost all clients with learning disabilities feel overwhelmed and anxious because they are unable to manage the complexity of life. They are stressed because they need to use four steps to accomplish what others do in two, or they need to use set, almost ritualistic, procedures to accomplish relatively simple tasks. Extra steps mean extra energy expended, increased fatigue, and a sense that there is never enough time. For example, telephone messages and numbers need to be double-checked for errors. Simple computation requires a calculator, but first the calculator must be found. Avoiding making mistakes keeps the person anxious and "on edge."

Low self-esteem.

"I'm dumb. It won't work. I can't." Adults with learning disabilities have spent years developing low self-esteem as a result of the sense of incompetence in meeting their own and others' expectations. Standards such as timeliness and accuracy, so common to most adults, impede the performance of intelligent adults with learning disabilities. Persons who, from childhood on, internalize beliefs of incompetence have a monumental task in disputing them and developing beliefs in their own competence.

Dependence on others often reinforces beliefs of incompetence. Successful learners view appropriate reliance on others (e.g., an editor) and on mechanical devices (e.g., a calculator) as means to an end. In contrast, adults with learning disabilities often view such reliance as one more indicator of incompetence. An inappropriate belief that everyone else is self-reliant is reinforced if, in the workplace or in the classroom, providing accommodations is viewed as unfair.

Low self-esteem also leads to fear of new learning situations. Change is the worst enemy of some adults with learning disabilities. Learning has often been laborious and painful, and the need to begin again in a new situation is terrifying. Although some trepidation in a new environment is common to everyone, a new situation with unpredictable demands can be debilitating to an adult with a learning disability.

Finally, self-esteem problems are heightened when attention and concentration problems add to feelings of incompetence. The inability to attend or concentrate means that the person misses important data. Names, telephone numbers, and formulas fly away with embarrassing results. Many adults have no idea that their attention problems may be amenable to cognitive therapies and to medication, where appropriate. For many, the first crucial step toward competence is referral to a physician familiar with the medications effective in the treatment of attention deficit hyperactivity disorder (ADHD) in adults.

CASE EXAMPLE

Chris, a college sophomore, lived in chaos. Her apartment was a wreck, her schoolwork disorganized, her personal appearance in disarray. She was on the verge of failing in school and was anxious and depressed, certain that she was just no good. In a counseling intake, the counselor had to take notes just to keep track of the content of Chris's rapid, disorganized talk. Chris recognized in herself ten of the fourteen behaviors associated with ADHD (American Psychiatric Assocation, 1987), but she did not know that there was treatment for her wandering attention and disorganization. A trial of Ritalin had no apparent immediate effect, but one day Chris arrived in the office in tears. For the first time in her life, she had completely cleaned her bathroom without being distracted. While seemingly minor in the universe of her problems, this feat symbolized a change in her life. With the help of the medication, Chris began to mobilize her energy and apply it to learning the cognitive and behavioral strategies necessary to organizing her life.

Unresolved grief

"Why did this happen to me? Nobody understands! It hurts so much! I hate my life and myself. It's not fair." Rage, anguish, guilt, sadness, betrayal, fear, jealousy—all of the feelings associated with grieving a major loss—are common to adults with learning disabilities. The intensity depends on how painful the experiences were and how skillfully they were masked from awareness. Many adults with learning disabilities have never grieved their losses: what they cannot do that other people do easily, the loss of academic and personal self-esteem, the opportunities for the future that are out of reach. Others have never been able to vent their rage at parents, spouses, siblings, teachers, friends, co-workers, employers, and others who failed or continue to fail to support and understand. Although unresolved grief is virtually never the presenting problem of adults with learning disabilities, it is almost always not too far beneath the surface and needs to be recognized for the power it contains and the barrier it erects to further growth. Counselors of adults with learning disabilities need to be especially sensitive to the likely presence of grief and especially patient in helping clients to recognize it, express it, and eventually move beyond it.

CASE EXAMPLE

Eric, a 35-year-old college-educated salesman, had been out of work for six months. Although he and his wife had no significant financial problems, he came to counseling at her urging, ostensibly to discover what might be going wrong in his unproductive job search. He presented himself as cocky, brash, and defensive, seeking counseling only to appease his wife. He knew that he was dyslexic but saw no relationship between that and his problems in the work setting. He denied any need to address behaviors that might be related to the learning disability. Eric's anger erupted when he discussed his wife's belief that it should be easy for him, with all his skills and experiences, to find an appropriate job. His grief was barely below the surface, and his rage exploded when he finally realized that his wife had never understood how difficult life could be for him.

Helplessness.

"I can't get through college. I was never destined to be a professional anyway. I'm 'special ed.' I have a learning disability." Feelings of helplessness can stem from limited understanding of learning disabilities and of learning *abilities*. Successful adults with learning disabilities understand both their learning disabilities and their learning abilities, and are therefore able to set realistic goals based on their strengths (Gerber, et al., 1992). Most adults with learning disabilities in therapy have lost sight of their competencies.

CASE EXAMPLE

Beth, who weekly assembled Sunday dinner for seventeen relatives and who had memorized all of Handel's *Messiah*, did not view herself as able to organize tasks or remember words well enough to read and comprehend the medical technology lab manuals at work. Beth had no idea that the organization and memory strategies that she used outside of work were indicative of what she could do within the work environment. Once she understood these strengths, she was able to set realistic goals and move up the ladder in her work environment.

Theoretical Rationale

A thorough discussion of the various approaches to counseling and psychotherapy is clearly beyond the scope of this chapter. Nevertheless, some appreciation of the major approaches to therapy, as well as our recommended integration of these theories, especially as they pertain to the counseling of adults with learning disabilities, provides the background from which treatment planning and interventions are derived.

Although many authors classify as many as 10 to 12 major theoretical approaches to counseling and psychotherapy, we find four major categories, based roughly on the major focus of the approach, to suffice for thinking about the totality of clients' experience. These four, when integrated, provide a comprehensive picture of clients who are influenced by their early learning, by what they do, by what they think, and by how they feel. If we think about all human beings as composed of unconscious motives, and by thoughts, behaviors, and feelings, we can choose to intervene with a particular client in any of those realms. Although some counselors approach every client from one of the four basic approaches described below, we believe that counselors can be most effective by consciously choosing an intervention based on their analysis of its potential power to influence a particular client at a particular time in terms of self-understanding, of changing thought processes, of doing something differently, or of altering destructive feelings. In this way the counselor operates from a theoretical base of conscious integration or reasoned eclecticism, and intervenes with purpose and direction based not on a single theoretical orientation but on an analysis of client needs.

The first approach is that of the psychoanalytic (more recently termed *psychodynamic*) theorists, who emphasize unconscious processes, learned early, which lead to thinking, feeling, and behaving in the present. The second is that of the behaviorists, who emphasize the important role of what we do in influencing how we think and feel. The third is that of the cognitive therapists, who believe that our perceptions and beliefs determine how we feel and be-

have. Finally, the fourth is that of the humanistic, or person-centered, theorists, who believe that how we feel is of primary importance in influencing how we think and behave. We believe that all four understandings are important in working with adults with learning disabilities. To better clarify the focus of each of the approaches, let us analyze the case of an imaginary adult woman with a learning disability and process how a therapist oriented from each of these four perspectives might approach working with her.

CASE EXAMPLE

Susan is a 23-year-old college sophomore who was diagnosed as dyslexic when she was in the tenth grade and who finished high school in a program designed specifically for adolescents with dyslexia. Susan is the middle of three children; her oldest brother is in his last year in a prestigious law school and already has job offers with starting salaries well above $50,000. Her sister, just 10 months younger than Susan, is in her last year of college and has been accepted into a graduate program in clinical psychology. Susan has come to therapy because of her feelings of anxiety, low self-esteem, and lack of career direction. She has taken general education requirements, has a 2.1 grade point average (out of 4.0), and needs to declare a major.

A *therapist from a psychodynamic background* would likely focus on Susan's early family environment and learning. She would probably assume that Susan's anxiety and low self-esteem are the product of Susan's not being able to fulfill her parents' expectations of her, as well as Susan's perceptions that she doesn't measure up to the competencies displayed by her siblings. The therapist would probably ask Susan to recall early experiences in her family and would focus on helping her to gain insight into the origins of her anxiety and low self-esteem. This therapist would believe that once Susan has gained the necessary insight into the origins of her feelings, the insight itself would provide the means for changing them and for setting new directions for herself.

In contrast to the insight-oriented approach, a *behavioral therapist* would focus on what Susan is doing, in the present, to create her anxiety and low self-esteem. This therapist would assume that Susan fully understands her problems and so would not spend a great deal of time exploring her feelings, her background, or her understanding of her dyslexia; rather a behavioral therapist would focus on collecting specific data about what Susan *does* to create her anxiety and negative thoughts and feelings, and would prescribe specific action-steps leading to anxiety reduction and increased self-esteem. This therapist would be likely to focus on what Susan needs to do to change her life to make it more fulfilling and would ask Susan to confront the reality of her situation, to accept it, and to work positively within it. The therapist would likely have Susan identify both the antecedents and the reinforcers of her negative behaviors and then determine ways to change both sets of stimuli. Susan would probably sign contracts that would help her to practice new, more self-enhancing behaviors, including stress-reduction exercises, medication if appropriate, and appointments with faculty to discuss career options in various majors.

A *cognitive therapist* would approach Susan with the belief that it is her cognitive processing and negative thoughts that create her anxiety and low self-esteem. This therapist would emphasize the role of cognition in behavior and would be active and directive in helping Susan to confront her irrational ideas about her competence, especially as compared to that of her siblings, and about her future. The emphasis would also be on solving problems with rational, realistic thinking.

A *humanistic, person-centered therapist* would be most interested in providing a safe and nurturing environment in which Susan would feel free to take the risk of exposing her negative feelings and thoughts. This therapist would rely most heavily on support and encouragement to help Susan feel worthwhile and competent and would assume that once Susan felt better, other aspects of her life would fall into place.

All four approaches have considerable merit in working with adults with learning disabilities, who clearly present issues of negative feelings, thoughts, and behaviors, and who frequently received strong negative messages in their early lives. Nevertheless, to work most effectively with adults with learning disabilities, we believe that the therapist should start from a humanistic, feeling-oriented framework, designed primarily to establish trust and support for clients who may have little reason to trust their environments. But with adults with learning disabilities, trust and support are simply not sufficient. Based on the counselor's exploration of the clients' background and concerns, a thorough exploration of early messages and their resultant thoughts and feelings may be necessary for the clients to understand how they may have come to perceive themselves as they do. Some clients may also need a thorough explanation and understanding of their particular disability and its implications. It is never safe to assume that just because clients are adults, they understand their disabilities. Once a supportive environment is established, and once the counselor is certain that the client has insight and understanding into both the disability itself and into early learnings resulting from the disability, it is probably necessary to move to what is likely to form the crux of the therapy: cognitive interventions designed (1) to help the clients to learn to organize thoughts and to process them appropriately; (2) to confront erroneous beliefs both about their disabilities and about their perceptions resulting from the disabilities and from feedback received from others; (3) to use learnable cognitive skills designed to increase the use of cognitive organizers and perception checks; and (4) to challenge their assumptions about the world. Although the

Client centered Approach

main focus of therapy for adults with learning disabilities may well be in the cognitive realm, significant attention is likely to be needed to change behavior as well. Because of their frequently faulty perceptions, adults with learning disabilities do not always behave appropriately, especially in social situations, so the counselor must help the clients to identify self-destructive behaviors and to develop more productive and enhancing coping strategies.

Treatment Plan

An appropriate treatment plan fits the unique cognitive, emotional, and social needs of the client. Developing the plan depends on an empathic investigation of the client's learning abilities and disabilities. This process facilitates developing the therapeutic alliance and designing appropriate interventions.

Diagnostic Process

The therapist needs to be an astute interviewer and observer, working to understand the client's world view while remembering that this client may not receive, organize, or express information in expected ways. As the client's story unfolds, the therapist may need to do more clarifying and reframing than is usual, supplying words to keep the narrative progressing and taking notes to organize the seemingly chaotic story the client tells.

The counselor must look for behavior clues to the client's underlying cognitive processing. These include the inability to maintain attention, to perceive stimuli accurately, to remember, to attach meaning to symbols, to form concepts by differentiating among and combining meanings, and to understand the nature and process of one's own learning. The therapist needs to understand the inferred relationship between observed behaviors and underlying cognitive processes

in order to form hypotheses about how the person learns and to develop intervention strategies based on these hypotheses.

In addition, the therapist must discuss observations and hypotheses with the client and then evaluate their efficacy from the client's perspective.

CASE EXAMPLE

In his initial interview, Bryan appeared easy-going, attentive, and friendly. He maintained eye contact, smiled, said socially appropriate things, and nodded agreeably. On the surface, he appeared completely engaged in the discussion. However, within the first ten minutes, he twice chuckled and commented that he tended to forget little, unimportant things. Suspecting a possible problem with distractibility, the counselor asked about the "little things." Bryan's comments minimized what proved to be a major unrecognized problem with internal distractibility, which severely affected his work, his relationship with his fiancee, and his coursework in college.

The therapist needs to listen carefully to the client's language and to observe visual and verbal processing in the interview. Inability to recall names and familiar data and misused vocabulary may signal word-retrieval problems. Poorly organized sentences with incorrect syntax may reflect language organization and expression problems. Some clients cannot process visual and verbal information simultaneously, so while the counselor is explaining how to fill in the registration form, they are distracted by the visual stimuli and do not hear a word of the instructions. They may spell their names or addresses incorrectly, or they may avoid filling out a form at all. They may smile and nod agreeably while assimilating little of what is said.

The counselor needs to watch for defensive behaviors, both the client's and the counselor's own. One of the gifts of many of these clients is their ability to protect themselves from embarrassment by manipulating others. They may redirect attention away from themselves by focusing on the counselor, questioning the counselor's credentials, or telling a longwinded and irrelevant story, all to avoid discussing the real problem. These defensive behaviors need to be noted and confronted once a therapeutic alliance has been formed.

Throughout the diagnostic phase, the therapist needs to glean information about the client's learning disabilities and how they influence daily life. What are the roles of reading, writing, mathematics, speaking, and listening skills in the client's daily life? What happens in the workplace and at home? How and where does the learning disability interfere with competence? How does the client approach new situations? How unpredictable and inconsistent are the problems? How much variation exists in the client's abilities? How are feelings about the disabilities expressed behaviorally? Are there tendencies toward repetitive, anxious behaviors? Is the client behaving obsessively? Hypercritically? Are characteristics of depression evident?

Equally important is evidence of the client's successes, even if they appear meager. What does he or she enjoy doing? How does he or she spend leisure time? What successes has he or she experienced? What is the client good at? It is within this framework that both counselor and client can identify the cognitive abilities that can become the foundation on which to rebuild self-esteem and develop new skills.

It is also essential to know as much as possible about the residual effects of school failure and of parental and personal reactions to it. Most adult clients have emotionally charged recollections of teachers whom they perceive as embarrassing them, belittling them, or criticizing their intelligence. Some have equally painful recollections about parents and other family members. It is crucial that the therapist understand these experiences, not only for their impact on the client, but also because the client is likely to project onto the therapist the anger and hurt learned from parents and teachers.

Educational, work, and family histories are all needed. If they are available, the therapist should read the evaluations that have been done over the years. Old report cards, school records, and work evaluations can provide data about abilities as well as disabilities. A family genogram is useful to organize family information concretely for both the counselor and the client.

Last, the therapist needs to use the diagnostic phase to examine social relationships and behaviors. Do clients use socially appropriate language and behavior? Can they track the counselor's dialogue while organizing and expressing their own? Are they aware of the counselor's behavior and their own simultaneously? Do they view the work in dichotomies because they can only take one perspective at a time? Do they accurately read body language and tone of voice? Do they use personal space appropriately?

Therapeutic Alliance

As the therapist is developing hypotheses about the client's learning abilities and disabilities through observations and history-taking, the therapist is also forging the therapeutic alliance essential for healing and growth and for confronting defensive, self-defeating behaviors. Here the humanistic, person-centered approach is most appropriate.

Adults with learning disabilities are often keenly sensitive to possible rejection and disapproval. The therapist therefore needs to be authentic, empathic, and accepting. Respecting the client's values and lifestyle and maintaining confidentiality are also crucial. Some young adults have little confidence that their privacy will be respected. Many have been tested and discussed by numerous professionals over the years and therefore may not trust that their personal lives will be kept confidential.

The therapist must also remain aware of the client's processing style and adapt his or her behavior to accommodate that style. For example, if the client processes speech slowly, the counselor must slow his or her speech to the client's pace. Some clients have difficulty with word retrieval. Although some may welcome the therapist's help in locating the right word, others resent it. It is the therapist's responsibility to adjust accordingly.

With the development of an appropriate therapeutic alliance, the client feels accepted, respected, and trusted. Only when the client feels such safety can the counselor begin to foster independent growth, expose and confront inappropriate social behavior, and begin to help the client toward the resolution of confusing issues and feelings.

Interventions

Interventions come from all four basic therapeutic approaches, with the addition of processing interventions that are not usually necessary with non-learning-disabled clients. Traditionally psychotherapy preparation rarely includes training in how to adapt therapy techniques to a client's unique cognitive processing abilities. With adults with learning disabilities, such adaptations are crucial both to building and maintaining the therapeutic alliance and to helping the client learn new cognitive and behavioral skills.

The importance of understanding both the nature of the disability and the early learning associated with it has already been discussed. The profound impact of learning disabilities on these factors cannot be underestimated, and the therapist needs to be especially vigilant in ensuring that the client understands both.

From the humanistic therapeutic approach the therapist needs to utilize the importance of empathy, authenticity, and respect and to add consistent support and encouragement. Adults with learning disabilities make errors and continually feel inadequate, so therapists need to reward effort and process rather than outcomes alone. Clients need to know that it is impossible for them to "fail" therapy. There are no grades,

no performance standards, no stupid questions, no need to feign understanding. Clients need the freedom to say when they don't understand and to acknowledge when they have been distracted and have processed nothing that has occurred.

In addition to the traditional cognitive strategies, counselors of adults with learning disabilities need to understand client's cognitive processing and use specific cognitive organizers far more than do counselors of the non-learning disabled. Teachers of persons with learning disabilities know that they need to organize and present data systematically, using the client's most efficient perceptual processing system. Reading, writing, listening, and speaking skills are often developed using multisensory strategies. Self-monitoring strategies are taught to enable the development of the metacognitive abilities needed to focus and maintain attention and to evaluate environmental feedback. Like these teaching procedures, therapy techniques for adults with learning disabilities need to be adapted to processing styles and are most effective when they are multisensory, organized, systematic, and self-reinforcing.

Cognitive interventions should model information-processing adaptations applicable to other relationships. "Perception checks" are one useful adaptation. The process for using these checks is explicitly taught and used collaboratively to assess whether each is perceiving communication similarly. Frequent, simple comments such as, "Let's pause and see if we both are following a similar train of thought," allow for sharing and for clarification by both counselor and client.

Clients with learning disabilities need structure and techniques that encourage independence. Since they often lack internal direction, they benefit from clearly stated, time-limited, mutually established, and realistic goals. Setting such realistic goals prevents the frustration and failure of the cycle of unattainable goals that often characterized their lives before therapy and raises esteem and builds confidence.

These clients also frequently benefit from concrete organizers, including planning calendars, appointment books, digital watches, and taperecorders. They may also need graphic organizers, such as decision-making charts, mindmaps, and drawings that structure dates visually and help compensate for memory problems.

Therapists need also to know their community resources for remedial and compensatory education, since the cognitive organizers useful in therapy may not be sufficient. Many clients will need assistance with addressing their learning and work-related problems. Others need tools to free them from the drudgery imposed by the disability. For some, word processors become lifelines to independence. Sometimes a simple handheld spelling checker relieves more anxiety than hours of therapy.

Finally, strategies borrowed and adapted from behavioral therapy are essential. Some adults are not aware of their physiological responses to thoughts, events, and feelings. Learning to recognize the physiology of emotions helps them to recognize their feelings and to begin to gain control over both their bodies and their emotions and to avoid inappropriate behavior. For example, recognizing that a clenched jaw signals the building of anxiety and frustration allows the client to intervene with appropriate relaxation techniques or compensatory strategies.

The therapist must confront self-defeating behaviors and attitudes without discouraging the client. In addition to neurologically based learning disabilities, a client may have developed what Byrne and Crawford (1990) call "learned disabilities," behavioral compromises that protect the individual from anxiety and depression. These generally appear either as psychoneurotic symptoms, which mimic the learning disability (e.g., poor short-term memory), or neurotic character traits (e.g., manipulativeness to cover weaknesses). To give up the "learned" disability, the client needs to learn to differentiate between the learning disability and the resultant learned disability, to validate the reason for the existence of the learned disability, and to understand its implications for the future. The therapist's task is to listen for the pain—the overt and disguised anger, the anxiety, the helplessness, and the grief—and to assist the client in understanding how these have led to the development of the learned disability.

One way to deal with the pain is to reach out to others and then to share successful coping strategies.

CASE EXAMPLE

Margie's greatest delight as she began to deal with her problem of reversals and confusion of letter forms was to teach everything she learned to her 7-year-old nephew. Together they shared tricks to remember letter forms and wrote letters in the air and on each others' backs and in each others' palms. Weekly she brought to therapy stories of their accomplishments.

Therapy's stress management

Three useful strategies for work with adults with learning disabilities borrowed from behavioral therapy are assertiveness training, social skills training, and stress-management techniques. Learning to advocate for themselves with employers, instructors, and family members is essential for adults with learning disabilities. Younger adults, especially, have often not learned to negotiate for their rights and for appropriate accommodations in school or in the workplace. Some clients, because of their inefficient perceptual processing systems, have not intuitively learned appropriate social skills. These need to be directly taught, since poor social skills are significant roadblocks to success at work and to building relationships. Lastly, stress is ever present in the lives of these clients. Stress-reduction activities, proper diet, exercise, and adequate rest are vital. This may be especially true for those clients who exhibit attention deficit problems, for whom diet and exercise are as critical to success and self-monitoring of attention as is appropriate medication.

Learning disabilities persist throughout the client's lifetime (Blalock, 1981; Gerber et al., 1990). These clients may need counseling and psychotherapy intermittently across all developmental stages. Support for them needs to focus on helping them to understand and cope with the disability as it is affecting life goals and developmental needs and must be adapted to the unique processing style of each individual. Adults with learning disabilities can be highly successful in many facets of their lives, but they will likely need assistance as they confront new life issues and demands and discover that previously successful coping strategies need adjustment for new circumstances.

References

American Psychiatric Association. (1987). *Diagnostic and statistical manual of mental disorders* (3rd ed., revised). Washington, DC: American Psychiatric Association.

Blalock, J. W. (1981). Persistent problems and concerns of young adults with learning disabilities. In Cruickshank & Silver (Eds.), *Bridges to tomorrow.* Syracuse: Syracuse University Press, pp. 35–56.

Byrne, T. P., & Crawford, A. (1990). Some theoretical and practical issues in counseling the learning disabled student. *Journal of College Student Psychotherapy, 5* (1), 75–85.

Gerber, P., Ginsberg, R., & Reiff, H. B. (1992). Identifying alterable patterns in employment success for highly successful adults with learning disabilities. *Journal of Learning Disabilities, 25* (8), 475–487.

Gerber, P. J., Schnieders, C. A., Paradise, L. V., Reiff, H. B., Ginsberg, R., & Popp, P. (1990). Persisting problems of adults with learning disabilities. Self-reported comparisons from their school-age and adult years. *Journal of Learning Disabilities, 23* (9), 570–573.

Chapter 8

Personal Perspectives on Learning Differences: Coming Out of the Shadow

KEN DRUCK, PH.D.

I was surrounded by the school counselor, the principal, a psychologist, and two special education teachers from "the district." The school counselor spoke first: "After extensive testing, we recommend that your daughter attend *special* classes, Dr. Druck." Before I could think about what all this meant, I was hit by a wave of sadness rising up from deep inside me. My mind flashed back thirty years. . . . I was sitting in the school counselor's office with my mother. The counselor, Mr. Malamud, began, "Mrs. Druck, your son's test scores are below average but don't worry . . . he can always be a janitor, gym teacher, or *something*."

It was 1961 and 12-year-old Kenny Druck had been given a battery of *aptitude* tests. A 40-year-old gym teacher, doubling as the school guidance counselor, was trying to make the best of a difficult parent meeting. What he said that day both hurt and enraged me, and was destined to shape the course of my life. Thirty years later, sitting at my daughter's special education staffing, little Kenny was still alive inside me; I could feel his anguish. I realized, in order to help my daughter, I had to go back in time, find "little Kenny," and help him overcome the feeling

This chapter is dedicated to my gifted daughter, Stephanie Druck, age 14

that he was stupid. Unless I did, I would be of little use to my daughter.

That night I had a vivid dream. I imagined myself standing in a large grassy field. In the distance was a small boy, walking toward me. As he got closer, I realized it was the 9-year old Kenny. He looked so innocent, so young, and my heart swelled as he approached. Soon he was standing in front of me. I reached across, brought him close, and embraced him. We walked to a large rock just a few feet away and sat down together. We had a lot of catching up to do. "Kenny, tell me how you are."

Kenny told me he was sad because he was stupid. School had been a problem since he began kindergarten at Wilson Elementary School. He could read but didn't remember what he had read; he could do math but only after it had been explained to him many times. This had angered his impatient father who accused him of being lazy and undisciplined and not trying hard enough. Kenny confessed that sometimes he didn't put out his best effort because he didn't understand the instructions and felt stupid asking for help. Nine-year-old Kenny couldn't keep up with the kids his age. He thought something must be wrong with him. His mother's encouragement and her explanation that he was "just a little slow," didn't help. He hated school, except for recess, where he was one of the top athletes.

Each new school year, Kenny would take his place in the back of the room, terrified he'd be called on and make a fool of himself. He told me that he felt betrayed by his own mind. He wished he was "like other boys and not a dummy." Kenny joked and acted self-assured with the other kids, but inside, he felt lost, confused, and ashamed. At times he'd go into a rage. He tried hard but fell further and further behind. Life hurt too much for a boy of nine.

Toward the end of the dream, I asked young Kenny, "What is your deepest need?" "To be held and loved," was his reply. He wanted me to tell him that I knew he was smart and that he would grow up to be a fine man. I looked directly into the eyes of this vulnerable young boy and told him, "Kenny, I *know* you are smart," and it brought tears to his eyes. That is where the dream ended.

Overcoming Learned Stupidity

Since then I have realized how the torturous years in elementary school and junior high school convinced me that I was stupid. School was war, and I fought for my life each day. To avoid being left back I had to attend summer school every year. One year I was allowed to go to summer camp if I'd make up a class at the local school. I would sneak in and out of camp each morning, living in constant fear of being caught by the other campers. Throughout childhood I felt like a dummy.

I had enough fight and pride (or was it fear) in me to survive. I did not allow myself to be consumed by the idea that I was a dumb kid. I had to save myself. My survival plan was to learn to "fake it" at school. I learned every trick in the book, including cheating and becoming friends with the smart kids. I made sure my teacher liked me and used whatever verbal skills I had to demonstrate understanding in class. Next, I got in with the popular kids by being a tough guy and a good athlete. I surrounded myself

with the smart kids, rich kids, and athletes. I found myself drawn to kids who suffered from low self-esteem and who had troubled lives. My best friend, Roger, had been abandoned by his parents at age 10 and lived with his bartender brother in a small apartment. It was easier for me to feel sorry for others than to deal with my own pain. I became a resource for any of my friends, or girlfriends, who needed help or were having a problem. I secretly admired and envied from afar the bright kids who did well in school. I competed with them in sports, where I had great success. Sports helped me salvage my self-esteem. On the playground and after school, I practiced hard. There were days after a good game when high school basketball felt like my ticket to respectability and success. Hiding in the back of the geometry class the very next day, I would cherish each unforgettable play.

Learning to Compensate

The word "compensate" most accurately describes the first 30 years of my life. I lacked intelligence. Why else would I be failing in school? To make up for my deficiency, I worked extra hard, listened intently in class, went for tutoring after school, cheated on tests, became a teacher *pleaser*, and got people to help me with my homework. When I didn't understand how to do something in school, I made up my own shortcuts and invented crazy, roundabout methods. I kept my stupidity a secret and taught myself. I slowly discovered how to learn, although it took great concentration and patience for me to grasp new concepts. Somehow, year after year, I squeaked by.

Compensating was survival at first. These compensatory skills became the basis for my psychological style, or approach, to work, relationships, and school. They also became the reason for my success. I knew how to make up for what I lacked by being charming, by working excessively long hours, by inventing verbal solutions, and by recruiting assistance. I developed confidence in my ability to compensate in even the most challenging situations. But this style became increasingly dysfunctional.

Intent on proving my worth, I began overcompensating. As a young psychologist, I was a tireless worker, determined to save the world from all human suffering. I routinely overextended myself. My compulsion to prove myself got in the way of my better judgment. I was in over my head but drove myself harder and harder. To fail was an admission that I was a dummy after all. I compensated in every way imaginable, anything to pass as smart. This became a destructive pattern in my adult life for many years. I would overcommit myself and then turn to my *compensatory bag of tricks* to bail me out. Without them, I feared the "real" me wasn't enough. Compensation had become a kind of dependency.

My unrelenting drive and persistence grew out of fear, my ambition out of insecurity. I competed against powerful and successful men to bolster my confidence. I was always testing myself. My insecurities led to hypercritical and hypersensitive behavior. Like a defiant gambler, I faced each new challenge, trying to beat the odds. I hedged my bets against being judged as stupid or revealed as an impostor.

As I approached the age of 30, it became clear that I had to reverse this unhealthy pattern. I would *not* spend the next 20 years doubting myself, living in fear of being found out, playing roles, trying to prove that I was smart. I had to strip myself of my compensatory *skills*, the adult defenses protecting "little Kenny." I was not little Kenny any more. I had to learn that I *was* smart enough, that there was nothing else I had to do or be. It had become so automatic, I had to learn how *not* to adapt, or compensate. I was enough. After 30 years, with this new and unfamiliar belief in hand, I began to accept that I was different, not disabled.

What I share in this chapter comes from the heart of a wounded boy, not from statistical science. The more I heal, the better I understand my daughter and the challenges of all the children who are *different*. It has taken me years to understand my learning differences and to change my fundamental belief about being stupid. Healing the emotional wounds has required forgiving those who didn't know any better and making peace with my worst, unrelenting critic all those years . . . myself. Some wounds will remain with me for the rest of my life, and the anguish I felt as a boy was reawakened at my daughter's school staffing.

I no longer believe that I am stupid. I accept that some things are going to take me longer to complete. Others I will not do very well. This is O.K. I learn at a different pace, but I am not disabled. I was unable to compute and perform learning tasks in the traditionally acceptable ways, but I have been given a blessing. I have developed my intuitive abilities more than most people have. I approach my work creatively, often by using my own unorthodox methods. For example, I researched my doctoral thesis by personally interviewing scholars, rather than reading their works. This enabled me to learn about my subject in greater depth and scope. In addition, I frequently requested and took oral exams to demonstrate mastery of a subject. I played drums and wrote songs on the piano, yet I could not learn to read music no matter how I tried. On national TV shows such as CNN, HBO, Oprah, and Donahue, I was unable to memorize and retain printed material. Instead, I would develop an elaborate string of fresh associations in my *mind's eye* that I called up instantly during the show. No amount of memorization could have matched those spontaneous responses. For these same reasons, I have never given a prepared speech. Words roll off my tongue, yet they come from a reservoir of ever-growing, intuitively organized ideas inside me. This is the same process that enables me to write books (and chapters like this) without an outline.

Another blessing is my wife of 20 years, Karen. Karen has been an inspiration and tutor. When writing projects were taking *too* long, she was a voice of patience. When I felt awkward and stupid, she was a reminder to me that I am bright. When I couldn't understand directions, for example, installing our new VCR, she read them to me and I was able to do the rest (I'm better with the "hands on" part). Together, we make a great team.

Difference does not necessarily mean disability. Howard Gardner's pioneering work with multiple intelligences, outlined in his 1983 book, *Frames of Mind*, demonstrates at least seven ways to teach the same subject. Teachers and administrators who continue to approach learning from only one direction discriminate against children who cannot follow traditional educational curricula. We must identify and take advantage of our children's learning strengths and minimize their weaknesses without labeling them *dumb, disabled,* or *stupid.* Parents, educators, researchers, and administrators must fashion and embody a vision of children who possess an inborn drive to learn and create, including those who do not follow *customary* learning paths. As educators and parents, we must work as allies to emphasize to these students that being different does not mean being better—or being worse. We must do everything in our power to uproot destructive, outdated biases within ourselves and then within our learning institutions. Few things are as widely destructive to children's self-esteem as myopic academic discrimination.

Our sense of purpose in life, as well as our unique talents, often come from our deepest wounds. By reliving my past and dispelling a crippling myth, I feel empowered to stand by my daughter. This incredibly bright young women, of whom I am so very proud, is on her own journey, as are all children with learning differences. I know in my heart she is gifted, not only because she is a talented athlete and scored off the charts on the WISC-R performance scale, but also because she possesses the spirit of an adventurer and desperately wants to learn. I will still cringe when she tells me she's in the class "for retarded kids," and I will probably continue to well up with emotion every time I remind myself that children like little Kenny and Stefie still walk around feeling stupid.

> "Einstein was a daydreamer who played fancifully with images in his mind, but in the process, he created an objective image of the universe that transformed forever our view of physical reality. Einstein had trouble learning and remembering facts, words and text but he was teacher to the world. He was slow to speak but in time the world listened."
>
> Thomas G. West,
> from In The Mind's Eye, p. 129

References

Gardner, H. (1983). *Frames of Mind.* New York: Basic Books.

West, T. G. (1991). *In the mind's eye: Visual thinkers, gifted people with learning difficulties, computer images and the ironies of creativity.* Buffalo, NY: Prometheus Books.

PART III
EDUCATIONAL ISSUES

Chapter 9

Transition of Youths with Learning Disabilities to Adulthood: The Secondary Education Foundation

SHARON DEFUR, ED.D
HENRY B. REIFF, PH.D.

Transition, commonly defined as a change or passage from one place to another, implies progression from a less developed to a more developed stage. In contemporary life, almost all of us experience numerous transitions throughout our lives. Adolescence is a particularly difficult period of transition, marked by both desire for and fear of independence. Increasingly, young adults must extend their dependency on families as career training takes longer and, at least in the economy of the early 1900s, employment opportunities decrease. The transition from school to work, from adolescence to adulthood, is a difficult adjustment for all youths, with or without a disability. Having a learning disability or any disability compounds the pressure to achieve independence. On leaving the security of public schools, individuals who have disabilities face a reality of little or no employment, low income, social isolation, and inadequate residential or other services (Edgar, 1987; Hasazi et al., 1985; Mithaug & Horiuchi, 1983; Rusch & Phelps, 1987; Wehman et al., 1985). As a result, the development of mechanisms that

foster movement toward independence for youths with disabilities has received considerable attention in recent years.

"Conventional wisdom" has suggested that youths with learning disabilities do not face significant barriers to independence. Although youths with learning disabilities may typically attain greater post-secondary success than many other individuals with different disabilities, they do not achieve post-secondary independence to the degree or with the ease that is often assumed (Gerber & Reiff, 1991). Yet this assumption is both persistent and pervasive and may interfere with the development of transition goals and assistance for youths with learning disabilities.

In spite of resistance to the need for transition services for youths with learning disabilities, we are entering a new era in which the lifelong impact of learning disabilities is gaining recognition. Yet much remains to be done. This chapter describes transition policy and legislation affecting secondary education programs and transition planning for youths with learning disabilities. It also addresses the role of secondary education in helping youths with learning disabilities develop the competencies needed to achieve the goals of late adolescence and the role of special educators in facilitating the transition process. The chapter concludes with recommendations to extend and improve existing services.

What Are the Policy and Legislative Influences on Transition Services?

Disability legislation and initiatives in special education, vocational education, and vocational rehabilitation have been widespread during the past 25 years (Table 9-1). During this period, both depth and breadth of services increased and a general awareness of the need for transition services for youths with disabilities developed. The theme of coordination of transition efforts across many fields can be found throughout all legislation passed during the evolution of "transition from school to work" (Will, 1984).

During the early 1980s, the fields of vocational rehabilitation, vocational education, and special education focused attention on the development of interdisciplinary transition services for youths with disabilities (Edgar, 1987; Rusch & Phelps, 1987; Sitlington, 1986; Szymanski & Danek, 1985). P.L. 98–199, Section 626 of the Education of the Handicapped Amendments of 1983, commonly referred to as the "transition authority," directed special educators to address the development of practices and programs that would improve opportunities for youths with disabilities for successful entry to postsecondary education or training, empowerment, and community living. P.L. 98–524, The Carl Perkins Vocational Education Act, echoed the intent of P.L. 98–199 and specifically addressed the provision of services to individuals with disabilities in each of the titles within this act. These legislative initiatives underscore the commitment begun in the early 1980s to the development of transition services and emphasize the importance of interagency cooperation as integral to this process.

Recent amendments to these laws continue to strengthen the commitment to transition services to youths with disabilities. The Carl Perkins Vocational Education and Applied Technology Act of 1990 maintained the assurances for special populations and strengthened the role of vocational education in the provision of transition services to youths with disabilities. Transition policy efforts culminated in amendments to P.L. 94–142 in 1990. P.L. 101–476, now named Individuals with Disabilities Education Act (IDEA), defines transition, mandates the identification of needed transition services on the individualized education program (IEP) of all youths receiving special education no later than age 16, and places secondary special education in a clearly defined role as coordinator of transition planning.

The bridges from school to work model (Will, 1984) became a framework for both developing programs (i.e., the commencement of the transition process) and evaluating the transition process (i.e., employment outcomes). Will stated that this "definition emphasizes the *shared responsibility* of all partners for transition success, and extends beyond traditional notions of service coordination. . ." (p.2). Recent models of transition do extend beyond the concept of school-to-work transition and include school to postsecondary education and training and transition to independent community living.

Current transition-related legislation, policy statements, and funding initiatives call for cooperative planning from the federal level (Everson & Moon, 1987; Sarkees & Scott, 1986; Wehman et al., 1988). The provision of transition services is already the first major federally funded program for individuals with disabilities that actively encourages collaborative efforts of vocational education programs and special education. The American Rehabilitation Counseling Association takes a stronger stance in recommending federal regulations to require coordination between special education and rehabilitation (Szymanski & Danek, 1985).

Table 9-1. Selected Federal Legislation and Policy Related to Transition Services for Youths with Learning Disabilities

---

1969

P.L. 91–230 Elementary and Secondary Education Amendments of 1969: Title VI of the 1969 amendments established the Education of the Handicapped Act. One new feature added to Title VI was programming to serve children with specific learning disabilities.

1973

P.L. 93–112, Rehabilitation Act of 1973: Section 503 requires employers receiving federal contracts to take affirmative action to recruit, hire, train, and promote individuals with disabilities. Section 504 is considered the first civil rights law protecting the rights of individuals with disabilities. Section 504 statute reads:

> No otherwise qualified handicapped individual in the United States shall, solely by reason of his handicap, be excluded from participation in, be denied the benefits of, or be subjected to discrimination under any program or activity receiving Federal financial assistance.

This section also includes requirements that (1) individuals with disabilities must have opportunities to participate in or benefit from services equal to those that are provided to other individuals; for example, excluding children or youth with disabilities from any education programs because of their disability violates their civil rights; (2) colleges and post-secondary programs that receive federal funds may not discriminate against applicants on the basis of disability; in addition these post-secondary institutions must make reasonable accommodations to make it possible for qualified students with disabilities to participate; and (3) all programs must be barrier-free. Programs or institutions that fail to comply with these requirements risk losing all federal funds received by the institution or agency. Benefits of this legislation for youths with learning disabilities include increased access and support in institutes of higher education and community college.

1975

The Education of the Handicapped Act of 1975 (P.L. 94–142) mandated free, appropriate public education for all children and youth with disabilities, including special education and related services. A written individualized education program (IEP) must be developed and implemented for all children and youth eligible for special education or related services. Specific learning disability was included as one disability area to benefit from the rights and requirements of P.L. 94–142.

1976

The Vocational Education Act Amendments of 1976 (P.L. 94–482) extended the provision of vocational education services to disabled individuals of all ages. Secondary and post-secondary programs receive funds, of which a percentage must be spent on special populations. Vocational education plans for youths with disabilities must be coordinated with youth's IEP. Youth with learning disabilities participating in vocational education are afforded the same assurances guaranteed by Section 504 and P.L. 94–142.

1981

The Rehabilitation Comprehensive Services and Developmental Disabilities Act (P.L. 95–602) of 1978 was interpreted by the Rehabilitation Services Administration to allow persons with severe learning disabilities to receive rehabilitation services.

1982

Job Training Partnership Act (JTPA) (P.L. 97–300) established programs to prepare youth and unskilled adults for entry into the labor force and to afford job training to those economically disadvantaged persons, and other persons facing serious barriers to employment. Persons with disabilities are eligible for JTPA training. Youth with learning disabilities can participate in programs funded under JTPA programs while in secondary school as well as after exiting secondary school.

1983

The Education of the Handicapped Act Amendments of 1983 (P.L. 98–199) established a new grant authority to fund programs to improve secondary special education and transitional services for youth with disabilities (Sec. 626). Many programs offering transition services for youth with learning disabilities have been initiated using these funds.

Table 9-1. *Continued*

1984 and 1986
The Rehabilitation Act Amendments (P.L. 98–221 and P.L. 98–506) increased the emphasis on services to youth with disabilities. In the 1986 amendments to the Rehabilitation Act, the state plan requirements were changed to require states to: (a) plan for individuals who are making the transition from school to work, and (b) reflect how the state rehabilitation agencies will implement the new supported employment program.

1984 and 1990
The Carl D. Perkins Vocational Education Act of 1984 (P.L. 98–524) strengthened provisions and assurances to youth with disabilities, including access to the full range of vocational program offerings in the least restrictive environment and the provision of vocational assessment prior to students entering vocational education.

In 1990, this act was renamed the Carl Perkins Vocational and Applied Technology Education Act (P.L. 101–392). Significant funding changes were made in this legislation, but the assurances for special populations were maintained and the emphasis on transition support increased. In addition, vocational education is expected to coordinate efforts with vocational rehabilitation as well as special education. This legislation established a technical preparation program (Tech Prep) that begins with two years of preparation in secondary school, followed by two years of training in community college.

Vocational education offers youth with learning disabilities training and occupational preparation that will facilitate participation and placement in post-secondary employment options.

1990
The Individuals with Disabilities Education Act (P.L. 101–476, formerly Education of the Handicapped Act), or IDEA, defined transition services as follows (Sec. 602(a)19)): a coordinated set of activities for a student, designed within an *outcome-oriented* process, which promotes movement from school to post-school activities, including post-secondary education, vocational training, integrated employment (including supported employment), continuing and adult education, adult services, independent living, and community participation. The coordinated set of activities shall be based upon the individual student's needs, taking into account the student's preferences and interests, and shall include: instruction, community experiences, the development of employment and other post-school adult living objectives, and, when appropriate, acquisition of daily living skills and functional vocational evaluation.

In Sec. 602(a)(20) a requirement was added that IEPs include a statement of the needed transition services for students beginning no later than age 16 and annually thereafter (and, when determined appropriate for the individual, beginning at age 14 or younger), including, when appropriate, a statement of the interagency responsibilities or linkages (or both) before the student leaves the school setting.

Will's (1984) policy paper both implicitly and explicitly addressed this emphasis on cooperative planning and involvement between school and adult agencies. The framers of P.L. 98–199 recognized the necessity of interagency coordination among all educational and adult service agencies, including mental health, mental retardation, public employment, vocational rehabilitation, and employers themselves, in order to facilitate the planning and developing of transition services, thereby achieving successful transition outcomes. Policy from the national level has become increasingly explicit and consistent with regard to interagency activities, particularly as they relate to the provision of transition services. Cobb and Mikilin (1985) state that the ". . . articulated interagency planning, much discussed in the late 1970s, may become a reality in the 80's" (p. 13). Transition planning and services require agencies that typically function independently to establish ways to function interdependently. The provision of transitional services requires the disciplines involved to reassess the traditional roles and responsibilities of personnel within and between agencies.

Why Are Transition Planning and Services Important for Youths with Learning Disabilities?

Prior to 1969 when Congress passed the Children with Specific Learning Disabilities Act, federal law did not recognize learning disabilities. The field emerged with an almost exclusively childhood orientation buttressed by assumptions that learning disabilities would disappear in adulthood (Gerber & Reiff, 1991). As a result, initial efforts at transition tended to overlook persons with learning disabilities. Data that have emerged over time do not support such assumptions and instead argue the need for transition services.

In contrast to the belief that youths with learning disabilities successfully graduate from high school, the National Longitudinal Transition Study (Wagner, 1989) reports a graduation rate of 61% for youths with learning disabilities compared to 56.2% for all youths with disabilities and 71 to 75% for the general population. Thirty-five percent of youths with learning disabilities drop out of school, frequently leaving school at age 16 with minimal academic skills and before having received any vocational training. Because most students with learning disabilities receive their secondary education within the regular education program and opt for general education training rather than vocational education training, the majority currently leave school without any specific training in career or vocational areas. Many of these youths are not aware of the nature of their disabilities, nor have they developed the self-awareness or self-advocacy skills needed to advocate for services once they leave secondary education (Aune, 1991; Gerber & Reiff, 1991; Smith, 1988).

Definitions of learning disabilities often carry an assumption of average to above-average ability allowing entry into higher education or community college following secondary school. In actuality, only 16.7% of students with learning disabilities surveyed participated in any type of post-secondary education or training, with less than 9% attending community or four-year colleges. Comparatively, 50% of the general population attends post-secondary education training programs (Wagner, 1989).

Adults with learning disabilities may achieve success in the employment world more readily than other individuals with disabilities, but youths with learning disabilities do experience greater difficulties than their nondisabled peers. Post-secondary outcome data for youths with learning disabilities show high rates of unemployment or underemployment and low participation in post-secondary education or vocational training (Wagner, 1989). Of particular concern, underemployment and resulting lower levels of independence, job status, and income tend to plague many adults with learning disabilities (Okolo & Sitlington, 1988; Gerber & Reiff, 1991; Sitlington, Frank, & Carson, 1990).

Currently, educational outcomes for all students with disabilities are receiving attention, and students with learning disabilities represent the largest disability group. Increasingly, policymakers, educators, service agency professionals, employers, and parents recognize the need to ensure that youths with learning disabilities receive transition services. Youths with learning disabilities stand to benefit from the policies now in place that require secondary special education to address the needed transition services. Furthermore, a shift in philosophy is accompanying these policies. A theme of developing independence in individuals with disabilities, including those with learning disabilities, permeates the current vision driving disability policy. Consequently, programs for youths with disabilities increasingly emphasize preparation for adult independence and functional skill development.

What Are Transition Services for Youths with Learning Disabilities?

Initially, proponents of transition services such as Will (1984) emphasized employment as the means to secure adult independence and the endpoint of transition efforts. Consequently, transition services concentrated almost exclusively on vocational or prevocational programs. Models of post-secondary outcomes now reflect a broader focus.

Halpern (1992) conceptualizes transition as encompassing "all appropriate dimensions of adult adjustment and involvement in the community" (p. 203). Secondary transition services then become those programs and activities in education or related services that assist youths with disabilities in accessing adult options, including postsecondary education, community living, and employment. School exit or graduation can no longer represent an endpoint for students but rather a transition point, continuing the preparation for ongoing adult adjustment and increasing independence.

Secondary special and general education are finding new ways to offer many transition support services. Interagency transition planning teams identify and develop new services and programs. Assessment, appropriate instructional programming, professional development, and interagency cooperation are some of the key components in the transition of youths with learning disabilities from school to productive lives. The inclusion of transition services does not constitute a major change in current secondary education options. Rather, the change comes from (1) the inclusion of purposeful planning, based on long-range goal setting and accounting for functional as well as academic goals; and (2) deliberate collaboration and cooperation both within secondary education staff and among staff, students, families, and community representatives.

How Should Planning Secondary Education Transition Services for Youths with Learning Disabilities Take Place?

P.L. 101–476 (IDEA) suggests that transition planning, developing, implementing, and monitoring are ongoing parts of the IEP process. Successful transition practices require the involvement of a multidisciplinary team that keeps the student's present and future needs firmly in the center of decision-making. Following a logical series of steps should benefit those involved in the transition process in achieving successful outcomes.

Step I: Prepare the Youth to Begin the Transition Process

CASE EXAMPLE

Tommy, a student with severe learning disabilities, and his family began discussing Tommy's transition goals with members of his IEP team early in his high school career. The IEP team recommended an extensive vocational evaluation of Tommy. The results of this evaluation and discussion with Tommy and his family enabled the IEP team, including Tommy, to plan for his vocational education program. Inservice training helped prepare school staff for developing transition plans. Training also familiarized staff with other adult service agencies that could offer Tommy support after high school.

P.L. 101–476 requires that "transition services are to be identified for students receiving special education no later than age 16 and annually thereafter (when deemed appropriate for the individual beginning at age 14 or younger)." Yet many youths with disabilities drop out of school at age 16, and they are set on this course of action several years earlier. In actuality, career education should begin in early childhood and elementary school with career-awareness activities. During middle and early high school years, career exploration builds a natural foundation for more intensive and direct transition services. IEPs should address the goals of these periods formally as a precursor to secondary transition planning.

Planning and developing transition services depend on effective assessment, ranging from simple interest inventories and informal interviews to comprehensive vocational evaluations. This assessment can reveal a student's interests and aptitudes, a valuable asset for choosing either appropriate occupational training in school or preparation for post-secondary education. Many students with learning disabilities do not plan for their future in a realistic and systematic fashion (Reiff et al., 1989); support services that facilitate a well-conceived adult orientation are more likely to lead to successful transition programs and practices.

Step II: Putting the Transition Component in the IEP

CASE EXAMPLE

The IEP team decided that Tommy should participate in an occupational training sequence and consequently developed appropriate goals and objectives. Tommy's special education teacher, working with the vocational instructor, identified and taught the academic competencies Tommy needed for the vocational program, while the vocational instructor helped Tommy master the occupational competencies in his training area. The IEP team continued to identify annual goals that would direct activities in furthering the development of skills needed to achieve his desired post-secondary outcomes. Together they set objectives such as participation in a summer youth employment program prior to graduation. Linkage with the local vocational rehabilitation counselor occurred during Tommy's junior year when the counselor offered an after-school workshop in self-advocacy skills on the job. Tommy participated on his IEP transition planning team throughout high school. He assumed responsibility for some of the activities to reach identified objectives. For example, Tommy arranged for driver's training support and agreed to take the test on his own. His special education teacher agreed to include the driver's manual as one textbook for a unit on reading manuals. The guidance counselor helped

the team identify classes that would develop personal management skills needed for independent living.

Historically, special education has been something "done" to children and youths with disabilities and their families. The new model of thinking, in both special and general education, requires the student to participate actively in educational decision-making, including membership on the IEP transition planning team. This role promotes ownership, encourages responsibility, and fosters self-awareness, all key components to adult success (Gerber et al., 1992).

The IEP transition planning team also should include special, general, and vocational educators; adult service personnel; and any other person involved in providing transition support to the youth with learning disabilities. Team membership may vary depending on the critical area being addressed by the IEP transition team. As part of the IEP process, the team needs to identify the type and nature of the post-secondary outcomes relevant to the student's needs and abilities. The desired outcomes include long-range plans for post-secondary education or training, employment, and independent living. Once the team agrees on desired outcomes, it then decides if the student requires specialized transition services to achieve those outcomes. If transition services are necessary, the team determines appropriate annual goals that promote moving in the direction of the outcomes.

As in the development of the IEP, annual objectives serve as the basis for activities leading to the transition goals. Identified objectives should drive services, not the converse. For example, a tenth-grade student and the IEP team might identify employment after high school as a desired post-secondary outcome. A related annual goal calls for developing employability skills such as job seeking, job punctuality, and work endurance. One objective centers on work experiences. Guidance and counseling services may facilitate sound occupational training choices. Services could also include unpaid job shadowing in school or paid employment after school or in the summer. In some cases, agencies may not follow through on agreed-on services. In that event, the IEP team should reconvene and explore alternative services to meet the same objective. For example, a paid summer employment program may not materialize; some type of volunteer work might represent the strongest alternative that addresses the objective of work experience.

Identification of desired goals and objectives involves scrutiny of the different demands of different adult options. Post-secondary educational options must extend beyond vocational training to include advanced technical training, two- and four-year colleges, and postgraduate possibilities. For youths opting for college, developing functional skills that will assist them in coping with very different academic and social challenges is often an integral component of the long-term goal.

For others, career exploration opportunities will lead to greater awareness of the post-secondary employment resources such as those offered by rehabilitation and employment services. These services can also assist the individual student in locating meaningful employment in the desired community. Planning within the context of the local community, active participation of the individual student and family, sharing of school and community resources such as vocational rehabilitation, school–business linkages, and the involvement of vocational training personnel in schools are all critical elements (Everson, 1990; Wehman, 1990).

The transition planning team should establish criteria and time lines to evaluate and monitor goals, objectives, and activities; identify the person(s) or agency (including the student or family when appropriate) accountable for each transition area; and review these areas at least annually. Transition goals and desired post-secondary outcomes are likely to change with the natural changes in career and self-awareness typical of adolescence. Consequently, flexibility to

modify transition plans should be endemic to the process.

Systematic development of adult functional skills needs to occur throughout curricula. An emphasis on adult adjustment as a natural part of education will facilitate long-term mastery of these skills. Educators of students with learning disabilities should assess individual social skills needs and, when warranted, assign high priority to social skills programming on the IEP. Curricular modifications may also include building intrapersonal skills and knowledge, characteristics correlated with successful employment and overall adult adjustment (Maslow, 1954). Beginning this process early in education ensures an adequate period of time to review and to try alternative practices when indicated. Ongoing review, evaluation, and modification throughout high school help build the bridge from school to adulthood.

Step III: Beginning Adult Independence—Establishing Linkages

CASE EXAMPLE

Tommy decided that he wanted to work following high school. The IEP/ITP team requested that Tommy be assessed regarding his job readiness skills. A job placement specialist from an adult agency assisted Tommy in finding a job and provided follow-up after graduation. Tommy and his family were also given information regarding post-secondary training options such as vocational training and community college. Tommy left secondary school with skills in an occupational area, a first job, and resources to assist him if he decides to seek a different job or to return to school.

Graduation or school exit marks the beginning of new transitions for youths with learning disabilities. Many youths with learning disabilities have had transition plans in place since high school only to find these plans failing to materialize once they leave. These students are not guaranteed adult services, nor will adult or college support services necessarily seek out individuals with learning disabilities. In order to connect young adults wtih disabilities to adult support systems, successful transition programs require a firmly established school/post-school linkage. This linkage necessitates a follow-along system that fosters the "hand-off" of the lead responsibility from secondary education and identifies the adult agency or person(s) who will assume responsibility for monitoring and evaluating progress.

Perhaps the greatest transition revolves around the issue of labels. School exit means an end of "being labeled" and the beginning of choosing whether or not to disclose the label of learning disabilities. Decisions about self-identifying may raise confusion or even conflict for young adults struggling to shed a special education label. For the first time in many cases, these young adults will determine if they want services and to what extent.

College-bound youths who self-identify their learning disabilities benefit from meeting the on-campus support services coordinator. Face-to-face meetings make it easier for the student to seek out the services offered. Support services normally include accommodations and adaptations to meet individual learning needs such as modifications to test formats (e.g., untimed, oral instead of written, essay instead of multiple choice), content area tutoring and study skills development, course selection and other advisement, peer mentoring, and support groups. Colleges increasingly are emphasizing school-to-work transition services for their students. For college students with learning disabilities, this post-secondary transition planning process not only assists in finding employment after graduation, but increases the likelihood of retention by helping students focus on academic areas of strength.

Youths with learning disabilities may also be eligible for transition services through other agencies, including Job Training Partnership Act (JTPA) programs and/or rehabil-

itative services. In addition, each state offers employment services for individuals seeking employment within that state. Because state employment services do not have eligibility requirements, young adults with learning disabilities do not need to self-identify to access services. However, they may choose to disclose their disability and receive additional job-seeking assistance within those agencies.

Support groups for adults with learning disabilities comprise another critical component for providing on-going, post-educational transition support. The adult world offers few opportunities for individuals with learning disabilities to access services geared specifically to their issues. Support groups, a relatively recent innovation, are one exception, a source of respite from a world that is not yet attuned to concerns of adults wtih learning disabilities. Adult chapters of the Learning Disabilities Association (LDA) as well as independent groups (such as the National Network for Learning Disabled Adults and Marin Puzzle People) are growing. These organizations may be able to assist young adults in coping with vocational and social challenges of adulthood.

What Are the Roles of Secondary Educators, Adult Service Providers, Parents, and Students?

A partnership of secondary special, general, and vocational educators is necessary to address the curriculum needs for transition success of youths with learning disabilities. These students will profit from both academic and functional skills and an understanding of the relationship of the two areas. An orientation toward desired post-secondary outcomes in education, employment, and independent living should drive the development of the individualized education program. Annual goals and objectives can result directly from these expectations.

Secondary special educators have the role of initiating interaction with adult or outside agency service providers. In taking on this position of acting as a case manager extending beyond in-school services, secondary special educators will need to become knowledgeable of the community services and adult agencies. These services encompass rehabilitation, post-secondary counseling, employment services, job training or placement services, and, increasingly, support groups for adults with learning disabilities.

To facilitate an awareness of existing resources, adult agencies should market their services to secondary special and vocational educators as well as to parents and students. This involvement with the school community may not only alleviate problems due to lack of knowledge of services or how to access them but provide technical assistance to educators who try to predict and advise transition steps. In many cases, students may initiate some adult services while still in school. Establishing this type of linkage between schools and adult services and creating collaborative partnerships that accept follow-up or follow-along responsibility for young adults with learning disabilities enhance the likelihood of post-secondary transition success.

Transition is a shared responsibility, and the student and the family plan key positions. Without the active participation of parents and students in all phases of transition planning and implementation, service providers can neither guarantee delivery of services nor ensure the quality and coordination of those services. Case management also falls to the family and the individual with learning disabilities. Assuming a more proactive role, especially for young adults with learning disabilities, means accepting responsibility in confronting the very real academic, vocational, and social challenges imposed by learning disabilities. Gerber and co-workers (1992) concluded that this process, which they term "reframing the learning disabilities experience," has catalyzed successful adult outcomes in many individuals with learning disabilities. In many ways, reframing embodies a pervasive spirit of the transition initiative, the drive for independence. The development of skills of self-determination and self-advocacy provides the strongest preparation for adult adjustment. Clearly, the family and, perhaps most importantly, the individual have central and critical roles and responsibilities in the transition process.

Conclusions

Broader frameworks for transition goal-setting for youths with learning disabilities had been articulated before Will's (1984) transition initiative. For example, Erikson (1968) outlines goals for the transition to young adulthood: to develop a stable identity; to establish some independence from family; to formulate career plans; to achieve a mature sexual identity; and to develop moral and ethical values and behaviors consistent with those of society. Erikson presented a full agenda that may supersede the purview of IEP transition planning. Yet transition planning and activities need not proceed solely through formal outlets.

In many ways, successful adaptation to adulthood may depend on the basic nature and philosophy of the entire educational experience. For students with learning disabilities, fundamental reconceptualizations of the educational process, particularly in terms of expected competencies, may be necessary. Similar to reforms in general education, curricular revision for students with learning disabilities should include the infusion of problem-solving and decision-making skills and strategy development with academic skills. Adaptability to changes in demands, ability to acquire new skills, and a willingness to forge new directions may represent critical components of successful adult adaptation (Naisbitt & Aburdene, 1990). Certainly, even a cursory reading of Piaget and other developmentalists reveals transition as an ongoing process from one developmental stage to another. Consequently, the time leading up to formal transition planning, from elementary to early secondary years, should contribute developmentally to the accomplishment of Erikson's goals. Opportunities abound in home, school, and community to incorporate a philosophy of transition within the developmental process.

Halpern (1992) defines transition as "a period of *floundering* that occurs for at least the first several years after leaving school as adolescents attempt to assume a *variety* of adult roles in their communities" (p. 203). In addition, almost any adult is likely to admit that adulthood is filled with periods of floundering, that transitions are part of a lifespan process. Thus, part of preparation is developing a willingness to flounder. To accept such an outlook might be difficult enough for any adolescent; it will be particularly challenging for youths with learning disabilities who are often resistant to any kind of change (Lerner, 1985). Perhaps the essential requisite for "rolling with the punches" of adulthood is a strong and healthy self-esteem. Transition efforts that facilitate recognition, understanding, and acceptance of learning disabilities, a process termed *reframing* by Gerber and associates (1992), may offer the best preparation for coping with the myriad demands of adulthood.

Bridges (1980) presents a paradigm suggesting a predictable sequence of events in transitions: (1) a time of letting-go; (2) a time of in-betweeness; and (3) a launching forth into new situations. Perhaps all transition planning for youths with learning disabilities should incorporate such an overview that helps the individual understand the process as well as the various components. As adults, individuals need to generalize the transition process from one situation to another. Armed with this knowledge and an experiential base of systematic planning and implementation, young adults with learning disabilities will be better able to face and negotiate future transitional events.

References

Aune, A. (1991). A transition model for postsecondary-bound students with learning disabilities. *Learning Disabilities Research & Practice, 6,* 177–187.

Bridges, W. (1980). *Transitions: Making sense of life's changes.* Reading, MA: Addison-Wesley.

Cobb, R. B., & Mikilin, E. (1985). *Implementing the special needs provisions of the Carl D. Perkins Vocational Education Act of 1984.* Position paper presented to the American Vocational Association.

Edgar, E. (1987). Secondary programs in special education: Are many of them justifiable? *Exceptional Children, 53,* 555–561.

Erikson, E. (1968). *Identity, youth, and crisis.* New York: W. W. Norton.

Everson, J. M. (1990). A local team approach. *Teaching Exceptional Children, 23,* 44–46.

Everson, J. M., & Moon, M. S. (1987). Transition services for young adults with severe disabilities: Defining professional and parental roles and responsibilities. *Journal of the Association of the Severely Handicapped, 12,* 87–95.

Gerber, P., Ginsberg, R., & Reiff, H. (1992). Identifying alterable patterns in employment success for highly successful adults with learning disabilities. *Journal of Learning Disabilities, 25,* 475–487.

Gerber, P., & Reiff, H. (1991). *Speaking for themselves: Ethnographic interviews with adults with learning disabilities.* Ann Arbor: University of Michigan Press.

Halpern, A. (1992). Transition: Old wine in new bottles. *Exceptional Children, 58,* 202–213.

Hasazi, S., Gordon, L., & Roe, C. (1985). Factors associated with the employment status of handicapped youth exiting from high school from 1979–1983. *Exceptional Children, 51,* 455–469.

Lerner, J. (1985). *Learning disabilities: Theories, diagnosis, and teaching strategies* (4th ed.). Boston: Houghton-Mifflin.

Maslow, A. (1954). *Motivation and personality.* New York: Harper & Row.

Mithaug, D.E., & Horiuchi, C. (1983, September). *Colorado statewide follow-up of special education students.* Denver: Colorado Department of Education.

Naisbitt, J., & Aburdene, P. (1990). *Megatrends 2000: Ten new directions for the 1990's.* New York: Morrow.

Okolo, C.M., & Sitlington, P. (1988). The role of special education in LD adolescents' transition from school to work. *Learning Disability Quarterly, 9,* 141–155.

Reiff, H., Evans, E., and Anderson, P. (1989, October). *Vocational preferences of secondary students with learning disabilities.* Paper presented at the International Conference of the Council for Learning Disabilities. Denver, CO.

Rusch, F. R., & Phelps, L. A. (1987). Secondary special education and transition from school to work. *Exceptional Children, 53,* 487–492.

Sarkees, M. D., & Scott, J. L. (1986). *Vocational special needs* (2nd ed.). Homewood, IL: American Technical Publishers, Inc.

Sitlington, P. (1986). *Transition, special needs and vocational education.* Columbus, OH: The National Center for Research in Vocational Education (ERIC Document Reproduction Services No. 272 769).

Sitlington, P., Frank, A., & Carson, R. (1990). *Iowa statewide follow-up study: Adult adjustment of individuals with mild disabilities one year after leaving school.* Des Moines: Iowa Department of Education.

Smith, S. (1988). Preparing the learning disabled adolescent for adulthood. *Children Today, 17,* 4–9.

Szymanski, E. M., & Danek, M. M. (1985). School-to-work transition for students with disabilities: Historical, current, and conceptual issues. *Rehabilitation Counseling Bulletin, 29,* 81–88.

Wagner, M. (1989). *The transition experiences of youth with disabilities: A report from the national longitudinal transition study.* (USDOE, OSEP Contract # 300-87-0054). Menlo Park, CA: SRI International.

Wehman, P. (1990). School-to-work: Elements of successful programs. *Teaching Exceptional Children, 23,* 40–43.

Wehman, P., Kregel, J., & Seyfarth, J. P. (1985). Employment outlook for young adults with mental retardation. *Rehabilitation Counseling Bulletin, 29* (2), 90–99.

Wehman, P., Moon, M. S., Everson, J. M., Wood, W., & Barcus, J. M. (1988). *Transition from school to work: New challenges for youth with severe disabilities.* Baltimore: Paul H. Brookes.

Will, M. (1984). *Bridges from school to working life.* Washington, DC: Department of Education, Office of Special Education and Rehabilitative Services.

Chapter 10

Post-secondary Education and Vocational Training: Keys to Success for Adults with Learning Disabilities

ESTHER H. MINSKOFF, PH.D.

If individuals with learning disabilities are to achieve their potential in adulthood, a full range of post-secondary educational, vocational training, and psychosocial services must be provided. This range of services is necessitated by the heterogeneity of the population of adults with learning disabilities. The heterogeneity is due to definitional differences and the natural diversity of the population. However, even if appropriate educational and vocational training and psychosocial services are provided, other factors are still required for success. Some of these factors are amenable to change, and some are not. The purpose of this chapter is to examine the various factors related to success in adults with learning disabilities, with special emphasis on post-secondary education and vocational training.

Definitions of Learning Disabilities

Definitions of learning disabilities vary depending on the underlying purpose. Almost all schools in the United States use either the original or a modified version of the P.L. 94–142 definition of learning disabilities, which emphasizes the concept of discrepancy between potential and academic achievement (Mercer et al., 1990). Since the purpose of this definition is educational, the academic aspect of learning disabilities is highlighted. The definition used for vocational rehabilitation purposes emphasizes factors that are significant for employment (e.g., psychological process deficits such as remembering oral directions; psychosocial deficits such as getting along with co-workers; and employability factors such as punctuality) (Rehabilitation Services Administration, 1985). Identification of adult learning disabilities is further complicated by the lack of a definition of learning disabilities in Section 504 of the Rehabilitation Act, which is the basis for the provision of college and university services.

Use of different definitions at different age levels is inevitable because of varying purposes; however, this may lead to discontinuity of services when an individual is diagnosed as learning disabled by the schools and not so diagnosed by vocational rehabilitation agencies or colleges and universities.

Such discontinuity can be detrimental if it leads to the denial of needed services. However, it is unlikely that one definition of learning disabilities applicable to all age levels will ever be agreed on because of differing purposes.

Factors Related to Success in Adulthood

Over the past ten years I have worked with adults wtih severe learning disabilities who were receiving vocational rehabilitation services, adults with mild learning disabilities who were enrolled in a selective four-year university, and adults with mild, moderate, and severe learning disabilities who were assessed at a university-based diagnostic clinic. Some of these adults have attained outstanding achievements beyond the expectations of their parents and teachers, and others have failed in all endeavors and have experienced despair and breakdown. Based on my experiences, I have identified the following six factors as being significant for the success or failure of adults with learning disabilities: (1) severity of learning disabilities; (2) family support; (3) socioeconomic status (SES); (4) completion of high school; (5) quality of educational services at the elementary and secondary levels; and (6) quality of post-secondary educational, vocational training and psychosocial services.

Severity of Learning Disabilities

It is generally recognized that learning disabilities continue through the lifespan, but of greater significance is the indication that learning disabilities may become more severe in adulthood. In a comparison of high school seniors and adults with learning disabilities, the latter reported more problems in learning, daily living skills, social skills, personal adjustment, and vocational adjustment (Minskoff et al., 1988). These results may be caused by two possible factors: lack of accurate self-perception of problems by the high schoolers because of overprotection of special educators and parents, and/or the inability of the adults to cope with the "real world" and the resulting increase in problems. Gerber and co-workers (1990) found that even successful adults with learning disabilities reported deterioration in academic and psychological processing areas over time.

Judgments regarding severity of learning disabilities are complex and should be based on the following seven variables: (1) level of general intelligence; (2) special talents or specific intelligences; (3) psychological processing abilities; (4) language abilities; (5) academic achievement level; (6) psychological/social adjustment; and (7) vocational/employability skills.

Level of General Intelligence. IQ has been identified as the best predictor of academic and vocational success (Hohenshil et al., 1985). Most definitions of learning disabilities do not specify a level of general intelligence for the diagnosis of learning disabilities; and if they do, they merely mention the requirement of average intelligence (Mercer et al., 1990). Consequently, the IQ levels of persons with learning disabilities may range from 70 (the cut-off for the diagnosis of mental retardation) to the upper limits of giftedness.

In a comparison of the intelligence of various groups of adults with learning disabilities, Minskoff, Hawks, Steidle, and Hoffman (1989) found that groups receiving vocational rehabilitation had full-scale WAIS-R IQ means in the 80s, whereas groups in post-secondary education programs had means in the 100s. Faas and D'Alonzo (1990) found that higher scores on the WAIS-R comprehension and information subtests and the verbal IQ were the most important WAIS-R variables for job success. When both the WAIS-R verbal and performance IQs are low or when the verbal IQ and verbal scale subtests are low, then the individual should be judged as being severely disabled on this variable.

Special Talents or Intelligences. There is increasing recognition that intelligence is multidimensional (Gardner, 1983; Sternberg, 1989) and that intelligence tests primarily measure two types of intelligence, linguistic and logical–mathematical. Adults with learning disabilities must be evaluated to determine if they have talents in music, spatial, bodily–kinesthetic, interpersonal, intrapersonal, or practical judgment/common-sense areas. Smith (1992) has described adults with learning disabilities who have become successful because their special talents were developed (e.g., Greg Louganis's talent in bodily-kinesthetic areas). When such talents are recognized and nurtured, the probability of success in adulthood is enhanced. An individual with no special talents should be considered severely disabled in this dimension.

Psychological Processing Abilities. Deficits in psychological processes such as attention, reasoning, perception, and memory must be evaluated in relationship to the demands for these processes in vocational training and post-secondary education. Obviously, attention and memory are critical for success in understanding a lengthy verbal description of how to run a new photocopy machine or how to write a term paper in a history class. The more psychological processes found to be deficient, the more likely the person is severely disabled in this dimension.

Language Abilities. Deficits in receptive oral language make it difficult to take telephone messages when training for office work or to understand new vocabulary in a sociology class. Deficits in expressive oral language make it difficult to present a speech in a communications class or in a sales training program to explain to a customer how a VCR works. For an individual with a deficit in the auditory processing area of auditory figure–ground discrimination, it may be difficult to work in an environment with a noisy background. If receptive and expressive language skills and auditory processing are impaired, the individual should be considered severely disabled on this variable.

Academic Achievement Level. Adults with learning disabilities range in academic achievement from those with practically no reading or math skills to adults with high-level competencies in all academic areas. Increasingly higher levels of academic achievement are necessary for the changing workplace (Carnevale et al., 1990) and for post-secondary education. Adults in vocational rehabilitation were found to have academic skills at the fourth- to fifth-grade level, making success unlikely in daily living skills, jobs, and post-secondary education (Minskoff et al., 1989). Individuals who are below functional literacy or functional numeracy (variably defined as sixth to eighth grade) should be considered as having severe deficits on this variable.

Psychosocial Adjustment Psychological adjustment is especially important for getting and keeping a job. In a study of adults with learning disabilities who were vocational rehabilitation clients, 16% reported that their personal problems made it difficult for them to get or keep a job (Hoffman et al., 1987). Employers have identified social skills as an important skill for job maintenance (Minskoff et al., 1987). Probably the most frequently cited problem of persons with learning disabilities is a low self-concept (Ness & Price, 1990). Related to this is the finding that many adults with learning disabilities are not aware of their disabilities and lack the self-understanding necessary to build a healthy self-concept (Aune, 1991). Individuals with deficits in psychological adjustment (e.g., depression, anxiety), social skills, and/ or low self-concept should be considered severely disabled on this variable.

Vocational/Employability Skills. A number of studies have indicated that adults with learning disabilities have difficulty getting and keeping jobs despite having received special education (Wagner, 1989). Problems in this area may stem from lack of knowledge of how to get a job or educational and vocational services, poor work behaviors (e.g., punctuality, taking criticism), and lack of specific vocational skills. A history of unemployment and frequent job changes should be indicative of being severely disabled on this variable.

Family Support

Persons who achieve adult success are likely to come from supportive, loving homes where the parents believed in their children's abilities often in spite of disbelief by others, especially school personnel. In my contacts with mothers of successful adults with learning disabilities, I have found that many returned to college to study special education so that they could better understand and help their own children as well as other children with learning disabilities. Supportive parents serve as advocates for their children, thereby obtaining the best possible services. For children who experience failure at school, a loving home provides a haven of safety and support for the development of a good self-concept despite school failure.

Socioeconomic Status

Persons having middle-class status value education as a means of having their children attain middle-class status for themselves. When their children with learning disabilities have school difficulties, they actively advocate for their children's needs. Many parents in the lower SES have little education themselves and do not value education. When their children with learning disabilities do poorly in school, they may not be overly concerned. Furthermore, persons living in poverty may be more concerned about more critical issues such as obtaining food, clothing, and shelter than about school. Some parents with lower SES do want better services for their children with

learning disabilities but do not know how to advocate for such services.

Completion of High School

Unemployment rates for school dropouts (whether they have learning disabilities or not) are twice the rates for high school graduates (U.S. Department of Labor, 1987). Recent studies have found that the dropout rates for students with learning disabilities range from 36% (Wagner, 1989) to 53% (Zigmond & Thornton, 1985). It is unlikely that dropouts with learning disabilities will achieve success without vocational training and/or post-secondary education, both of which they probably do not know how to access once they leave school.

Quality of Education at Elementary and Secondary Levels

Students who are given appropriate special and regular education have a strong foundation for achieving post-secondary success. At the elementary school level, remediation of the students' learning disabilities and compensatory programs for circumventing their disabilities to master the academic content of the regular curriculum must be provided. An appropriate educational program is one that builds success and avoids failure and the resulting low self-concept. An appropriate secondary program contains transition services including pre-college preparation and comprehensive vocational training programs.

Quality of Post-secondary Educational and Vocational Training and Psychosocial Services

Many persons with learning disabilities need post-secondary services because their disabilities are severe and the services provided at the elementary and secondary levels are not enough to ensure mastery of adult challenges. Others need post-secondary services because they did not receive adequate services in school. Quality school services are easier to provide than quality post-secondary services because the former involves only one institution. Quality post-secondary services are harder to provide because they must be coordinated by different institutions, such as colleges, universities, vocational rehabilitation, and community mental health agencies.

Postsecondary Educational and Vocational Training

Some of the factors related to success in adulthood are amenable to change, and some are not. Factors that cannot be changed are severity of learning disabilities and SES. The factor of family support is exceedingly difficult to change and involves intensive counseling services. Factors that *can* and *must* be changed involve provision of dropout prevention programs; strong elementary programs of remedial and compensatory education and strong secondary education programs, including transition to post-secondary education and/or training; and appropriate post-secondary educational and vocational training programs.

While a student with learning disabilities is in school, it is necessary to use a life-planning approach (Schumaker et al., 1985) so that post-secondary options can be pursued well before a student is ready to exit school. Post-secondary plans must be based on comprehensive psychoeducational and vocational assessments. Hawks and co-workers (1990) have developed a model diagnostic battery to assess intelligence, psychological processes, language, academics, coordination, psychological adjustment, and vocational skills for adults and adolescents wtih learning disabilities. A comprehensive vocational assessment should examine career awareness, interests, aptitudes, special needs, learning styles, work habits and behaviors, personal and social skills, values and attitudes toward work, self-concept, and

work tolerances (NICHCY, 1990). The results of these assessments must be used as the basis for deciding the most appropriate post-secondary option at that time. Selection of a post-secondary option is not a one-time occurrence. Most persons with learning disabilities will need assessment and counseling at different times during adulthood. Individuals with learning disabilities may need assistance whenever job changes are necessitated by technological and societal advances or changed personal goals.

Two major options involving special services are available after high school: college/university programs and vocational training. Not all adults with learning disabilities need special services. Some persons with mild learning disabilities can successfully enter competitive employment, the military, or post-secondary education and vocational training. However, even for adults with mild learning disabilities such options are difficult to attain because they must compete with non–learning-disabled persons who have higher-level skills. Therefore, even some adults with mild learning disabilities may need special assistance at different periods during their lifetimes.

Post-secondary Education

Although there have been many articles about college and university programs for persons with learning disabilities, relatively few persons with learning disabilities actually select this option. In a study of 245 students with learning disabilities one to two years after leaving high school, Wagner (1989) found that 16.7% were taking courses from a post-secondary institution (9.6% at a vocational or trade school, 6.9% at a two-year college, and 1.8% at a four-year college) compared with 56% of the general population.

College and university education is most appropriate for students with mild learning disabilities who have higher IQs and academic competencies. Although comprehensive psychoeducational batteries such as the Hawks battery, described above, are available, there are no measures of assessing higher-level skills in college/ university students. In my work evaluating students with learning disabilities at a university diagnostic clinic, I have experienced the lack of such measures (e.g., a test of advanced visual perception skills for a nursing student who was having difficulties rotating figures in an organic chemistry course).

Training students with learning disabilities to be successful in college must start high school. High school students must take college preparatory classes, master study and organizational skills, learn to understand and accept themselves, use accommodations, and advocate for themselves (Aune, 1991; Strichart, 1990). Most students with learning disabilities opt for a two-year college rather than for a four-year college (Miller et al., 1991). For most students this is the best choice because the differences between high school and a two-year college are less dramatic than with a four-year college, more support services are usually available at a two-year college, and it is not necessary to master independent living skills.

Rose (1991) recommends providing three categories of support services for college/ university students with learning disabilities: (1) reasonable accommodations under Section 504 of the Vocational Rehabilitation Act (e.g., priority registration for courses, tape recording of lectures, notetaker at no costs); (2) remedial services (e.g., skill tutoring, which is found more frequently at two-year colleges than at four-year colleges); (3) and special support services (e.g., tutoring by learning-disability specialists). Rose further recommends that students with learning disabilities at the college/university level be given assessment, learning strategies, counseling, and academic skills intervention. Aune (1991) described a transition program where skills such as accommodations and self-advocacy that were developed in the senior year of high school were expanded in the first year of post-secondary education. This model seems effective in readying a student for the challenges of college and then providing assistance

when confronted with the actual college challenges.

Strichart (1990) has advised many parents of students with learning disabilities about college options, but has warned that college is not an appropriate option for all students with learning disabilities. For some parents, attendance at college is a status symbol, which they want despite the possibility of failure by their children. The most important prerequisite for college attendance for students with learning disabilities is *motivation*. If a student is not willing to work harder despite the parents' motivation, success will not be achieved.

The motivation of George, a student with learning disabilities I knew at a four-year university, exemplifies the degree of work that may be necessary for success. George tape recorded all class lectures while taking notes. As soon as he went home, he integrated the notes and the information from the tape and typed the integrated notes on a word processor. He then color coded the typed notes for main and subordinate ideas. George successfully completed a rigorous university program in business and computers in five years because of intelligence, academic skills, computer talents, and, most importantly, motivation.

Vocational Training

The major means for obtaining special services for vocational training involves the provision of vocational rehabilitation. The vocational rehabilitation services most often needed by persons with learning disabilities are evaluation, counseling, job training, job placement, and job follow-up. To qualify for vocational rehabilitation services, individuals must meet the criteria that the disorder must result in a substantial handicap to employment and that there is a reasonable expectation that vocational rehabilitation services may benefit the individual in terms of employability (Rehabilitation Services Administration, 1985). The issue of underemployment is significant to these criteria.

For example, persons with learning disabilities employed at entry-level positions (e.g., food preparation in a short-order restaurant) may be found ineligible for vocational rehabilitation because they are employed despite the belief by parents and professionals that they are capable of higher-level positions if given the appropriate training.

Vocational rehabilitation services are most effective when built on a strong foundation of career education and vocational education provided at the secondary level. Assessment for vocational rehabilitation purposes should be based on a comprehensive psychoeducational battery such as the one devised by Hawks and associates (1990) and a comprehensive vocational assessment battery (NICHCY, 1990). Although such evaluations may have been done in high school, it is necessary to update them in adulthood because there may be substantial changes. I have found that academic levels decrease in many adults with learning disabilities because of disuse of such skills. In addition, psychosocial problems often increase because of vocational and social failures experienced after exiting school.

Counseling and guidance, another needed vocational rehabilitation service, may be difficult because some persons with learning disabilities have unrealistic goals that they cannot achieve at a particular point in time. The vocational counselor must not "burst the person's bubble," but must clearly delineate the skills and training necessary to perform the desired job, analyze the individual's skills and training in relation to the requirements, and identify the means of attaining the needed skills and training. Then the counselor must help the individual to identify a more realistic vocational goal in the same general area of the original desired goal or a different area. For example, a person with learning disabilities may want to be a pilot despite fifth-grade reading and math levels and attentional deficits. The counselor must clearly lay out the requirements for securing a pilot's license and the means for attaining these requirements. Then the counselor should discuss jobs in the transporta-

tion field that may be more attainable at that particular time (e.g., airport baggage handler) or identify other areas of interest.

Vocational training may be provided at a specialized or regular school. Regular trade and technical schools prepare students for employment in occupations such as dental assistants, welders, and secretaries. Almost all trade and technical schools require a high school diploma or a graduate equivalent diploma (GED), which may be a significant obstacle for many dropouts with learning disabilities. When a student with learning disabilities is enrolled in a regular trade or technical setting, it is important that the instructor be educated about the person's special training needs to compensate for his or her deficits. For example, the student may need shorter training periods because of an attentional deficit. Making the instructor aware of the individual's learning problems may, however, engender bias unless the instructor is educated about what learning disabilities are and how they can be accommodated in the training program.

Another vocational training program that may be available to persons with learning disabilities is provided through the Job Training Partnership Act (JTPA), which was designed to increase the role of private business and industry in training and employment of disadvantaged youth. Persons with learning disabilities may be eligible for JTPA-funded training programs because they are economically disadvantaged or because they have a mental disability that constitutes a substantial handicap to employment. Another form of vocational training may involve on-the-job training (OJT), which enables an individual to work on a job while learning the skills and duties from a co-worker or a supervisor. Internships and apprenticeship programs also provide training and may be provided by local unions (NICHCY, 1991).

Vocational placement, another needed vocational rehabilitation service, is successful when the requirements of the job match the skills and interests of the individual. Vocational placement involves the difficult decision by persons with learning disabilities about self-disclosing their learning disabilities to prospective employers. The concern about employer knowledge of an individual's learning disability may be well founded in light of the findings on employer attitudes toward hiring persons with learning disabilities. Minskoff, Sautter, Hoffman, and Hawks (1987) found that only one-half of the 326 employers they surveyed stated that they would hire persons with learning disabilities for the jobs that they supervised. If individuals with learning disabilities self-disclose their learning disabilities, there is a risk of not being hired despite the provisions of the Americans with Disabilities Act (ADA). If individuals do not self-disclose, then employers cannot make the reasonable accommodations that are federally mandated. When counseling individuals with learning disabilities on such situations, it is recommended that if they do not want to self-disclose their learning disabilities, they should assertively point out their strengths (e.g., hard worker, punctual, careful) and weaknesses (e.g., difficulty following oral directions and therefore the need to have them repeated and/or written) and how they are strongly motivated to compensate for their weaknesses.

Another necessary vocational rehabilitation service involves job follow-up. Some persons with learning disabilities need assistance with job performance over a long period of time. If this is not provided, they may lose their jobs and eventually drop out from the vocational rehabilitation service network. Some persons may also lose their jobs because of economic factors or may decide that the job was not what they wanted. Therefore, continuous job monitoring is necessary.

Other Necessary Adult Services

Many adults with learning disabilities need other services to enable them to achieve success in adulthood. A large number of dropouts with learning disabilities need re-medial education to obtain their GED so that they can pursue post-secondary education or training. Other persons with learning disabilities need to improve and/or maintain their academic skills, especially since academic skills seem to decrease with disuse. Teachers in Adult Basic Education (ABE) programs and literacy programs usually provide such remedial education. However, many ABE teachers and literacy instructors report that they have limited knowledge of learning disabilities and the means for providing services to such individuals (Martin-Ross & Osgood-Smith, 1990). The Lab School of Washington has an excellent night-school program for academic remediation for adults with learning disabilities that is provided by persons trained in learning disabilities (Smith, 1992); however, it can reach only a limited number of persons in need.

Many adults with learning disabilities desperately need assistance with difficulties in psychological and social adjustment. When the years of school failure are compounded by years of vocational failure in adulthood, many persons with learning disabilities are overwhelmed by feelings of inadequacy and further deflation of their self-concepts. Such individuals need psychological counseling from professionals knowledgeable about learning disabilities. Currently, most mental health agencies and private practitioners are not knowledgeable and therefore may not provide appropriate counseling or therapy.

Many adults with learning disabilities cannot adjust to the social demands on the job or in their interpersonal lives. They may have been overprotected by special educators and their families, and are victims of learned helplessness. Such individuals need to develop appropriate social skills for the job and for interpersonal satisfaction. At this time, the means for developing such skills are limited. Self-help groups composed of and led by persons with learning disabilities are effective avenues for providing training in self-awareness and self-advocacy, but again such groups are provided infrequently.

Summary

Although there is general consensus that learning disabilities are a lifelong condition, there is not concomitant recognition that lifelong services must be available. Post-secondary education, vocational training, and services to improve psychosocial adjustment must be widely expanded to meet the needs of the many adults with learning disabilities requiring such services. All individuals who work with persons with learning disabilities in colleges, universities, and training schools; employers; ABE teachers; literacy instructors; and mental health providers must be trained to understand learning disabilities and to provide appropriate services so adults with learning disabilities can realize their potentials.

References

Aune, E. (1991). A transition model for postsecondary-bound students with learning disabilities. *Learning Disabilities Research & Practice, 6,* 177–187.

Carnevale, A., Gainer, L., & Maltzer, A. (1990). *Workplace basics.* San Francisco: Jossey-Bass.

Faas, L. A. & D'Alonzo, B. J. (1990). WAIS-R scores as predictors of employment success and failure among adults with learning disabilities. *Journal of Learning Disabilities, 23,* 311–316.

Gardner, H. (1983). *Frames of mind.* New York: Basic Books.

Gerber, P. J., Schnieders, C. A., Paradise, L. V., Reiff, H. B., Ginsberg, R., & Popp, P. A. (1990). Persisting problems of adults with learning disabilities: Self-reported comparisons from their school-age and adult years. *Journal of Learning Disabilities, 23,* 570–573.

Hawks, R., Minskoff, E. H., Sautter, S., Sheldon, K. L., Steidle, E. F., & Hoffman, F. J. (1990). A model diagnostic battery for adults with learning disabilities. *Learning Disabilities: A Multidisciplinary Journal, 1,* 94–101.

Hoffman, F. J., Sheldon, K. L., Minskoff, E. H., Sautter, S. W., Steidle, E. F., Baker, D. P., Bailey, M. B., & Echols, L. D. (1987). Needs of learning disabled adults. *Journal of Learning Disabilities, 20,* 43–52.

Hohenshil, T. H., Levinson, E. M., & Heer, K. B. (1985). Best practices in vocational assessment for handicapped students. In A. Thomas & J. Grimes (Eds.), *Best practices in school psychology* (pp. 215–228). Kent, OH: National Association of School Psychologists.

Martin-Ross, J., & Osgood-Smith, J. (1990). Adult basic educators' perceptions of learning disabilities. *Journal of Reading, 33,* 340–347.

Mercer, C. D., King-Sears, P., & Mercer, A. R. (1990). Learning disabilities definitions and criteria used by state education departments. *Learning Disability Quarterly, 13,* 141–152.

Miller, R. J., Rzonca, C., & Snider, B. (1991). Variables related to the type of postsecondary education experience chosen by young adults with learning disabilities. *Journal of Learning Disabilities, 24,* 188–191.

Minskoff, E. H., Hawks, R., Steidle, E. F., & Hoffmann, F. J. (1989). A homogeneous group of persons with learning disabilities: Adults with severe learning disabilities in vocational rehabilitation. *Journal of Learning Disabilities, 22,* 521–528.

Minskoff, E. H., Sautter, S. W., Hoffmann, F. J., & Hawks, R. (1987). Employer attitudes toward hiring the learning disabled. *Journal of Learning Disabilities, 20,* 53–57.

Minskoff, E. H., Sautter, S., Sheldon, K. L., Steidle, E. F., & Baker, D. P. (1988). A comparison of learning disabled adults and high school students. *Learning Disabilities Research, 3,* 115–123.

National Information Center for Children and Youth with Handicaps (NICHCY). (1990). *Vocational assessment: A guide for parents and professionals.* Washington, DC: NICHCY.

National Information Center for Children and Youth with Handicaps (NICHCY). (1991). *Options after high school for youth with disabilities.* Washington, DC: NICHCY.

Ness, J., & Price, L. A. (1990). Meeting the psychosocial needs of adolescents and adults with learning disabilities. *Intervention in School and Clinic, 26,* 16–21.

Rehabilitation Services Administration. (1985). *Operational definition of specific learning disability for VR purposes.* Program Policy Directive, RSA-PPD-85-7.

Rose, E. (1991). Project TAPE: A model of technical assistance for service providers of college students with learning disabilities. *Learning Disabilities Research & Practice, 6,* 25–33.

Schumaker, J. B., Hazel, J. S., & Deshler, D. D. (1985). A model for facilitating postsecondary transition. *Techniques. A Journal of Remedial Education and Counseling, 1,* 437–446.

Smith, S. L. (1992). *Succeeding against the odds: Strategies and insights from the learning disabled.* Los Angeles: Tarcher, Inc.

Sternberg, R. J. (1989). *Learning and individual differences: Advances in theory and research.* New York: W. H. Freeman.

Strichart, S. S. (1990). College opportunities for students with learning disabilities: Issues and practices. *Learning Disabilities: A Multidisciplinary Journal, 1,* 119–127.

U.S. Department of Labor, Bureau of Labor Statistics. (1987). *Occupational outlook handbook.* Washington, DC: U.S. Government Printing Office.

Wagner, M. (1989). *Youth with disabilities during transition: An overview of descriptive findings from the National Longitudinal Transition Study.* Menlo Park, CA: SRI International.

Zigmond, N., & Thornton, H. (1985). Follow-up of postsecondary age learning disabled graduates and dropouts. *Learning Disabilities Research, 1,* 50–55.

Chapter 11

Adult Literacy and Learning Disabilities

C. WILSON ANDERSON, M.Ed.

For many reasons the lack of adult literacy is an enormous and complex problem facing American society and the American workplace, as evidenced by the emergence of Literacy Plus and literacy classes in many corporations. Moreover, it has also become a major problem in colleges and universities across the country. In most parts of the United States, it is still assumed that adult illiteracy is the result of poor school attendance and unavailability of education, as well as a lack of commitment on the part of the student. This is no longer true. In fact, most adult illiterates have high school diplomas. Clearly, America's schools are blamed as the major producers of illiterates.

Just what is and who is the adult illiterate is really not debated because there is near universal agreement on the definition of the skills necessary to function on an acceptable level in the many environments where adults work and live. The unacknowledged part of the illiteracy definition and question is that more and more demands are being placed on American workers as they shift to an "information and service economy" after 60 years of a skilled labor orientation (Johnston, 1987). However, when the issue turns to why there are so many adult illiterates, the temperature rises, fingers point, and territorialism and denial set in.

One of the major problems in the area of adult literacy is the unresolved question and yet persistent belief that one-half of all adult illiterates are in fact learning disabled. This largest portion of the group labeled *learning disabled* is sometimes referred to as *language learning disabled* or by the older term, *dyslexic*. Many professionals in education and psychology, as well as in other related fields, still don't "believe" in dyslexia, the other subtypes of learning disabilities, or even in the concept of learning disabilities. Yet these professionals have a difficult time explaining why there are so many illiterate Americans, many of whom have high school diplomas. Attention to the multiple causes of adult illiteracy is critical if the correct remedial strategies are to be used. It is obvious to all but those "nonbelievers" that the "one size fits all" approach to reading, written expression, and spelling did not work well for many students and will not work for the adult illiterates who have adequate intelligence and good exposure to school, who come from families where success is expected, and who have no other disabilities such as blindness or deafness.

On a national level, less than 4% of school-age children are in programs for the learning disabled (see Table 11-1) and current estimates state that up to 15% of any population is affected by learning disabilities. It then follows that 11% of the learning-disabled population falls through the cracks and does not receive the services that were promised under P.L. 94-142. Many believe this is attributed to 49 of the 50 states resorting to the use of discrepancy formulas in order to protect themselves financially from the consequences of fully implementing P.L. 94-142.

Virtually every school district in the United States publishes data as one of many attempts to prove that each district is doing its best possible job of educating students. As it turns out, almost all schools report that their district's students are all above average. This fact has been dubbed the "Lake Wobegon effect." Most schools have local and state testing programs, which means that four weeks of the school year are dedicated to preparing the students for tests. President Bush's Education 2000 program proposes to add a battery of national tests, which in reality will divert another two weeks on top of the other four weeks of testing from an already overcrowded curriculum. This means that even less time will be spent teaching and learning the basic skills of reading, written expression, spelling, math, and humanities and sciences. President Clinton's plan has not yet been formalized, but is expected to call for national testing.

People inside and outside of the educational community agree that adult illiteracy exists, but there is much disagreement about the cause and even more disagreement about treatment methods and strategies. In reality, adult illiterates are a group made up of very diverse populations. Tradition has it that these adult illiterates are a small homogeneous group, but nothing could be further from the truth.

Adult Illiterates

Adults who are illiterate have many individual differences despite being placed in a "homogeneous grouping." Nine subgroups exist when grouping adult illiterates who are learning disabled. They are:

The traditional learning-disabled group
The group who used to be labeled educable mentally retarded
Adults who have not had educational opportunities

The dropouts or push outs
The slow learners
The fall-through-the-cracks students
The student from poor quality schools
The English-as-a-second language group
Unwed mothers

The first group of adult illiterates consists of those individuals who are indeed learning disabled, and who were appropriately identified according to the discrepancy formula in state learning-disabilities regulations, but were not well remediated. Most of their special education programs were spent in keeping the student organized, current in homework, and successful in academic classes. Generally, this group contains no more than 4% of any school population (see Table 11-1).

The second group is made up of people who used to be diagnosed and labeled as educable mentally retarded (EMR or EMH) and who now, in many schools, are simply relabeled as learning disabled. The older EMR or EMH group has better literacy skills than the younger group. Teachers speculate over and over again that the older EMR population was better taught, skill-wise, than their mainstreamed successors. The teachers' concerns about these students' capabilities have been effectively silenced by the demands of vocal parents that their children be mainstreamed rather than placed in special classes for skill development.

The third group consists of those adults who have not had educational opportunities for whatever reason. Although they are now fewer in number, they do exist. Bob Sheppard, Director of Topeka's Literacy Council, estimates that about 25% of the Literacy Council's clients did not have educational opportunities after the fourth grade. Most of these adults are the children of sharecroppers or migrant workers.

The fourth group of students had educational opportunities but did not take advantage of them and for many reasons dropped out of school or became "push outs." As for those who found themselves in prison, their educators have come to accept the rule of

Table 11-1. Percentage of 6- through 21-Year-Olds in Special Education 1988–89

States	All Conditions*	Learning Disabilities	Speech Impaired	Mentally Retarded	Emotionally Disturbed
Alabama	9.37	3.18	2.22	2.97	0.62
Alaska	9.76	5.25	2.08	1.49	0.42
Arizona	6.38	3.69	1.42	0.53	0.42
Arkansas	7.38	3.96	1.16	1.91	0.05
California	6.32	3.78	1.45	0.38	0.18
Colorado	6.51	3.18	1.04	0.43	1.19
Connecticut	8.46	4.52	1.32	0.56	1.70
Delaware	8.17	4.62	1.06	0.83	1.17
District of Columbia	5.71	2.75	0.88	0.92	0.81
Florida	7.97	3.38	2.39	1.02	0.90
Georgia	5.46	1.60	1.16	1.43	1.10
Hawaii	4.60	2.61	0.83	0.48	0.31
Idaho	6.89	3.93	1.18	1.07	0.18
Illinois	8.34	3.86	2.09	1.01	1.04
Indiana	7.56	2.88	2.63	1.48	0.33
Iowa	7.93	3.50	1.43	1.61	1.01
Kansas	6.92	2.90	1.90	0.99	0.77
Kentucky	7.38	2.39	2.34	2.00	0.31
Louisiana	5.56	2.24	1.62	0.94	0.34
Maine	9.03	3.95	1.97	1.00	1.45
Maryland	8.13	4.15	2.39	0.55	0.40
Massachusetts	10.92	3.85	2.51	2.31	1.50
Michigan	6.61	2.94	1.48	0.90	0.89
Minnesota	7.42	3.52	1.40	1.06	1.89
Mississippi	7.69	3.74	2.47	1.21	0.03
Missouri	8.24	3.87	2.14	1.29	0.69
Montana	7.30	4.07	1.82	0.59	0.33
Nebraska	7.69	3.33	2.01	1.15	0.65
Nevada	6.49	3.92	1.34	0.48	0.39
New Hampshire	6.64	4.07	1.10	0.48	0.66
New Jersey	9.57	4.83	2.97	0.37	0.85
New Mexico	7.90	3.79	2.29	0.55	0.83
New York	6.90	4.09	0.61	0.58	1.12
North Carolina	6.96	3.02	1.55	1.38	0.60
North Dakota	7.04	3.37	2.19	0.96	0.27
Ohio	7.47	2.91	1.94	1.70	0.30
Oklahoma	7.62	3.63	2.00	1.47	0.19
Oregon	7.47	4.03	1.88	0.59	0.45
Pennsylvania	7.31	3.11	1.97	1.34	0.69
Rhode Island	8.54	5.68	1.37	0.48	0.78
South Carolina	7.96	3.15	2.06	1.75	0.70
South Dakota	7.37	3.32	2.19	0.93	0.31
Tennessee	8.25	4.28	1.98	1.17	0.22
Texas	7.03	3.97	1.39	0.58	0.57
Utah	7.64	3.37	1.42	0.62	1.74
Vermont	8.98	3.89	2.59	1.30	0.68
Virginia	7.16	3.66	1.67	0.98	0.57
Washington	6.39	3.32	1.17	0.71	0.41
West Virginia	9.13	4.17	2.34	1.88	0.50
Wisconsin	6.83	2.04	1.13	0.44	0.88
Wyoming	7.74	4.18	2.04	0.57	0.47

*Includes deaf, blind, hearing-impaired, visually handicapped, multiply handicapped, orthopedically impaired, and other health-impaired conditions, as well as the conditions listed separately on the chart.

Notes: Percentage of children served is based on the Census Bureau's estimated resident population counts for July 1988. Includes students served under the Education of the Handicapped Act and Chapter 1 state-operated programs for disabled students.

Source: Education Department. Reprinted from *Education of the Handicapped*, July 18, 1990

thumb: "Whatever grade was the inmate's last grade in school, subtract three years and that will be the estimated reading level" (unpublished personal communication). The results of the South Dakota Penitentiary Program Project Success (1977) confirms this rule of thumb. A 1982 study suggested that youths with reading disabilities were over-represented in the juvenile delinquent population by a ratio of 60% (Hogenson, 1974).

The fifth group contains the students with the moniker of *slow learner*. These are the students who "gutted it out" and worked as well as they could. Typically, they were not behavior problems in their classes. Generally speaking, it is widely believed that this is the current population receiving services under the learning disabilities label.

The sixth and largest of the groups consists of those students who were never eligible for services under the various state discrepancy formulas, yet were struggling enough that the teachers referred them for help because the teachers knew that their teaching skills would not help these kids. According to Hirsch (1988), around fourth grade, those who lack the initial knowledge required for significant reading begin to be left behind permanently.

The seventh group is made up of those who have not been exposed to good education opportunities even though they faithfully attended schools. Specifically, this group is the group that is of most concern to college professors and the directors of college learning-disability programs across the country. The professors' dilemma is to fail the students, "water down" the curriculum, and/or end "open door" admissions policies. Colleges clearly find themselves in a bind with this type of student, and further the colleges and universities lack financial resources to develop appropriate remedial programs to meet academic and student needs.

Students in the eighth group are those for whom English is a second language. These people have not been taught and/or have not learned standard American English well enough to function in an English-speaking business community. While the educational debate continues, these individuals are forced to accept low-paying jobs in a segregated community, not because of desire or intelligence, but because of inadequate skills needed to function in mainstream America (Chisman, 1989).

The ninth group is the least acknowledged group in the field of illiteracy, and its composition has not been studied because its first symptom is so overwhelming that no one looks for secondary causes. This group is generally known as junior high and high school unwed mothers. Although there are programs designed to keep them in school, in reality most drop out, continue to have children, and rely on welfare payments. Moreover, their children are at-risk to repeat the cycle. How many of these young women fit the previous eight categories is a complicated and as yet unanswered question.

All nine of these groups exist, and the threads of attention deficit hyperactivity disorder (ADHD) and drug and alcohol abuse run through all of them. As Silver (1990), a psychiatrist who is a specialist in learning disabilities, points out, "ADHD means that the child is not available for learning."

The abuse of chemicals has the residual effect of limiting learning potential and memory, as well as affecting motivation. Those adults who began heavily using drugs and alcohol in their junior high and high school years, for all practical purposes stopped their social and emotional growth and plateaued in intellectual growth.

Another factor that is just beginning to surface is the issue of lead poisoning and its residual effects on future generations (Epstein, 1991). The jury is still out as to the effect that lead poisoning has had and is having on those children from the inner city as well as on the suburban children of parents who were from the inner city. The hypothesis is that lead poisoning leeches to the fetus.

Adult illiteracy is clouded by many issues, but the largest subpopulation in the adult literacy crusade is the population of individuals with learning disabilities, with or without a diagnosis. Even though this group exists, it is often ignored. The threads of the problems mentioned earlier further complicate the issue.

The solutions to the adult literacy problem must take into account the conditions found in the nine major subgroups as well as the three, and possibly four, common threads of alcoholism, chemical abuse, environmental poisoning, and ADHD that may also be found as factors. This is not happening. As with most educational problems, the cry is to fix it without much thought about how it is going to be fixed. For most of the six of the nine subgroups, the students have been exposed to a traditional education, at least to the ninth grade. Yet educators and politicians persist in believing that if the student did not learn the first time, "We'll just do more of the same thing the second time and if that doesn't work, we'll vary the rate and vary the pace of more of the same the third time." Study after study has shown that in most cases, retention does not "fix" the problem (Shepard & Smith, 1990; Solorzano & Smith, 1990).

Order must be brought to the current chaotic programs that are at odds and inconsistent with each other on local, state, and federal levels. Young and Anderson (in press) observed, "Despite the success adults with learning disabilities have made in gaining recognition as a legitimate handicapped group, much of federal, state and local government does not take learning disabilities into account when planning for adult literacy programs." The result is that many adults with learning disabilities who are in need of services will again fail in educational settings that are not geared to meet their needs. This failure only adds to the frustration felt by those who have limited literacy skills and do not have an understanding of the underlying cause. Mental health professionals recognize that these individuals continue to blame themselves for their academic and vocational failures. With society blaming the victim and the victim believing that he or she is to blame, serious social, economic, and individual consequences are created.

It is also important to mention that there are legitimate educational disagreements as to what is appropriate intervention. Common sense would dictate that each of the nine groups needs to be examined with regard to what constitutes accurate identification and what constitutes appropriate intervention to guarantee success in the shortest amount of time possible. This means, of course, that time and resources must be allocated to appropriate past history and diagnosis before persons are placed in the most beneficial literacy program. In the long run, appropriate diagnosis will be less expensive and less destructive to the individual than another round of failure experience and dropping out. Current estimates by the various literacy groups is that half of their clients who are believed to be bright enough to learn drop out of proven literacy programs (Chisman, 1989).

Caution needs to be exercised by those who believe that federal funding is the answer. Most people are unaware that approximately 20% of the money allocated ever reaches the Chapter One classrooms; the rest is used to pay administrative costs. As with many programs, the call to "fix" something is left to the very same people who "didn't do it right to begin with"; as a result, adult illiterates are back in the same hands with more of the same dressed up in a "new proposal," like old wine in new bottles. In addition, pseudo-solutions, such as writing reports and brochures, arguing and rearguing the problem, and calling for conferences to discuss the issue, take the time, money, energy, and focus away from the problem and force the resources to be allocated elsewhere. In the widely read and much touted booklet *Jump Start: The Federal Role in Adult Literacy,* (Chisman, 1989), funded by 21 knowledgeable and prestigious groups, not one word is mentioned about learning disabilities, let alone the role played by the learning disabilities population in the adult literacy problem. The same thing is true of the U.S. Department of Labor's publications entitled *The Workplace Basics: The Skills Employers Want* (Carnevale & Gainer, 1989b) and *The*

Learning Enterprise (Carnevale & Gainer, 1989a). The same problem faces the Job Training Partnership Act (JTPA), the Adult Education Act, and the Family Support Act (JOBS program). The counselors in the state departments of vocational rehabilitation services recognize learning disabilities but lack sufficient referral resources and the finances to help. Those persons who receive services through the Carl Perkins Vocational Education Act will be successful only because of the skills of their individual remediator, not because of the program.

Remedial technology and approaches have been well established for the past 60 years. The problem is that they are well-guarded secrets. Generally speaking, more of the same is not going to work any better than it did the first time. Very few illiterate individuals are total nonreaders. Programs that regiment a semi-literate person to page one of workbook one will not hold the person's attention, let alone build his or her self-esteem. Most adults will give a program a fair chance for several hours. If progress is not felt by those individuals, they will bail out in order to save what is left of their pride. Remediators forget or do not know that their clients have been led down the rosy path before, and these clients will bolt rather than be hurt or humiliated. It does not matter if the threatened hurt or humiliation is real or perceived.

As mentioned before, the illiterate population is heterogeneous. It is not the fact that illiteracy exists that is so important; it is the reason(s) for illiteracy and the kinds of problems that need remediation that determine the appropriate intervention strategy(ies). This can only be accomplished through obtaining an educational history, a cognitive ability assessment, and a thorough diagnosis of reading, written expression, and spelling ability, including carefully evaluated error patterns. A good diagnosis will also include a session of clinical teaching in order to decide which approach or combination of approaches will be appropriate for the client.

An educational history of the client is very critical. First, it will establish in which

of the nine subgroups the client will fit. If there is no history of learning problems and the client does not appear to fit any subgroup, and if problems are recent or rapidly deteriorating, a medical referral is appropriate to confirm or deny the existence of neurological problems such as a tumor or stroke.

It is generally agreed that those persons who are language learning disabled will not score as well on standardized IQ tests. Still, it is important to the remediation process for the teacher to know if the client is educable mentally retarded, a slow learner, or learning disabled. Remediation strategies and length of time estimated for remediation are all related to the client's potential to learn. It is true that a skilled teacher, after working with an individual, can discern the intellectual ability of the client, but the time it takes to determine the information and the amount of time needed to change tutoring strategies are enormous when compared with an hour-and-a-half test.

The same is true of a good diagnostic examination of reading, written expression, and spelling skills. Error analysis of both reading and spelling is critical for determining the remediation process to be used in teaching the client. Spelling tests must be encoded tests, not the traditional "proofreading tests" where the student chooses the one correct or the one incorrect spelling out of four choices. Clinical experience indicates that those clients who have reading abilities above the fourth-grade level will be easier to remediate than those who fall below the fourth-grade level. Fourth grade is the time the curriculum shifts from learning to read to reading to learn. Fourth grade is also the level where the language systems of reading, writing, and spelling come together. Those tests that yield scores only and are so global that error analysis cannot be used are not helpful, and other tests should be used or at least be supplemented to obtain a more global view of the learning disability.

Based on error analysis, a session of clinical teaching should begin. If the client cannot read words in isolation, can he or she read those same words in context? If he or she cannot spell bigger words, can he or she spell those same words when given in syllable form? If he or she spells "phonetically" does he or she know the alternative spelling choices for the sounds and does he or she know the "place value" for each of the symbols for those sounds? If he or she does not know sight words, will practice using the Fernald approach work? Can the person work and learn in a small group of three, or will that person need one-on-one tutoring?

The final and most important reason for appropriate and careful diagnosis and evaluation is that with the passage of the American Disabilities Act (ADA) (1990) those adults who "fell through the cracks" or were not properly diagnosed have the opportunity to make gains through the implementation of the "reasonable accommodation" provision of ADA. Most employers would rather keep an employee than have to search for, hire, and train a new employee.

Some employers will "talk a good literacy" game, but they are really only interested in providing those literacy skills necessary for the person to succeed on the job. If the client is a car painter, the employer may only be interested in sponsoring that person in order that he or she can read, write, and spell the job order. That includes ordering the parts of the car that need painting, reading paint names, reading instructions and warnings, writing what was done to the car, and computing time spent on the job as opposed to the "book rate." Some employers may want word-processing skills, invoice-reading skills, and other job-related items, such as the ability to use indexes in order to cross-reference parts. In this case the best practice for the client would be to secure all the print materials that the employer wishes the client to learn. Vocabulary/reading words can be isolated, broken into syllables, and pre-taught before the employee begins the chapter. Study guides can be developed with the important information highlighted so that the employee knows what needs to be learned. For other words, the tutor/teacher uses work materials to

teach reading and does not teach reading and eventually apply it to work materials.

Large numbers of well-trained, dedicated individuals and groups of individuals across the United States have the ability, the time, and the expertise to provide the necessary remediation strategies for illiterate Americans. The key problems are not in person power, but in diagnosis and payment for services. Unless the client has some personal investment beyond time or threatened job loss, there is not much motivation to improve skills or to stick with a program long enough to gain results.

Adequate financing is available from several different sources. The problem is letting the sources know that effective and efficient professional services exist. Professionals in state social service and welfare agencies, JTPA programs, vocational rehabilitation programs, local businesses, private schools, and vocational schools are eager to find programs that have successful track records. Note: One mistake that some welfare programs make is to insist that all recipients must receive a graduate equivalent diploma (GED). Even with the appropriate documentation and oral testing, a GED is not a possibility for many people. An alternative is to spend the time and money to return to school and earn a diploma. According to the GED program coordinator in the Topeka, Kansas 501 Unified School District, it is currently believed that one-third of present high school students could not pass a GED examination. This would be possible with several dedicated and creative teachers who could set up such a program within school districts. The cost to states would be less than spending years trying to prepare people for an unobtainable GED.

It will take time to cultivate various programs to meet the needs of adult illiterates and to subcontract through various educational services, but it can be done. There are several such models in existence throughout the United States. One such model is the Literacy in the Work Place Program, administered through the Menninger Clinic in Topeka, Kansas (Anderson, 1991). In this program, directors of human services in local businesses are contacted. Those employees who want or need to improve literacy skills are identified by the company. The cost of establishing the diagnosis is paid for by the company. If tutoring or small group classes are needed, the cost is borne by both the employee and the employer. The exact ratio of employee–employer cost is determined by each company. After the diagnostic and clinical teaching sessions are completed, if appropriate, clients enroll in eight sessions of tutoring or small group work with the option of renewing for another eight sessions. Clients are grouped according to skill needs, personality factors, and appropriate instructional methodology. The instructor is chosen accordingly and is carefully matched with the group. Tutoring sessions or small group classes meet twice a week. The times range from early afternoon through early evening. Each adult student has a notebook with a realistic remedial plan spelled out that has been agreed on by the client, the diagnostician, and the instructor. As skills are mastered and assignments are completed, they are recorded and filed in the student's notebook. The notebook belongs to and stays with the student. This is a useful record for the student, because it means the student can begin again without extensive diagnostic work, and the instructor can "see" what has happened in past performance. If the approach proves to be inappropriate, the record shows what has been tried but did not succeed. In this way the blame is placed on the remedial approach rather than on the client. It is important to remember that traditional approaches did not work, and several of the alternative approaches may not work either. Whatever the case, a record of successes and setbacks has been created.

Menninger tutors and small group instructors are trained in the traditional approach of basal, whole language. In addition, they receive training in linguistics, Orton-Gillingham (synthetic, multisensory phonics), and Fernald (multisensory whole word).

Menninger-trained teachers and tutors are part of a two-year training program (Anderson, 1992). Some of the tutors and supervisors receive training in Laubach and other alternative approaches. Menninger works closely with other agencies in the communities across the state and also gives and receives referrals to agencies with appropriate programs.

Summary

Thirty million Americans are estimated to be illiterate. Half of these persons are suspected of being learning disabled, with or without "an official diagnosis." The issue is further complicated by the inattention given to persons with learning disabilities by federal, state, and local agencies in their guidelines and programs. Each day there are increasing literacy demands on our current workforce. American schools are releasing more illiterate persons into the workforce. With increasing skill demands on personnel and lack of skill development in the area of literacy, effective solutions are mandatory. Until professionals and policymakers effectively tackle this growing issue of learning disabilities and literacy, the human costs will continue to mount.

References

Americans with Disabilities Act. (1990). P.L. 101-336.

Anderson, C.W. (1992). Menninger Center for Learning Disabilities Teacher Training Program.

Anderson, C.W. (1991). *Tutoring, and adult evening school, literacy in the work place program.* Topeka, KS: Menninger Clinic.

Carnevale, A.P., & Gainer, L.J. (1989b). *The workplace basics: The skills employers want.* Alexandria, VA: American Society for Training and Development.

Chisman, F.P. (1989). *Jump start: The federal role in adult literacy.* Southport, CT: Southport Insititue for Policy Analysis.

Epstein, H. (1991). Personal correspondence.

Hirsch, E.D. (1988). *Cultural literacy.* New York: Houghton Mifflin Publishers.

Hogenson, D.L. (1974). *Reading and juvenile delinquency. Bulletin of the Orton Society.* Towson, MD: Orton Dyslexia Society.

Johnston, W.B., & Packer, A.H. (1987). *Workforce 2000: Work and workers of the twenty-first century.* Indianapolis: Hudson Institute.

Shepard, L.A., & Smith, M.L. (1990). Synthesis of research on grade retention. *Educational Leadership.*

Silver, L.B. (1990). *ADHD Staff Development Presentation to the Menninger Clinic's Children's Division.* Topeka, KS.

Solorzano, L.A., & Smith, M.L. (1990). Will staying back help or hurt? *Ladies Home Journal.*

Young, G., & Anderson, C.W. (in press.). Literacy and learning disabilities—disconnected policies of federal, state and local agencies.

Chapter 12

Services for Students with Learning Disabilities in the Community Colleges

DARYL F. MELLARD, PH.D.

Rick had finished high school and from his perspective was finished with school. His schooling experience had been painful. For as long as he could remember, school had been anything but a rewarding experience. Rick couldn't express himself well either in writing or in oral expression. In response to his frustrations, he adopted defiant behaviors and an angry demeanor. Those difficulties of expressing himself were not only part of school but also of life at home. The sullen, unhappy youngster of elementary school grew into the sullen, unhappy adolescent. If Rick had been bigger, he would likely have developed a more physical response to dealing with his frustration, but he didn't. Perhaps the support he had received tempered his responses.

Rick received assistance and understanding from several important sources. Rick's parents helped his educational achievement and offered assistance as best they could. The learning disabilities services through school helped him earn passing grades. The efforts of his parents and teachers plus his own interests in music supported him through the school system. Getting him through high

school, however, did not provide him with the preparation for taking responsibility for his own independence—living on his own or earning a living wage. As an older adolescent, Rick realized his need for help in a way that had been less evident in high school. In his case the assistance seemed to be best accomplished through courses at the community college and working with the vocational rehabilitation counselor.

The long-term outcome to Rick's story is not known. From his own report and his parents' comments, he did benefit from the assistance through vocational rehabilitation and the community college. Rick earned his vocational certificate in construction technologies and currently is working full-time. His plans include "quickly" finding a residence outside his parents' house. For Rick the combination of educational and vocational rehabilitation services provided a valuable means of ensuring a successful outcome. In contrast, most students with learning disabilities encounter a much lower level of success (Gerber & Brown, 1991) and a very low probability of participating in post-secondary education. A primary statistic of these academic and related difficulties is the significant percentage of students who withdraw from high school. Five follow-along or follow-up studies (Adelman &

I gratefully acknowledge the assistance of Karen Halliday and Richard Lau in the writing of this chapter, and Bill Dodd, Sally Fasteau, and Carol Toppel for their helpful comments in reviewing this chapter.

Vogel, 1990; Cobb & Crump, 1984; Edgar, 1987; Malcolm et al., 1990; Valdes et al., 1990) reported dropout rates of 36%, 42%, 42%, 56%, and 32%, respectively. These figures should be considered conservative estimates since an additional number of students had likely exited the school system prior to the selection of students for these studies. Furthermore, while some of the students who withdrew eventually may return to complete high school or its equivalency, the number of students who do so is small.

In comparison to their nondisabled peers, students with learning disabilities are unlikely to participate in any post-secondary education (Fairweather & Shaver, 1991; Valdes et al., 1990). Valdes and associates (1990) reported that approximately 15% of the youth with learning disabilities that they followed had completed a post-secondary course in the year prior to their study. Fairweather and Shaver (1991) reported that 17% of the youth with learning disabilities who exited high school enrolled in a post-secondary educational program, whereas 56% of their nondisabled counterparts enrolled.

Rick's outcome is unique because he was employed in an area that matched his training and at a level above the base wage. These outcomes provided a strong likelihood that he could sustain himself with a standard of living above the poverty level. Sitlington and Frank (1990) found in their state-wide follow-up that students' employment did not correspond to their areas of technical or vocational training. This mismatch between educational training and employment would hinder the likelihood of a living wage. Cobb and Crump (1984), Edgar (1987), Fourqurean and co-workers (1991), Haring and associates (1990), Malcolm and colleagues (1990), Scuccimarra and Speece (1990), Shapiro and Lentz (1991), Siegel and Gaylord-Ross (1991), Sitlington and Frank (1990), and Valdes and co-workers (1990) all reported that the individuals' employment was primarily at entry-level positions. Consequently, the income level corresponded to a base wage that resulted in an annual income

bordering on the poverty line. Although these studies might be considered as generally bleak, other studies have described more positive outcomes but had more limited generalization because they included more selective or restrictive samples of individuals with learning disabilities (e.g., Adelman & Vogel, 1990; Gerber & Reiff, 1991).

Rick and other students with learning disabilities seeking post-secondary education do have a number of opportunities. Unfortunately, these opportunities are disparate in a number of critical dimensions, including the likelihood of a successful outcome (White, 1985). For example, post-secondary educational experiences are increasingly provided by companies as part of the training experience for their work (Fourqurean et al., 1991; Scuccimarra & Speece, 1990; Sitlington & Frank, 1990). In these circumstances, however, the training focuses on content and skill knowledge directly related to the job, rather than on broader educational objectives. An alternative would be a four-year college or university (see chapter 13). Yet, unless the college is specifically oriented to a student population with learning disabilities, the admissions requirements, course requirements, and graduation requirements may be burdensome. At the same time, supportive services may be very limited, thereby making the matriculation process very laborious.

Fairweather and Shaver (1991) reported positive outcomes for students with disabilities who participated in post-secondary vocational education. The curricular emphasis on occupational training and the apparent stronger links with high schools were suggested as possible reasons for improved outcomes. These positive outcomes have not been reported as frequently for two-year and four-year colleges. Fairweather and Shaver noted that one would expect more positive outcomes with the two-year colleges, in particular because of their efforts to recruit and serve diverse populations and their focus on vocational curricula. The authors also thought that the cost of attending a community college compared favorably with the cost of attending a proprietary vocational institution.

Attributes of Community Colleges

The preceding paragraphs identify several of the issues and problems potentially confronting young adults with learning disabilities seeking post-secondary educational opportunities. The remainder of the chapter describes factors that might influence one's choice for a post-secondary educational setting in a community college. A variety of attributes are described that might help the reader develop an informed opinion about community colleges and provide a context for understanding learning disabilities services.

Colleges differ from one another in their missions, curricular emphases, structures, resources, and other features. In particular they differ in the services available for students with learning disabilities (Bursuck et al., 1989; Mangrum & Strichart, 1988; Sclafani & Lynch, 1989). Thus, the listed attributes are not intended as a generalization of all community colleges. Based on the following discussion, however, the reader should have information for comparing and selecting among community colleges and other post-secondary settings.

Accessibility. Community colleges generally offer one of the most inclusive models for post-secondary opportunities. *Inclusive* here means that students are more likely to encounter lower admissions standards at a community college than at a college or university. The four-year institutions may require a special admission procedure to review a student's application (McGuire et al., 1990). From this perspective, then, the community college setting is more accessible since a prospective student can gain admission more readily. Few, if any, admissions standards such as a specified high school grade-point average or performance on any of the college entrance tests (such as the Scholastic Aptitude Test or College

Boards) are required to be met. In some instances, no admissions requirement exists. The student is admitted just by registering for the classes of his or her choice.

Course Offerings. Community colleges frequently offer a variety of course work. That variation in courses permits a student to choose a track of classes that might lead to a degree such as an associate of arts or to a vocational certificate. Another option would be courses that are oriented toward a degree but that also prepare the student for transfer to a four-year college program and a bachelor's degree. This variety of courses offered should help the students explore available career opportunities corresponding to their interests, strengths, and weaknesses.

Moreover, in the area of course offerings, community colleges differ from other colleges by offering a greater range of remedial or developmental courses and adult education courses. The community college is a community resource and, as such, will attract a wide range of students in the community. To accommodate this diverse group, course work includes the preparatory classes needed so the students can complete upper-division course requirements. A recent study in the California community colleges (Chancellor's Office, 1991) reported on the curricular choices by current students. Of the new students, 52% enroll in transfer and general education courses, 26% in basic skills courses, 11% in vocational education, and 5% in noncredit classes. Since one in four of all two-year college students is attending a community college in California, these numbers reflect a significant population of students.

For students seeking financial assistance, enrollment in the remedial or developmental classes can help in meeting the requirements for that assistance. Although the unit or half-unit for enrollment generally does not apply to a degree and is nontransferable, the unit will count toward a required minimum number of enrolled credits for financial assistance. So, in effect, the students are assisted in meeting a requirement for financial assistance and simultaneously are enrolled in course work that should increase the likelihood of success in their academic or vocational courses.

Community Responsiveness. Few four-year colleges are linked to the community's interests as closely as community colleges are. Although community colleges may have difficulty defining their mission in relation to high schools, colleges, and universities, a close association generally exists for responding to the needs of the local community. Even if a community college offers student housing, the majority of students are commuters from the nearby communities. In this way, the community college may be able to adapt to a small but supportive representation from the community. As a consequence of this sensitivity to the community, administrative, curricular, and supportive changes are more likely to accommodate the needs of a defined segment of the student body, especially if the community's interests are clearly described.

Transition Services. Associated with community responsiveness is the characteristic of integration with agencies and services in the community. The implication for this integration is that students from the local and neighboring communities' high school programs are more likely to have a smoother transition to the community college setting. This transition is helped by the existing ties among the local high schools, department of rehabilitation services, and the college (Fairweather & Shaver, 1991). For example, such agreements might permit students to attend the colleges for college credit while they are still high school students. This integration is not unique to the community college but overall is better developed and more frequently observed in community colleges than at four-year universities.

Instructional Orientation. Community colleges focus on instruction and service to the local communities. This focus is not necessarily unique to community colleges, but it is a benefit of the colleges' community orientation. Community colleges differ from four-year colleges in providing instruction that might be targeted toward an associate degree, a vocational certificate, or personal enrichment through adult education and other noncredit or remedial courses. Thus, the community college might be more tolerant to variation in students' instructional interests and needs, which should help students in planning and completing a course of study. The accommodations, substitutions, and waivers for students might be better tolerated at a community college, given the diversity of the curriculum and of the student population.

An advantage of such course offerings is that students might use the community college to complete the initial or requisite courses required at four-year institutions. San Louis Obispo is home to both Cuesta College, a community college, and California State Polytechnic, a four-year college. This city serves as an example for communities with both a community college and a four-year college. The situation works well for those students who want co-enrollment for the advantages available to each setting. In this example, the services for students with disabilities are particularly desirable to students who might travel from outside the neighboring communities to attend a college.

Community Representation

As the "community's" college, the setting provides an opportunity to interact with a wide range of individuals representing various ages and ethnic, social, and academic backgrounds. The introductory class in written composition might be equally suited to recent high school graduates and to older individuals who want to improve their writing skills as a means of advancing to better jobs. This representation from so many dimensions is likely to ensure that the students experience the perspectives from people with different backgrounds. A college with more selective entrance requirements or higher associated financial costs would seemingly offer a narrower representation of the educational, cultural, social, and economic classes of society.

Similarly, the community college is an integrated setting in the sense that students with learning disabilities are more likely to encounter the demands of a traditional college setting than those students attending a segregated program that includes only students with learning disabilities. An integrated educational setting should foster integration into a community. Thus, this aspect of integration should help students succeed in transitioning into successful community roles and assuming broader social responsibilities.

Some community colleges have enrollments nearly equal to those of the largest colleges and universities. Larger communities will have large enrollments, which might make the campus atmosphere seem more like a large college or university setting. Yet, even with these large enrollments, the majority of the student body is likely to live in the local community. With some exceptions, few students travel from out of state to attend a particular community college. Therefore, the student body will reflect the local community.

Associated Costs. Living in the local community should also mean that attending the college should be less expensive than traveling to another community and attending college. In addition, the costs of tuition and fees are lower in a community college.

The lower cost can be more appealing to a student with a learning disability. Students with learning disabilities are generally identified as such in a school setting in part because of the extreme difficulty they encounter in learning and demonstrating their achievement. Those difficulties would likely inhibit them from pursuing further education. On the other hand, if the financial cost seems reasonable, the value of continuing their education may be deemed worthwhile. In addition, since a number of studies have

demonstrated that the students with learning disabilities are likely to be living with their parents and depending on them for financial support (e.g., Sitlington & Frank, 1990), the students might have a greater financial incentive and support for attending college.

Considerations for Learning Disabilities Services

Service Providers. Colleges are required to provide reasonable accommodations to otherwise qualified individuals with disabilities as part of the 1973 Vocational Rehabilitation Act (Rothstein, 1986; Scott, 1991). As Mangrum and Strichart (1988) described, this law has resulted in a great variation in the available services. In considering a postsecondary institution, potential students might want to inquire about (1) the range of services provided to students encountering similar difficulties, (2) the people providing these service, and (3) the manner in which these services are administrated. Students can further ask: Does the college have a set of core services that are readily available? Are the services provided by the college's faculty or by its staff? Are the services from the Dean of Instruction or through an Office of Disabled Students?

The more that a college's faculty rather than its staff is involved in the services might indicate that the college has a broader, more integrated approach to working with students with disabilities. This perspective is certainly debatable. Nonetheless, if college faculty provides the services, these faculty members are more likely to be involved in the academic and administrative issues of the college than staff members would be. All faculty members by the nature of their positions have more responsibilities and representation throughout the college; consequently they might help in modifications to particular classes or courses of study (CAPED, 1992). Previous experience has shown that if any alteration of the course is required, the issues are usually resolved through negotiations with the student, an advocate, and the course instructor.

Educational and Psychological Assessments. A service that might be of particular interest is the availability of educational and psychological assessments. The student could inquire about what assessments are available and about any associated costs. In the California community colleges the assessments that are part of the eligibility process or placement are provided without additional costs to the student with learning disabilities. Thus, a student might complete an assessment to determine his or her eligibility for learning disabilities services at the college. In California's university and state university systems, in contrast, these assessments are a requirement for students if they intend to receive learning disabilities services, and the student pays associated costs. Given the potential costs involved in an assessment of intellectual ability, academic achievement, adaptive behavior, and other self-report measures, this difference can be significant. Assessment services and the completed report can be valuable to college planning and also in seeking assistance from vocational rehabilitation services.

Available Learning Disabilities Services and Classes. The community colleges are likely to have as much variation in the available services as any other educational institution, but they also provide special classes to students with learning disabilities. In California these services have been described in a directory (Chancellor's Office, 1988). The directory includes a description of each college, with the name and a telephone number of a college contact person, plus a listing of the generic services available. Such a listing is useful not only for knowing the offerings of the colleges but also for comparing settings outside California's community colleges. The directory has broadly organized services to include program management services, assessment services, instructional intervention services, counseling services,

and other designated services (e.g., parking assistance, interpreter services, and transportation services).

Service Delivery. The two most critical issues confronting the colleges' learning disabilities service provider are, first, initially choosing an eligibility model and, second, establishing an efficacious intervention model. Choosing an eligibility model is critical because the eligibility model is the basis on which students are evaluated for services, and also one would expect that services would be tailored for the eligible students. Students who meet the eligibility model are entitled to the special services available through the college. Mellard and Deshler (1984) described three conceptual issues important to establishing such an eligibility model: distinguishing classification decision errors, describing population parameters, and contrasting clinical versus statistical decision models. Addressing these issues in a post-secondary setting has been particularly difficult for several reasons, including the lack of an organizational structure for dealing with such issues across colleges. Within a college a frequently encountered problem is not having a qualified staff member who can evaluate students' assessment results and judge their eligibility. One way that colleges seem to be addressing these issues is to interpret the need for services and eligibility decisions in a very narrow framework from the 1973 Rehabilitation Act (Gerber, 1981).

Students who meet the learning disabilities eligibility model are entitled to the colleges' services and accommodations. As suggested above, those services would be geared toward the needs of the students who are eligible. Since colleges likely already offer remedial and developmental courses, the repetition of such classes for learning disabilities would seem unnecessary. Most likely, colleges would want to distinguish their learning disabilities services from other forms of student assistance. One way to make that distinction is on the basis of characteristics of students receiving and being denied those services. Eligible students with learning disabilities should have different characteristics and learning needs than the students in the colleges' remedial and developmental courses.

Minskoff, Hawks, Steidle, and Hoffman (1989) identified the needs of adults with learning disabilities that would have curricular implications: vocational counseling, vocational training, vocational support, functional academics, coping, social skills, pragmatics of language, self-awareness, job-seeking, and personal counseling. An apparent difficulty, however, is the diversity of the college students with learning disabilities. The college population with learning disabilities has some students for whom such a focused curriculum is entirely appropriate. Other students, however, who intend to transfer should expect a very different focus to the services and classes (e.g., learning strategies curriculum, an advocacy model, or tutorial assistance). The college staff is unable to provide adequate instruction with such different focuses, let alone any additional special requirements, owing to severe deficits evidenced by some students. In comparing colleges, students should carefully investigate the curricular orientations of the services and classes.

Special classes may be offered through the colleges, with curriculum and instructional methods specifically for the students with learning disabilities. Students need to consider carefully if enrollment in such special classes is desirable. The horror stories of introductory classes in English and math that discourage students from continued enrollment at a college are disconcerting to students with learning disabilities. In such a situation the special class offering might be of interest and a valuable alternative to increase the likelihood of a successful college experience. We have little data evaluating different service-delivery options in the post-secondary setting. Lacking that data, recommendations are mere best guesses. The student should exercise some careful judgment and seek academic counseling both from disabled students programs and services and the other academic counselors to assess the suitability of alternative options.

Additional Learning Disabilities Issues. Other attributes of the college are important to identify and evaluate. For example, the proportion of students who transfer and are retained in a four-year setting may be important if the student is interested in pursuing a bachelor's degree. To what colleges do the students obtain admission and graduate? For students seeking vocational certificates, an important determinant might be the successful placement and job retention of the program's graduates. How successful are the graduates in finding employment in their chosen field? At the secondary level, several authors (Okolo & Sitlington, 1988; Shapiro & Lentz, 1991; Sitlington & Frank, 1990) have questioned the sustained value of vocational programs as those programs currently are implemented. The repeated finding is that the students lack sufficient preparation to qualify for employment in their chosen area of study. The jobs they find are in areas different from their areas of education or training.

The descriptions included about colleges would seem to make them an ideal choice for everyone. On the other hand, the general statements offered about such attributes as accessibility, variation in course work options, and support services are variable across the college settings. Similarly, some students with learning disabilities may be particularly prepared for the requirements of the college or university setting and would have little to gain from a two-year stint at a community college.

General Issues in Post-secondary Education

Post-secondary educational settings have not always been so tolerant of nontraditional students, including students with disabilities. In some ways the problems of inappropriate or lack of college preparation and negative attitudes among college faculty cited by Prater and Minner (1986) and Putnam (1984) are persistent. Before concluding this chapter a few general comments seem appropriate about general issues in post-secondary educational settings for students with learning disabilities.

Definition and Eligibility Issues. Most practitioners in the area of learning disabilities would like to think that the students and adults with learning disabilities have a demonstrated disability that was accurately and objectively identified by a multidisciplinary team. With that perspective, the Learning Disabilities Association (1990) adopted a position paper arguing that once a valid diagnosis is made the individual should remain eligible for needed services. However, considerable data are available to suggest that identification and eligibility decisions are made for reasons other than objective and accurate evidence. For example, one is hard pressed to find any public school definition and eligibility criteria within one state that uniformly identify the same individuals as the definition and eligibility criteria used by other state departments of education, professionals with vocational rehabilitation services, or psychologists using the American Psychiatric Association's *Diagnostic and Statistical Manual* (1987). State departments of education have adopted wide variations in their definitions and eligibility criteria (Frankenberger & Fronzaglio, 1991; Mercer et al., 1990). In these circumstances, college staffs are appropriately wary of accepting previous diagnoses without first reviewing the available information and applying their own standards and eligibility models.

The issue for the student with learning disabilities is knowing who will make that determination and on what basis the determination will be made. Some settings have adopted definitions and eligibility models for use throughout the state, such as in California's community colleges (Mellard, 1990). To facilitate that review of eligibility, the student wants to be certain that a variety of information is available. The student would want the information available that origi-

nally was used in establishing the diagnosis as well as the most recent results of any comprehensive evaluation. Students with such documentation would possibly find that the college staff would be better able to facilitate the review and provision of needed services.

In the California community colleges, approximately 11,000 students were evaluated for eligibility for learning disabilities services in 1990 to 1991. Many of these students were not evaluated previously for a learning disability or for services. So the college may be the first opportunity for them to learn about learning disabilities and its broad areas of impacts. Thus, the issues raised previously about the need for a clearly described and equitable assessment model are particularly important. For those students who have encountered academic difficulties, the college provides an important source for helping them understand possible explanations for those difficulties. Jorgenson and Mellard (1988) described the results for several students who completed the colleges' eligibility assessment. For some students, the eligibility decision was less important than the understanding they gained about their academic strengths and weaknesses and possible interventions. On the other hand, the learning disability eligibility decision provided resources that they considered important to their success in college.

Financial Support. One quick test of a state's or college's commitment to serving students with disabilities is to inquire whether supplemental moneys are available for needed services. Students can inquire if the college or state has a means of reimbursing or supporting the direct excess costs associated with educating students with disabilities. Although this standard certainly isn't sufficient to judge a program's quality, the financial support provides one visible means for judging the extent to which the college or state is willing to ensure appropriate educational opportunities for those students encountering significant, chronic learning and achievement problems in post-secondary settings.

Levels of Support. The reader is possibly familiar with the legal requirements for students with disabilities established under Section 504 of the 1973 Rehabilitation Act and related federal legislation. This legislation was critical to allowing students with disabilities access to higher education. Discrimination became illegal, and the law mandated that the post-secondary settings provide access and accommodations to students who might otherwise be excluded. (See Scott [1991] for a full review of the implications of Section 504 and related legislation.) This legal directive has numerous consequences, including a provision of adjustments to class requirements (e.g., length of time for completing degree requirements, substitution of specific courses for satisfying degree requirements, and adaptation of the instructional methods to allow taped texts, text readers, and note-taking assistance). An important fact to recall is that college personnel determine these adjustments on the basis of the individual with disabilities rather than allowing these adjustments to all students with a comparable disability (e.g., all students with learning disabilities).

These provisions are examples from the federal law. Adjustments and accommodations may also be available under existing state laws and regulations. For example, in California the students with learning disabilities in community colleges are entitled to the protections and accommodations afforded under Section 504 and existing community college regulations. Additional resources might be available to students who are eligible under the regulations specific to the community colleges, because of the state's financial and legal supports to students with learning disabilities. For example, special classes are not prescribed in Section 504, but a student with learning disabilities who meets the community colleges' learning disabilities eligibility model may have such an intervention as an option. The effect is that students with a history of learning disabilities would receive the accommodations provided under Section 504, and yet if these students do not meet the community college's eligibility model, other services may or may not be available. Given the diversity and confusion associated with learning disabilities, the colleges' adoption of their own eligibility model seems reasonable. One outcome is protecting the state's interest of ensuring that the additional expenditures are reaching the intended students.

These comments about the diversity of definitions, eligibility criteria, financial support, and level of support are intended to raise the reader's awareness that a host of issues surrounds the provision of services to students with learning disabilities in post-secondary settings. Careful study and questioning are needed to ensure that the educational opportunity provided is valued and valuable to the student. An unfortunate consequence of current debates in education is that post-secondary education has been excluded from most policy debates and research initiatives at a system level. Indeed, little information would appear available to describe colleges' services accurately to students with learning disabilities (Bursuck et al., 1989). Without research, anecdotal information would seem to be the best available to assess the outcomes of services to this important population.

Summary

Community colleges provide a unique opportunity for students committed to post-secondary educational opportunities. Such features as easy access, open admissions, and lower costs make community colleges a worthwhile consideration. The diversity of the student population of the colleges also could potentially ease some hesitancy about continuing educational opportunities. The colleges include students across the widest possible age and ethnic ranges seeking their own goals, which are likely more diverse than found in a four-year college.

In the selection of a community college, however, several other attributes are important. The advocacy for students with disabilities, the curricular offerings, and the transition planning are variable across these post-secondary settings. The integration of students with disabilities and the on-campus services for students with disabilities are important considerations. If the office for student assistance is not visibly integrated into the campus, students are even less likely to be accommodated. Advocacy is very important as issues of waivers, course substitutions, and access are addressed at the college.

As suggested previously, the curricular offerings from a college should be clearly described. "Helping students realize their potential" is a laudable goal and one that most educators would agree is important. The question for the student seeking postsecondary educational opportunities is how does the college accomplish that goal for a student who presents unique instructional and curricular challenges due to his or her learning differences and resulting demands. Similarly, the curricular options must respond to the variability in the students' goals for attending a post-secondary setting (e.g., personal enrichment for an improved or different occupational status, vocational training for entry into a meaningful employment setting, and academic preparation to ensure transfer to a four-year college). These different curricular emphases would pose significant challenges on any college attempting to provide them all.

The last area of special concern is the area of transitional planning and support. The evidence is almost unequivocal that for students with learning disabilities, their community participation, uses of community resources, and vocational success are very limited. Although particular individuals might be judged successful on a variety of standards (Adelman & Vogel, 1990; Gerber & Reiff, 1991; Rogan & Hartman, 1990), these individuals are the exceptions. The clear majority of students with learning disabilities are not as successful. Thus, the options for a post-secondary setting must be carefully weighed in light of clearly defined goals and the college's impact on assisting students to achieve those goals. Transition planning seems critical to that role as a means to providing better outcomes to the students' formal educational experiences (Dalke & Franzene, 1988).

The community colleges are an important resource for students seeking the opportunities afforded from post-secondary education. The colleges provide opportunities for the student to learn to direct his or her learning and how to meet the demands of a college setting. In that setting the student can make further plans for career development and exploration that fulfill the perspective of learning as a lifelong experience.

References

Adelman, P.B., & Vogel, S.A. (1990). College graduates with learning disabilities—employment attainment and career patterns. *Learning Disability Quarterly, 13,* 154–156.

American Psychiatric Association. (1987). *Diagnostic and statistical manual of mental disorders.* (3rd ed., revised). Washington, DC: American Psychiatric Association.

Bursuck, W.D., Rose, E., Cowen, S., & Yahaya, M.A. (1989). Nationwide survey of postsecondary education services for students with learning disabilities. *Exceptional Children, 56,* 236–245.

California Association of Post-Secondary Educators of the Disabled. (1992). *Accommodating students with specific learning disabilities in post-secondary education.* Sacramento, CA: Accommodations Committee of the Division of Learning Disabilities.

Chancellor's Office. (1988). *California community colleges' directory of programs and services for adults with learning disabilities.* Sacramento, CA: California Community Colleges, Disabled Students Programs and Services.

Chancellor's Office. (1991). *Important trends for California community colleges.* Sacramento, CA: California Community Colleges, Research and Analysis Unit.

Cobb, R.M., & Crump, W.D. (1984). *Post-school status of young adults identified as learning disabled while enrolled in public schools: A comparison of those enrolled and not enrolled in learning disabilities programs.* Birmingham: University of Alabama, Department of Education. (ERIC Document Reproduction Service No. 253 029).

Dalke, C., & Franzene, J. (1988). Secondary-postsecondary collaboration: A model of shared responsibility. *Learning Disabilities Focus, 4,* 38–45.

Edgar, E. (1987). Secondary programs in special education: Are many of them justifiable? *Exceptional Children, 53,* 555–561.

Fairweather, J.S., & Shaver, D.M. (1991). Making the transition to postsecondary education and training. *Exception Children, 57,* 264–270.

Fourqurean, J.M., Meisgeier, C., Swank, P.R., & Williams, R.E. (1991). Correlates of postsecondary employment outcomes for young adults with learning disabilities. *Journal of Learning Disabilities, 24,* 400–405.

Frankenberger, W., & Fronzaglio, K. (1991). A review of states criteria and procedures for identifying children with learning disabilities. *Journal of Learning Disabilities, 24,* 495–500.

Gerber, P.J. (1981). Learning disabilities and eligibility for vocational rehabilitation services: A chronology of events. *Learning Disability Quarterly, 4,* 422–425.

Gerber, P.J., & Brown, D. (1991). Report of the pathways to employment consensus conference on employability of persons with learning disabilities. *Learning Disabilites Research and Practice, 6,* 99–103.

Gerber, P.J., & Reiff, H.B. (1991). *Speaking for themselves: Ethnographic interventions with adults with learning disabilities.* Ann Arbor, MI: The University of Michigan Press.

Haring, K.A., Lovett, D.L., & Smith, D.D. (1990). A follow-up study of recent special education graduates of learning disabilities programs. *Journal of Learning Disabilities, 23,* 108–113.

Jorgenson, M., & Mellard, D.F. (1988). *Qualitative survey of programs for students evaluated for learning disabilities.* Sacramento, CA: Chancellor's Office, Disabled Students Programs and Services, California Community Colleges.

Learning Disabilities Association. (1990). LDA position paper: Eligibility for services for persons with specific learning disabilities. *LDA Newsbrief, 25* (3), 2a–3a.

Malcolm, C.B., Polatajko, H.J., & Simons, J. (1990). A descriptive study of adults with suspected learning disabilities. *Journal of Learning Disabilities, 23,* 518–520.

Mangrum, C.T., & Strichart, S.S. (Eds.) (1988). *Peterson's colleges with programs for learning disabled students.* Princeton, NJ: Peterson's Guides.

McGuire, J.M., Norlander, K.A., & Shaw, S.F. (1990). Postsecondary education for students with learning disabilities: Forecasting challenges for the future. *Learning Disabilities Focus, 5,* 69–74.

Mellard, D.F. (1990). The eligibility process: Identifying students with learning disabilities in California's community colleges. *Learning Disabilities Focus, 5,* 75–91.

Mellard, D.F., & Deshler, D.D. (1984). Modeling the condition of learning disabilities on postsecondary populations. *Educational Psychologist, 19,* 188–197.

Mercer, C., King-Sears, P., & Mercer, A.R. (1990). Learning disabilities definitions and criteria used by state education departments. *Learning Disability Quarterly, 13,* 141–152.

Minskoff, E.H., Hawks, R., Steidle, E.F., & Hoffman, F.J. (1989). A homogeneous group of persons with learning disabilities: Adults with severe learning disabilities in vocational rehabilitation. *Journal of Learning Disabilities, 22,* 521–528.

Okolo, C.M., & Sitlington, P. (1988). The role of special education in LD adolescents' transition from school to work. *Learning Disability Quarterly, 11,* 292–306.

Prater, G., & Minner, S. (1986). Factors inhibiting the performance of learning disabled students in postsecondary settings. *Reading, Writing, and Learning Disabilities, 2,* 273–277.

Putnam, M.L. (1984). Post-secondary education for learning disabled students: A review of the literature. *Journal of College Student Personnel, 25* (1) 68–75.

Rogan, L.L., & Hartman, L.D. (1990). Adult outcome of learning disabled students 10 years after initial follow-up. *Learning Disabilities Focus, 5,* 91–102.

Rothstein, L.F. (1986). Section 504 of the Rehabilitation Act: Emerging issues for colleges and universities. *Journal of College and University Law, 13,* 229–265.

Sclafani, A.J., & Lynch, M.J. (1989). *College guide for students with learning disabilities 1988–1989.* Miller Place, NY: Laurel Publications.

Scott, S. (1991). A change in legal status: An overlooked dimension in the transition to higher education. *Journal of Learning Disabilities, 24,* 459–466.

Scuccimarra, D.J., & Speece, D.L. (1990). Employment outcomes and social integration of students with mild handicaps: The quality of life two years after high school. *Journal of Learning Disabilities, 23,* 518–520.

Shapiro, E.S., & Lentz, F.E. (1991). Vocational-technical programs: Follow-up of students with learning disabilities. *Exceptional Children, 58,* 47–59.

Siegel, S., & Gaylord-Ross, R. (1991). Factors associated with employment success among youths with learning disabilities. *Journal of Learning Disabilities, 24,* 40–47.

Sitlington, P., & Frank, A.R. (1990). Are adolescents with learning disabilities successfully crossing the bridge into adult life? *Learning Disability Quarterly, 13,* 97–111.

Valdes, K.A., Williamson, C.L., & Wagner, M.M. (1990). *The national longitudinal transition study of special education students: Statistical almanac, volume 2: Youth categorized as learning disabled.* Palo Alto, CA: SRI International.

White, W. (1985). Perspectives on the education and training of learning disabled adults. *Learning Disability Quarterly, 8,* 231–236.

Chapter 13
College and University Programming

STAN F. SHAW, ED.D.
JOAN M. MCGUIRE, PH.D.
LORING C. BRINCKERHOFF, PH.D

Major changes are occurring in regard to students with learning disabilities attending four-year, graduate, and professional schools. Although the definition of *learning disabilities* has always contained some reference to average or above-average intelligence, until recently many students and parents, as well as high school and college personnel, have not been fully cognizant of the viability of this post-secondary option. In fact, during the 1980s the number of voluntarily self-identifying college students with learning disabilities increased tenfold (*Learning Disability Update*, 1986), substantiating that at least 1.3% of college freshmen are students with learning disabilities (*Profiles of Handicapped Students in Postsecondary Education*, 1987). Henderson (1992) reported that since 1985 the percentage of first-year, fulltime college students with disabilities who indicated they had a learning disability has grown from 15% to 25%.

This growth has resulted from a number of factors affecting both secondary and post-secondary institutions.

1. P.L. 94-142, which was implemented in 1977, has required mandated special education services for recent high school graduates with learning disabilities throughout their public school experience. These students have often succeeded in school and expect that success to continue in college with the assistance of support services.

2. Emphasis on placing students with disabilities in the least restrictive environment has resulted in many students with learning disabilities taking sufficient academic course work as a prerequisite to qualify for four-year colleges.

3. More than half (50.1%) of the students with learning disabilities exiting school in 1988–1989 graduated with a diploma (*Thirteenth Annual Report to Congress*, 1991). This cohort of more than 66,000 students annually has become increasingly attractive as a viable student market to colleges' admissions offices as the number of high school graduates has plummeted in recent years.

4. Awareness of college options has resulted from the efforts of advocacy groups such as the Learning Disabilities Association (LDA) and publication of post-secondary learning disability guidebooks such as Peterson's and Lovejoy's. Students and their parents are effective advocates for program development because they know both their needs and their rights.

5. Federal regulations now require individual transition plans beginning no later than age 16 (but earlier if appropriate) [U.S. Department of Education, 1992, p. 44804]. Such plans have helped students focus on college early enough in their secondary program to take the necessary prerequisite courses for competitive four-year colleges.

6. The increasing availability of computers and other compensatory technology has helped to foster student access and independence. In particular, the advent of spelling checkers, voice-activated computers, and voice synthesizers has made it possible for students with learning disabilities to compete with their nondisabled peers.

7. Increasing numbers of high school special education programs have moved away from the remedial or content tutoring models to instruction in learning strategies, metacognition, self-advocacy, and social skills necessary for college success (Phillips, 1990; Shaw et al., 1991; Spector et al., 1991). In addition, regular classroom teachers who are working with these students in high school content classes are beginning to develop effective instructional skills with a focus on problem solving and training for independence (Decker et al., 1992).

8. Section 504 of the Rehabilitation Act of 1973 is a civil rights act providing equal access and reasonable accommodations for "otherwise qualified" college students with disabilities (Scott, 1990). In recent years, case law and decisions by the Office of Civil Rights based on Section 504 have provided the impetus for four-year colleges, graduate schools, and professional schools to revise admissions policies, provide accommodations, and develop support services (Brinckerhoff et al., 1992; Scott, 1991).

These significant events are evidence of a longitudinal process of participation in education by students with learning disabilities. In the 1970s, support services were available in most elementary schools. By the late 1970s and early 1980s, this cohort of elementary students moved up to secondary schools, encouraging the development of resource rooms and related services at the secondary schools as well. The 1980s heralded a constant increase in the number of students enrolling in post-secondary education (*Learning Disability Update*, 1986). According to data from the National Longitudinal Transition Study (Wagner, 1989), these students typically enrolled in vocational or community colleges, rather than in four-year colleges. On exiting from high school, 9.6% of youth with learning disabilities attended vocational or trade schools and 6.9% attended two-year colleges, whereas only 1.8% attended four-year colleges. It is clear, however, that as the factors described previously impact on more students, schools, and colleges, increasing percentages of students with learning disabilities will be accessing four-year schools and graduate programs.

For example, preliminary data recently gathered in Connecticut indicate that the number of self-identified students with learning disabilities in four-year colleges is greater than in two-year colleges (J. McGuire, personal communication, October 18, 1991). Information from the *Profile of Handicapped Students in Postsecondary Education* (1987) has documented the developmental progression of *all* students with disabilities accessing advanced programs. While 10.5% of college students report at least one disability, only 8.4% of graduate students and 7.3% of students in professional schools indicate a disability. Movement into postbaccalaureate programs is documented by Parks, Antonoff, Drake, Skiba, and Soberman (1987), who found that almost half of the 223 graduate and professional schools that responded to their survey offered some type of support services for these students.

As four-year colleges and universities, as well as graduate and professional schools, develop and publicize support services for students with learning disabilities, enrollment will grow throughout the 1990s despite demographic trends indicating the continual decline in the number of traditional college-age students. In addition, when these institutions clarify policies and procedures regarding admission, accommodations, and academic adjustments, students with learning disabilities will more confidently approach the challenge of acquiring an undergraduate or graduate degree (Davie, 1990).

The following sections of this chapter describe the array of support service models currently in operation and discuss the challenging issues facing four-year, graduate, and professional schools as they try to meet the needs of students with learning disabilities within the context of Section 504.

Learning Disability Support Service Models

Many colleges and universities are in the process of planning, developing, or refining support services for college students with learning disabilities. Mangrum and Strichart (1988) report that over 950 two- and four-year colleges and universities throughout the United States are now offering support services specifically for students with learning disabilities. With appropriate support services, these students seem to have a more successful retention and graduation rate than many other students (American College Testing, 1988; McGuire et al., 1989; McGuire et al., 1991). In order to effectively serve the increasing number of students with learning disabilities enrolling in post-secondary institutions, colleges and universities need to establish effective procedures for communication and coordination of effort among existing academic and service departments (Brinckerhoff, 1991; Vogel, 1982). It is imperative that learning-disability support services are not viewed as an "add-on" or as a duplication of existing campus services, but as an integral part of the academic support

network available to students (Brinckerhoff et al., 1993).

Determining Types of Services

It is important to clarify the terminology used to describe the range and scope of support services available to students with learning disabilities. *Support services* are typically coordinated by a part-time or full-time staff member who is responsible for providing students with learning disabilities a variety of "academic adjustments" that are mandated under Section 504 of the Rehabilitation Act of 1973. Instructional modifications often include test-taking modifications, readers, notetakers, use of taperecorded textbooks, and access to adaptive technology. The individual who provides these core supports is often instrumental in linking students with learning disabilities with other support services on campus (e.g., writing lab, math tutorial, academic development center, and so forth).

In contrast, a *learning disability program* is characterized by a variety of functions and typically includes a full-time coordinator or director with additional staff who deliver a comprehensive menu of support services, coordinate diagnostic services, provide specialized tutorial support, screen admissions applicants, assist students in arranging for priority registration, and lead learning-disability support groups. An additional fee may accompany this type of program. Service providers and higher education administrators need to think carefully before deciding whether to offer a learning-disabilities program since these two words imply a multitude of expectations from students and their parents regarding the services to be offered. Some college students with learning disabilities will perform best in a setting where they can negotiate the system independently with minimum support. For these students a support-services model might be the best match. For students who need intensive support and frequent monitoring, a learning disability program may be more suitable.

Continuum of Services

Regardless of which service-delivery model is adapted, each institution should provide support services that will comply with Section 504 and ultimately increase student independence and decision-making. A continuum highlighting the various forms of post-secondary learning-disability support services (McGuire & Shaw, 1989) should help administrators and learning-disability service providers in conceptualizing the "best fit" for services on their campus (Figure 13-1).

1	2	3	4	5
No Services Available	**Decentralized and Limited Services**	**Loosely Coordinated Services**	**Centrally Coordinated Services**	**Data-Based Services**
• Meets minimal requirements under Section 504	• No formal contact person • Limited services • Few established policies • Students dependent on sympathetic faculty	• Contact person available • Generic support services available • Peer tutors available to help at-risk students • Students referred to other on-campus resources • Services available only during the academic year	• Full-time learning disability coordinator • Services often housed in disability student services office • Accommodations provided for testing and coursework • Established policies on admissions and service delivery • Strong emphasis on student self-advocacy • Peer support groups • Specially trained tutors may be available • Student required to provide documentation of learning disability • Services available throughout the year	• Full-time learning disability director • Learning disability assistant coordinator • Full range of accommodations provided • Development of Individualized Semester Plans • Tutoring available from trained staff and graduate-level interns • Data-based contact records and service use profiles generated for annual report

Figure 13-1. Continuum of postsecondary LD support services. Adapted from *Resource Guide of Support Services for Students with Learning Disabilities in Connecticut Colleges and Universities*, edited by J. M. McGuire and S. F. Shaw, 1989. Storrs: A. J. Pappanikou Center on Special Education and Rehabilitation: A University Affiliated Program, University of Connecticut. Reprinted with permission.

The first category, *no services available,* is certainly a possibility, but most college and university administrators recognize that some minimal services are required to meet the legal mandates under Section 504 (Brinckerhoff, 1986). The second level of support is *decentralized and limited.* Support services in this category are characterized as lacking any formal learning-disabilities contact person and having few established policies for serving students with learning disabilities. Compliance with Section 504 is often handled by an individual who has no direct contact with students or with adjunct support staff. The limited services that may be offered are often those services available to all students on campus in need of academic assistance. These students are often dependent on availability of sympathetic faculty or staff.

The third level, *loosely coordinated services,* includes a contact person who often has no specific training in the area of learning disabilities but is interested in helping these students succeed at the institution. These services may be found in the academic development center, where emphasis is placed on helping all students who are at risk for failure. Typically, peer tutors are available to work with these students, and computer lab assistance may be provided. The individual directing these services needs to be a liaison with faculty and knowledgeable about other campus and community resources. These services are often available only during the academic year.

The fourth level, *centrally coordinated services,* is typically offered through the disabled student services office where learning-disability services are administered by a full- or part-time coordinator who has some training in learning disabilities. The coordinator can assist students with learning disabilities with a variety of functions, including ordering taped textbooks, arranging for testing accommodations, supporting student requests for course substitutions, and linking students to academic, peer, or personal counselors. Other services available may include priority registration and priority housing assignments, special provisions for a reduced course load, and written policies on admissions. Typically, there is a strong emphasis on teaching students to self-advocate with professors and support staff. Professional staff can also facilitate peer support groups. Specialized tutorial support offered by trained staff or graduate student interns is sometimes beneficial. If there is no previous history of a learning disability, then a diagnostic in-house testing component is frequently provided in this level of service. Centrally coordinated offices are usually staffed throughout the year.

The final category, *data-based services,* involves a full-time director with advanced training and experience in learning disabilities. The director usually has a variety of other support staff, including a full-time assistant coordinator. These individuals are responsible for providing all the services noted under the previous category as well as developing individualized semester plans (ISP) based on diagnostic testing, and serving as a liaison with other staff on campus. Typically, decision making in these learning disability programs is data-based. Contact records are maintained and service use profiles are generated for an annual report.

Regardless of what support model is ultimately adopted, the goals and scope of the services provided should be subject to annual review. Feedback should be solicited from students, ancillary support staff, and faculty concerning the quality of the services offered. This input can help to shape future program development. If the level of service is not meeting the present need, it may be appropriate to consider other options on the service-delivery continuum.

Current Issues on Service Delivery

Given the present climate of fiscal austerity in higher education, colleges and universities may want to develop a core of support services for students with learning disabilities and not attempt a comprehensive program until long-term institutional support is ensured. One cost-effective approach that higher education administrators have found successful is to designate a staff person who has already shown an interest in learning disabilities as the campus contact person for students with learning disabilities. Individuals who are given the responsibility for providing learning-disability support services often come from a variety of different fields, including psychology, special education, counseling, social work, curriculum and instruction, rehabilitation, and allied health areas. Frequently, their job duties are expanded to encompass college students with learning disabilities. Within a year or two, part-time duties often evolve into full-time "learning specialist" positions. During the period of rapid growth of learning disability support services, the newly appointed learning specialist often looks for additional resources and contact persons who can assist in the development and refinement of the service delivery model.

The literature in this area is still sparse, and few resource persons are available to provide the necessary technical assistance. Consequently, developing post-secondary learning disabilities services can be a challenging opportunity as well as a lonely and frustrating undertaking. Sandperl (1990) pointed out that in the future, programs will need to be more thorough in the range of services they provide to these students. However, even in times of budgetary crisis, some of our best guides in the development of learning disability services and programs may be the consumers who use these services. We must look to them for further input on how to refine these services so that they can succeed.

Challenges Facing Colleges and Universities

P.L. 94-142 was recently amended (P.L. 101-476) as the Individuals with Disabilities Education Act. It requires elementary and secondary schools to provide a free, appropriate, public education to all eligible students according to clearly stated principles and a detailed framework for delivery (Rothstein, 1990). In contrast, Section 504 requires colleges and universities to ensure nondiscrimination on the basis of disability. The regulations accompanying Section 504 provide no detailed framework for post-secondary institutions to follow, thus allowing for a broad range of individual interpretation of key constructs such as "substantially limits," "otherwise qualified" and "reasonable accommodations." This lack of regulatory specificity contributes to a number of challenging issues that post-secondary administrators and service providers will continue to grapple with until clear legal precedent or best practice is established. Included in these challenges are the following: (1) determining "otherwise qualified" applicants with learning disabilities who are seeking admission to undergraduate and graduate programs; (2) judging what constitutes acceptable documentation to support a student's eligibility under Section 504; and (3) deciding on reasonable accommodations and appropriate academic adjustments such as course substitutions or waivers while weighing the essential requirements of a program.

Admissions

In their consideration of access to highly selective post-secondary institutions, Shaywitz and Shaw (1988) summarized the admissions quandary in a way that can be generalized across settings: "Is the presence of a learning disability compatible with pursuit of scholarship . . . ?" (p. 81). Scott (1990) addressed this concern from the perspective of applying the construct "otherwise qualified." One of the most provocative dilemmas in rendering admission decisions centers on which criteria should be considered, since grade-point average (GPA) and performance on standardized admissions tests have the potential to discriminate against the applicant with a learning disability (Scott, 1990).

Most four-year undergraduate and graduate programs require standardized test scores on the Scholastic Aptitude Test (SAT), the American College Testing (ACT) Program, the Graduate Record Exam (GRE), the Law School Admission Test (LSAT), or the Medical College Aptitude Test (MCAT). Yet, there is limited research on the predictive validity of these tests for students with disabilities.

In order to better understand the relationship between selected variables and future first-year college performance as indicated by GPA, Braun, Ragosta, and Kaplan (1986) conducted research on the predictive value of SAT scores, high school grades, and combined scores and grades. Results indicated that the academic performance of students with learning disabilities was overpredicted when only SAT scores were used. In other words, the grades received by these students were lower than what would be predicted for nonhandicapped peers based on SAT scores alone. A combination of SAT scores and high school GPA yielded better predictions, but the authors advised caution in interpreting these overall results due to regression toward the mean because of sample characteristics.

Regulations for Section 504 indicate that post-secondary institutions are not required to alter academic and technical standards substantially when considering whether an applicant is "otherwise qualified." Balancing these two constructs places admissions personnel in the difficult position of rendering judgments about acceptance without clear and reliable standards to guide them. Section 504 also requires that post-secondary institutions conduct periodic validity studies to determine the correlation between criteria used for admission decisions (e.g., standardized test scores, academic performance) and subsequent student performance. Yet, evidence indicates that admission personnel do not conduct these studies (Spillane et al., 1992). This suggests that unbiased decision-making in the admission process may be compromised by virtue of depending on traditional criteria, which

may not be the most valid predictors for students with learning disabilities.

Alternative factors such as unique strengths and talents, personal qualities, persistence, and motivation are frequently cited as important variables for consideration (Mangrum & Strichart, 1988; Scheiber & Talpers, 1987), yet how to measure and weight these criteria when considering an applicant is unclear. Ensuring nondiscrimination on the basis of a learning disability in light of these challenges will remain problematic until more research is conducted to verify alternative approaches that incorporate nonstandard criteria.

Documentation to Determine Eligibility

On admission, a student with a documented learning disability is eligible for protection under Section 504 if that student (1) has a physical or mental impairment that substantially limits one or more major life functions; (2) has a history of such impairment; or (3) is regarded as having such an impairment. It is incumbent on the student to self-identify, since colleges and universities are prohibited from any preadmission inquiry about a disability (Rothstein, 1986). On self-identification, it is reasonable for college personnel to require documentation of the specific learning disability, not only for verification of this "hidden handicap" but also for use in determining appropriate accommodations and academic adjustments. Yet, the regulations for Section 504 do not address the question of what constitutes reliable and valid documentation.

Rothstein (1986) stated that determination of the existence of a learning disability under P.L. 94-142 while a student was in public school would likely carry substantial weight. Documentation such as an individualized educational program (IEP) or school records such as minutes from placement team meetings, which substantiate a formal diagnosis of a specific learning disability, would unequivocally support a history of a disability. Yet, at the elementary and secondary levels, there is evidence that inconsistent and indefensible criteria are used for the purpose of identification (Ysseldyke et al., 1983). Furthermore, the use of outdated assessment data for rendering individual judgments about appropriate accommodations have questionable relevance. The issue of the validity of documentation based on diagnosis of a learning disability for previously unidentified adults is fraught with measurement problems, including the absence of norms based on an adult population and the lack of adequate test reliability and validity. Because the match between the nature of the disability and specific accommodations is critical, adequate documentation is paramount. Brinckerhoff et al. (1992) pointed out that blanket accommodations do little to build on students' strengths and do not ultimately equip them to deal with challenges after graduation.

The issue of acceptable documentation becomes further clouded in instances where students have been diagnosed by private consultants, psychologists, or individuals with questionable credentials. Given the lack of consensus in the field about the definition of a learning disability, opportunities for abuse of the label and misdiagnosis are rampant. There are a number of controversial theories and therapies associated with the diagnosis of a learning disability, including tinted lenses, orthomolecular interventions, visual training, and cerebral-vestibular dysfunction (Rooney, 1991). Whether a diagnosis based on any of these treatment modalities constitutes valid evidence to ensure protections under Section 504 remains open to interpretation.

Reasonable Accommodations and Academic Adjustments

Otherwise qualified undergraduate and graduate students with learning disabilities must be assured of equal educational opportunity that includes reasonable accommodations and academic adjustments. Section 504 regulations specify examples of aca-

demic adjustments such as a reduced course load, extended time for completion of degree requirements, and course substitutions (Section 104.44). Use of auxiliary aids and modifications in course examinations (e.g., extended time, alternate format) are also stipulated in the regulations. Yet given heterogeneity of the population, each request should be handled on an individual basis, and therein lies the challenge of interpretation.

Emerging case law provides some guidance for post-secondary learning disability service providers as to operationalizing the term "reasonable." In the *Campbell A. Dinsmore v. Charles C. Pugh and Regents of the University of California* (1990) civil suit, which was settled outside of court, the dyslexic plaintiff (student) had been denied additional time on an examination because the faculty member flatly rejected his request. As a result of the settlement, the university was required to develop a policy and procedures for considering requests for accommodations, and the professor was required to pay monetary damages (Brinckerhoff et al., 1993).

The issue of modifying the format of a test as a reasonable accommodation was addressed in *Wynne v. Tufts University School of Medicine* (1990). The medical student maintained that his specific learning disability adversely affected his ability to take multiple-choice examinations and requested an alternate test format (oral), which was refused (Heyward et al., 1991). Tufts argued that test format constituted an educational, not judicial, decision and that the skill of passing a multiple-choice exam was essential to the job of a physician. The court ruled that post-secondary institutions have specific obligations in instances of denying a requested accommodation. Excerpts from the ruling warrant serious consideration on the part of college and university personnel:

> There is a real obligation on the academic institution to seek suitable means of reasonably accommodating a disabled person and *to submit a factual record indicating that it con-*

scientiously carried out this statutory obligation [emphasis added].

The institution must submit undisputed facts demonstrating that the relevant officials within the institution considered alternative means, their feasibility, cost and effect on the academic program, and came to a rationally justifiable conclusion that the available alternatives would result either in lowering academic standards or requiring substantial program alterations. (Heyward et al., 1991, p. 6)

When determining whether a request for an academic adjustment such as a course substitution is valid, post-secondary personnel have limited research to guide them in decision-making. These requests frequently involve the area of foreign language, where a substantial number of students with learning disabilities have difficulty (Ganschow et al., 1989). In general, blanket substitutions are not recommended, given the importance of establishing a case based on the student's strengths and weaknesses as well as the context in which the student is functioning (Lerner et al., 1991). However, it appears that there is great variability in policy, which can create confusion on the part of students and their advisors (Ganschow et al., 1989; Goodman et al., 1990) as well as the potential for discrimination.

Legal precedent regarding what constitutes essential requirements of a specific program, reasonable accommodations, and evidence that a student with a disability is "otherwise qualified" is provided in the Supreme Court's ruling in *Southeastern Community College v. Davis* (1979). In spite of the disability, an "otherwise qualified" student with a disability must be able to meet all of a program's requirements given the provision of reasonable accommodations that do not fundamentally compromise the essential aspects of a program.

It is clear, however, that interpretation of these constructs has the potential for far-reaching implications, especially in light of the Americans with Disabilities Act of 1990, which will extend protections into the workplace. As students with specific learning disabilities graduate and seek licensure in fields such as teaching, law, and the medical and health-related professions, challenges now facing post-secondary learning disability service providers will require more precise determinations.

Summary

In their recent ethnographic research on adults with learning disabilities, Gerber and Reiff (1991) found that successful adjustment to the challenges of adult living is possible despite the disability. The concepts of giftedness, creativity, and learning disabilities are not mutually exclusive and there are references in the literature (Aaron et al., 1988) to individuals such as Thomas Edison and Hans Christian Anderson who may very well have experienced significant reading disabilities. By definition, a learning disability exists with accompanying average to above-average aptitude or intelligence and the potential for achievement (Lerner, 1988). Admittedly, learning disabilities are divergent in type and degree, as manifested in a heterogeneous distribution. Realistic goals must be fashioned that take into account a student's strengths and weaknesses. However, as adults with learning disabilities continue their quest for post-secondary education and employment opportunities, it is important to bear in mind the potential contributions these individuals can and will make to society. Given issues such as reasonable accommodations (e.g., use of adaptive technology), adjustments (e.g., job restructuring), and nondiscrimination on the basis of the specific learning disability, the next decade may very well herald the realization of civil rights for these individuals based not only on the results of best practice but also unquestionably on legal precedents emerging from litigation.

References

Aaron, P. G., Phillips, S., & Larsen, S. (1988). Specific reading disability in historically famous persons. *Journal of Learning Disabilities, 21* (9), 523–538, 545.

American College Testing. (1988). *ACT high school report.* Iowa City, IA: Author.

Braun, H., Ragosta, M., & Kaplan, B. (1986). *The predictive validity of the Scholastic Aptitude Test for disabled students.* Princeton, NJ: Educational Testing Service.

Brinckerhoff, L. C. (1986). Accommodations for college students with learning disabilities: The law and its implementation. In *Support services for LD students in postsecondary education: A compendium of readings, Vol. 1* (pp. 1–7). Columbus, OH: Association on Handicapped Student Service Programs in Postsecondary Education.

Brinckerhoff, L. C. (1991). Establishing learning disability support services with minimal resources. *Journal of Postsecondary Education and Disability, 9,* 184–196.

Brinckerhoff, L. C., Shaw, S. F., & McGuire, J. M. (1992). Promoting access, accommodations, and independence for college students with learning disabilities. *Journal of Learning Disabilities, 25* (7), 417–429.

Brinckerhoff, L. C., Shaw, S. F., & McGuire, J. M. (1993). *Promoting postsecondary education for students with learning disabilities: A handbook for practitioners.* Austin, TX: PRO-ED.

Campbell A. Dinsmore v. Charles C. Pugh and the Regents of the University of California. Berkeley (N.D. Cal., Sept. 23, 1990).

Davie, A. (1990, Spring). Access for students with learning disabilities to graduate and professional schools: A cautious beginning. *Latest Developments,* pp. 2–4.

Decker, K., Spector, S., & Shaw, S. F. (1992). Teaching independence and responsibility to high school students with mild handicaps: The role of the regular classroom teacher. *The Clearing House, 65* (5), 280–284.

Ganschow, L., Meyer, B., & Roeger, K. (1989). Foreign language policies and procedures for students with specific learning disabilities. *Learning Disabilities Focus, 5* (1), 50–58.

Gerber, P. J., & Reiff, H. B. (1991). *Speaking for themselves: Ethnographic interventions with adults with learning disabilities.* Ann Arbor, MI: The University of Michigan Press.

Goodman, J. F., Freed, B., & McManus, W. J. (1990). Determining exemptions from foreign language requirements: Use of the Modern Language Aptitude Test. *Contemporary Educational Psychology, 15,* 131–141.

Henderson, C. (Ed.). (1992). *College freshmen with disabilities: A statistical profile.* Washington, DC: American Council on Education.

Heyward, S., Lawton, D., & Associates. (Eds.). (1991). *Wynne v. Tufts University: The contro-versy continues. Disability Accommodation Digest, 1* (2), 6. Columbus, OH: Association on Handicapped Student Service Programs in Postsecondary Education.

Learning Disability Update. (1986, May). Information from HEATH, p. 3.

Lerner, J. (1988). *Learning disabilities: Theories, diagnoses, and teaching strategies.* (5th ed.). Boston: Houghton Mifflin.

Lerner, J. W., Ganschow, L., & Sparks, R. (1991). Critical issues in learning disabilities: Foreign language learning. *Learning Disabilities Research and Practice, 6,* 50–53.

Mangrum, C., & Strichart, S. (1988). *College and the learning disabled student.* (2nd ed.). Orlando, FL: Grune & Stratton.

McGuire, J. M., Harris, M. W., & Bieber, N. (1989). Evaluating college programs for learning disabled college students: An approach for adaptation. In *Support services for LD students in postsecondary education: A compendium of readings, Vol. II* (pp. 131–138). (Also in ERIC Document Reproduction Service ED 322 675).

McGuire, J. M., Litt, A. V., & Shaw, S. F. (1991). *Moving beyond the basics in postsecondary learning disability programming: A case study.* Unpublished manuscript, The University of Connecticut, Postsecondary Learning Disabilities Unit, A. J. Pappanikou Center on Special Education and Rehabilitation: A University Affiliated Program, Storrs.

McGuire, J. M., & Shaw, S. F. (Eds.). (1989). *Resource guide of support services for students with learning disabilities in Connecticut colleges and universities.* Storrs: The University of Connecticut.

Parks, A. W., Antonoff, S., Drake, C., Skiba, W. F., & Soberman, J. (1987). A survey of programs and services for learning disabled students in graduate and professional schools. *Journal of Learning Disabilities, 20,* 181–187.

Phillips, P. (1990). A self-advocacy plan for high school students with learning disabilities: A comparative case study analysis of students', teachers', and parents' perceptions of program effectiveness. *Journal of Learning Disabilities, 23,* 466–471.

Profiles of Handicapped Students in Postsecondary Education. (1987). Washington, DC: U.S. Department of Education, National Center for Education Statistics.

Rooney, K. J. (1991). Controversial therapies: A review and critique. *Intervention in School and Clinic, 26* (3), 134–142.

Rothstein, L. F. (1986). Section 504 of the Rehabilitation Act: Emerging issues for colleges and universities. *Journal of College and University Law, 13,* 229–265

Rothstein, L. F. (1990). *Special education law.* New York: Longman.

Sandperl, M. (1990). Towards a comprehensive model of learning disabilities service delivery. In *The next step: An invitational symposium on learning disabilities in selective colleges proceedings* (pp. 181–191). Cambridge, MA: Harvard University Press.

Scheiber, B., & Talpers, J. (1987). *Unlocking potential: College and other choices for learning disabled people.* Bethesda, MD: Adler and Adler, Inc.

Scott, S. S. (1990). Coming to terms with the "otherwise qualified" student with a learning disability. *Journal of Learning Disabilities, 23,* 398–405.

Scott, S. S. (1991). A change in legal status: An overlooked transition to higher education. *Journal of Learning Disabilities, 24,* 459–466.

Shaw, S. F., Brinckerhoff, L. C., Kistler, J. K., & McGuire, J. M. (1991). Preparing students with learning disabilities for postsecondary education: Issues and future needs. *Learning Disabilities, 2,* 21–26.

Shaywitz, S. E., & Shaw, R. (1988). The admissions process: An approach to selecting learning disabled students at the most selective colleges. *Learning Disabilities Focus, 3* (2), 81–86.

Southeastern Community College v. Davis, 422 U.S. 397 (1979).

Spector, S., Decker, K., & Shaw, S. F. (1991). Independence and responsibility: An LD resource room at South Windsor High School. *Intervention in School and Clinic, 26,* 159–167.

Spillane, S. A., McGuire, J. M., & Norlander, K. A. (1992). Undergraduate admission policies, practices, and procedures for applicants with learning disabilities. *Journal of Learning Disabilities, 25,* 665–670, 677.

Thirteenth Annual Report to Congress on the Implementation of the Education of the Handicapped Act. (1991). Washington, DC: U.S. Department of Education.

U.S. Department of Education. (1992). Individuals with Disabilities Act (IDEA): Rules and regulations. *Federal Register, 57* (189), 44794–44852.

Vogel, S. A. (1982). On developing LD college programs. *Journal of Learning Disabilities, 15* (9), 518–528.

Wagner, M. (1989). *Youth with disabilities during transition: An overview of descriptive findings from the National Longitudinal Transition Study.* Menlo Park, CA: SRI International.

Wynne v. Tufts University School of Medicine, 89-1670 (1st Circuit, 1990).

Ysseldyke, J. E., Thurlow, M. L., Graden, J. L., Wesson, C., Deno, S. L., & Algozzine, B. (1983). Generalizations from five years of research on assessment and decision making. *Exceptional Education Quarterly, 4,* 75–93.

Chapter 14

Assistive Technology for Adults with Learning Disabilities: A Rationale for Use

MARSHALL H. RASKIND, PH.D.

Technology means change. It has changed the way we travel, the way we communicate, the way we work, and the way we play. It has enabled us to explore space, promote health, and even sustain life. Although technology has significantly changed the lives of most people, perhaps the greatest changes—and the greatest benefits—have been realized by persons with disabilities. Technology has enabled paralyzed individuals to gain mobility through electronically controlled wheelchairs, people who are blind to read through optical character recognition systems, persons with hearing impairments to hear with hearing aids, and those who are non-speaking to talk through speech synthesizers.

Realization of how technology can improve the quality of life of persons with disabilities has prompted the development of a subfield of disabilities called *assistive technology* and has given rise to numerous assistive technology publications, conferences, centers, and products. According to the Technology-Related Assistance Act of 1988 (P.L. 100-407), an *assistive technology device* refers to "any item, piece of equipment, or product system, whether acquired commercially off-the-shelf, modified, or customized, that is used to increase, maintain or improve the functional capabilities of individuals

with disabilities." For purposes of this chapter, assistive technology will be further delineated as any technology that enables an adult with a learning disability to compensate for specific deficits. In some instances the technology may assist, augment, or supplement task performance in a given area of disability, whereas in others it may be used to circumvent or "by-pass" specific deficits entirely. Assistive technology is not intended to "cure," "fix," or remediate learning disabilities, nor is it intended to teach or instruct (as is computer-aided instruction, CAI). Furthermore, it strives to accentuate strengths rather than weaknesses, to enable expression of abilities at a level commensurate with intelligence, and, ultimately, to enhance the quality of life of persons with learning disabilities.

Although assistive technology has gained considerable attention in regard to persons with visual, mobility, and communication impairments, assistive technology for persons with learning disabilities has received little attention. At the writing of this paper there are no articles devoted to assistive technology in the leading refereed learning disability journals (to be differentiated from literature dealing with computers as instructional/remedial tools; e.g., Chiang, 1986; Jones, Torgesen & Sexton, 1987), no texts on the subject, no centers focusing on learning disabilities and assistive technology, few presentations on the subject at learning disability conferences, and only one product currently on the market (a screen-reading/speech-synthesis system) specifically designed for persons with learning disabilities. Furthermore, although technology for persons with learning disabilities has been mentioned in learning disability literature (e.g., Gray, 1981; Vogel, 1987), as well as in sources "outside" the field of learning disabilities (e.g., Enders & Hall, 1990; Green & Brightman, 1990), discussions are generally brief or limited in scope.

Assistive technology is a viable area of study that unfortunately has been neglected at the expense of persons with learning disabilities. Why then is it important? Why should any effort, time, or money be directed toward this area? This chapter will be directed to these very questions and will present a rationale for the use of assistive technology by persons with learning disabilities.

Overview of Assistive Technology for Adults with Learning Disabilities

In order to develop a rationale for the use of assistive technology by persons with learning disabilities, it is imperative to first have knowledge of available technologies. This section will provide a brief description of several technologies that may be helpful in assisting adults with learning disabilities compensate for their difficulties in such areas as reading, writing, math, organization, listening, and memory. (For a more detailed discussion of these technologies, see Raskind & Scott, 1993). Difficulties in these areas have been described frequently in learning disability literature (e.g., Buchanan

Portions of the "Overview" section are drawn from Raskind, M. H., & Scott, N. G. (1993). Technology for postsecondary students with learning disabilities. In S. A. Vogel & P. B. Adelman (Eds.), *Success for college students with learning disabilities* (pp 240–279). New York: Springer-Verlag.

& Wolf, 1986; Hoffman et al., 1987; Johnson & Blalock, 1987). Although this overview is not intended to be all-inclusive, it is hoped that it will provide the reader with a sampling of the more significant assistive technologies for adults with learning disabilities that have emerged over the past decade, as well as provide a "spring board" from which to identify other potentially beneficial technologies. Not all the technologies discussed will be appropriate for all adults who are learning disabled. Adults with learning disabilities comprise a heterogeneous group, each person having a unique profile of strengths, weaknesses, interests, and experiences. Therefore, a technology that might be a blessing for one person could spell disaster for another. Similarly, a technology that may be appropriate in one context may be inappropriate in another. It is of paramount importance that specific technologies be chosen relative to the individual, the function to be performed, and the context of interaction (see Raskind & Scott, 1993).

Word Processing

A word processor is a computer-based writing system, which, unlike conventional methods of writing with pencil and paper or typewriter, enables the user to write without having to be overly concerned about making errors, as the text first appears on the computer screen before it is printed out on paper and thus can be easily corrected. Omitted words may be added, inappropriate words or blocks of text deleted, sentences or paragraphs moved, and spelling and punctuation corrected. In addition, specified text is easily "bolded" (highlighted), underlined, or centered. The "freedom to make errors" and easily alter and manipulate text may serve to release persons with written language deficits from the "mechanical" aspects of writing and enable them to redirect their efforts toward the "meaning" of their written communication, as well as to help reduce the anxiety or fear associated with writing. Word processors are available as personal computer (PC)–based systems, which consist of a computer, keyboard, monitor, word-processing software program, and optional printer, as a self-contained "stand-alone" devices that do only word processing.

Spell-Checking

Spell-checkers are available as part of word-processing programs (or as "add on" software) and as battery-operated stand-alone devices in desktop and pocket sizes. Word-processing–based programs match the words in a document against words in the spell-checker's dictionary to verify spelling. If a match is not found, the user is alerted by a visual or auditory cue (e.g., the word might be highlighted on the screen). Generally, when spell-checkers find a misspelled word, they present the user with a list of words from which to choose the correctly spelled word. The user selects the correct word and the computer automatically corrects the misspelled word in the text.

On stand-alone spell-checkers, the user enters a word (via a small keyboard) the way he or she thinks it is spelled. The more basic units will simply verify and correct spelling on a liquid crystal display (LCD). More sophisticated devices also include a dictionary for access to word definitions and a thesaurus for synonyms. Some of these spell-checkers are equipped with speech synthesizers, so the user can hear as well as see the word in question.

Proofreading Programs

Proofreading software programs work in conjunction with word processors. They scan documents and alert the user to probable errors in punctuation (e.g, missing question marks), grammar (e.g., subject–verb agreement), word usage (e.g, homonyms), structure (e.g, transition words), spelling, style (e.g., trite words), and capitalization (e.g., "i"). Most of these programs can be used either to mark probable errors or mark the error along with a commentary (e.g., "Be sure you are using 'is' with a singular subject."). Once probable errors have been flagged, the document may be edited from within the proofreading program.

Proofreading programs are not completely accurate and on the average pick up only about 25% of the grammatical errors and 80% of the "objectionable phrases" in a document (Frankel, 1990). They may also make incorrect suggestions, prompting the user to correct parts of writing that are not really incorrect. Furthermore, such programs may be demeaning and demoralizing, in that they criticize the user's writing and may contribute to his or her preexisting feelings of incompetence and negative self-image as a writer.

Outlining/"Brain Storming"

Outlining programs for use on personal or laptop computers enable the user to approach writing tasks by "dumping" information in an unstructured manner ("holistic" as opposed to "linear")—information that subsequently can be placed into appropriate categories and ordered more easily. This approach may be particularly helpful to those individuals who have difficulty getting that first word or sentence down on paper, as well as later organizing, categorizing, and sequencing what has been generated.

The user types in any idea or thought on a specified topic without regard to overall organization. The outlining program automatically creates the Roman numerals for "major headings" and letters and Arabic numbers for "subordinate headings" through the use of a few simple keyboard commands. There is no need for preoccupation with order, levels of importance, or categories, because text can be easily moved at a later time. After basic ideas have been written down, related ideas and thoughts can be grouped together as major headings or categories. Ideas that fall under any major heading can be easily reduced to any level of subordinate heading.

If the user determines at a later time that an idea does not belong under a certain heading, it can be easily moved within the outline—as many times as may be necessary. Roman numerals, letters, and Arabic numbers designated for specific headings will be automatically reorganized by the program. There is another advantage to outlining programs in that they enable the user to limit what is viewed on the computer screen to only the major headings and thus facilitate an overview of what has been generated, without the distraction of details. Alternately, it is possible to select only one heading and view all information under it for a detailed analysis. In other words, outlining programs allow the user to "collapse" all subordinate headings under the major headings or to "expand" any particular heading in order to display all subordinate headings and details. In this way, the user has the option of either seeing the "forest" or the "trees."

Abbreviation Expanders

Abbreviation expansion programs allow users to create their own abbreviations for frequently used words, phrases, or standard pieces of text. When used in conjunction with word-processing programs, these programs save keystrokes and ultimately the amount of time it takes to prepare written documents. This is an important factor considering that some adults with learning disabilities may take longer to complete tasks than their nondisabled peers (Blalock & Johnson, 1987). Abbreviations are expanded by simply typing the abbreviation and pressing the spacebar on the keyboard (e.g., "la" to "Los Angeles"). Abbreviation expansion programs are "memory resident" and operate simultaneously with the word-processing program. Abbreviations are easily recorded by pressing a predetermined "hot key" and executing a few simple commands, and they may be saved from one writing session to the next.

Speech Recognition

Speech recognition systems operate in conjunction with personal computers (and specific laptops) and consist of speech recognition hardware (internal board), software, headphones, and a microphone. These systems enable the user to operate the computer by speech. Such a strategy may be particularly helpful for those adults whose oral language exceeds their written language abilities. When used in conjunction with word processors, sophisticated systems (e.g., DragonDictate) enable the user to dictate to the computer at 40 to 70 words per minute (depending on the speed of the particular computer in which the system is installed) and the system converts oral language to written text. These systems automatically learn the phonetic characteristics of each person's voice while that person dictates to the system.

The user dictates through a microphone with a calculated pause (at least $\frac{1}{10}$ second) between words. The word that the system "thinks" the person has spoken is placed on the screen. If the word is incorrect, the user can choose the correct word from a menu/list of "similar sounding" words that also appear on the screen. Similarly, all keyboard editing and control commands (e.g., "delete word") can be controlled through speech.

Speech Synthesis/Screen Review

Speech synthesis refers to a "synthetic" or computerized voice output system usually consisting of an internal board or external hardware device. In conjunction with "screen reading" software, a speech synthesizer will read back text displayed on a computer screen so that the user can hear as well as see the text. Depending on the specific system, text can be read back a letter, word, line, sentence, paragraph, or "screen" at a time. The speed, pitch, and tone of voice can generally be set to accommodate individual preferences. Voice quality between speech synthesizers varies considerably, from more "human" to more "mechanical" sounding, as does pronunciation accuracy and intelligibility.

Speech synthesis/screen review systems can be used to review text on a computer screen that has been written by the user, as well as to review materials generated by others, including software tutorials, on-line help systems, letters, reports, and "books on disk." The ability to hear what has been written (in some cases in addition to seeing it and in others in lieu of seeing it) may help alert the user to errors in grammar or punctuation, as well as to the "semantic integrity" of a document. This may be especially useful to those persons with learning disabilities who have oral language abilities superior to their written language abilities.

Optical Character Recognition Systems/Speech Synthesis

Optical character recognition (OCR) systems provide a means by which to directly input text/printed material (e.g., a page in a book, a letter) into a computer. Text is input by using either a hand-held scanner that the user moves across (or down, depending on the particular system) a page of text or a full-page scanner, on which a page of text is placed face down. Once the text has been scanned into the computer, it can then be read back to the user by means of speech synthesizer, thus creating what might be thought of as a "reading machine." The user is able to access print by hearing as well as seeing text.

OCR systems are available as stand-alone or PC-based systems. Stand-alone systems have all components built into one device, including the scanner, OCR software/hardware, and speech synthesizer. The PC-based system consists of a number of components that are hooked up to a PC, including a full-page (desktop) or hand-held scanner, an OCR board and/or software, and a speech synthesizer. Automatic document feeders are now available for some systems.

Personal Data Managers

Personal data managers allow the user to store and retrieve vast amounts of personal information easily and are available as computer software programs or as self-contained hand-held units. Data are input and retrieved via a keyboard/keypad and shown on a computer monitor or LCD display. Personal data managers vary considerably, having numerous capabilities and offering a number of diverse combinations of functions. Typically, features include monthly calendars, daily and weekly planners, clocks/alarms, memo files, "to do lists," name/address books, telephone directories (some with electronic dialers), and bankbooks/check registers/ "money managers." Such features may be quite useful to an adult with learning disabilities who has organizational and/or memory difficulties.

Free-Form Databases

Free-form databases are software programs that might be thought of as "computerized Post-It" note systems. They can be used independently, or as memory resident programs which can be activated while in a word processor or other programs by simply pressing a predetermined "hot key." The user can create notes of any length and on any subject, in much the same way a person uses Post-It notes, a notepad, or scraps of paper to jot down important information. However, free-form databases store notes electronically in the computer's memory, rather than on tiny pieces of paper that can be easily misplaced.

Perhaps more important than how the information is stored is how it is retrieved. Any note can be retrieved by typing in any piece or fragment of information contained in the note. For example, the note below could be brought up on the computer's screen by inputting any of the following information, including (but not limited to) "Mike," "Gold," "Pacific," "Ave.," "Wood," and "818."

Mike Goldman, President
Pacific Electronics
5455 Temple Ave.
Woodland Hills, CA 91364
(818) 395-7015

Like personal data managers, free-form databases may be of value to individuals with organizational and/or memory problems.

Variable Speech-Control Taperecorders

Variable speech-control (VSC) taperecorders are portable units that, unlike standard/conventional taperecorders, enable the user to play back audiotaped material (e.g., lectures, books-on-tape) at a slower or faster rate than that at which it was initially recorded, without the loss of intelligibility (e.g., "chipmunk"-like speech at faster speeds). Intelligible speech at varying rates is achieved by simply adjusting pitch- and speed-control levers on the unit to the desired settings.

Speech rates can be reduced to more comprehensible levels for those who have difficulty processing at standard rates, and conversely, the rates can be increased in order to reduce the amount of time it takes to re-listen to taped material (e.g., class lectures or prerecorded text). Most of these recorders can reduce the speech rate by approximately 25% and increase playback speed up to 100% without the loss of intelligibility. The use of such devices may be helpful to adults with learning disabilities who process auditory stimuli at rates significantly slower than their nondisabled counterparts (McCroskey & Thompson, 1973), as well as to those who take considerably longer to complete tasks than their nondisabled peers (Blalock & Johnson, 1987).

Listening Aids

Personal frequency modulation listening systems or listening aids consist of two basic components: a wireless transmitter with a microphone and a receiver with a head-set or earphone. These devices essentially carry a speaker's voice directly from the "speaker's mouth" to the "listener's ear," thus making the speaker's voice more salient. The speaker (e.g., professor) "wears" the transmitter unit (about 2″ × 3″), while the user wears the receiver unit (also about 2″ × 3″). The transmitter or receiver is easily clipped to a belt or shirt pocket. The microphone is only about 1 ½ inches long and also can be easily clipped to clothing (e.g., a tie). Volume is controlled by a dial on the receiver. Transmitter units are also available to handle multiple speakers (e.g., in a meeting). Personal listening systems may be of benefit to those adults with learning disabilities who have difficulty focusing auditorially on a speaker (Hasbrouck, 1980).

Talking Calculators

A talking calculator is simply a calculator with a speech synthesizer. When number, symbol, or operation keys are pressed, they are "vocalized"/"spoken" by a built-in speech synthesizer. In this way, the user receives simultaneous auditory feedback in order to check the accuracy of visual-motor operations. Once a calculation has been made, the number (answer), which appears on the calculator's display, can be read back via the synthesizer, providing additional feedback in much the same way as a screen-reading/speech-synthesis system does with text. This may be quite useful when numbers are being transferred from calculator to paper, as it enables users to double-check what they have written down for possible errors (e.g., transpositions, inversions, additions, deletions). These devices can slow down the speed at which calculations are performed, because it takes longer to have operations spoken than to simply display them visually.

Rationale for the Use of Assistive Technology

A rationale for the use of assistive technology by adults with learning disabilities extends beyond the above-described technologies and their possible benefits in helping to compensate for specific learning disabilities. A number of other issues also warrant the use of, or at least should encourage the exploration of, assistive technology as a compensatory strategy for adults with learning disabilities. These issues are discussed below.

Persistence of Learning Disabilities

The first consideration in justifying the use of assistive technology for persons with learning disabilities is the recognition that learning disabilities persist into adulthood. There would be no need to endorse the use of technology by adults with learning disabilities if the difficulties experienced in childhood had subsided or been alleviated by adulthood. However, research does indicate that learning disabilities are neither cured nor outgrown (e.g., Chelser, 1982; Hoffman et al., 1987; Johnson & Blalock, 1987; White, 1985), and in many cases they may even worsen (Gerber et al., 1990) as the demands of adulthood (e.g., managing a home, pursuing a career, raising children) are faced. The problems persisting into adulthood represent the wide range of difficulties associated with children and adolescents with learning disabilities. These include deficits in reading, writing, speaking, listening, spelling, math, organization, memory, attention, social functioning, and psychological adjustment. These deficits are manifested in such areas as independent living, managing a home, managing money, job retention and success, post-secondary education, and social interaction (Chesler, 1982; Fafard & Haubrich, 1981; Hughes & Smith, 1990; Johnson & Blalock, 1987). Children with learning disabilities become adults with learning disabilities, and although the contexts in which they function may change, the disability remains. Learning disabilities are not restricted merely to early phases of adulthood (e.g., ages 17 to 22), but rather extend throughout the entire lifetime (Polloway, Smith & Patton, 1988). Consequently, adults with learning disabilities may have to face "double jeopardy" as the aging process itself brings about a gradual decline in cognitive (e.g., memory), motor (e.g., visual-motor coordination), and sensory (e.g., visual acuity) abilities (Bromley, 1990; Cavanaugh, 1990; Whitbourne, 1985).

Knowledge that learning disabilities persist into adulthood must provide an impetus to find ways to help adults with learning disabilities cope successfully in the adult world. The necessity to assist adults who are learning disabled is especially important considering the suggestion that traditional approaches for treating/remediating learning disabilities have failed; even when specific coping skills or strategies appear to have been learned, they often are not maintained over time (Poplin, 1988). Assistive technology may be one of the ways to help adults with learning disabilities compensate for their difficulties and increase their chances of leading a rewarding and fulfilling life. Of course, such a determination cannot yet be made and requires further study. However, even at this time evidence suggests that technology can be of benefit in enhancing the lives of persons with learning disabilities.

Positive Reports on the Effects of Assistive Technology

Perhaps the most convincing reason for fostering the use of assistive technology by adults with learning disabilities is a body of reports indicating its effectiveness in compensating for specific learning disabilities. For example, Collins (1990) and Primus (1990) found that the use of word processors enhanced the writing abilities of postsecondary students with learning disabilities. Brown (1987) and Norris and Graef (1990) have reported that speech synthesis in conjunction with word processing improves the quality and quantity of written language production. C. Brown (personal communication, January, 1992) and N. G. Scott (personal communication, February, 1991) have indicated that the use of speech-recognition systems enhances the quality of written language production in adults with learning disabilities. Cutler (1990) reported that spell-checkers were useful in helping college students with learning disabilities compensate for spelling difficulties. In addition, a number of authorities in learning disabilities (e.g., Gray, 1981; Mangrum & Strichart, 1988; Scheiber & Talpers, 1985; Vogel, 1987) have indicated that taperecorders, calculators, and OCR systems can be useful for adults with learning disabilities. It is interesting to note that P. J. Gerber (personal communication, August, 1991) stresses that highly successful adults with learning disabilities tend to be users of assistive technology.

The majority of these reports on the effectiveness of technology are anecdotal and are not the result of controlled experimental paradigms. However, they do provide enough evidence to at least continue the exploration of assistive technology as a compensatory strategy for adults with learning disabilities.

Compensation versus Remediation

Despite years of remedial intervention aimed at improving areas of deficiency, the problems of childhood and adolescence find their way into the lives of many adults with learning disabilities. Continued efforts to remediate, alleviate, or "fix" deficiencies often replicate the past by yielding little or no improvements. Learning disabilities may remain despite years of intervention, regardless of the theoretical/instructional model used to "treat" the problem. As previously discussed, there has been a failure to successfully remediate/alleviate learning disabilities, irrespective of the historical model used (Poplin, 1988).

Given the failure of historical approaches for remediating learning disabilities, the use of assistive technology appears to offer a viable alternative or at least a supplement to traditional approaches for dealing with the

problems experienced by adults with learning disabilities. It does not try to improve deficits that have shown resistance to remedial approaches but rather allows for a compensatory approach that seeks to circumvent or "work around" deficits while capitalizing on strengths. Several authors have emphasized the importance of using compensatory approaches with adults with learning disabilities (e.g., Gray, 1981; Mangrum & Strichart, 1988; Vogel, 1987).

The compensatory approach offered by assistive technology is also warranted because many adults with learning disabilities suffer from what may be termed "remedial burn-out." An extreme negative attitude or aversion toward remedial methods characterizes "remedial burn-out." This attitude is more than likely the consequence of years of remedial instruction and the effort and frustration associated with it, which yielded little or no benefit in alleviating specific learning dysfunctions. For many adults with learning disabilities, the use of assistive technology is appealing, since it offers a more immediate solution to a particular problem than that promised by a remedial approach. An employee with a severe reading disability, who is saddled with the task of reading a 200-page report overnight, would be in a better position to accomplish the feat by using an OCR/speech-synthesis system than by attempting to improve reading skills through "phonic training." Similarly, a postsecondary student with a reading disability would probably have a better chance of getting through the 400-page text assigned for a midterm exam if the book were put on audiotape, rather than trying to remediate the reading deficit. Adults with learning disabilities often require immediate solutions with immediate results and do not have the "luxury of time" to receive remedial training. The intention here is not to suggest that remedial approaches have no value or should not be used, but rather that a compensatory approach through the use of assistive technology may offer the most expeditious means of addressing specific difficulties within particular contexts.

Independence

The move toward independence is difficult for many persons with learning disabilities. Adults with learning disabilities have been found to be overly dependent on others, including parents, siblings, friends, peers, co-workers, and teachers, and across a variety of settings, including home, school, and work (Blalock & Johnson, 1987; Chesler, 1982; Fafard & Haubrich, 1981; Mangrum & Strichart, 1988). It may be a question of relying on parents for living arrangements, on a friend to proof school work, or on a co-worker to check mathematical calculations. Such over-reliance on others and the inability to solve one's own problems and to take responsibility for one's own life make the transition to adulthood difficult and ultimately deter the attainment of a satisfying and rewarding adult life. This is particularly true for individuals with learning disabilities who may already suffer from low self-esteem (Blalock & Dixon, 1982; Chesler, 1982) and learned helplessness (Grimes, 1981). Furthermore, overdependence places adults with learning disabilities at the "mercy" of other people's availability and/or willingness to provide assistance. Such constant concerns can serve to raise anxiety levels, place stress on relationships, and foster guilt—the last thing needed by persons who may already be prone toward such psychological difficulties as anxiety and frustration (Cox, 1977) and social problems such as difficulty in making friends and maintaining friendships (Hoffman et al., 1987).

While the use of personal support (e.g., clerical in the workplace and readers and transcribers in post-secondary settings) may be a necessary strategy for survival, the use of assistive technology can facilitate the move toward independence by reducing reliance on others. Tasks such as reading, writing, listening, and organizing may be accomplished through reliance on a specific technology, something that the adult with a learning disability possesses and controls, rather than on the whims or availability of another person. This may in turn foster a sense of pride through independently accomplishing a particular task or resolving a particular problem. The benefits of independent accomplishment in persons with learning disabilities have been stressed by Polloway and co-workers (1988). For the most part (barring any technical problems), the technology will be there when and where it is needed, and it should reduce the psychological stress and possible negative social ramifications of having to continually rely on others.

Contexts of Interaction

Historically, learning disabilities have primarily been considered relative to the school environment (Poplin, 1988). However, adults with learning disabilities function not only in educational settings but also in work, home, and social contexts, and therefore must have their problems addressed relative to all the environments in which they function (Gray, 1981; Polloway et al., 1988). Optimally, approaches for helping adults with learning disabilities deal with their difficulties need to be effective in various contexts. Unfortunately, the skills and strategies for coping with learning disabilities taught through historical models do not tend to generalize across situations (Poplin, 1988).

The use of assistive technology, on the other hand, offers a method of coping with learning disabilities across various contexts. With the advent of laptop computers, "hand-held" and "pocket" technologies (e.g., spell-checkers, taperecorders, personal data managers) it is easy to transport assistive technology from one setting to another and thus employ the compensatory strategies for dealing with specific difficulties in a variety of settings. For example, a laptop computer with a word processor and speech synthesizer could be used in a post-secondary setting to write a term paper, at work to generate a business plan, and at home to write a letter to a friend. A variable speech-control taperecorder might be utilized to record a lecture at school or an important business meeting at work, or to listen to an audio-book at home. Similarly, a personal data manager with a calendar/scheduler could keep track of meetings and deadlines at work, exam and assignment dates at school, and personal appointments at home (e.g., social engagements, medical appointments). As the computer/electronics industry moves toward greater standardization, the compatibility among products will be enhanced, which in turn will further facilitate the use of technology among various contexts of interaction.

As previously noted, adults with learning disabilities may also manifest social difficulties, and therefore assistive technology must be considered in regard to the social settings in which adults with learning disabilities function. Although the applications may not be quite as obvious or direct, assistive technology can be useful in social situations. For example, a personal data manager with an appointment calendar may help ensure timely appearances for social engagements. An OCR/speech-synthesis system could be instrumental in accessing printed materials (e.g., popular books, magazines, newspapers), which in turn can provide "topics of conversation" at social gatherings. Similarly, a calculator might make the difference between full participation in or isolation from recreational activities (e.g., bowling, darts, card and board games). Finally, as technology becomes more and more a part of society and of our daily lives, it will emerge more frequently as a conversational focal point. Knowledge and familiarity with technology will place adults with learning disabilities in a better position from which to participate in such discussions during social interaction.

Conclusion

Every effort should be made to promote the exploration of assistive technology as a means for enhancing the quality of life for persons with learning disabilities. Such an effort should include conducting further controlled research regarding the benefits/effectiveness of assistive technology, dissemination of information to promote greater awareness, identification of specific assistive technology products, establishment of effective service- and product-delivery systems, and the development of new technologies for adults with learning disabilities. Technology means change, and it is time that technology be utilized to change the lives of persons with learning disabilities.

References

Blalock, G., & Dixon, N. (1982). Improving prospects for the college-bound learning disabled. *Topics in Learning and Learning Disabilities, 2*, 69–78.

Blalock, J., & Johnson, D. (1987). Primary concerns and group characteristics. In D. J. Johnson & J. W. Blalock (Eds.), *Adults with learning disabilities: Clinical studies* (pp. 31–45). Orlando, FL: Grune & Stratton.

Bromley, D. B. (1990). *Behavioral gerontology: Central issues in the psychology of ageing.* New York: John Wiley & Sons.

Brown, C. (1987). *Computer access in higher education for students with disabilities.* Washington, DC: Fund for the Improvement of Postsecondary Education, U.S. Department of Education.

Buchanan, M., & Wolf, J. S. (1986). A comprehensive study of learning disabled adults. *Journal of Learning Disabilities, 19*, 34–38.

Cavanaugh, J. C. (1990). *Adult development and aging.* Belmont, CA: Wadsworth Publishing.

Chesler, B. (1982). ACLD vocational committee completes survey on LD adult. *ACLD Newsbriefs, 5* (146), 20–23.

Chiang, B. (1986). Initial learning and transfer effects of microcomputer drills on LD students' multiplication skills. *Learning Disability Quarterly, 9*, 118–123.

Collins, T. (1990). The impact of microcomputer word processing on the performance of learning disabled students in a required first year writing course. *Computers and Composition, 8*, 49–68.

Cox, S. (1977). The learning disabled adult. *Academic Therapy, 13*, 79–86.

Cutler, E. (1990). Evaluating spell checkers, thesauruses, dictionaries and grammar editors for the community college student with learning disabilities. In H. J. Murphy (Ed.), *Proceedings of the Fifth Annual Conference on Technology and Persons with Disabilities, 5*, 163–175.

Enders, A., & Hall, M. (1990). *Assistive technology resource book.* Washington, DC: RESNA Press.

Fafard, M., & Haubrich, P. A. (1981). Vocational and social adjustment of learning disabled young adults: A follow up study. *Learning Disability Quarterly, 4,* 122–130.

Frankel, S. (1990, May 27). Write right. *The Sunday Oregonian,* pp. K1, B4.

Gerber, P., Schneiders, C. S., Paradise, L. V., Reiff, H. B., Ginsberg, R. J., & Popp, P. A. (1990). Persisting problems of adults with learning disabilities: Self-reported comparisons from their school-age and adult years. *Journal of Learning Disabilities, 23,* 570–573.

Gray, R. A. (1981). Services for the LD adult: A working paper. *Journal of Learning Disabilities, 4,* 426–431.

Green, P., & Brightman, A. J. (1990). *Independence day: Designing computer solutions for individuals with disability.* Allen, TX: DLM.

Grimes, L. (1981). Learned helplessness and attribution theory: Redefining children's learning problems. *Learning Disability Quarterly, 4,* 91–100.

Hasbrouck, J. M. (1980). Performance of students with auditory figure-ground disorders under conditions of unilateral and bilateral ear occlusion. *Journal of Learning Disabilities, 13,* 548–551.

Hoffman, F. J., Sheldon, K. L., Minskoff, E. J., Sautter, S. W., Steidle, E. F., Baker, D. P., Bailey, M. B., & Echols, L. D. (1987). Needs of learning disabled adults. *Journal of Learning Disabilities, 20,* 43–52.

Hughes, C. A., & Smith, J. O. (1990). Cognitive and academic performance of college students with learning disabilities: A synthesis of the literature. *Learning Disability Quarterly, 13,* 66–79.

Johnson, D. J., & Blalock, J. W. (Eds.) (1987). *Adults with learning disabilities: Clinical studies.* Orlando, FL: Grune & Stratton.

Jones, K. M., Torgesen, J. K., & Sexton, M. A. (1987). Using computer guided practice to increase decoding fluency in learning disabled children: A study using the hint and hunt I program. *Journal of Learning Disabilities, 20,* 122–128.

Mangrum, D. T. II, & Strichart, S. S. (1988). *College and the learning disabled student.* Philadelphia: Grune & Stratton.

McCroskey, R., & Thompson, N. (1973). Comprehension of rate controlled speech by children with specific learning disabilities. *Journal of Learning Disabilities, 6,* 29–35.

Norris, M., & Graef, J. (1990). Screen reading programs for student with learning disabilities. In H. J. Murphy (Ed.), *Proceedings of the Fifth Annual Conference on Technology and Persons with Disabilities, 5,* 491–499.

Polloway, E. A., Smith, J. D., & Patton, J. R. (1988). Learning disabilities: An adult developmental perspective. *Learning Disability Quarterly, 11,* 265–272.

Poplin, M. (1988). The reductionist fallacy in learning disabilities: Replicating the past by reducing the present. *Learning Disability Quarterly, 7,* 389–400.

Primus, C. (1990). *Computer assistance model for learning disabled.* (Grant # G008630152-88). Washington, DC: Office of Special Education and Rehabilitation Services, U.S. Department of Education.

Raskind, M. H., & Scott, N. (1993). Technology for postsecondary students with learning disabilities. In S. A. Vogel & P. Adelman (Eds.), *Success for college students with learning disabilities.* New York: Springer-Verlag.

Scheiber, B., & Talpers, V. (1985). *Campus access for learning disabled students.* Washington, DC: Closer Look.

Technology-Related Assistance for Individuals with Disabilities Act of 1988, P.L. 100-47, 29 U.S.C. 2201, 2202 (1988).

Vogel, S. A. (1987). Issue and concerns in LD college programming. In D. J. Johnson & J. W. Blalock (Eds.), *Adults with learning disabilities: Clinical studies* (pp. 239–275). Orlando, FL: Grune & Stratton.

Whitbourne, S. K. (1985). *The aging body: Physiological changes and psychological consequences.* New York: Springer-Verlag.

White, W. J. (1985). Perspectives on the education and training of learning disabled adults. *Learning Disability Quarterly, 8,* 231–236.

Chapter 15

Personal Perspectives on Adult Educational Issues

ELISABETH H. WIIG, PH.D.

The Dilemma

What Do I Do Now?

I struggled during all of my school years with a learning disability that included dyslexia, dyspraxia, and visual perceptual deficits. Now everyone thought I was finally there—I was about to graduate from high school. Only I wondered, "*So, what do I do?*" It was difficult for others to understand the turmoil I was facing. I had to face the realities and imposed limitations of learning disabilities and make choices in a world of adult education that did not at that time (in the 1950s) have a label or sympathy for my problems or support systems to help me reach my potential.

The Academic Path

In Denmark I had passed most of the academic hurdles I had confronted because of my inherent dysfunctions, among them learning to read, learning basic math, and learning Latin. Some of the academic hurdles I had, fortunately, been allowed to skirt. When I kept getting hurt in gym and no one wanted to have me on the team, my gym teacher asked me to assist her in teaching. She would demonstrate games and exercises. I would direct with words and remind everyone of rules. When I failed geometry for three semesters in high school, I was granted a waiver from the State Department of Education. In lieu of geometry, I completed directed studies in recording and analyzing children's schoolyard games and in philosophy and logic. Little did I or they know that the flexibility and deviations in academic requirements I had been afforded would influence my life's trajectory and place me in a position to be asked to share personal perspectives on adult education.

Talents, Expectations, and Realities

During the school years, I had been identified as having a promising voice. I received voice and singing training after regular school hours through junior and senior high school and gave recitals. Everyone anticipated that a career in opera would allow me to avoid the adult academic requirements. No one actually took my learning disabilities seriously the last year of high school. The expectations of my future life had been defined. I followed those expectations, a path of least resistance, and spent a year in opera school.

Obviously, I was not meant to live my life on a stage as a singer. Two concomitants of my learning disabilities made that option an illusion. First, a significant component of my learning disability consists of an inability to deal with movement in space, social imperception, and a very real problem in recognizing faces. In opera, all these deficits proved impossible to handle, especially in view of the second component. That component is a mood disorder, primarily taking the form of seasonal depression but also containing a touch of mania. The mood disorder (manic–depression) surfaced around puberty and became more intrusive in the late teens and early twenties. At that time, none of the modern medicines was available to level my moods. I could not face the demands of a career as a performing artist. I needed to face the reality of being a high school graduate with no artistic talent to fall back on. The realities of adult education faced me, and I believed myself to be ill prepared.

The Resources

A Self-Inventory

When I look back, the approach I chose to overcome my problems was to make an inventory of skills, knowledge, organizational abilities, reasoning, and creativity. My special education teacher, who was trained by Maria Montessori, had taught me this strategy, albeit with rods and squares, when I entered her class in the third grade.

Skills

How did I fare? Probably not unlike many of my peers with learning disabilities. I found that I had auditory memory and recall strengths in areas related to all language learning. In the early grades I had escaped identification as a nonreader by memorizing texts and using the accompanying pictures as cues for content. I was not identified until the pictures were removed in the third grade. I had weaknesses in visual memory and recall, visuo–spatial–motor integration, and social perception that would affect areas such as gym, math, geometry, sciences, and nonverbal aspects of communication. In ad-

dition, I had little or no sense of time or orientation in space. This automatically ruled out professions such as dentistry, medicine, engineering, accounting, and architecture. The strengths inventory gave me options such as becoming a translator, foreign language teacher, or lawyer.

Knowledge

The inventory of knowledge fared much better. I had proven I had academic knowledge in areas such as foreign languages (excluding Latin), social studies (e.g., geography, but excluding history), natural sciences (e.g., botany and zoology), and philosophy. I also had tacit knowledge of disabilities and emotional disorders, gained from my years in special education and having a "buddy" who was a polio victim. I added child development and psychology to my list of educational options.

Organization

I then considered my strengths and weaknesses in organizational abilities at that point in time. I had entered the special education setting without abilities or strategies for organizing anything in the environment or any physical task. My teacher taught me a rule or strategy for compensating that has served me all my life. She taught me to start by categorizing everything and then making organizational decisions and setting priorities. Nonetheless, organizing the environment was, and still is, a glaring weakness for me. Although my slate looked dismal on the spatial side, it looked better on the verbal side. I had organized games all my life, the first being an intricate spy game of Nazis versus Allies. Obviously, jobs that required teaching, interviewing, or writing appeared open to me.

Conceptualization and Reasoning

My greatest assets in school had been my abilities to conceptualize and reason. My teacher pointed out early that I had excellent ability to recognize patterns in behavior, characterizations, language, and social study areas. In those domains, I could form hypotheses, test them, develop strategies, and generalize to new instances. I also found that I could alternate between looking at the parts and looking at the whole. Visual–spatial patterns, especially those based in movement, escaped me, however. As a result, I formed few or no hypotheses, could not develop strategies, and did not generalize. Needless to say, in visual domains I was concrete and not a risk taker. The inventory of conceptualization and reasoning strengths and weaknesses further strengthened my belief in the educational options I had identified. I added to them the option of becoming a researcher in some field related to language or development.

Creativity

Creativity is an important variable in evaluating one's educational options as an adult. I had shown creativity in areas that used language as a vehicle. I told creative "tall" or scary stories when a child. I could be dramatic and used dialogue well. I could play act and stage games that required verbal cunning. However, although I had perfect pitch and a good voice, I could not create with music. Again, the areas of creativity suggested staying in fields that required language as the medium and might involve research, writing, and designing materials of some kind. After completing the inventory of my resources, I settled on pursuing a career in education and psychology. The career path was as yet undefined, but I embraced it wholeheartedly. My only question was, *"How can I pass the qualifying tests and examinations?"*

The Qualifiers

College Entrance

Every educational system has qualifiers for college entrance. In the Danish system, the high school grades and qualifying examinations for graduating from high school are the most important. Without tutoring in Latin, getting a waiver for geometry, and serving as an assistant to the gym teacher, I would never have been able to meet grade requirements. The qualifying examinations are the same nationwide and include both written and oral components in selected subject areas. Luckily for me, the examinations that year emphasized modern languages, literature, geography, and botany. I was able to qualify by both the grade and examination criteria, received a high school diploma, and was accepted to a university.

In Denmark we did not have multiple-choice college entrance examinations such as the SAT. Instead, we had a qualifying year of studies that include psychology, philosophy, symbolic logic, and math. Of these requirements, I failed math for three semesters. Again the system proved flexible and supported me. Since I had passed all other subjects, I was granted a waiver. Instead of completing the math requirement, I had to complete a directed study in psychology. This experience solidified my motivations for studying psychology and special education in some form.

Graduate School

After receiving an undergraduate degree in educational psychology and working for a year, I decided to pursue graduate studies. I was accepted at Western Reserve University in Cleveland, Ohio, provided I could pass the graduate school entrance examinations during the fall of my first year. Another obstacle was in my way. The qualifying examinations were the Miller Analogies Test (MAT). I scored six on that test. The minute I saw the format, which required analogous reasoning, I knew I was in hot water. Analogous reasoning was always my weakest area even when the comparisons were verbal. My grade record luckily saved me from extinction as a graduate student. The MAT requirement was waived.

The Process

A Holistic Perspective

As I look back on the adult educational process I went through, there were several events that gave me an opportunity to reach my potential. Danish education is realistic and holistic in its assessment of students. It considers a student as an integrated whole, rather than as a configuration of individual strengths or weaknesses. I had learned from the third grade to develop insights into the nature and ramifications of my learning disabilities. I had acquired a degree of self-knowledge that allowed me to take inventory at critical decision points. I had, however, not arrived at total acceptance of myself as a person with a learning disability. That happened much later, in my late thirties, after I had received a doctorate and published. Even then, I did not accept myself as a person with a mood disorder. This occurred only in my forties. I can now say that those acceptances freed me as an individual. I no longer had to cover up, suppress, role play, feel guilty, or give excuses.

Academic Flexibility

Another consequence of the realistic, holistic perspectives of Danish education was that it gave me academic waivers. It only gave the waivers after it had been established that I had tried my level best. Without them I might never have qualified for college. In the United States, only the flexibility of the faculty of my university made it possible for me to continue in graduate school. The longer I work with students with learning disabilities, the more convinced I become that the attitude that students with learning disabilities are essentially like normal students, only slower, leads to inflexibility, lost opportunities, and a shallow emphasis on remediating deficit areas. They, like me, often have valuable strengths that are worth nurturing and pursuing.

Motivation from Success

Motivation is often cited as the most important ingredient in succeeding. I think we are overrating its potency. To me, conceptualization, reasoning, and creativity are the ingredients of success. Motivation follows. I personally started most school subjects with motivation and anticipation. My motivation sank in those subject areas that were negatively affected by my learning disabilities. It soared in subject areas that required my profile of strengths. I hated gym with a venom until my teacher asked me to assist her in teaching. After that, every gym session became an opportunity. We tend to treat motivation as if it can be created "by pulling oneself up by one's bootstraps." Instead, motivation follows when areas of strength are fostered, curricula are adapted, potentials are identified, and successes are rewarded.

Support Systems

As I stated earlier, I did not have the benefits of the support systems that are now available to college students with learning disabilities. I did not have modern technology in college to help me compensate. I did not have counselors, learning centers, and special programs. I had only the strategies I learned in elementary and high school to help me succeed. Conceptualization, reasoning, and strategy acquisition were emphasized early in my education. I applied specific strategies, such as using categorization, hierarchical arrangements, and priority setting, to many tasks. These strategies translated into study skills, organization in task and study management, concentration, and perseverance. Without those pieces of mental luggage my travels through adult education would have been difficult, even in the rather flexible educational systems I was fortunate to be part of.

Technology Use

Over the years, I have availed myself to all of the modern technologies to support my potential. I have acquired the most powerful and user-friendly computers of their times. It was emphasized early during my years in special education that I should use all available tools to support my performance. I was allowed to use multiplication and other math tables, including statistical tables, to help me pass required math courses. I typed everything, and only a minimal amount of handwriting was required of me. My teacher constantly initiated and supported problem solving in how to compensate for disabilities by using available tools, equipment, and resources. Her only requirements were that I had to have the basic skills and understand the underlying concepts in a domain before I used support systems. I consider the cost of compensatory supports over my lifetime to be far less than their value.

Conclusion

In conclusion, my experiences as an individual with learning disabilities and as a speech–language pathologist and special educator are that we can educate persons with learning disabilities successfully at the post-secondary level. It appears, however, that educators in general may need to change perspectives, processes, and procedures. The current educational perspectives and procedures are often deficit-driven. To support students with learning disabilities to achieve their highest potentials, the perspectives of assessment and interventions should be strength-driven. We need policy and procedural changes to give educators permission and ability to tailor-make educational programs that maximize individual strengths in students with learning disabilities. We also need to take better advantage of current and future technologies, both in academic settings and in life after academia, to allow for compensation and provide for support of strengths and creativity. Last, but not least, we need to substitute short-term, product-oriented planning perspectives with long-term, quality- and process-oriented planning to achieve the positive changes that will give equal educational and quality-of-life opportunities for individuals with learning disabilities.

PART IV
VOCATIONAL ISSUES

Chapter 16

Serving Individuals with Specific Learning Disabilities in the Vocational Rehabilitation System

CAROL A. DOWDY, ED.D.
TOM E. C. SMITH, ED.D.

Although vocational rehabilitation (VR) services have been available to eligible persons with specific learning disabilities (SLD) only since 1981, this disability population is nationally the fastest-growing disability population in the state/federal VR program. Fiscal year 1988 data from the Rehabilitation Services Administration (RSA) indicate that 10,733 of the 29,000 SLD cases in the VR program were closed as successfully rehabilitated, with a rehabilitation rate of 67%, which was slightly higher than the rate for non-SLD clients (64%). In fiscal year 1989, SLD comprised 5.3% of all clients rehabilitated, compared with only 1.3% in fiscal year 1983.

This dramatic increase is the direct result of the major efforts undertaken by RSA and state VR agencies since 1981 to expand and improve the nature and scope of available rehabilitation services to individuals with SLD. Key to this expansion have been the numerous service demonstration and training projects funded by RSA since 1981. With service projects serving as catalysts in pro-gram development and expansion initiatives, the training programs, particularly those designed to impact VR counselor functioning and the contributions of psychologists to the rehabilitation process, served as supports in the improvement of services to individuals with SLD. In spite of these major efforts, state VR agencies may still be underserving this population in light of the statistics that 47.7% of the students in special education settings have SLD (U.S. Department of Education, 1990). Thus, it appears that in the foreseeable future there will be a continuing need on the part of rehabilitation personnel for information and training with respect to SLD, particularly regarding the heterogeneous nature of persons with SLD and the difficulties they face in getting and keeping a job (Biller & White, 1989). The need to plan and implement service programs designed to address the unique rehabilitation needs caused by functional limitations will require continuing RSA commitment.

The purpose of this chapter is to describe the rehabilitation process for clients with learning disabilities. The first section discusses SLD in terms of the RSA definition, diagnosis, and characteristics. The second

The authors would like to acknowledge the significant contribution of Jerry Abbott, Rehabilitation Services Administration, Region III, Philadelphia, Pennsylvania.

section addresses key decision points within the VR process, that is, eligibility and severity of disability determinations, and planning effective individualized written rehabilitation programs (IWRP) designed to meet the specific and unique rehabilitation needs of an individual with SLD.

Definition, Diagnosis, and Characteristics

Definition

In 1985, RSA promulgated the following operational definition of SLD for use by state VR agencies:

> A specific learning disability is a disorder in one or more of the central nervous system processes involved in perceiving, understanding, and/or using concepts through verbal (spoken or written) language or nonverbal means. This disorder manifests itself with a deficit in one or more of the following areas: Attention, reasoning, processing, memory, communication, reading, writing, spelling, calculation, coordination, social competence, and emotional maturity (Rehabilitation Services Administration, 1985).

An understanding of the central nervous system (CNS) as referenced in this definition is pivotal to the understanding of SLD (Dowdy, 1992). The CNS works much like a computer. Input is obtained primarily through visual, auditory, or haptic stimuli, allowing a person to learn through seeing, listening, and/or touching or moving the body. The preferred input channel is often identified as an individual's learning style.

New information is sent to the brain for analysis, integration, and storage (Chalfant & Schefflin, 1969). To assimilate new information, one must pay close attention to relevant detail and classify the new information efficiently to store for later retrieval (memory). The brain creates filing systems. If the files are well organized, the new information can be easily and efficiently retrieved. Persons with SLD generally have difficulty associating new information correctly and efficiently with previously learned information. The result is an inefficient memory system that fails to retrieve information often assumed to be easily remembered. Persons with SLD often appear disorganized. Sometimes this is manifested in appearance, but it is especially prominent in their time-management activities. For example, it is common for a person with SLD to arrive on the wrong day, but at the correct time of day, for an appointment.

Unfortunately, VR counselors may easily interpret some of these characteristics to mean they have an unmotivated, uncommitted client. To do so would be similar to holding a person who is blind responsible for seeing. Indeed, it is often stated that a person with SLD may be misunderstood and sometimes underserved because of the hidden nature of the disability.

Finally, a person's output is a way of demonstrating that the new information has been successfully learned. Output responses can be in the academic areas of oral language and written language. Nonacademic output includes one's social interaction, body language, and coordination (Dowdy, 1992). A person with SLD may have difficulty taking in information, trying to make sense of it, or attempting to apply or use the information or concepts. The frustrations experienced as individuals encounter these problems daily and in a variety of environments often lead to low self-esteem, social skills deficits, and emotional immaturity. Each of these behaviors can potentially be a significant vocational limitation that the VR counselor must address during determination of eligibility and the writing of the rehabilitation plan (Zwerlein et al., 1984).

One difficulty in understanding SLD is that the disability can occur anywhere in the CNS process and can be in one or more of several areas. For example, one individual might have difficulties with attention, reading, and written language, whereas another might have deficits in oral expression, listening, and time management, with good skills in reading and written language.

Given the complexity and heterogeneity of SLD, it can be seen that a comprehensive diagnostic study and an accurate assessment of the information generated by the evaluations in terms of the individual's functional capacities and limitations and learning/working styles are pivotal to the identification of the appropriate services required by the individual to receive a suitable vocational goal.

Diagnosis

Although the VR counselor is not responsible for the diagnosis of SLD, it is important for this individual to understand the diagnostic process in order to be an informed consumer of psychological services. Because state VR agencies require the use of a licensed physician or psychologist to obtain the diagnosis, the *Diagnostic Statistical Manual, 3rd edition, revised* (DSM-III-R) (American Psychiatric Association, 1987) is generally used as the standard tool that establishes the criteria. Psychologists are often not as familiar with applying the diagnostic criteria to adolescents and adults as they are in applying them to young children. Psychologists may also not be aware of the VR counselors' need to obtain a comprehensive evaluation that identifies functional limitations and strengths.

The categories primarily used in the diagnosis of SLD include specific developmental disorders and disruptive behavior disorders. The specific developmental disorders include academic, language, speech, and motor skills. The deficits in these areas must not be due to demonstrable physical or neurological disorders, a pervasive developmental disorder, mental retardation, or a lack of educational opportunities. Under the disruptive behavior disorders category only the attention deficit hyperactivity disorder (ADHD) and undifferentiated attention deficit disorder (UADD) are used for diagnosis of SLD. A list of specific characteristics and other criteria are provided in DSM-III-R (1987) to facilitate diagnosis of these conditions.

Because many people think of SLD as primarily a reading or math deficiency, evaluators have tended to apply a limited assessment battery to this population. However, due to the heterogeneity of individuals with SLD, a very extensive testing process is required to obtain a comprehensive diagnosis (McCue, 1989; Vogel, 1989). The diagnostic battery should include, but should not be limited to the following: (1) intelligence, (2) reading, (3) arithmetic, (4) expressive writing, (5) receptive language, (6) attention–hyperactivity, (7) medical assessment (to screen hearing/visual acuity and to rule out neurological disorders), and (8) vocational assessment or a separate measure of coordination (Dowdy, Smith, Nowell, 1992) Simpson & Umbach, 1989).

Results of a national survey of VR agencies conducted by Sheldon and Prout (1991) indicated great variability regarding specific diagnostic practices. Differences were noted in specific tests used and cut-off scores for diagnosis. Only 6% required a neuropsychological assessment; however, 28% did recommend the use of this testing procedure.

An individually administered test of intelligence is always required for an SLD diagnosis. In general, persons with SLD have average or above-average intelligence. Comprehensive referral information may assist in reducing the number of additional tests needed; however, if limited referral information is available, the diagnostic battery must assess all of the possible areas where an SLD may exist.

It is also important for counselors to realize that clients may come to them because of other problems, but they should not rule out the potential of SLD. This may be the case particularly when the SLD is hidden or secondary to another presenting problem such as an industrial injury. A medical evaluation is also important with this population in order to rule out primary vision, hearing, and neurological disorders.

The diagnosis should include a comprehensive assessment of the SLD with particular emphasis on the functional capacities and limitations of the person. Academic deficits are the obvious manifestations of SLD, but these are only the "tip of the iceberg." Nonacademic processes may be the most important in terms of functional limitations with respect to employment. For example, poor time management skills and inattention will create problems in the workplace, just as these skills interfered with academic achievement in the school setting. These and other characteristics should be identified during the diagnostic process to assist in determining eligibility and developing an effective IWRP.

Possibly the single most important area to be investigated during the diagnostic process is a client's learning style. *Learning style* is the term given to one's preferred methods of taking in information, understanding the information, and/or acting on the information. We all learn and think differently and prefer to express ourselves in different ways. For some individuals with SLD, this learning style or preference can be so strong that identification of the preferred style is critical in planning the diagnostic assessment procedures and in developing appropriate IWRPs. Accommodating an individual's learning style may be as important as providing oral instructions for a nonreader. Accommodations may be necessary for a variety of SLD characteristics in order for individuals to be successful in training or employment settings.

Counselors may need to assess learning style informally during the intake process or arrange for the assessment to be included in the evaluation process. Inventories of learning styles are available commercially; however, additional research is needed in this area.

Characteristics

During the diagnostic process, information about the characteristics of SLD that the client possesses is necessary to document functional capacities and limitations. This assessment is particularly important because nonacademic characteristics may have greater implications for vocational planning than those characteristics associated with poor academic performance. Many of the characteristics may simply be observed during diagnostic testing.

For example, a person with an attention deficit may be easily distracted and have difficulty remaining seated throughout the intake interview and during a test. An individual with a reasoning deficit may display disorientation to time and poor decision-making skills. A client with a processing deficit may take longer to do a job than others and may require a concrete demonstration. There may be a critical need for oral or written directions. A memory deficit may be observed when a client has difficult recalling his or her case history or has difficulty following multiple directions. A client who has difficulty expressing thoughts coherently and has a limited vocabulary may have a communication problem.

Coordination problems may manifest themselves during fine-motor or balancing tasks. Deficits in social competency and emotional maturity may be observed as inappropriate interactions with peers and supervisors, poor eye contact, or lack of awareness of consequences of behavior. Deficits in reading, writing, and math are more easily observed and measured through testing.

The University of Alabama at Birmingham Learning Disabilities Project, funded by RSA special service and training grants, recognized the importance of documenting observations of the behavioral characteristics of SLD and developed a checklist that may be used in several ways. The *Learning Disability Checklist* (Dowdy, 1990) was structured according to the manifestations of SLD as delineated in RSA's definition (1985). After extensive research, the checklist has been reduced to 76 characteristics, which may be observed by parents or other family members, teachers, vocational evaluators, and others. These data may be important for the counselor in identifying vocational limitation to employment that can be used to substantiate eligibility and severity of disability determination and to develop appropriate IWRPs.

Key Decision Points

Eligibility

The gateway to obtaining a comprehensive program of rehabilitation services to enable an individual to achieve suitable employment is the determination of eligibility for VR services. Both RSA data and the findings of the Berkeley Planning Associates (BPA) (1989) evaluation of VR services to persons with SLD suggest that individuals with SLD, when compared to non-SLD individuals, experience major problems in accessing the rehabilitation service system. This is particularly true in terms of even getting to the point where a decision regarding eligibility can be made. The BPA data indicate that while 23% of non-SLD applicants for VR services never make it to the point where an up or down decision on eligibility can be made, 37% of applicants with SLD do not make it to this gateway decision point.

If, however, persons with SLD can get through the diagnostic phase of the rehabilitation process, current data suggest they are just as likely to be found eligible on the basis of a substantial disability as the applicants with other disabilities. They also are less likely than applicants with other disabilities to be found ineligible as too severely disabled to meet the eligibility requirement that the individual has a reasonable expectation of benefiting from VR services (BPA, 1989). Thus, based on available statistical data, SLD does not appear to present any more problems to VR counselors than other disabilities do with respect to the application of the VR program eligibility criteria. This conclusion appears to be confirmed by various surveys of state VR agencies and VR counselors (BPA, 1989).

Although the eligibility criteria must be applied in the same manner to persons with SLD as to persons who do not have SLD, the nature of SLD as an "invisible" or "hidden" disability often creates problems in the identification process and makes the application of the eligibility criteria difficult. Characteristics of SLD are often subtle and may appear as other types of problems, such as lack of motivation or emotional disorders. This is particularly true when the counselor uses a limited diagnostic approach that may not adequately identify the individual's functional capacities nor the limitations caused by the SLD.

To gather vocationally relevant diagnostic information on which to make an eligibility determination, the counselor needs to use a broad range of assessment strategies such as work evaluations, standardized tests, standardized assessments, role plays, and a review of the individual's history (Gerber, 1981). In many instances, the ideal assessment approach is the direct observation of the individual when confronted by the demands of the work environment.

Severity of Disability

Persons with SLD historically have been significantly underrepresented in comparison with other individuals in the VR program vis-à-vis the determination of the existence of a severe disability. RSA data indicate that whereas 68.5% of all persons in the VR program are classified as individuals with severe disabilities, only 52% of individuals with SLD are so classified. Again, findings of the BPA (1989) study suggest that the severity determination is a policy area in which VR counselors were experiencing major difficulties. It is hypothesized that many VR counselors have an a priori tendency to see individuals with SLD as being only mildly disabled by the disability. This presumption is difficult to counter when the diagnostic work-up is not sufficient in scope and sensitivity to accurately identify the serious functional limitations associated with the SLD.

Recently, RSA promulgated comprehensive guidelines regarding the determination of whether a person has a severe disability for VR program purposes, such as an order of selection (Rehabilitation Services Administration, 1990). In this case, a service priority is afforded individuals with severe disabilities when the agency determines it cannot serve all eligible individuals because of resource constraints. The need for such guidance was prompted by the above-referenced facts and the concern that individuals with SLD, although determined eligible for VR services, may not receive needed services if the state VR agency invokes an order of selection mandate.

The core of the RSA guidance focuses on the identification and assessment of an individual's functional limitations within the context of behavioral excesses or deficiencies in terms or their intensity, frequency, duration, and appropriateness as manifested throughout an individual's life, particularly with respect to their impact on employment considerations. Thus, serious functional limitations may result from behaviors that occur too frequently or too intensely, last too long, or when and where they should not normally occur. Conversely, serious limitations may also result from behaviors that fail to occur with sufficient frequency, adequate intensity, in the appropriate form, or under socially acceptable conditions (Rehabilitation Services Administration, 1990).

Individual Written Rehabilitation Plan

The IWRP has been an integral part of the VR process since 1975. It provides the formal mechanism by which the client and the counselor, based on the findings of the diagnostic phase of the VR process, develop a formal, written plan of action. To develop the plan, the counselor, in collaboration with the client, considers the client's capabilities, limitations, interests and other such information and determines an appropriate vocational outcome (goal). In addition to the goal, the action plan includes the delineation of intermediate objectives that must be attained to achieve the goal and the specification of the services required to attain the intermediate objectives.

One of the fundamental legal principles guiding the state/federal VR program is that of "individualization." This requires the VR program to focus on the specific rehabilita-

tion needs of the individual client. Thus, the policies, processes, and procedures of a state VR agency must be flexible enough to accommodate and respond to the unique dimensions of each client's rehabilitation needs. At the service-delivery level, the IWRP operationalizes this legal mandate; thus, VR services must be planned, coordinated, and delivered to address the particular rehabilitation needs of a given client. Considering the subtle and highly idiosyncratic presentations of SLD, the identification of appropriate services tailored to the rehabilitation needs of the individual is necessary to achieve the IWRP's objectives (Gerber & Brown; 1991; Dowdy, 1992). Again, as with the eligibility and severity of disability determinations, the findings of the diagnostic evaluations, in terms of the individual's functional capacities and limitations, are pivotal to (1) the identification of an appropriate long-range vocational goal, (2) the delineation of realistic intermediate objectives, and (3) the specification of a suitable array of services configured to meet the unique rehabilitation needs of the individual with SLD.

In developing IWRPs with their clients, VR counselors typically utilize rehabilitation intervention strategies to remediate deficits, accommodate and compensate for the client's limitations, and capitalize on the individual's strengths. While important for all clients, such strategies are imperative for the development of appropriate and successful IWRPs for individuals with SLD, given the highly idiosyncratic presentations of the disability and the need for creative rehabilitation thinking and solutions to address unique rehabilitation needs.

Based on the RSA-funded work at the University of Alabama at Birmingham, such strategies have been structured in a document, *Compensations, Accommodations, Modifications, and Strategies* (CAMS) (Dowdy, In Press). This document also includes the vocational impact of common characteristics of learning disabilities (Dowdy, in press). For example, appropriate jobs may be identified for clients in which their characteristics are circumvented. A client with hyperactivity and feelings of restlessness might avoid sedentary jobs and seek employment such as landscaping, which requires movement. Often a higher-level job can be secured if CAMS can be identified to reduce the impact of the characteristic. For example, CAMS for a client who is easily distracted might include (1) minimize distractions, (2) highlight significant characteristics of the activity, (3) isolate the worksite, (4) use earphones/plugs, and (5) provide a step-by-step checklist and ask the client to record or monitor his or her own behavior.

The question of whether appropriate IWRPs are being developed and implemented for individuals with SLD is partially answered by the outcomes achieved; however, current outcome data do not give a clear picture in this regard. While the rehabilitation rate for persons with SLD is slightly higher than for clients with disabilities excluding SLD, the proportion of the rehabilitations with SLD in competitive employment is substantially higher than for non-SLD clients (94% vs. 82%). There appears to be a major problem in terms of underemployment, with SLD clients holding service occupations (particularly food service and janitorial positions) to a substantially larger degree than non-SLD clients, and with most clients with SLD being placed in entry-level positions, many on a part-time basis and at relatively low wages. These outcomes, however, must also be interpreted within the context of the major differences in the mean age of clients with SLD (20.7 years) and that of non-SLD clients (31.5 years) (Mars, 1991).

While the VR program has made impressive strides in the past 10 years to expand and improve its services to individuals with SLD, much more needs to be done, particularly in regard to the problems identified in this article. In 1990, the RSA Commissioner, Nell Carney, established an internal RSA SLD work group, which is being aided by a panel of national experts, to develop and recommend program improvement initiatives for this population. Through this kind of leadership and ongoing priorities in funding for service and training efforts, the future rehabilitation efforts will continue to successfully build on the achievements of the past decade.

References

American Psychiatric Association. (1987). *Diagnostic and statistical manual of mental disorders*. (3rd ed., rev.). Washington, DC: American Psychiatric Association.

Berkeley Planning Associates (BPA) (1989). *Evaluation of services provided for individuals with specific learning disabilities: A final report*. (Vol. I & II). Prepared for U.S. Department of Education (Contract #300-87-0112).

Biller, E. F., & White, W. J. (1989). Comparing special education and vocational rehabilitation in serving persons with specific learning disabilities. *Rehabilitation Counseling Bulletin, 33* (1), 4–17.

Chalfant, J., & Schefflin, M. (1969). *Central processing dysfunction in children: A review of research*. (NINDS Monography No. 9). Bethesda, MD: U.S. Department of Health, Education, and Welfare.

Dowdy, C. A. (In Press). *Compensation accommodations, modifications, and strategies for adults with learning disabilities in the workplace*. Training manual submitted for publication.

Dowdy, C. A. (1992). Identification of characteristics of specific learning disabilities as a critical component in the vocational rehabilitation process. *Journal of Rehabilitation, 58* (3), 51–54.

Dowdy, C. A., Smith, T. E. C., & Nowell, C. H. (1992). Learning disabilities and vocational rehabilitation. *Journal of Learning Disabilities, 25* (7), 442–447.

Dowdy, C. A. (1990). *Learning disability checklist*. Assessment instrument submitted for publication.

Gerber, P. J. (1981). Learning disabilities and eligibility for vocational rehabilitation services: A chronology of events. *Learning Disability Quarterly, 4*, 423–425.

Gerber, P. J., & Brown, D. (1991). Report of the pathways to employment consensus conference on employability of persons with learning disabilities. *Learning Disabilities Research and Practice, 6*, (2).

Mars, L. I. (1991). Personal communication. Case services report—RSA—911 raw data. Persons rehabilitated in state agencies in F.Y. 1989 (October 1, 1988–September 30, 1990).

McCue, M. (1989). The role of assessment in the vocational rehabilitation of adults with specific learning disabilities. *Rehabilitation Counseling Bulletin, 33* (1), 18–37.

Rehabilitation Services Administration. (1985, January 24). *Program policy directive.* Washington, DC: U.S. Office of Special Education and Rehabilitation Services.

Rehabilitation Services Administration (1990, September 28). *Program Assistance Circular.* Washington, D.C.: U.S. Office of Special Education and Rehabilitation Services.

Sheldon, K. L., & Prout, H. T. (1991). Vocational rehabilitation and learning disabilities: An analysis of state policies. *Journal of Rehabilitation, 51* (1), 59–61.

Simpson, R. G., & Umbach, B. T. (1989). Identifying and providing vocational services for adults with specific learning disabilities. *Journal of Rehabilitation, 9,* 49–55.

U.S. Department of Education. (1990). *Twelfth annual report to Congress on the implementation of the Education of the Handicapped Act.* Washington, DC: U.S. Office of Special Education and Rehabilitation Services.

Vogel, S. A. (1989). Adults with language learning disorders: Definition, diagnosis, and determination of eligibility for post secondary and vocational rehabilitation services. *Rehabilitation Education, 3,* 77–90.

Zwerlein, R. A., Smith, M., & Diffley, J. (1984). *Vocational rehabilitation for learning disabled professionals.* Albertson, NY: Human Resources Center.

Chapter 17

Supported Employment: Issues and Applications for Individuals with Learning Disabilities

KATHERINE J. INGE, M.ED., O.T.R.
GEORGE TILSON, ED.D.

One strategy that is beginning to change the bleak employment outlook for adults with disabilities is supported employment. Supported employment as defined by the 1986 Rehabilitation Act Amendments is competitive work in integrated settings:

> for individuals with severe handicaps for whom competitive employment has not traditionally occurred, or

> for individuals for whom competitive employment has been interrupted or intermittent as a result of a severe disability, and who, because of their handicap, need on-going support services to perform such work (P.L. 99-506, Title I, Sec. 103,i).

Key Components of Supported Employment

Several unique features distinguish supported employment from other models of vocational services. Most importantly, supported employment uses a "place and train" approach, in contrast to rehabilitation strategies that focus on providing services prior to job placement (Kiernan & Stark, 1986; Rusch, 1986). Individuals are assisted by a job coach, also known as an employment specialist, to find an appropriate job and then are trained on work tasks and job-related skills while actively employed (Moon et al., 1986; Wehman & Melia, 1985). Some of the training also can take place at other sites to include transportation training, use of banking facilities, eating in a restaurant, or other work-related activities. The job coach assists the supported employment consumer to overcome the obstacles of maintaining employment while on the job site. Thus, this approach addresses the issue of skill generation from a training site to an actual work environment.

Another distinctive feature of supported employment is the amount and type of training or supervision that are provided. The employment specialist assesses the consumer's needs on the worksite and provides only as much training and support as necessary for the individual to meet the job requirements. A number of supported employment models have evolved around this concept of ongoing support. Three of the most popular include the mobile work crew, the enclave, and the individual placement model (Hughes & Wehman, 1992).

The mobile work crew and enclave models were designed for individuals with severe disabilities who require continual support, and typically the consumers are paid less than minimum wages (Bellamy et al., 1988; Bourbeau, 1985; Rhodes & Valenta, 1985). The mobile work crew consists of four to eight workers with severe disabilities and a work crew supervisor that operates out of a human service agency such as a sheltered workshop or supported employment program. The agency develops contracts with local businesses and industry to complete general maintenance tasks such as housecleaning, grounds work, and janitorial and other similar services.

The enclave model consists of no more than eight workers with severe disabilities and a work supervisor from a human service agency. Unlike the mobile work crew, this group of individuals is stationary within a community business or industry (Rhodes & Valenta, 1985). Jobs are identified within the business, and the consumers receive continual support and training from the human service worker. Wages are based on the production of each individual and are paid either directly to the consumer or through the human service agency. As in the mobile work crew, the trainer is always present at the worksite to provide support.

In the individual placement model, the consumer receives assistance from the job coach to identify and obtain competitive employment. He or she is hired at or above minimum wage by a business and is then provided training on the job site by the employment specialist (Moon et al., 1986). Initially, the consumer may require assistance throughout the work day; however, as he or she adjusts to the work demands and social requirements of the job, the coach gradually "fades" from the setting until the consumer is working independently. By federal definition, a consumer in an individual supported employment placement must receive at least bimonthly follow-along visits from the employment specialist. These visits may focus on identifying skill deficits that need additional training, social skills development,

facilitating co-worker supports, or training additional job duties that have been assigned to the consumer. The amount of support may vary across the length of the consumer's employment and should be determined by ongoing assessment and monitoring by the employment specialist.

Clearly, the provision of ongoing support based on the consumer's needs is critical in the success of supported employment placements. The amount of on-going support required for job success may vary from continual support as in the enclave and mobile work crew models to only bimonthly visits for individual placements. Individuals who can maintain employment without this intensive long-term follow-up should not be considered for supported employment services.

National Status of Supported Employment Programs

A major challenge of the 1990s for supported employment is to include individuals with all types of severe disabilities and not just those with mental retardation (Hughes & Wehman, 1992). A number of demonstration projects exist that have included individuals with brain injury, dual sensory impairments, and cerebral palsy. In addition, several attempts nationally have included individuals with learning disabilities in supported employment demonstration projects. The remainder of this chapter focuses on the appropriateness of supported employment for this group of individuals and explores strategies for application and implementation.

Is Supported Employment Appropriate for Adults with Learning Disabilities?

One may argue that successful employment of any individual, with or without a disability, is dependent on the type and degree of support available to that individual. Support in this generic sense refers to many things, including sufficient wages and benefits, good training, cordial atmosphere, collegiality among workers, adequate supervision and assistance, variety of work tasks that use a person's interests and skills, reasonable working conditions, and so forth. These basic elements encourage employees to contribute valued service to their companies. The greater the incentive, the greater the employee's contribution will be.

Supported employment, as previously defined, refers to a policy that guides services aimed at successful integration of people with severe disabilities within community jobs. The reader might question whether (1) the category "severe disability" includes individuals who have learning disabilities and (2) whether ongoing support is needed by this group of adults. These are legitimate questions.

The Rehabilitation Act Amendments of 1986 do cover individuals with learning disabilities provided their disability poses a significant vocational disability. Although there is no clear consensus on what constitutes a "severe" learning disability as opposed to a "mild" learning disability, some model employment programs for adults with learning disabilities have made distinctions between mild and severe disabilities based on functioning levels and adaptive behavior (Luecking et al., 1991; Neubert et al., 1989; Thomas et al., 1990; Tilson et al., 1991). Thus, in terms of supportive employment, severity of a learning disability pertains to its impact on employability.

The question remains, "Is supported employment appropriate for meeting the needs of adults with learning disabilities?" According to Rusch and Hughes (1990), supported employment is intended for "those who cannot function independently in employment without intensive ongoing support services and require these ongoing services for the duration of their employment." Clearly, there are individuals whose learning disabilities pose substantial obstacles to their vocational training, employment, and independent living (Kerr et al., 1987). Many of these individuals might therefore benefit

from some type of supported employment. By the same token, many adults with learning disabilities do not need specialized supports; they are able to succeed in their pursuits using support systems available to their nondisabled peers. Programs providing supported employment services must carefully develop a screening process to determine those individuals who do not need the ongoing support provided by supported employment models.

If the argument is accepted that supported employment has relevance for certain individuals with severe learning disabilities, then the issue becomes one of determining the appropriate method for providing support. The most likely approach appears to be the individual placement model. As previously described, the individual placement model uses the services of an employment specialist to assist an individual in locating a position within a community business and then provides training and support as needed. The five main components of the individual placement model include consumer assessment, job development, job placement, job site training, and follow-along (Moon et al., 1986). The subsequent sections of this chapter cover some of the "how to" issues within each of these categories for providing supported employment to adults with severe learning disabilities.

Consumer Assessment Issues

The purpose of assessment for supported employment is to obtain the necessary information for identifying an appropriate job in the community (Moon et al., 1986). Assessment should also focus on the identification of those individuals who need the intensive ongoing support provided by this model. It is not intended to exclude individuals based on their readiness for employment or to be used for the identification of skill deficits to design training programs prior to a job placement.

Consumer assessment should identify the consumer's strengths, needs, and preferences in order to compare these to job requirements at potential employment sites. In addition, assessment should provide the needed information for selecting training procedures and job site modifications or accommodations during the other phases of supported employment. This process is referred to as job "matching."

For instance, an individual with severe dyslexia may not be considered for a chef's position based on formal vocational assessment that indicates that he or she reads on a first-grade level. However, with the intensive job site analysis and training provided by the supported employment model, a job may be located and modified that would allow this individual to pursue his or her employment objective. For this person with severe dyslexia, it may mean matching him or her with a job at the local deli or pizza restaurant, as the majority of the food preparation tasks at such sites do not require extensive reading ability.

Consumer Interviews

Clearly, it is imperative to obtain the consumer's input when conducting an assessment for supported employment services. However, an individual with a severe learning disability may not have a clear understanding of his or her disability and the implications for employment (Getzel & Gugerty, in press). In addition, the individual with a communication difficulty may need several different explanations prior to understanding what is being asked during the assessment process. Therefore, the employment specialist must be sure that the consumer fully understands by verifying that he or she comprehends what is being said (Getzel & Gugerty, in press). Table 17-1 provides a list of sample questions that may be useful in designing a consumer interview for supported employment assessment.

Situational/Behavioral Assessment in Supported Employment

A situational or behavioral assessment in a real work environment is the best predictor of an individual's performance for a supported employment placement (Moon et al., 1990). The employment specialist is able to see what the consumer can accomplish under normal working conditions. This type of assessment can provide information regarding specific worker characteristics as well as help the consumer explore work options that he or she might enjoy (Revell & Peterson, 1991). In fact, one of the major goals of supported employment should be to encourage

Table 17-1. Sample Interview Questions for Consumer Assessment

- What are some of your strengths that would be useful on a job? What do you do well?
- What jobs would you be interested in pursuing?
- What skills do you have that would allow you to perform these jobs?
- What things/help will you need to perform the jobs that you have identified?
- Tell me about your work experience. What work experience did you enjoy most and why?
- What work experience did you enjoy least? Why?
- What changes could have made this work experience better?
- What is the best way for you to learn a new task?
- Have you ever used any accommodations (tricks) to help you perform an activity
  or job that was hard for you?
- How would you feel about having an employment specialist work with you to learn a job?
- What could an employment specialist do that would result in your being employed?
- Have you ever been on a job interview? Tell me about it.
- What was the best part of the interview? What was the hardest part?
- Do you see yourself needing any assistance during the job interview process? If so,
  what would you need?
- Is there anything else that I need to know that would be important when finding you a job?

the job seeker to exercise personal choice (Inge et al., 1992).

Moon and colleagues (1990) suggest conducting assessments that are representative of the types of jobs that can be found in the local community and that will be available to the consumers in the supported employment program. In order to conduct this type of assessment, the supported employment program first establishes a rapport with several businesses in their communities and analyzes jobs that would be appropriate for the consumers. The assessments are then scheduled within a real work environment at the convenience of the employer. This allows the employment specialist to evaluate the consumer's responses to naturally occurring environmental cues (Pancsofar, 1986). Typically situational assessments last for 4 hours and take place in a variety of local community businesses.

Observation of the potential employee in a number of different jobs can determine the types of support that will be needed, identify job accommodations, indicate the type of training needed, and specify the skills and strengths the individual has that can be used in employment settings. Once the assessments are completed, the employment specialist should develop a written report to

include how the person responded to the various work tasks as well as the training needs that should be considered when developing a job for this individual in the community. Some of the individual's work characteristics to evaluate when conducting a situational assessment can be found in Table 17-2.

Job Development and Placement Issues

A number of components to the job development process include (1) conducting a local labor market analysis, (2) determining consumer preferences, (3) job site/ecological analysis, (4) matching the consumer's characteristics to potential jobs, (5) developing resumes for job seekers, and (6) the interview process. Highly successful employment specialists consistently pay close attention to the needs of the employers with whom they are associating as well as to the needs of the targeted jobseeker.

Analysis of the Local Labor Market

The process of job market analysis requires that the employment specialist analyze the

Table 17-2. Assessment of Consumer Characteristics

Availability to work	Unusual behaviors
Transportation	Attention to task; perseverance
Physical/sensory characteristics	Independent sequencing of job duties
Ambulation/physical mobility	Initiative; motivation
Sight	Adaptability to change
Hearing	Reinforcement needs
Fine motor skills/dexterity	Family support
Strength; lifting and carrying	Financial needs
Endurance	Discrimination skills
Orienting	Time skills
Independent work rate	Reading skills
Independent problem solving, judgment	Math skills
Appearance	Ability to handle criticism, stress
Communication	Aggressive actions or speech
Social Skills	Travel skills
Relating to employer/co-workers	Benefits needed
Relating to public/customers	

From Moon, M. S., Goodall, P., Barcus, J.M., & Brooke, V. (1986). *The supported work model of competitive employment: A guide for job trainers.* (2nd ed.). Richmond: Virginia Commonwealth University, Rehabilitation Research and Training Center.

community in which the supported employment program is located and identify jobs that are appropriate for the consumers served (Moon et al., 1986; Pancsofar, 1986). Moon and colleagues (1990) suggest that the employment specialist ask the following questions when conducting a job market analysis:

1. Who are the major employers in my community?
2. How many employees are hired by these companies/employers?
3. Which companies or types of employment have the largest turnover rate?
4. What companies are known to have hired individuals with learning disabilities?
5. What have been the employment outcomes for individuals with learning disabilities in my community?
6. How can these employment opportunities be expanded?

Answers to these questions will assist the employment specialist in determining the labor needs of the community as well as how these needs can be met by the supported employment program.

Job development is community specific as well as individual specific. Employment specialists should identify those jobs in their communities with the highest frequency, availability, and appropriateness to the individuals served by the supported employment program (Moon et al., 1986). Information can be obtained from the local chamber of commerce, by reading the newspaper ads, by looking in the telephone yellow pages, by completing follow-up contacts with school graduates, and by contacting other adult service agencies such as the Department of Rehabilitative Services or other supported employment programs. In addition to identifying job categories that may be targeted for supported employment, considerable time and effort should be spent in getting to know the "ins and outs" of each company (Luecking & Tilson, in press; Moon et al., 1986). For instance, how is the company structured? What are the company's products and ser-

vices? Who are the personnel in charge of hiring decisions? What is the environment like? In essence, what is the "culture" of the targeted workplace?

The job seeker and his or her advocate should devote substantial time to building a network of contacts. While following up on announced job vacancies is important, it is equally important to establish key contacts (Bissonnette, 1986). As positions become available for which the job seeker is qualified, many of these contacts are likely to pay off in the form of job opportunities.

Identifying Consumer Job Preferences

Young employees with learning disabilities who base their career goals on personal interests and preferences may be more likely to build successful job histories than their counterparts who have had little or no input into the job placement process (Thomas et al., 1990). In addition, special attention should be given to the type of work setting or environment that is preferred by the job seeker. For example, a clerk typist may prefer to work for an autobody shop where the setting is very informal, rather than for a large, formal corporation. Too often this factor is overlooked, resulting in a job "mismatch" and subsequent dissatisfaction with, or even termination of, employment.

Job Site/Ecological Analysis

After completing a general screening of the community and determining the preferences of the consumers to be placed into jobs, the employment specialist can identify specific jobs available. Some of the general information that should be obtained on the initial employer contact would be the specifics about job duties, education and skill requirements, hours, location, transportation needs, wages, and benefits (Moon et al., 1986). This initial information will assist the employment specialist in determining if the job should be pursued for any of the consumers in the supported employment referral pool.

An environmental analysis that provides specific information about the job opening is the next step in the job analysis process. A number of supported employment programs have developed various forms for gathering the necessary information for matching potential consumers to job openings (Moon et al., 1986; Pimental et al., 1991; Sarkees & Scott, 1985). Whatever forms are utilized, the employment specialist should evaluate the worksite characteristics in the same areas as addressed in the consumer-assessment process. For instance, the consumer-assessment process should reveal an individual's ability to orient in an unfamiliar or familiar work environment (i.e., small work area, building wide, or work grounds), orient to a schedule, keep track of time, and other issues. Likewise, a job analysis should determine what orienting skills the employee would need to complete the job duties.

For instance, an employment specialist might identify an opening as a grounds crew member at a large corporate headquarters as a potential supported employment position. Analysis of the job reveals that the potential employee must be able to use a small tractor and trailer to travel around the grounds to plant and care for the various flowers and shrubs, mow the lawns, and remove trash. Clearly, orienting skills around the maintenance building as well as throughout the corporate grounds are job characteristics. The employment specialist would then review the potential employees to determine if any of them are interested in this type of work and whose current skill level matches this requirement. In addition, the employment specialist should consider what modifications or adaptations may be provided during job site training that could assist in meeting the job requirements. For an individual who has difficulty with directions and is unable to orient around a large corporate complex, a map, co-worker support, or other compensatory strategy could be used to facilitate a match between the consumer and the job.

Matching the Consumer's Characteristics to Potential Jobs

After the job analysis is completed, the employment specialist can identify a job/consumer match. This entails reviewing each job requirement and related individual skills and characteristics to determine which consumer in the supported employment program best matches the job opening (Moon et al., 1986). The employment specialist is attempting to identify the consumer whose current skills match the requirements of the job. Skill deficits are addressed through direct training and accommodations on the job site and not by preemployment training in the supported employment model.

Developing Resumes for Job Seekers

An important step in the job placement process is developing the job seeker's "marketability." In the business world, marketability refers to all of the factors that would make a company want to buy a product or service (McCormack, 1984). This principle certainly applies to individuals who aim to convince prospective companies of their marketability as potential employees.

A unique challenge to an employment specialist is to assist job seekers with learning disabilities to "sell" their skills, abilities, and personality. Some organizations that provide supported employment services to young adults with learning disabilities have found it beneficial to provide training in employability skills to include role playing the employment process, from how to dress for an interview to how to prepare a resume that will catch an employer's eye (Katski et al., 1987). The image that an applicant conveys to a prospective employer can make or break the employment opportunity.

It is recommended that the employment specialist work closely with the consumer as well as with all the individuals who know the job seeker well to design a resume that highlights specific skills, previous work experiences (including paid and unpaid jobs and internships), vocational training, and, when possible, a list of references from previous employers. This may be a particularly challenging task in the case of an adult with a learning disability who has a very limited vocational background. The Bridges project, sponsored by the Marriott Foundation for People with Disabilities (Donovan, 1990), assists young adults and their families to identify skills used in the pursuit of hobbies and leisure-time activity, or skills used around the home that can be used on a resume to demonstrate work-related skills. A concise, professional-looking resume should target the consumer's positive attributes that can take the focus off the disability.

The Interview Process

American employers rely heavily on interviews as a means of determining whether or not an applicant would make a suitable employee. Verbal communication is a deficit area for many adults with learning disabilities (Kerr et al., 1987). Although instruction in answering typical interview questions and practicing through role playing may be very useful, some interviewees may experience continued frustration and failure in actual interview situations. We recommend that, in addition to helping the job seeker to improve his or her interviewing skills, the employment specialist consider preparing the *employer* as well. For instance, an employment specialist who knew her consumer would have difficulty with verbal instructions told the employer this information prior to the interview. As result, when the employer asked questions concerning the use of a computer at the job site, he used a list of written questions and instructions as a guide for the consumer.

Increasingly, company recruiters are encountering non–English-speaking applicants. Rather than relying solely on formal face-to-face interviews, the applicant is asked to demonstrate performance of given tasks. Emphasis is therefore taken off the

ability to converse and placed on the ability to actually perform the required tasks. This may be an excellent strategy for applicants with learning disabilities. The employment specialist should bear in mind that the Americans with Disabilities Act mandates "reasonable accommodations" for all aspects of employment, including the recruitment process. Certainly negotiating for a "working interview" could be considered a reasonable option, or accommodation, for an applicant with a learning disability who may have extreme difficulty with a sit-down interview.

In assisting the applicant, the employment specialist must remember to take a "backseat supporting role." The employment specialist's role during the interview process should be one of facilitator. After he or she has determined that the consumer's skills match the potential job, it is the employer's responsibility to determine whether the applicant is qualified and suitable.

Job Site Training

Many adults with learning disabilities struggle with a number of the same problems on the job that affected their performance while in school. Some of the difficulties include making frequent errors, having a greater number of accidents than the average worker, demonstrating difficulty learning the sequences of tasks, displaying deficiencies in academic skills, and impulsivity (Getzel & Gugerty, in press). Add to this that these individuals often deny having learning disabilities (Bender, 1992; Kerr et al., 1987; Thomas, 1990) and there is potential for many difficulties occurring during employment.

Supported employment can overcome these problems and provide the assistance necessary to make individuals with severe learning disabilities successful in the workplace. It is the role of the employment specialist to identify the areas in which the employee needs training, support, and accommodations in order to complete job requirements. In addition, this support should be provided in the least intrusive manner that will not stigmatize the new employee. Many workers with learning disabilities, while in need of support, have expressed dismay at being treated "differently" on the worksite (Luecking et al., 1991; Thomas et al., 1990).

Natural Supports

The first step in job site training should therefore be the identification of naturally occurring supports and cues. For instance, what existing resources does the company have that can assist the new employee? Are co-workers and the employer open to learning how to provide assistance to the consumer? Is there a co-worker willing to provide natural supports to the consumer such as acting as a "mentor" during particularly difficult portions of a job task?

Typically, support does occur naturally in the work environment (Nisbet & Hagner, 1988). The type and amount of support can vary based on the physical proximity of the consumer to other workers, length of employment, type of job duties performed, and so forth. Often in supported employment, natural sources of support are overlooked for support provided by the employment specialist (Nisbet & Hagner, 1988). However, in order for this model to work for individuals with learning disabilities, natural supports are critical.

Luecking and co-workers (1991) have referred to this as providing internal supports for the worker with a learning disability. These authors recommend working with a manager to determine (1) how the employee learns, (2) the areas in which the employee may have difficulty, and (3) strategies for capitalizing on strengths while minimizing limitations. Some of the areas of difficulty for the employee may be visual, auditory, motor, academic, organizational, and social. Table 17-3 provides a sample of suggestions for employers and employment specialists when working with an individual with severe learning disabilities.

Naturally Occurring Cues

A natural cue represents some component or feature of the work environment that signals the employee what to do next (Moon et al., 1990). Examples of naturally occurring cues might be the placement or location of work materials (e.g., paper coming out of the copy machine), presence of a co-worker, a mechanical device such as an indicator light, and pictorial instruction such as diagrams over the salad-preparation bar at a fast-food restaurant. An individual with a learning disability who has difficulty organizing work tasks may not attend to these naturally occurring cues in the workplace. In this instance, the employment specialist should work with the consumer, co-workers, and supervisor to identify those cues that could assist the individual in completing his or her tasks successfully. Initially, an added artificial cue may assist the person in attending to the natural cue, such as color coding, using a beeper on a watch, and so forth. These extra cues can be gradually eliminated as the individual begins to attend to the naturally occurring ones. Finally, the consumer should always be involved in identification and use of natural cues, as he or she will then feel ownership of the strategy.

Naturally Occurring Reinforcers and Contingencies

Natural reinforcers on a job site may include the worker's paycheck, co-worker and supervisor praise, supervisor evaluations, social interaction with co-workers, praise from customers, pay raises, free meals or break snacks, and so forth. Naturally occurring contingencies may include such things as co-worker or supervisor feedback about the employee's performance. As previously stated, individuals with learning disabilities often complain that they are treated "differently" than their co-workers. In these instances, the employment specialist should assist the co-workers and supervisor to interact with the consumer in a normal fashion

Table 17-3. Strategies for Employer/Co-worker Support

Modifications for Visual Difficulties

- Identify a proofreader to review the employee's written work.
- Demonstrate the task several times and allow the employee a chance to practice with feedback on the performance.
- Provide tape recorded instructions or directions that the employee can use whenever necessary.
- Draw diagrams or pictures to illustrate job duties.

Modifications for Auditory Difficulties

- Allow the person to work in quiet surroundings.
- Realize that the employee may need repeated directions.
- Make sure you establish eye contact prior to giving directions.
- Provide written or pictorial instructions. Allow the employee to repeat the instructions back to you. Better yet, ask the employee to demonstrate what needs to be done.
- Ask questions to be sure that the individual has paid attention to details.
- Use short sentences that are "to the point."
- Provide a written outline or agenda of topics to be discussed.
- Encourage the person to take notes or tape record the instructions for review.

Modifications for Organizational Difficulties

- Encourage the person to use a daily checklist. Be sure to make the checklist time-oriented if this is a problem for the employee.
- Provide a system for filing important written information such as a workbook or three-ring binder.
- Develop a system for organizing work surfaces such as in/out boxes, files, etc.
- Break multistep or complex instructions into smaller steps.
- Pair the person with a co-worker who can reinforce the schedule or work sequence.

Modifications for Social Difficulties

- Communicate directly with the person in a flexible manner; address issues as they occur.
- Avoid the use of sarcasm, indirect hints, or hidden messages that might be misunderstood.
- Offer praise and reinforcement for tasks done well.
- Be careful to pair verbal and nonverbal cues when talking with the individual.
- Provide an opportunity for the individual to participate in work-related social activities in which his or her co-workers are involved.

Adapted from Luecking, R. G., Tilson, G., Jr., & Willner, M. (1991). *Corporate employee assistance for workers with learning disabilities*. (Available from TransCen, Inc., 234 N. Washington Street, Rockville, MD 208950).

and to provide the same feedback and reinforcement that would be afforded any employee of the company. Sometimes the mere presence of the employment specialist will create unnatural situations such as the supervisor telling the employment specialist when a problem arises rather than relating it directly to the employee. The employment specialist should always direct the co-workers and supervisor to go to the consumer rather than "run interference" for the individual. Some of the suggestions in Table 17-3 may prove helpful for these situations.

Providing Instruction for Job Site Independence

Planned instruction for job completion may still be necessary for individuals with the most severe disabilities even after natural supports, naturally occurring cues, and naturally occurring contingencies and reinforcement have been identified. The employment specialist should work the job at least one day prior to introducing the new employee to the work environment in order to completely familiarize himself or herself with the position requirements. Job duties should be thoroughly analyzed in order to establish a routine and time schedule for task completion. During this process, the employment specialist should identify, isolate, and describe each job skill that the new employee will be required to perform, including any special tools or machinery to be used (Buckley, 1988; Chadsey-Rusch & Rusch, 1988; Moon et al., 1990). This activity has been referred to as *job duty analysis* and *task analysis* (Barcus et al., 1987; McLoughlin et al., 1987; Moon et al., 1986). This systematic organization of the job site should prove especially beneficial to individuals with learning disabilities.

Actual instruction of job duties can include the use of response prompts such as verbal, model, gestural, and physical cues. It can also include extra stimulus prompts/cues such as job accommodations or compensatory strategies and self-management strategies. In any case, instruction should be specific to the individual and his or her learning style. Additionally, the consumer should be closely involved in designing any compensatory strategy or self-management procedure to ensure successful implementation.

Observation and evaluation of the worker's performance should be monitored to determine when the worker can perform the task without assistance. This information will assist in determining when the employment specialist should fade from the job site. Table 17-4 provides some examples of self-

management and job site accommodation strategies.

Follow-Along Strategies

As the new employee settles into his or her job, the employment specialist, employee, and employer should determine the type(s) and amount of follow-along support needed. By federal definition, follow-along must include a minimum of two visits to the job site per month for job site training. A follow-along schedule should be negotiated that would include these two visits as well as any other additional contacts such as phone interviews, consumer off-site visits, parent/guardian contacts, and so forth.

On-site visits should be conducted that result in a minimal amount of intrusive behaviors by the employment specialist. It is suggested that a slow time of day be selected for observation to ensure that the normal workflow is not interrupted (Moon et al., 1986). This may allow the employment spe-

Table 17-4. Self-management and Job Site Accommodation Strategies

Strategy	Example
1. Self-recording	*Individual has difficulty tracking work completed within specified time limits.* Employee charts his or her performance on a graph or chart, such as length of time to complete a specific job duty. Feedback provided by the chart assists the person to stay within time limits or job expectations.
2. Worksheets	*Employee has difficulty reading copy requests to determine work assignments.* Develop a form with supervisor input that highlights relevant features of the task, such as a "thick outlined box" for number of copies requested.
3. Picture cues	*Employee cannot read recipe to complete food preparation.* Design picture diagrams and cues to complete food preparation responsibilities. *Employee has trouble remembering sequence for cleaning and assembling machinery.* Design a picture diagram with the appropriate sequence.
4. Pretaped instruction	*Employee has difficulty remembering supervisor's instructions.* Use a portable cassette tape recorder to record instructions that can be played back when needed.
5. Checklist	*Employee has difficulty remaining organized and often forgets to complete certain job duties.* Employee uses a checklist of job duties to monitor responsibilities.
6. Visual cue	*Employee has difficulty discriminating between similar tools for machinery assembly.* Color code or number the tools in order of their use.

cialist to talk with the consumer as well as the employer and co-workers. The consumer's work performance should also be monitored using data-collection methods that were implemented during the job site training to determine if additional supports or training is necessary for successful task completion.

In terms of long-term adjustment to the job, it is important that both the employee and his or her direct supervisor have access to the employment specialist or adult agency when difficulties arise. Adults with learning disabilities who are receiving supported employment should be encouraged to advocate for themselves whenever possible. Self-advocacy may mean knowing when and how to access outside assistance. Employers also need to be informed of resources that can help supervisors when problems do not appear readily solvable.

In addition to support for learning and performing job tasks, much has been written about the importance of social integration in and outside the workplace (Clement-Heist et al., 1992; Fabian & Luecking, 1991; Germino-Hausken, 1992). Job clubs may be one strategy for providing ongoing support to young adults with learning disabilities, in addition to the more traditional forms of supported employment follow-along (Thomas et al., 1991; Tilson et al., 1991).

Funding Supported Employment Services

Supported employment opportunities with job site training and support have become increasingly available nationally through the development of interagency programs involving vocational rehabilitation and a variety of public and private provider and extended-service funding agencies (Revell & Peterson, 1991). Typically, three funding sources can be accessed: discretionary funding sources; vocational rehabilitation (VR); and state offices for persons with developmental disabilities, mental illness, and problems associated with substance abuse (Hill et al., 1987).

Discretionary funding sources are usually time-limited and distributed through contracts or grants for specific targeted initiatives. Discretionary funding sources can be both public and private and are distributed at the discretion of agencies such as the department of education, Goodwill, and private corporations. The funding may be in the form of gifts, grants, or contracts in response to proposals submitted.

The state department of rehabilitation can also be a source for initial funding, management, and provision of supported employment services (Hill et al., 1987; Revell & Peterson, 1991). One way VR funds supported employment is through a fee-for-service strategy. A vendor is approved by the state agency to provide the service for a specified period of time. A vendor can be defined as a service agency that has developed a program to provide services to individuals with disabilities (e.g., supported employment) and has been approved by VR.

VR will fund supported employment through the consumer assessment, job development/job placement, and job site training phases. Once the consumer has become stable on the job site and the employment specialist has faded from the site, the VR case is closed and an extended funding source assumes responsibility for the consumer. In fact, the VR counselor will not consider a consumer for supported employment unless a source for long-term funding has been established prior to job placement.

Therefore, if individuals with learning disabilities are to access money through VR for supported employment services, a long-term funding source must be identified. As previously stated, some programs serving these individuals are using discretionary funds. Another possible source may be the Plan for Achieving Self-Support (PASS) through Social Security regulations (O'Mara, 1989; U.S. Social Security Administration, 1987). In order to access a PASS, the individual must be eligible for Social Security, demonstrate a vocational goal, show a clear connection between the vocational goal and increased earning, and develop a plan that meets criteria established by the Social Security Administration. PASS can make it possible for an individual with a disability to hire a job coach. Support services could include job development, job site training, and follow-along support up to a maximum of 48 months (Brooke et al., 1990).

In some states, VR agencies are accepting natural supports or those supports provided by the employer and/or co-workers as extended services providers (V. Brooke, personal communication, March 16, 1992). This seems to be an extremely viable option for individuals with learning disabilities, since they often refuse more traditional VR services. Programs using this strategy would need to develop an individual work-related plan (IWRP) with VR that specifies how the employer and/or co-workers intend to implement natural supports.

Summary

This chapter describes the federal supported employment initiative that was mandated through the Rehabilitation Act Amendments of 1986 (P.L. 99-506). Supported employment may be appropriate for individuals with severe learning disabilities that substantially affect their ability to obtain and retain employment. This group is not likely to include those individuals who successfully complete post-secondary education and enter professions requiring college degrees. A wide range of characteristics make this group highly heterogeneous. Because learning disabilities are manifested in many different ways, from individual to individual, employment support must be customized. Further, many adults with learning disabilities seek to hide their disabilities from employers, fearing stigmatization and rejection. This poses a real problem for those individuals who may be in need of assistance but refuse to accept traditional rehabilitation approaches.

We present the notion of facilitating "internal company supports" whenever pos-

sible, that is, using the services of an employment specialist to increase the employer's confidence in supervising and working with people with learning disabilities. Ample documentation exists that many adults with learning disabilities require unique supports to become successfully employed. Little has been said about the relevance of the federally defined supported employment model for this group. The intent of this chapter is to generate discussion and encourage further investigation.

References

Barcus, M., Brooke, V., Inge, K., Moon, S., & Goodall, P. (1987). *An instructional guide for training on a job site: A supported employment resource.* Richmond: Virginia Commonwealth University, Rehabilitation Research and Training Center.

Bellamy, B. T., Rhodes, L. E., Mank, D. M., & Albin, J. M. (1988). *Supported employment: A community implementation guide.* Baltimore: Paul H. Brookes.

Bender, W. N. (1992). Learning disabilities. In P. J. McLaughlin & P. Wehman (Eds.), *Developmental disabilities* (pp. 82–95). Boston: Andover Medical Publishers.

Bissonnette, D. (1986). *Training for job developers: A supervisor's guide.* Northridge, CA: Milt Wright & Associates, Inc.

Bourbeau, P. (1985). Mobile work crews: An approach to achieve long-term supported employment. In P. McCarthy, J. M. Everson, M. S. Moon, & J. M. Barcus (Eds.), *School to work transition for youth with severe disabilities* (pp. 151–166). Richmond: Virginia Commonwealth University, Rehabilitation Research and Training Center.

Brooke, V., McGill, J. K., O'Mara, S., & Inge, K. J. (Fall, 1990). *Social security and supported employment: Reaching out to people with disabilities.* Richmond: Virginia Commonwealth University, Rehabilitation Research and Training Center.

Buckley, J. (1988). *Employment training specialists: Job description, training, and evaluation.* Eugene, OR: University of Oregon, Specialized Training Program.

Chadsey-Rusch, J., & Rusch, F. R. (1988). Ecology of the workplace. In R. Gaylord-Ross (Ed.), *Vocational education for persons with handicaps* (pp. 234–256). Mountain View, CA: Mayfield.

Clement-Heist, K., Siegel, S., & Gaylord-Ross, R. (1992). Simulated and in situ vocational social skills training for youths with learning disabilities. *Exceptional Children, 58* (4), 336–345.

Donovan, M. R. (1990). Envisioning links from school to work. *Rehab USA*, Summer, 3–4.

Fabian, E., & Luecking, R. (1991). Doing it the company way: Using internal company supports in the workplace. *Journal of Applied Rehabilitation Counseling, 22* (2), 32–35.

Germino-Hausken, E. S. (1992). *A survey of the career development outcomes of individuals with mild disabilities after completing a post-secondary transition-to-work program.* Unpublished doctoral dissertation, George Washington University, Washington, DC.

Getzel, E. E., & Gugerty, J. J. (in press). Designing and implementing individual transition plans: Applications for students with learning disabilities. In P. Wehman (Ed.), *Transition from school to adulthood.* Baltimore: Paul H. Brookes.

Halpern, A. S. (1990). A methodological review of follow-up and follow-along studies tracking school leavers from special education. *Career Development for Exceptional Individuals, 13* (1), 13–28.

Hill, M., Inge, K. J., Moon, M. S., & Wehman, P. (1987). Possible funding mechanisms for supported employment. *Funding supported employment, 4* (1), 4. Richmond: Virginia Commonwealth University, Rehabilitation Research and Training Center.

Hughes, T., & Wehman, P. (1992). Supported employment. In P. J. McLaughlin & P. Wehman (Eds.), *Developmental disabilities* (pp. 184–205). Boston: Andover Medical Publishers.

Inge, K. J., Brooke, V., Hall, V., Peters, P., Slaughter, G., Toth, T., Turner, E., Urofsky, S., Wehman, P. (Spring, 1992). *Consumer leadership in supported employment.* Richmond: Virginia Commonwealth University, Rehabilitation Research and Training Center Newsletter.

Katski, M., Mendelson, M., Foster, J., Tilson, G., & Neubert, D. (1987). *Transitional programming for mildly disabled out of school young adults: An implementation manual.* (Available from the George Washington University, Department of Teacher Preparation and Special Education, 2201 G Street, N.W., Suite 524, Washington, DC 20052.)

Kerr, M. M., Nelson, C. M., & Lambert, D. L. (1987). *Helping adolescents with learning and behavior problems.* Columbus, OH: Merrill Publishing Company.

Kiernan, W., & Stark, J. (1986). *Pathways to employment for adults with severe developmental disabilities.* Baltimore: Paul H. Brookes.

Luecking, R. G., & Tilson, G., Jr. (in press). Public-private partnerships in transition services: A systems case management approach. In C. Kochhar & D. Hiltenbrand (Eds.), *Patterns in the mosaics: Interagency service coordination for transition from school to independence for youth with special needs.* Horsham, PA: LRP Publications.

Luecking, R. G., Tilson, G., Jr., & Willner, M. (1991). *Corporate employee assistance for workers with learning disabilities.* (Available from TransCen, Inc., 234 N. Washington Street, Rockville, MD 20895.)

McCormack, M. H. (1984). *What they don't teach you at Harvard Business School.* Toronto: Bantam Books.

McLoughlin, C. S., Garner, J. B., & Callahan, M. (1987). *Getting employed, staying employed: Job development and training for persons with severe handicaps.* Baltimore: Paul H. Brookes.

Moon, M. S., Goodall, P., Barcus, J. M., & Brooke, V. (1986). *The supported work model of competitive employment: A guide for job trainers.* (2nd ed.). Richmond: Virginia Commonwealth University, Rehabilitation Research and Training Center.

Moon, M. S., Inge, K. J., Wehman, P., Brooke, V., & Barcus, J. M. (1990). *Helping persons with severe mental retardation get and keep employment: Supported employment issues and strategies.* Baltimore: Paul H. Brookes.

Neubert, D., Tilson, G., Jr., & Ianacone, R. (1989). Postsecondary transition needs and employment patterns of individuals with mild disabilities. *Exceptional Children, 55* (6), 494–500.

Nisbet, J., & Hagner, D. (1988). Natural supports in the workplace: A reexamination of supported employment. *The Journal of the Association for Persons with Severe Handicaps, 13* (4), 260–267.

O'Mara, S. (1989). *PASS Manual.* Richmond: Virginia State Office of Supported Employment, Department of Rehabilitative Service.

Pancsofar, E. L. (1986). Assessing work behavior. In F. R. Rusch (Ed.), *Competitive employment issues and strategies* (pp. 93–101). Baltimore: Paul H. Brookes.

Pimental, R., Baker, L., & Tilson, G., Jr. (1991). *The Americans with Disabilities Act: Making the ADA work for you. Train the Trainer.* Northridge, CA: Milt Wright & Associates, Inc.

Revell, W. G., & Peterson, M. (1991). Assessing outside services and critically analyzing supported employment vendors. In S. Griffin & W. G. Revell (Eds.), *Rehabilitation counselor desk top guide.* (pp. 49–62). Richmond: Virginia Commonwealth University, Rehabilitation Research and Training Center.

Rhodes, L. E., & Valenta, L. (1985). Industry-based supported employment: An enclave approach. *Journal of the Association for Persons with Severe Handicaps, 10* (1), 12–20.

Rusch, F . R., & Hughes, C. (1990). Historical overview of supported employment. In F. R. Rusch (Ed.), *Supported employment: Models, methods, and issues.* Sycamore, IL: Sycamore Publishing Company.

Rusch, F. R. (1986). Competitive employment issues and strategies. In G. T. Bellamy, L. Rhodes, D. M. Mank, & J. M. Albin (Eds.), *Supported employment: A community implementation guide.* Baltimore: Paul H. Brookes.

Sarkees, M. D., & Scott, J. L. (1985). *Vocational special needs.* (2nd ed.). Homewood, IL: American Technical Publishers.

Thomas, J. L. (1990). *Acceptance of disability among learning disabled young adults: A developmental perspective.* Unpublished manuscript.

Thomas, J., Taymans, J., & Ianacone, R. (1990). *The George Washington University Model demonstration project: The evolution of transitional services for young adults with learning disabilities.* (Available from the George Washington University, Department of Teacher Preparation and Special Education, 2201 G Street, N.W., Suite 524, Washington, DC 20051).

Tilson, G., Jr., Taymans, J., & Germino-Hausken, E. (1991). *A descriptive study of young adults with mild disabilities who participated in a model postsecondary transition project.* (Tech. Rep. No. 2). Washington, DC: The George Washington University, Department of Teacher Preparation and Special Education.

U.S. Social Security Administration. (1987). *A summary guide to Social Security and Supplemental Security Income work incentives for the disabled and blind.* SSA Pub. No. 64-030 ICN 436900. Baltimore: Social Security Administration.

Wehman, P., & Melia, R. (1985). The job coach: Function in transitional and supported employment. *American Rehabilitation, 11* (2), 4–7.

Chapter 18

Employing People with Learning Disabilities

DALE S. BROWN, B.A.
PAUL J. GERBER, PH.D.

People with learning disabilities have entered into employment settings in greater numbers in recent years. Some individuals have never been identified as learning disabled and have found jobs to fit their talents and strengths. In such cases their learning disabilities have not become an issue, and their personal accommodations have allowed them to succeed, in some cases handsomely. Others with learning disabilities have struggled in their employment roles, working long hours and obtaining assistance from co-workers. Still a significant number of people with learning disabilities have found their disabilities to be insurmountable and are part of the structural unemployment problem facing this nation. Recently, the employment picture has changed dramatically for people with learning disabilities. With the passage (1990) and implementation (1992) of the Americans with Disabilities Act (ADA) people with learning disabilities will be afforded even more opportunity in the workplace, not only at job entry, but in job advancement and in supervisory and leadership roles.

Employment for people with learning disabilities has become one of the prominent concerns of the field of learning disabilities in the 1990s, and it has engendered intense interest from all concerned. The current state of the art is changing at a rapid pace, and more issues are developing in a variety of areas as time goes on. This chapter provides a discussion of the salient issues regarding employability and employment for individuals with learning disabilities.

The Current Situation: Employment of People with Learning Disabilities

Presently, employment of people with learning disabilities is a mixture of "good news" and "bad news." The good news is that many people with learning disabilities are succeeding in a diversity of jobs. Moreover, many are entrepreneurs and have started their own businesses. Society has become more acquainted with learning disabilities, which is making it easier for some people to disclose their disabilities and subsequently succeed in the workplace.

The National Longitudinal Transition Study of Special Education (NLTS), a study of over 8,000 secondary students who received special education services, showed that 57.7% of the graduates who had learning disabilities (n = 429) had a paid job at the time of the survey interview (SRI International, 1991). This compares with 45.9% of all youths with disabilities and 61% of youth without disabilities. For students with learning disabilities still in school, 62.9% had paid employment. This compares with 57 to 61% of young people without learning disabilities and 56% of all students with disabilities surveyed by the NLTS (pp. 8, 21). While these findings are viewed as generally positive, the issue of underemployment (Gerber, 1990) is not addressed and may be a hidden factor.

Other evidence, however, currently shows people with learning disabilities facing serious challenges in obtaining employment. According to a report by the U.S. Department of Labor (Employment and Training Administration, 1991), between 15 and 23% of participants in Jobs Training Partnership Act Title IIA programs have learning disabilities. Funds from Title IIA train and place economically disadvantaged persons. The report recommends that the Department of Labor consider establishing an interagency work group on learning disabilities and "reviewing the need for a research and technical assistance agenda to examine the learning disabled population and current practices for serving them" (p. ii).

Very few studies have investigated the unemployment rate of people with learning disabilities. Generally, it is thought that more people with learning disabilities are unemployed and underemployed than the general population (Gerber, 1990). In one survey of 567 adults with learning disabilities conducted by the Association for Children and Adults with Learning Disabilities (currently Learning Disabilities Association of America), 210 (or 37%) were unemployed (ACLD Vocational Committee, 1982).

Another important source of data is the Job Accommodation Network (JAN), an international accommodation information service sponsored by the President's Committee on Employment of People with Disabilities (Jacobs & Hendricks, in press). Approximately 1 in 25 (4.3%) of their inquiries involved a person with a learning disability. Data were analyzed from 371 people who called between January, 1987 and June, 1991. Of people with learning disabilities who called, 21% were job seeking versus 12% of people with other disabilities.

The evidence of widespread problems of people with learning disabilities in employ-

ment was serious enough that, in May of 1990, the President's Committee on Employment of People with Disabilities convened a national consensus building conference entitled "Pathways to Employment for People with Learning Disabilities." This conference brought together 61 of the nation's top educators, employers, helping professionals, people with learning disabilities, family members, and policy officials from government who were national leaders in a process designed to identify issues and develop a strategic plan to improve employment opportunities for people with learning disabilities (Brown et al., 1990). Recommendations from their work included:

1. Increasing public awareness of people with learning disabilities among the general public and specifically with employers
2. Improving cooperation among the agencies that have an impact on people with learning disabilities (both government and nongovernment)
3. Developing strong outreach to employers in training and assistance on accommodating the needs of people with learning disabilities at entry level and promotion
4. Strengthening national leadership and guidance to state and local areas.
5. Making greater efforts in developing stronger transition linkages from school to work
6. Aiding individuals with learning disabilities to take on the responsibility of finding and keeping employment

Barriers to Job Entry for People with Learning Disabilities

People with learning disabilities have significant problems in persuading employers to hire them. Traditional sources of locating job vacancies include classified advertising in newspapers and computer output at job services. Both of these sources are often difficult to read for many people with learning disabilities because of the format and print size. When the person locates a job vacancy or decides to apply at a particular job locale, the application may become a barrier. Although many people with learning disabilities can obtain help in filling out the form, many companies require that the person fill out the application at the site, thus exposing poor handwriting, problems with reading, spelling difficulties, or organizational problems, to name a few. A needs-assessment survey of 381 people with learning disabilities showed that filling out job applications presented a problem for 41% of them in getting or keeping a job (Minskoff et al., 1986).

Credentialing and testing requirements present a powerful barrier as well. Large companies and firms that hire temporary labor use paper-and-pencil tests that can screen out people with learning disabilities. Required credentials, such as advanced degrees or professional entry examinations, also can screen out people with learning disabilities, who would otherwise do an excellent job. The ADA (1990) forbids discrimination by using these requirements, stating that "examinations and courses related to applications, licensing, certification, or credentialing shall be offered in an accessible manner" (Title 1). It also says that in most cases it is discriminatory to use "qualifications standards, employment tests, or other selection criteria" (Title 1) to screen out people with disabilities. This civil rights approach contrasts with a current national trend toward testing and credentialing. Professions and jobs are increasing both pre-service and inservice testing (e.g., National Teachers Examination, the Commercial Truck Driver's License).

The interview process is difficult for many people as well. People with learning disabilities must make sure that their difficulties with directions, transportation, utilizing time, and organizing themselves do not cause them to be late. Their grooming must be excellent, a challenging process for some people who have visual perception problems and fine motor coordination difficulties. And, of course, the job interview itself is a set of complex social skills, which can be problematic for those with language disabilities or problems relating to others.

In addition, a decision must be made before the interview of whether or not to disclose the presence of a learning disability. Even though civil rights are currently guaranteed to people with disabilities, discrimination remains. If one discloses a disability during the interview and is rejected, it is extremely difficult to prove that the reason was that the interviewer was biased toward the person because of the disability. On the other hand, many people with learning disabilities who need accommodations prefer to make this clear from the outset. In traditional job hunting, the interview, particularly the initial interview, exists to screen out people. Conventional wisdom warns that any factor that could result in rejection should be avoided.

Nevertheless, it is appropriate and frequently helpful if applicants mention the learning disability in a positive sense, and explain how they would accommodate for their learning disability on the job. For example, one social worker who had significant difficulties reading and writing explained how she could work on a client's file by dictating into a tape recorder. When possible, it is important to accentuate the strengths of a learning disability. One hyperactive person explained how her extra energy was "markedly positive," enabling her to work long hours.

In order to overcome these barriers, people with learning disabilities need to explore their strengths and find jobs based on where they can excel. Chapter 19, on successful adults with learning disabilities in the workplace, by Ginsberg, Gerber, and Reiff, shows this well and describes success patterns.

The Changing Workplace

Several trends in the workplace have occurred over the past decade. These trends in technology and new organizational structures and systems have had both a positive and a negative impact on people with learning disabilities. Following are some of the latest developments in the workplace.

Teamwork is Replacing Hierarchy. This increases the social demands on the individual worker. Traditional chain of command demands a good relationship with one's direct supervisor. Today's workplace requires a myriad of relationships, an interpersonal demand that may overwhelm some persons with learning disabilities. On the other hand, it may be more possible for people to get help with their weaknesses when they can contribute strengths to the team.

Productivity Demands are Increasing. Work is required to be done faster and better. Quality demands are up. This is due to downsizing, restructuring, and the needs of organizations that are facing foreign competition. In addition, literacy requirements are growing. Many workers with learning disabilities who were once able to hide their disabilities are now negatively affected by new performance-appraisal systems, statistical process control systems, requirements for promotions, standardized tests, and other languages.

Technology Has Changed the Nature of the Working Day. Machines can save a great deal of time and assist many people with learning disabilities. They can also increase performance pressure. The fax machine has removed the relaxing few days while documents get to their destination. It increases the number of drafts possible as people work together on a document. Voice mail requires people to take their own messages and to depend on significant auditory memory. Computers monitor worker output and can now catch all "careless" and "dyslexic" errors. Sometimes this is used to correct workers, but too often it is used to fire them before they have a chance to prove themselves through other contributions. Word processors have increased ease of writing. Unfortunately they often mean it is easier to write

internal memos, increasing reading demands on the dyslexic worker. Now, advanced reading skills are essential. The professional worker must scan today's mass of written material and pick out the most important parts. In other words, the increase in written output means an increase in reading requirements. In addition, all new technology has to be learned. Instructions are often difficult for all employees, whether they have learning disabilities or not.

On the other hand, computers have made it possible for many people with learning disabilities to work. Spell-checkers, grammar-checkers, and desktop publishing have made it possible for many people with learning disabilities to write well.

Requirements for Educational Credentials and Passage of Standardized Tests are Increasing. Professions such as speech pathology, physical therapy, and sign language interpreting are phasing out their bachelor's level programs and requiring master's degrees. College degrees are replacing the high school diploma for many professions. Blue collar jobs such as truck driver, beautician and plumber now require licensing examinations. Although the ADA requires accommodation in licensing examinations, tests and degree requirements can be an insurmountable barrier for most people with learning disabilities. Organizations and agencies are depriving themselves of the human resource of creative and disciplined people who, for whatever reason, have difficulty with school and passing tests.

Developing Job Accommodations

Once employees are on the job, the effect of the learning disability should be systematically negated. If employees have jobs that provide a perfect match of their strengths with the needs of the employer, accommodation may not become an issue. For example, many executives with learning disabilities who have "understanding secretaries" have managed to hide their disabilities for decades.

In many cases, however, the match is not perfect and the disability becomes a problem. In this case, job accommodation is necessary. Job accommodation refers to the process of matching the communication style and expectations of the supervisor and the production system to ensure that the disability of the employee does not hamper his or her ability to produce quality products or services. Prior to beginning accommodation, the employer, counselor, and/or employee must locate the problem (e.g., the employee is not following instructions). The four-part process, based on the Shewhart cycle, involves improving quality and is familiar to the many employers who practice Total Quality Management (Ernst and Young Quality Improvement Consulting Group, 1990). The process is as follows:

1. *Plan.* The supervisor, the employee, and other team members find a way to resolve the situation. For example, the employee may suggest holding discussions in a quiet place or asking the supervisor to talk in shorter sentences. If an employee cannot give the necessary information, observing the employee at work will often yield the best idea. Supervisors should ask themselves questions such as, "Are there times when the employee was successful in following instructions?" These successes may give supervisors clues as to how to accommodate.
2. *Do.* After sufficient planning, the accommodation should be implemented. For example, one supervisor started giving the employee instructions in her office and avoiding the former practice of talking to the employee near his noisy machine.
3. *Check.* See if the accommodation works. If the employee is able to produce well without negative impact on other aspects of the organization, the accommodation works.
4. *Act.* If the accommodation does not work, it may be necessary to go through the cycle a second time. If the accommodation works, steps should be taken to institutionalize the accommodation

so the employee does not lose it with a change of supervisors or other company need.

In the planning process, the following three areas can be changed:

1. *The workstation.* The employer might color code files, make a machine knob larger, or locate the employee in a quiet place.
2. *Work distribution.* The employee might request that a co-worker do tasks that he or she cannot do in return for doing one that the co-worker dislikes. Sometimes the supervisor removes a difficult but unimportant duty from the employee's job and asks someone else to do it.
3. *Communication process.* The supervisor needs to know how the employee gets information best. Memoranda or written instructions might be read to a dyslexic employee. Or the supervisor might put all instructions in writing for an employee with an auditory disability.

Particular problems come up in accommodating people with learning disabilities. Supervisors and co-workers are more apt to ascribe the problems of the person with a learning disability to personality factors than to the disability. Invisible disabilities bring very little sympathy and few offers of help. In addition, many accommodations requested by people with learning disabilities, such as extra clerical help, quiet space, and better quality management, are wanted by all employees. The Pathways Conference (Brown et al., 1990) recommended that the term *reasonable accommodation* needs to be clarified, particularly how it applies to people with learning disabilities. This clarification will ultimately have much to do with success or failure in the workplace.

Job Accommodations for Particular Learning Disabilities

Many employees with learning disabilities have problems with written language. These problems range from mild to very severe. When these problems manifest themselves as trouble with reading, the term of choice is *dyslexia*. Spelling difficulties are often involved. When language problems manifest themselves as trouble with writing, the term of choice is *dysgraphia*. In the survey of people with learning disabilities who called the President's Committee's Job Accommodation Network (Jacobs & Hendricks, in press), 71% (140) said they had difficulty reading, 18% (36) said they had difficulty spelling, and 11% said they had difficulty with composing written language.

Following are some types of learning disabilities along with sample accommodations. Some examples come from the Polaroid Corporation and were compiled by Verna B. Lacey, Program Manager of Learning Disabilities Program of the Technology Readiness Program. Polaroid Corporation made a major effort to accommodate their hourly employees with learning disabilities and partially as a result won the EVE Award from the U.S. Department of Labor. These accommodation samples are not meant to be used as a "cookbook" but are offered to trigger the creative and problem-solving process of workplace accommodation. Here are some possible solutions, written as if a counselor or consultant were making recommendations to a supervisor:

1. Talk to employees rather than give written instructions.
2. Allow use of taped texts and put training manuals on tape.
3. Let employees know what is important to read. If necessary, have someone read to them. Many employees have hidden their dyslexia by having coworkers or family members read to them.
4. Design forms well. Print should be dark and clear. Sufficient white space should be provided, and each section should be distinct. These forms are frequently preferred by other employees.
5. Allow extra time for reading assignments and reviewing written materials.
6. Set up a buddy system with a coworker who can explain new vocabulary and terminology so that the person with dyslexia understands written instructions.
7. Use graphic presentations. Visual reminders such as drawings, diagrams, and flowcharts are helpful and can often be completed easily with desktop publishing.
8. Computer accommodations can be extremely helpful. Some computers have voice output. Spell-checkers and grammar-checkers can assist people with dyslexia. In addition, many people with dysgraphia can write easily using a computer keyboard.
9. Proofread the work of employees who are dyslexic. Correct numbers and make sure they are not reversed. Proof forms and ensure that the items are in the appropriate blocks.
10. If employees have difficulty composing text, it can be helpful if someone else provides an outline or fills in the blanks for routine correspondence. Also, some jobs can be restructured so that the employee does not have to write.

Problems of Employees with Specific Learning Disabilities

Visual Perception Problems. Some people with learning disabilities have difficulty processing visual information. This does not necessarily mean they are dyslexic, but it can have important implications for performance and productivity. Some accommodations are:

1. Arrange for neat and well-organized surroundings. Usually, these employees keep their desks clean. Management and co-worker cooperation might be needed, however, if employees have difficulty, for example, pulling the right tool out of a box crowded with many tools that were not sorted and organized.

2. Allow color coding and encourage the employees to keep their work possessions where they can see them, rather than in drawers.
3. Good lighting is helpful.

Auditory Perceptual Problems. Difficulties perceiving sound, particularly spoken language, are also common in the workplace. Although only 7% of the callers with learning disabilities told the President's Committee's Job Accommodation Network that they had auditory perceptual problems, this difficulty is common but usually not recognized. Typically, people are aware of difficulties reading, but will ascribe difficulties in understanding speech to "not listening hard enough" or poor directions from others. It is crucial for supervisors to sensitize themselves to know how well all employees comprehend their communications. The following accommodation ideas are also extremely helpful to employees who use hearing aids or have hearing impairments. These accommodations place responsibility on the employer for ensuring that employees understand directions and expectations. Here are some accommodations written as if a counselor or consultant were making recommendations to a supervisor:

1. Write down your instructions.
2. Talk clearly. Use short sentences. Avoid jargon and multisyllabic words. This is good advice for co-workers and subordinates as well as supervisors.
3. Allow employees to take notes as you speak. Give sufficient time for them to write.
4. Ask employees to repeat your words back and then listen carefully.
5. Let the employees use a taperecorder to record important instructions and procedures. They can use the playback as a review of what was said.
6. Show them what needs to be done and then let them show you.
7. Avoid hinting and recognize that they may not always hear the emotions in your tone of voice. For example, a sarcastic comment might be taken literally.

Many people with learning disabilities have both auditory and visual perceptual problems. They will need to use both of their modalities together to learn a task. They may require additional time for training. For the most part, they will need the same types of accommodations as people with auditory and visual perceptual problems.

Certain training techniques are effective for all workers but may be essential to people with learning disabilities. For example, it helps to use as many senses as possible. Videotaped training showing how a task is done can assist employees with both visual and auditory disabilities, since they see the task and hear it and have control over pace of instruction. An employer, while talking about a task, might show the employee how to do it and have the instructions in writing as a back-up. As with all employees, employers should observe to see if the task is done correctly, leave time for questions, and assure them that any problems can be remedied.

Temporal-Perceptual Problems. Some employees with learning disabilities will not observe the passage of time in the ordinary way. Reading a clock may be difficult for them. They may become absorbed in their work and not be aware of the time. They may lack an instinctive feel for the length of an "hour" or a "minute." Employees with learning disabilities may come in late and leave late. They are easy to distinguish from unmotivated employees who come in late but always leave on time. Employers should remind employees of deadlines and consider flextime. It is not always necessary to come in on time. Many employees with learning disabilities use timers and beeping watches to keep track of time.

Directional Difficulties. Many people have difficulty automatically distinguishing between left and right; learning north, south, east, and west; or learning the layout of a large symmetrical building. This directional problem can be particularly severe in people who have learning disabilities. When this problem is combined with other learning disabilities, serious functional limitations can result. Building design can aid people with this difficulty. Paint colors, pictures, and other decorations can give visual cues as to which direction the person is facing when he or she leaves an elevator or enters a building. Maps can be made available and hung on the wall at various places in the building. The employee with this type of learning disability will need more time to learn a route. It is helpful if a supervisor or co-worker shows the employee the way and is patient if the employee asks several times. Work-stations should not be symmetrical. They should have distinguishing features that facilitate spatial organization. Some people with this kind of learning disability put a piece of tape to the left or right of their computer or desk.

Short-Term Memory Problems.   People with learning disabilities often have difficulties remembering details such as names, numbers, and specific facts, particularly the first few times the information is presented. This difficulty was reported by 6% of the callers to JAN. Some helpful techniques for the employee and supervisor are:

1. Use mnemonic devices and acronyms to remember sequences, lists, and so forth.
2. Organize details on paper so they can be looked up quickly through diagrams, flowcharts, or cheat sheets.
3. Arrange drills and practice exercises using the new material.
4. Computer software can organize material and reduce reliance on memory. Well-designed menus and "Help" features are essential.
5. Teach and instruct employees using as many modalities (e.g., visual, auditory, tactile) as possible.

Getting Along with Others in the Workplace

The field of learning disabilities is gradually reaching a consensus that difficulties in social skills are often part of a learning disability. The report to the U.S. Congress completed by the Interagency Committee on Learning Disabilities (1992) contained a chapter on social skills deficits and stated that "recent research has documented its range and severity" (p. 211). Some leading experts in the field of learning disabilities (Blalock, 1981; Johnson & Myklebust, 1971) believe that social skills deficits can be the most debilitating parts of the learning-disabled experience.

Business literature also stresses the importance of social skills in obtaining and retaining employment. For example, John T. Molloy (1982), author of *Live for Success*, interviewed 1,000 executives of American corporations and found that 98.5% of those interviewed believed that "successful image—dressing correctly, moving correctly, and speaking correctly—is critical for getting ahead" (p. 54). In addition, studies of fired executives and workers have shown lack of ability to get along with others as the chief reason for failure in the workplace.

For this reason, assisting persons with learning disabilities in getting along with others is essential to their future progress in employment. Classes in social skills, support groups, and individual counseling are helpful. Many people with learning disabilities need to learn basic communication skills such as how to begin a conservation, enter a group of people, and respond assertively to put-downs.

The Pathways to Employment (Brown et al., 1990) conference made several recommendations in this area, which they called "socioadaptability." It was suggested that the social competence of adults with learning disabilities be assessed in the workplace. An effective curriculum for social competence needs to be developed. In addition, it was pointed out that "people with learning disabilities and other people in their social network must develop a greater awareness of the effect of various types of learning disabilities on the individual's performance in social settings, schools, and in employment settings." It is common for people with learning disabilities to try to find a mentor who articulates the hidden policies and the undercurrents of office politics.

It is also helpful if a supervisor can be direct and specific. Subtle hints often are not perceived by employees with learning disabilities. They may not "pick up" the day-to-day cultural mores that are not ordinarily articulated. Someone often needs to explain inappropriate behavior and help them to overcome it. For example, a person with difficulty perceiving depth stood too close to other employees while talking to them, which made them uncomfortable. Their boss suggested that the employee stand farther away. Employees with learning disabilities need to hear what actions are making others uncomfortable and what they can do about it.

In another example, a worker with a learning disability, when first hired, was very eager to learn about the organization. He persistently asked other employees many questions and made suggestions on how they could do a better job. His co-workers resented his advice. The rules of turf and territory on a job had to be explained to him. He learned that the department was the responsibility of his boss, whose role it was to consider suggestions.

People with learning disabilities want to be treated normally and are completely capable of conforming to most situations. Supervisors should apply the same standards and rules, although, of course, reasonable accommodation should always be provided. A thorough orientation is also helpful. Employers who are sensitive to these issues can help the person with a learning disability to succeed.

Job Advancement

Social abilities become more and more important as the employee advances through the pyramid of an organization. Failure at "office politics" can lead to being fired. Many people with learning disabilities, at high and low levels, reach a plateau and are unable to advance for reasons of personal matching.

Another barrier to job advancement is academic skills. Many people with learning disabilities refuse supervisory positions because of the reading and writing required. Many organizations are requiring credentials for their managers that sometimes are beyond the reach of the capabilities of individuals with learning disabilities.

The issue of job advancement was discussed during the Pathways to Employment conference. Some suggestions involved the role of the educational system in exposing students with learning disabilities to work environments during their school years and development of a curriculum of job advancement skills. Employers were asked to clearly communicate job advancement skills to educators and school administrators. In addition, it was recommended that, "Employers need to understand and respond to the particular needs of people with learning disabilities" (p. 30). People with learning disabilities were challenged with evaluating themselves and developing skills in areas such as self-advocacy, flexibility, independence, negotiation, and motivation. A strong self-image on the part of employees with a learning disability was recognized as critical to their future promotion potential.

Clearly, the strengths of many people with learning disabilities, such as creativity, self-discipline, and overcompensation, can assist the person with a learning disability to advance in employment.

Conclusion

People with learning disabilities attain their rightful place in the workplace by using their skills and abilities. Currently, they are doing so, but they are facing many barriers, some that are insurmountable at times. However, the workplace is a complex and ever-changing place. When they cannot contribute their abilities because of a lack of accommodation and other societal barriers, they become part of the problem of dependency and structural unemployment. Moreover, an undue toll is taken on self-esteem.

Through the work of national policymakers, service providers, employers, and people with learning disabilities themselves, people with learning disabilities can reach their potential. They can contribute by helping their business organization be an effective and efficient competitor in today's economy.

References

ACLD Vocational Committee. (1982). Preliminary report of ACLD Vocational Committee survey of learning disabled adults. *Newsbriefs*. Pittsburgh: Association of Children with Learning Disabilities.

Americans with Disabilities Act. (1990). P.L. 101–336.

Blalock, J. (1981). Persistent problems and concerns of young adults with learning disabilities. In W. M. Cruickshank & A. Silver (Eds.), *Bridges to Tomorrow* (pp. 35–46). Syracuse: Syracuse University Press.

Brown, D. S., Gerber, P. J., & Dowdy, C. (1990). *Pathways to employment for people with learning disabilities*. Washington, DC: President's Committee for the Employment of People with Disabilities.

Employment and Training Administration. (1991). *The learning disabled in employment and training programs*. Research and Evaluation Report Series 91-E. Washington, DC: U.S. Department of Labor.

Ernst and Young Quality Improvement Consulting Group. (1990). *Total quality: An executive's guide for the 1990's*. Homewood, IL: Business One Irwin.

Gerber, P. J. (1990). The problem, the future, the challenge: The issue of employability for persons with learning disabilities. In D. Brown, P. J. Gerber, & C. Dowdy (Eds.), *Pathways to Employment for people with learning disabilities* (pp. 3–9). Washington, DC: President's Committee for the Employment of People with Disabilities.

Interagency Committee on Learning Disabilities. (1987). *Learning disabilities: A report to the U.S. Congress*. Washington, DC: U.S. Department of Health and Human Resources.

Jacobs, A. E. & Hendricks, D. J. (in press). Job accommodations for adults with learning disabilities: Brilliantly disguised opportunities. *Learning Disability Quarterly*.

Johnson, D. & Myklebust, H. (1971). *Learning disabilities: Practices and procedures*. New York: Grune & Stratton.

Minskoff, E., Sautter, S. W., Sheldon, K. L., Streidle, E. F., & Baker, D. P. (1986). *Specific results: A comparative analysis of the survey responses of subgroups of adults with learning disabilities (Research Report B)*. Research and Demonstration Project for Improving Vocational Rehabilitation of LD Adults. Fishersville, VA: Woodrow Wilson Rehabilitation Center.

Molloy, J. T. (1982). *Live for success*. New York: Bantam Publishers.

SRI International. (1991). Youth with disabilities: How are they doing? *National Longitudinal Transition Study of Special Education Students*. Palo Alto: SRI International.

Chapter 19

Employment Success for Adults with Learning Disabilities

RICK GINSBERG, PH.D.
PAUL J. GERBER, PH.D.
HENRY B. REIFF, PH.D.

You have to decide that whatever you want to do, go for it. Don't worry if people say that you can't do it . . . there must be some way to achieve. You have to accept failure, recognize that the route you take may not be right, and accept the fact that you have to start over again. But if you want it bad enough, you'll do it.

You must learn where your strengths are and how you can use them, and where your weaknesses are and how to avoid them or compensate. I have learned to accept who I am, what I can do, and what I cannot do, who I should not try to be, and who I should try to be.

I think that probably my learning disability has helped me. Certainly, it has been a hindrance too . . . but things have a way of weighing themselves out, and I think in the long run it has been an asset. I don't ever think, "Gee, if I didn't have a learning disability just think of what I would have accomplished." I think probably my learning disability, because I had it, has brought out a different side to me that wouldn't be there if I didn't have it. It has been painful, but it has also brought out positive things.

Quotes from interviews with three highly successful adults with learning disabilities

Americans revere successful people. The phenomenon of billionaire Ross Perot's ill-fated quest for the presidency in 1992 is

evidence of the respect that people in contemporary America have for successful individuals. In advertising, kids sing that they "want to be like Mike" (Michael Jordan), as successful persons in a variety of fields are highly visible when promoting products, gracing magazine covers, and being held up as role models for children and adults alike. Why this love affair with success?

Americans and those in other industrialized nations share a common admiration for careers that offer high levels of status, wealth, and power (Etzioni, 1969). Professions such as medicine, law, university teaching, science and engineering, high finance, and accountancy as well as business entrepreneurs are held in higher esteem than many other occupations. Moreover, people in any field who make a lot of money or achieve some eminence are usually held in high regard. Along with earning high incomes, such individuals generally have much control over their daily work environment and go through rigorous training and intense experiences to develop their talents. They are respected for the work they perform. Such people have attained significant employment success.

The path to success is never easy. It requires much hard work, dedication, and risk. For those who must face challenges above and beyond the ordinary, attaining success is particularly elusive. People with learning disabilities struggle on a daily basis with common basic problems in such areas as reading, writing, calculating, concentrating, or memory. For some reason, they are unable to learn to process and conceptualize like the majority of other people. As an economist with dyslexia exclaimed during one of our interviews, "They are left-handed learners and thinkers in a right-handed world." Yet, despite the odds, many adults with learning disabilities overcome numerous hurdles and move on to greater heights. Indeed, many attain a level of success that would be the envy of most people.

This chapter presents the findings of a research study that entered the world of more than 70 adults with learning disabilities who beat the odds and became successful in their chosen professions. They beat the odds in that research has shown that learning disabilities do not disappear after schooling (Blalock, 1981) and that factors such as low reading levels, poor written language, feelings of inadequacy, fear of failure, attention disorders, organizational difficulties, and social learning problems can impede performance (Johnson & Blalock, 1987). Indeed, follow-up studies of children with learning disabilities indicate that the majority do maintain jobs and can support themselves and their families, but many have problems maintaining and/or obtaining positions (Cruickshank et al., 1980; Lewis, 1977; Rogan & Hartman, 1976).

Much has been written on success, including many popular personal accounts by media celebrities such as Donald Trump and Lee Iacocca and widely acclaimed studies of businesses (Peters & Waterman, 1982; Price, 1984). Studies have focused on success by examining a variety of people and variables, including successful women executives (Halcomb, 1979; Wilkens, 1987), successful black women (Sims, 1982), businessmen (Caddes, 1986; Garfield, 1986; McCormack, 1984), various achievement factors (Griessman, 1987; Jencks, 1979), and hundreds of success strategy plans. But the patterns described in the various studies concerning success are not necessarily relevant to those with learning disabilities. Simply put, although success for almost everyone requires some extraordinary effort, or drive, or talent, or some other such factor, persons with learning disabilities face an array of challenges foreign to their nondisabled counterparts.

Findings of previous research related to adults with learning disabilities share certain commonalities. The most striking of these is the pattern of persistence of learning disabilities into adulthood. The consistency of this finding suggests that learning disabilities represent more of a developmental deficit than a lag or delay. Persisting problems are manifested in diverse areas of functioning. And the impact of the childhood problems may emerge in different forms of adulthood. Studies by Menkes, Rowe, and Menkes (1967), Silver and Hagin (1964), Balow and Bloomquist (1965), Hardy (1968), Frauenheim (1978), Frauenheim and Heckerl (1983), Buchanan and Wolf (1986), Bowen and Hynd (1988), Kroll (1984), and McCue, Shelly and Goldstein (1986) all show that the various forms of problems associated with learning disabilities continue from childhood into adulthood. As Hoy and Noel (1984) noted, deficiencies in oral language, thinking and reasoning, interpersonal relationships, behavior, reading, mathematics, and written language were commonly reported in adults with learning disabilities.

Several studies have reported that success is possible for adults with learning disabilities. Research by Abbott and Frank (1975), Rawson (1968), Rogan and Hartman (1976), and Silver and Hagin (1985) all describe positive adult outcomes, particularly in the context of affluent family backgrounds and positive educational experience. Other studies provide evidence that successful school experiences in conjunction with other factors may predispose individuals with learning disabilities to greater success as adults. For example, Rawson's (1968) follow-up study of 56 adults who attended a special private school found that many were successful professionally and satisfied socially, although attributes such as affluent families, high intelligence, and mild learning disabilities were certainly contributing factors. Bruck (1987) even argues that functional limitations resulting from learning disabilities can be greatly reduced through proper intervention. Despite these positive indicators, the preponderance of data implies that adults with learning disabilities generally have a lower mean job status than the population in general (Gerber et al., 1988; White et al., 1983).

Unlike previous research, the study reported in this chapter went beyond examining personality dynamics and demographics of successful adults with learning disabilities, to explore the alterable variables and systems of interaction that have fostered high degrees of employment success. In other words, this study examined patterns of behavior that we feel are transferable to other individuals with learning disabilities. Qualitative research methods were utilized to more fully understand how learning disabilities present obstacles to success and how certain individuals were able to overcome these challenges. The main focus, therefore, was on examining those factors that led to success and should be transferable to the vast majority of the learning disabled population who have some difficulty in coping with their disability.

What follows is a brief presentation of the methods utilized in the research, as well as a discussion of the findings and the development of a model of employment success for adults with learning disabilities.

Methods

In order to understand the success patterns of adults with learning disabilities, we used retrospective interviews as the main source of data collection. We started with the effect of success and sought possible causes from the adults with learning disabilities we interviewed. In all, we interviewed a sample of highly successful adults with learning disabilities (n = 46) and a control group sample of moderately successful adults with learning disabilities (n = 25). Interviews followed an open-ended interview schedule and lasted from 3 to 8 hours. We drew our sample using a nomination process covering all of North America.

We defined success as involving five factors: income level, job classification, education level, prominence in one's field, and job satisfaction. For the most part, we selected these variables because they corresponded closely to the high levels of status, income, and power that characterize the most highly regarded professions. Job satisfaction was included to account for the affective side of success. We had a panel of five experts rate each candidate on the five factors as either high, moderate, or low. To be placed in the high category, participants needed at least four ratings of high and no ratings of low. Those with a majority of moderate ratings and no more than one low rating were placed in the moderate pool.

The final sample controlled for possible confounding factors by matching the two groups across key variables. The 71 interviewees came from 24 states and Canada. Twenty-six occupations were represented in the highly successful group, while fourteen were represented in the moderately successful group.

Data analysis focused on discovering the pattern of success of the adults with learning disabilities. Also, we compared the high-success and moderate-success groups to discern any distinguishing features of high degrees of vocational success. For purposes of validity, several researchers outside the project checked our findings and project staff shared and discussed results before final conclusions were drawn.

A Model for Successful Adults With Learning Disabilities

The findings suggest that the overriding factor leading to success is control. Successful adults with learning disabilities were able to

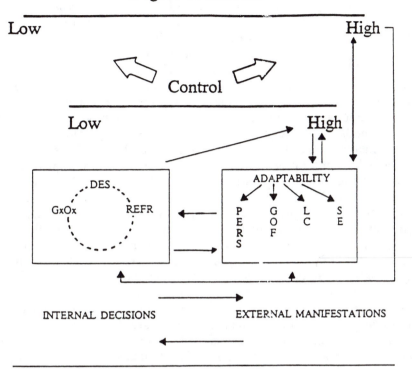

FIGURE 19-1 A model of vocational success for adults with learning disabilities. (From Gerber, P., Ginsberg, R., and Reiff, H. (1992). Identifying alterable patterns in employment success for highly successful adults with learning disabilities. *Journal of Learning Disabilities, 25,* 475–487.)

take control of their lives, and the greater the degree of control, the greater the likelihood for success. But taking control was characterized by several themes we categorize as "internal decisions" and "external manifestations." The internal decisions include what we call desire, goal orientation, and reframing. The external manifestations we depict as adaptability and include persistence, goodness-of-fit, learned creativity, and social ecologies. All these themes interact with one another, and the degree of control and, ultimately, the level of success are related to each individual's attainment within the various themes.

The most striking finding of our research was how well persons who are labeled as learning disabled are able to learn and ultimately succeed. They may not learn in the well-accepted ways of our culture, *but they* *can and do learn.* Given the differences in their styles, the road to success was often strewn with pain and frustration. But the patterns we discerned were common to all our successful adults and suggest a model for others to follow. Significantly, although both our high-success and moderate-success groups shared the patterns or themes we identified, the high-success group was more exceptional or attained a higher degree within each of these than did the moderate-success individuals.

Figure 19-1 presents the model for success for adults with learning disabilities. *Control* was the overriding theme that characterized all efforts geared at success. Control refers to the drive to manage one's life. This control involved a set of internal decisions and external manifestations that are represented on the figure beneath the issue of control. But attaining control is the key element for success. Adults with learning disabilities work throughout their lives to learn how to take control of their lives. It fuels their ultimate success.

Control was so important because individuals with learning disabilities do not learn or even think in traditional ways. They must forge an individualized path in order to accomplish something. Throughout their lives, the traditional culture they confronted sought to deprive them of their natural ways of learning and doing. After all, their approach was not acceptable to those without learning disabilities. Most times the adults with learning disabilities were reminded that their way was wrong! As we listened to the highly successful adults in our sample, we were continually reminded of the specific ways that they reached for control. A noted dentist said that, "I feel most confident when something is in my hands . . . when I have total control." A high-success school director explained, "Being dyslexic and having 75 cents can buy you a cup of coffee. . . . There is no percentage in being dyslexic unless you work to make it better." A woman executive stressed the need to anticipate problems to attain control. She reported, "If you can be an anticipator and look ahead and try to anticipate . . . you're ready. . . . LD people need to be taught strategies to anticipate problems."

Thus, control was a necessity. As the model predicts, high control is needed for high degrees of success, although success is still not automatic. Certainly, an array of uncontrollable factors (e.g., good or bad luck) may impact on an individual's level of success. Nonetheless, without a high degree of control, success for the adult with learning disabilities is unlikely. In our study, the higher degree of control attained clearly distinguished the highly successful group of participating adults with learning disabilities from the moderately successful group.

The model displays how control was achieved by our successful sample of adults. A set of interacting variables, which we call *internal decisions* and *external manifes-*

tations, characterizes control. Success must evolve, and the process, which spanned numerous years, began with a conscious set of decisions. Individuals must take a personal stance that they are going to try to gain better control of their existence and it is hoped, succeed. This beginning process we describe as the internal decisions. They are the internal components of gaining control. Then, the adults in our sample undertook certain activities that helped foster control and success. Thus, the internal decisions must be translated into actual behaviors. These coping strategies and techniques we refer to as the external manifestations, and all fall under the category of adaptability.

As the model suggests, these variables all interact closely with one another. As one masters the internal decisions (which are pictured in a circle to reflect that there is no clear beginning point, and that these three factors are all closely interrelated), greater adaptability is possible. But improved adaptability also fosters continually stronger internal decisions. As might be expected, as more control is achieved, and more success, the internal decisions and adaptability continue to strengthen and improve. Next, we briefly describe the components of the internal decisions and external manifestations.

Internal Decisions

Desire

Desire is an essential element if one is to excel. The adults in our sample took a stand for themselves at some point and decided it was the time to move ahead. Desire is certainly necessary for success for any individual, as we were vividly reminded by several of the highly successful adults in our sample who quoted former President Calvin Coolidge:

> Talent will not; there is nothing more common than unsuccessful men with talent. Genius will not, unrewarded genius is almost a proverb. Education alone will not; the world is full of educated derelicts. Persistence and determination are omnipotent.

But given that succeeding is such a great challenge for the adults with learning disabilities because of all the hurdles they confront, this desire was especially significant and was very conspicuous and powerful. In describing this perception, a number of individuals invoked metaphors related to fire. Their desire to prove that they could succeed felt like a fire was ablaze within them. Thus, we heard, "I've always had a kind of burning feeling . . . kind of like being on fire to succeed"; "You fight until you can't fight anymore, and then you fight some more. . . . You take the hurt and turn it inward and it becomes part of the burn. . . . It has to burn." Another summed it up this way: "You've got to have that inner sense that you're going to do it, want to do it. If you don't want to do it, you are not going to be successful. You might have to do one step at a time and go slower. But . . . you have to be determined in life if you are going to make it."

The tone of the desire among those in our moderately successful group was much more tempered. As one fellow described it, "I'm really just someone who is plodding along." Such an attitude would be foreign to those more highly successful adults with learning disabilities. The desire was certainly much more restrained for those we labeled as moderately successful.

Goal Orientation

Closely related to decisions concerning desire was being goal oriented. Adults with learning disabilities need to feel successful, and they are apprehensive about the possibility of a continuing pattern of failure. Thus, they set explicit goals to work toward. Goal setting allows persons with learning disabilities to have practical, attainable aspirations. It also provides greater focus for individuals who have experienced considerable difficulty in learning and other customary daily activities. In other words, the adults with learning disabilities do not waste a lot of time pursuing ends that will lead to failure. Finally, goal setting feeds on

itself. Once even minimal goals can be met, the feelings of success can be the basis for greater challenges. As a highly successful woman explained, "I have my goals . . . any kind of movement toward my goals feels very successful. Anything I am doing better than I did last week or three years ago feels successful." Another commented, "It (the learning disability) has greatly impacted my success by narrowing my field, not as a limitation, but as giving direction. It has pointed me to something I can do very well."

The goal setting for the highly successful group resulted in either short-term or long-term goals. But the key was that they set goals. One entrepreneur explained it this way: "Successful people have a plan. You have to have a plan, goals, strategy, otherwise you are flying through the clouds and then you hit the mountain."

The moderately successful group differed from their more successful counterparts in several ways. Some set much more short-term goals than the more successful individuals. Others appeared to be much more easily diverted from goals. Still others were much less goal oriented. Clearly, their goals were far less ambitious. One of the moderately successful adults, in explaining his thoughts about goals, remarked, "Successful people have goals . . . much of what happened to me just happened."

Reframing

The final component of the internal decisions was probably the most significant. A process we refer to as *reframing* is the set of decisions related to reinterpreting the learning disabilities experience from something dysfunctional to something functional. It is the acknowledgment that the major obstacle facing those with learning disabilities is not the disability itself, but instead the ability to brave the various challenges endured as one learns to live with the disability and overcome it. We discovered a number of stages to this process of reframing. Some moved through the stages almost in unison, whereas others systematically moved from one to the next.

The first is the need to *recognize* the disability. It is impossible to overcome a disability unless it is recognized.

Second, there must be a degree of *acceptance* attained. This can involve accepting both the negative and positive ramifications of having learning disabilities, but it is a need that is real and must be confronted. As a highly successful college professor explained, "I needed to be proud of myself. As long as I was ashamed of being learning disabled, it was difficult to succeed."

Third, there is a need for *understanding* the disability and all its implications. An understanding of one's strengths and weaknesses is a prerequisite for success. A lawyer described this component of reframing as follows: "As a dyslexic, you have to accept the degree to which you will and won't succeed in life. The biggest advantage is that once you realize you can't do all these things, you become good at finding alternative solutions and at making the best of what you have. . . ."

Finally, one must be willing to take *action*. All the recognition, acceptance, and understanding in the world is irrelevant without a conscious decision to take specific action toward goals. One person characterized herself this way, capturing the reframing process: "You must learn where your strengths are and how you can use them, and where your weaknesses are and how to avoid them or compensate. I have learned to accept who I am, what I can do, what I cannot do, who I should not try to be, and who I should try to be."

The moderately successful adults reframed as well. However, they generally did not progress through all four stages to the degree of the highly successful group. They did much more blaming and avoiding, and held back more than the more successful adults. A school director summed up this sense by explaining that, "I literally have approached life like I was a second-rate human being. Dyslexics don't feel as good about themselves as other people."

External Manifestations

Certain activities fostered control and success. The internal decisions had to be translated into actual behaviors. These approaches, behaviors, and techniques, which we call *adaptability*, were the keys for unleashing the potential within each person. Four such factors were identified.

Persistence

Successful adults with learning disabilities work extremely hard. Although desire was a necessary internal decision, externally it resulted in high levels of persistence. Thus, the desire to succeed was not enough; one had to be willing to sacrifice and persevere toward goals. This persistence became a way of life and no doubt was an outgrowth of having a learning disability. Comments indicated what an incredibly resilient group of people these were. For example, we heard, "I overcame my problem with sheer grit and determination"; "I made accomplishments by working harder than others and gutting it out"; "The learning disability positively affected my success . . . I learned to persist, to deal with pain and frustration . . . things don't come easy to me, but I work long and hard. This is central to my being."

The difference between the high-success and moderate-success adults with learning disabilities was distinct. While persistence was obvious for both groups, those who were moderately successful did not push with the tenacity of the more successful adults. The high-success adults displayed more drive, took more risks, and appeared more tenacious. As one moderately successful adult explained, "My non-assertiveness hinders my getting ahead."

Goodness-of-Fit

Along with persistence, an integral part of adaptability was the goodness-of-fit with the environment the adults with learning disabilities aspired toward. They tried to fit themselves to surroundings and environments in which they could succeed, where their skills and abilities could be optimized and their weaknesses minimized. These adults found work that they enjoyed and where they could be both comfortable and successful. Again and again, the successful adults explained to us how they carefully chose work that would allow them the chance for success. It was an empowering experience. For example, one man explained that, "For most of my life, I realized that I could not do what most people could. Therefore, I sought to be able to do things that others could not. With an aptitude in mechanics and a fascination with the human body, I chose biomedical engineering." A businesswoman succinctly told us, "Capitalize on your strengths . . . look at what you can do best and enjoy most."

Far fewer of the moderate-success people created their own work environments. Their autonomy was seemingly far more constrained in the workplace. In addition, they did not express the passion for their work so characteristic of the highly successful adults.

Learned Creativity

The essence of adaptability was learned creativity, or the various strategies, techniques, devices, and other mechanisms devised by the successful adults to enhance their ability to perform well. Since they had experienced some difficulty operating in the "regular" system, they bucked the company line and realized that there was little incentive to conform to a system that exposed their weaknesses. Instead, they came up with unique and personal ways to accomplish tasks. Thus, they manipulated the system to avoid highlighting what they could not do, and they tried to anticipate potential problem areas so they could compensate for their areas of weakness. As one high-success adult described this idea:

> Other people don't seem to look at the possibilities available to accomplish a task. When

I have been able to handle tougher jobs, it has always been because I could approach a problem in a different way, a little easier way. I have always tended to think of ways to do things that are a little unusual.

Both the high-success and moderate-success adults with learning disabilities used an array of coping strategies. Among the highly successful adults, techniques included color coding files, putting photographs of clients on files to assist with remembering the clients, special reading methods, and setting consistent morning and evening travel plans to avoid potential confusion getting to and from work. However, the moderate-success adults tended to focus much more energy on manipulation as a means for avoiding exposure of their disability. The high-success group was far more creative and attempted to build on their personal areas of strength.

Social Ecology

Finally, successful adults with learning disabilities willingly utilized supportive and helpful people. Also, they sharpened their skills by designing personal improvement programs. We call these support- and improvement-oriented processes their *social ecology*. Most of the successful adults established support networks with a spouse, a family member, a friend, or someone else they could rely on. In addition, they purposely selected their mentors. Some were luckier than others—their support came from family members or close friends they did not have to solicit. But having support readily available and actually making use of it are not always the same. In the case of successful adults, they recognized and took advantage of help they needed in overcoming hurdles, whether it be in the form of human support or training in areas of weakness. They avoided dependence, but rather achieved a balance between support and autonomy. One successful adult described the notion this way:

> You need other people to help . . . to help you believe in yourself. But you must be will-

ing to accept some help, from a secretary or anyone. Otherwise, you will waste too much time. You must learn to depend on others to a certain extent.

The distinction between the high-success and moderate-success adults concerning social ecologies revolved around two key factors: the level of support employed and the willingness to embrace support. The moderately successful were far more dependent on others than were the more highly successful adults. In contrast, the highly successful adults utilized support to help them gain control of their lives. In addition, the highly successful individuals were far more willing to seek support and help. As one moderately successful adult explained, "If I could do it all over again, I would ask for more help."

Conclusion

The implications of this research are closely aligned with findings from studies on multiple intelligences (Gardner, 1983; Gardner & Hatch, 1989) and variable thinking styles (Sternberg, 1990). Such studies suggest that individuals think and learn in different ways, and that schooling and training must be sensitive to these differences. Our research also shows that persons with learning disabilities do think and learn differently, but they can and do learn—they are just different learners. Our learning disabilities sample was most successful in the workplace given the right grit, determination, thought, application, and help.

We would also argue that each of the internal decisions and external manifestations discovered are variables susceptible to training. Individuals can be taught about desire, goal orientation, and reframing, and, as a result, they enhance the possibility of excelling in these areas. Similarly, people can be taught about the need for persistence, goodness-of-fit, learned creativity, and social support. Although such teachings may not always be effective, presenting how these themes have interacted for control and

success for others may play a significant role in altering children's lives.

References

Abbott, R., & Frank, B. (1975). A follow-up of LD children in a private school. *Academic Therapy, 19,* 291–298.

Balow, B., & Bloomquist, M. (1965). Young adults ten to fifteen years after severe reading disability. *Elementary School Journal, 66,* 44–48.

Blalock, J. W. (1981). Persistent problems and concerns of young adults with learning disabilities. In W. M. Cruickshank & A. A. Silver (Eds.), *Bridges to tomorrow: The best of the ACLD, Vol. 2* (pp. 35–56). Syracuse, NY: Syracuse University Press.

Bowen, S. M., & Hynd, G. W. (1988). Do children with learning disabilities outgrow deficits in selective auditory attention? Evidence from dichotic listening in adults with learning disabilities. *Journal of Learning Disabilities, 21,* 623–631.

Bruck, M. (1987). The adult outcomes of children with learning disabilities. *Annals of Dyslexia, 37,* 252–263.

Buchanan, M., & Wolf, J. (1986). A comprehensive study of learning disabled adults. *Journal of Learning Disabilities, 19,* 34–38.

Caddes, C. (1986). *Portraits of success: Impressions of silicon valley pioneers.* Palo Alto, CA: Tioga Publishing Co.

Cruickshank, W., Morse, W., & Johns, J. (1980). *Learning disabilities—The struggle from adolescence toward adulthood.* Syracuse, NY: Syracuse University Press.

Etzioni, A. (1969). *The semi-professions and their organization.* New York: The Free Press.

Frauenheim, J. (1978). Academic achievement characteristics of adult males who were diagnosed as dyslexic in childhood. *Journal of Learning Disabilities, 11,* 21–28.

Frauenheim, J., & Heckerl, J. (1983). Longitudinal study of psychological achievement test performance in severe dyslexic adults. *Journal of Learning Disabilities, 16,* 339–347.

Gardner, H. (1983). *Frames of mind.* New York: Basic Books.

Gardner, H., and Hatch, T. (1989). Multiple intelligences go to school. *Educational Researcher, 18,* 4–10.

Garfield, C. (1986). *Peak performers.* New York: Avon Books.

Gerber, P. J., Reiff, H. B., & Ginsberg, R. (1988). Studies on learning disabled adults: Methodological and substantive considerations. *Thalamus, 6* (7), 1–32.

Griessman, B. E. (1987). *The achievement factors: Candid interviews with some of the most successful people of our time.* New York: Dodd, Mead.

Halcomb, R. (1979). *Women making it: Patterns and profiles of success.* New York: Atheneum.

Hardy, M. (1968). Clinical follow-up of disabled readers. Unpublished doctoral dissertation. Toronto: University of Toronto.

Hoy, C. A., & Noel, G. K. (1984). *Description and definition of learning disabilities. Academic assessment and remediation of adults with learning disabilities: A resource series for adult basic education teachers.* Atlanta: Georgia State Department of Education.

Jencks, C. (1979). *Who gets ahead? The determinants of economic success in America.* New York: Basic Books.

Johnson, D. J., & Blalock, J. W. (1987). Summary of problems and needs. In D. J. Johnson & J. W. Blalock (Eds.), *Adults with learning disabilities: Clinical studies* (pp. 277–293). Orlando, FL: Grune & Stratton.

Kroll, L. G. (1984). LD's—What happens when they are no longer children? *Academic Therapy, 20,* 133–148.

Lewis, R. (1977). *The other child grows up.* New York: Time Books.

McCormack, M. H. (1984). *What they don't teach you at Harvard Business School,* New York: Bantam.

McCue, M. P., Shelly, C., & Goldstein, G. (1986). Intellectual, academic, and neuropsychological performance levels in learning disabled adults. *Journal of Learning Disabilities, 19,* 233–236.

Menkes, M., Rowe, J., & Menkes, J. (1967). A twenty-five year follow-up study on the hyperkinetic child with minimal brain dysfunction. *Pediatrics, 38,* 393–399.

Peters, T. J., & Waterman, R. H. (1982). *In search of excellence: Lessons from America's best run companies.* New York: Warner Books.

Price, J. (1984). *The spirit of enterprise: The best of the new entrepreneurs.* New York: Random House.

Rawson, M. (1968). *Developmental language disability: Adult accomplishments of dyslexic boys.* Baltimore: Johns Hopkins University Press.

Rogan, L., & Hartman, L. (1976). *A follow-up study of learning disabled children as adults.* Final Report (Project #443CH600100, Grant #OEG-0-74-7453), Washington, DC: Bureau of Education for the Handicapped, U.S. Department of Health, Education and Welfare.

Silver, A., & Hagin, R. (1964). Specific reading disability: Follow-up studies. *American Journal of Orthopsychiatry, 24,* 95–101.

Silver, A., & Hagin, R. (1985). Outcomes of learning disabilities in adolescence. In M. Sugar, A. Esman, J. Looney, A. Schwartzberg, & A. Sorosky (Eds.), *Adolescent psychiatry: Developmental and clinical studies* (Vol. 12). Chicago: The University of Chicago Press.

Sims, N. (1982). *All about success for the black woman.* Garden City, NY: Doubleday.

Sternberg, R. J. (1990). Thinking styles: Keys to understanding student performance. *Phi Delta Kappan, 71,* 366–371.

White, W. J., Deshler, D. D., Schumaker, J. B., Warner, M. M., Alley, G. R., & Clark, F. C. (1983). The effects of learning disabilities on post-school adjustment. *Journal of Rehabilitation, 49,* 46–50.

Wilkens, J. (1987). *Her own business: Success secrets of entrepreneurial women.* New York: McGraw-Hill.

Chapter 20

Personal Perspective on Vocational Issues

JOHN CORCORAN, B.S.

In order to provide a personal "perspective" on vocational issues, I must begin with the perspective I had before I learned to read, so that I can compare it to the way I see the workplace today. As I became a new reader, I developed a new perspective. I can't tell the world everything about literacy, but I can introduce my personal perspective as an employer, as an employee, and as an entrepreneur.

When I was young, I worked odd jobs where I wasn't confronted by the possibility of having to read. Whether it was digging a ditch, baling hay, or working in a service station, all I needed was my willingness to work hard and the drive to get the job done. These entry-level jobs were where I began developing my sense of a work ethic. I succeeded in the workplace because I understood that I was to provide a service to my employer, and that I would get paid for my efforts. I took pride in every job I had, and I always tried to give my boss more than he asked for. My area of confidence stemmed from the fact that I knew that if I could get the job, I could demonstrate my value by how hard I was willing to work. I succeeded when I had no paperwork to face in these types of jobs. My sense of competition carried me through these odd jobs.

Even though I was a failure in school and I couldn't read or write, I always knew that I could compete in the workplace, that I could excel, that I could succeed in that arena. I

had the need to excel, and this was the place that I was able to excel. The odds were overwhelmingly against me there. All the while, the marketplace was telling me that I needed an education to get ahead. I saw that paper was going to invade the successful arenas of my life only to easily pull me down. I knew that it was coming to get me. Paper became a symbol of failure to me. At school, that's all there was.

Growing up, I had known that I had many abilities that would allow me to succeed. I was competitive. I was creative. I could "read" any situation and react to it. As a paperboy at 9 years of age, I had to hold my own against 12- and 13-year-olds who would try to chase me off. It was these kinds of things that gave me self-confidence. Yet, what was devastating was being told by my teachers that I was lazy because I wasn't doing my language homework. Even though that was far from the truth, I didn't know that at the time.

Leadership was not a problem. When I was 18, I became a foreman with six men under me, all working for a crop duster. The hard work got me by. But eventually my dependence on pure work ethic became less reliable.

When I got a job in the mailroom as a college student, I experienced my first clash with my lack of literary skills in the workplace. This was still an entry-level job but I wanted a "clean hands" job. It was here that I began to grasp the idea of real-life competition.

For a while, I would be able to keep the monster from ruining me by creating my own environment. By becoming an entrepreneur, I was able to control the flow of paper, steering it away. But I always knew that I couldn't keep it up forever and that it would eventually catch up with me. Any confrontation with the paper was going to be a no-win situation. It was like fighting a war in which loss was certainly just a matter of time.

All the goals that I had were in constant jeopardy. As a contractor, I had learned to build a house, from digging the foundation to laying the rooftop, yet if any changes or improvements were to be made, it called for more paperwork. Unfortunately, the educational system had passed me by as a youth and it wasn't getting any better. Although I didn't have the reading skills of a second-grader, I was hoping that I would get it by osmosis or magic. I had heard from teachers and educators that it would develop like walking and talking. "Relax," I heard, "it will happen." It never did.

As I evolved in the workplace, I predicted my ultimate failure. What was true then is true now. As you climb the business ladder, as you get promoted, there is no way around facing "the paper." Anything that involved paper would spell my inevitable failure.

Eventually, my ambition told me that I had to increase my coping skills on my own. I couldn't allow myself to be passed by again. I believed that in order to go forward in the workplace I needed more "education." In my struggle against "paper," I tried to manipulate the papers without being master of them. I could obtain a high school diploma, a college degree, even a teaching credential, and yet I couldn't even read what was on them. The fact was I didn't have the language skills necessary to be able to acquire basic literary skills.

This manipulation that I speak of was how I coped with the literate world. By playing this dangerous game, I was constantly living on "the edge." I was in constant fear of failure and of being discovered or perceived as dishonest. I was as honest as I could be, but to the outside world, anyone who is illiterate is perceived as being stupid and lazy. These are the same people who give out the report cards and the paychecks. I call them the "gate keepers." In order to get past them, you have to be licensed. To be certified, you have to have the papers.

While I carried on the charade for so long, I never meant to hurt other people. I did it to enhance the quality of my life and to give myself some upward mobility. But the terrible side effect of this was that I was forced to go into a dishonest mode and put up a guard that never truly came down. I wish that my employers would have recognized my deficiency and helped me.

In the past, literacy was not an issue for the employer. An employer could get around the paper roadblocks. It was up to the employee to obtain his position with whatever skills he had. With this emerging awareness, there are now laws that require employers to aid these employees who confess to being illiterate.

For the modern employer, the minimum skills for any given job have increased. In a few places where one still does not need basic literacy skills, there is very little pay and no future. In the past, an employer depended on the public education system to provide him with a literate workforce.

Some employers who have become aware of the current extent of illiteracy would rather weed out the nonreaders by having them fill out the job application in front of them. The reality may be that it is time for employers to become active in the educational process for personal survival. A change of attitudes is being called for. Education need not end with a diploma, valid or not. Education should be a lifelong process.

It wasn't until recently that I found out that it was even possible for me to read. After the excitement of discovery wore off, I became infuriated because there is such a body of knowledge that remains untapped. There is a bureaucratic pecking order in the "paper world," and the "gate keepers" stand guard to prevent some truths from being revealed. I only wanted to be dealt a fair hand, but I ended up short-changed. I've been held hostage by the system for so long I was afraid they would blame me. It wasn't until I was 48 years old that I stopped running, by going to a library and asking for help.

I feel angry and bitter every time I think of how I was lost in the system. I was humiliated every time my teachers forced me to participate in the spelling bees each Friday, then made me stay in during recess when my spelling was incorrect. I was called on when they knew I couldn't read, and I was embarrassed in front of my peers. I was told I didn't try, that I didn't study. I was made to feel invisible. They had given up on me. They made me spiteful and mean toward innocent classmates just because these classmates knew the answers that I did not. I was forced to be dishonest. I was driven away from school.

My teachers could not admit to themselves that it might not be my fault that I wasn't able to read. They lied to my parents. They denied their inability to help me and didn't bother to try to understand, nor did they acknowledge my talents, strengths, hopes, dreams, or rights. They blamed no one but me.

I was made to feel criminal and worthless, as if there was something wrong with my brain and therefore I was completely incapable of learning to read. They didn't care about me. They reminded me of how important it was to learn, and then they didn't give me a chance to learn. They, the ignorant, cheated me.

Educators like these must be able to look in the mirror and admit what they see. I believe in what Plato once said: "Those who teach must never cease to learn." This not only applies to teachers in schools, but also to anyone who must play the role of the educator, be they employers, parents, or even policemen. They must acquire new information and commit themselves to being learners as well as teachers. Instead of pointing the finger of blame, they must seek the truth and reconcile themselves with the illiterate.

We have entered into the age of computers. In a time where our current technology actually seems futuristic, people seem to assume that our educational system is doing its job. But it's a lie.

Employers need to develop a spirit that supports the ongoing learning process and to accept the reality that everyone needs to participate in the teaching process. This transition will not be easy. Some will argue that the system is too big to do anything about it, or that we can simply dump money into the existing programs and they will be fixed. The fact is that we, as employers, as parents, as teachers, as individuals, need to reevaluate our attitudes about education in order to remain competitive.

Unfortunately, many employers will find legal ways to get around the laws. They need to realize that they will not be able to function properly without a literate workforce. Furthermore, education must be everyone's responsibility not just of the teachers or the employers, but of parents and friends as well. We must all bear part of the responsibility so that no one is skipped over by the system.

In earlier days, only the rich upper-class had the opportunity or means to learn to read and write. Illiteracy has always been associated with the have-nots. But literacy is no longer a privilege. It is a source of power that everyone should be given the opportunity to tap into. Educators today need to realize this and to see what history has shown us. In order for this country to continue to be a global economic power, everyone needs to take responsibility for our educational growth. Instead of getting distracted by extraneous side issues, we simply need to learn how to teach. Our children should be given language-processing skills, both oral and written. Teachers need to learn how to recognize those students who do not have language-processing skills necessary to acquire basic literacy skills. I want to give teachers another chance to teach us to read.

To be an illiterate or functional illiterate in America is a form of slavery. This slavery has created a second-class citizenry that is growing at an alarming rate in America today. America must regain its competitive edge, and it cannot do so with an illiterate workforce.

I want everyone to open up and become seekers of truth. We must humble ourselves in order to open ourselves to a learning process that has excluded us for all our lives.

Index